MODERN CHESS
FROM STEINITZ TO THE
21ST CENTURY

All sales or enquiries should be directed to Thinkers Publishing, 9850 Landegem, Belgium.

Email: info@thinkerspublishing.com
Website: www.thinkerspublishing.com

Managing Editor: Daniël Vanheirzeele

Typesetting: Primož Žerdin, Primož Riegler

Cover Design: Mieke Mertens

Graphic Artist: Philippe Tonnard

Production: Itagraf

ISBN 9789464201437
D/2022/ 13731/7

MODERN CHESS

FROM STEINITZ TO THE 21ST CENTURY

CRAIG PRITCHETT

Thinkers Publishing 2022

Thinkers Publishing

Table of Contents

Introduction

'I as though traced the evolution of chess thought and repeated its basic steps in my own development ... convinced that any player with high ambition should follow such a path'

Vassily Smyslov, *125 Selected Games* (1983)

This book takes the reader on a journey from early 19ᵗʰ century developments in the game up to the present-day. It takes in the revolutionary Wilhelm Steinitz's early summation and establishment of a firm positional basis for chess and the considerable contributions made by all of the subsequent world champions and certain other great players, including the contemporary computer phenomenon, AlphaZero.

Take note of Vassily Smyslov's wise words. Recalling a period of intense study in his father's chess library, Smyslov stressed that, without obtaining an understanding of the ways in which chess has developed over time, no aspiring player is ever likely to achieve his or her fullest potential. What went for Smyslov also applies to all of the inspirational players who appear in this book. Today's top players still borrow from the best games and ideas of past generations. Do join them!

I wrote this book primarily to explore, confirm and convey my own understanding of this grand sweep of chess history. To that extent it can only be a subjective work and readers may hold other opinions. Though I hope that much in this book is, indeed, persuasive, please feel free to reflect and draw your own conclusions. I also aimed at containing my account in one accessible volume, inspired by such succinct chess classics, as Richard Réti's, *Masters of the Chessboard*, Max Euwe's, *The Development of Chess Style*, and others.

We are all historically rooted, inescapably driven to constantly re-interpret the past to help make sense of our present and possible future. Indeed, the past often touches us when least expected. My working copy of Imre König's fine book, *Chess From Morphy to Botwinnik*, on loan from the Edinburgh Chess Club's 'Aitken' collection, is warmly inscribed by the author to his friend, Dr James M Aitken (1908-83), ten times Scottish chess champion.

That unexpected, near 70 year link to the middle age of one of my own illustrious countrymen, who, towards the very end of his chess career, was one of my own Scottish team colleagues, at the 1972 Skopje Olympiad, greatly encouraged me to pursue this project. Rarely, if ever, truly definitive, history moves on ceaselessly. The game itself changes. The context varies. Do enjoy the continuing journey!

Craig Pritchett
Dunbar, September 2021

From the Romantics to the Early Modern Age

'The indiscriminate and chiefly tactical kingside attack has been superseded by strategical manoeuvres, marches and counter-marches for gaining and accumulating small advantages at any point on the board'

Wilhelm Steinitz, *International Chess Magazine (April 1885)*

Wilhelm Steinitz (1836-1900), the first player ever to be formally acknowledged as 'world chess champion' (1886-1894), dominated the development of the game in the 19th century. He therefore forms the major focus of this chapter, which takes us from an earlier period that is often labelled 'Romantic' to what Steinitz considered to be superseded by what he called a 'Modern' school.

It isn't easy to define either of these terms exactly, as the development of chess thought unsurprisingly tends to reflect mainly subtle nuance and adaptation to existing understanding rather than radically polarised jolts. Steinitz's oft-quoted words at the top of this chapter do, however, neatly summarise the essential elements of change in the 19th century. Let them stand as a starting point.

Very broadly, earlier in the 19th century, in the absence of anything other than a fairly rudimentary body of openings theory and of a more profound strategic understanding of a later Steinitzian kind, the strongest players tended to exhibit an understandable tendency to consider the king the weakest link in an opponent's armoury and that the game's consequent primary aim was to topple it fast.

The Early Romantics
Bourdonnais and McDonnell

In his use of the phrase, 'indiscriminate, chiefly tactical kingside attack', Steinitz was certainly on to something of defining significance about the way much chess was played in the 1820s and 1830s. These two decades saw the discovery of the mercurial *Evans Gambit* and the first great international match series, at London 1834, between the world's two best players, Alexander McDonnell (1798-1835) and Louis-Charles Mahé de la Bourdonnais (1795-1840).

1. *Louis-Charles M. de la Bourdonnais*

In the visceral battles between these two – they played a punishing 85 games through the summer of 1834, which ended, +45 =13 -27, in Bourdonnais' favour – you can sense not just the brute nature of the mainly tactical and direct attacking nature of both of them, but also that they could rely on little in the way of available chess knowledge to help them orientate and nurture their attacks, other than their own calculating powers and powerful imaginations.

Such skills took them far but they were constrained by the limits of the age that they lived in. They understood the significance of material, time and spatial strengths and weaknesses, not least around vulnerable kings, but the idea that a player might best seek to accumulate 'small advantages at any point on the board', rather than to overwhelm an opponent's king directly, was largely beyond them.

Bourdonnais and McDonnell's chess may have been a touch naïve from the perspective of much better informed succeeding generations but their best games still nevertheless thrill with combinative excitement. We can still learn much from their attacking verve and considerable skill in concluding attacks with, at times, outstandingly conceived, beautiful and brilliant combinations.

Of the two, Bourdonnais was the stronger, more insightful and creative player, who to this day retains the deserved reputation of having been by far the most finished chess master in the early Romantic era. McDonnell, too, however, had a goodly share of his own brilliant attacking moments, as in the 50th game played in their 1834 series.

L-C. M. de la Bourdonnais – A.McDonnell

50th Game, London Series 1834

Queen's Gambit Accepted

1.d4 d5 2.c4 dxc4 3.e4 e5 4.d5 f5?!

The modern main line, 4.♘f3 exd4 5.♗xc4, is nowadays considered more challenging than Bourdonnais' more speculative 4.d5.

McDonnell's reply, however, takes huge risks with Black's kingside pawns and the light squares around his king. Of course, both players may already have been out of 1830s' 'theory', such as it was!

5.♘c3 ♘f6 6.♗xc4 ♗c5 7.♘f3 ♕e7 8.♗g5 ♗xf2+ 9.♔f1?!

A misjudgement: Bourdonnais should have played 9.♔xf2 ♕c5+ 10.♔e1 ♕xc4 11.♘xe5, and if 11...♕a6 12.♕b3, when, despite no longer being able to castle, White has a clear lead in development,

continuing light square pressure (including an ever latent threat of playing d6) and stands well.

9...♗b6 10.♕e2 f4 11.♖d1 ♗g4 12.d6 cxd6 13.♘d5?!

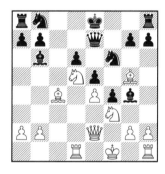

Playing this move, White no doubt hoped for either 13...♕d8?! 14.♘xf4, and if 14...exf4? 15.e5!, or the playable, but decidedly awkward retreat 13...♕f8. Black, however, two pawns to the good, opts for a wonderful sacrificial alternative, offering his queen for two minor pieces, a mighty post for his knight on e3 and a dangerous attacking initiative. His judgement appears to be good.

13...♘xd5 14.♗xe7 ♘e3+ 15.♔e1 ♔xe7

16.♕d3 ♖d8 17.♖d2 ♘c6 18.b3 ♗a5 19.a3 ♖ac8 20.♖g1 b5 21.♗xb5 ♗xf3 22.gxf3 ♘d4 23.♗c4

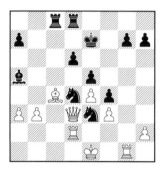

White may have had some way to stay in the game but defence was difficult. Now, however, he's certainly lost. White obtains a few spite checks but Black's perfectly safe king can fend off all serious threats and even assists in the final mating attack. Black's pieces and kingside pawns continue to dominate after the almost equally unconvincing alternative, 23.b4 ♘xf3+ 24.♔f2 ♘xg1, and if 25.bxa5 ♖c1 26.♕b3 g5.

23...♘xf3+ 24.♔f2 ♘xd2 25.♖xg7+ ♔f6 26.♖f7+ ♔g6 27.♖b7 ♘dxc4 28.bxc4 ♖xc4 29.♕b1 ♗b6 30.♔f3 ♖c3 31.♕a2 ♘c4+ 32.♔g4 ♖g8 33.♖xb6 axb6 34.♔h4 ♔f6 35.♕e2 ♖g6 36.♕h5 ♘e3 0–1

This dramatic kind of bare-knuckle contest still warms the soul. Full of wonderfully original and daring ideas, McDonnell's achievement has an attractive grandeur in its conceptual boldness and assured combinative flow. Over a century later, however,

Imre König, while sharing his admiration and indeed sense of wonder at this beautiful game, nevertheless felt duty bound to assert, in his book, *Chess From Morphy to Botwinnik*, that 'whilst some phases were beautifully played [they] are too disconnected and do not form a coordinated whole'.

Of course, peering so far back into a 'romantic' pioneering past, we can and must surely allow for many such retrospectively perceived, positional 'disconnects', of a kind that belong to a much better informed future age (and König does so). In context, Bourdonnais and McDonnell's most brilliant and best games certainly expanded the game's creative and combinative boundaries and still speak persuasively to us about skills that remain essential in any top player's armoury nowadays.

In his *Manual of Chess*, Emanuel Lasker draws out an especially valuable learning point. Quite taken by Bourdonnais' 'extraordinary genius', Lasker credits him as 'the father of the soundest plan known to the history of chess: to combat every developed unit of the enemy in the centre with a force at least equal to it and to follow the enemy, after having thrown him back in the centre, with a well-supported advance post in the heart of his position'.

This particular characteristic in Bourdonnais' chess is splendidly on show in the most famous game played in the 1834 series, a real gem that has scarcely lost its appeal since it was played almost 200 years ago. Bourdonnais' instincts for the development and exploitation of control in the centre provide a bridge between the 1830s and the full flowering of that powerful playing style, two decades later in the games of Adolf Anderssen and Paul Morphy.

A.McDonnell – L-C. M. de la Bourdonnais

62nd Game, London Series 1834

Sicilian Defence

1.e4 c5 2.♘f3 ♘c6 3.d4 cxd4 4.♘xd4 e5 5.♘xc6 bxc6 6.♗c4 ♘f6 7.♗g5 ♗e7 8.♕e2 d5 9.♗xf6 ♗xf6 10.♗b3 0–0 11.0–0 a5 12.exd5 cxd5 13.♖d1 d4 14.c4!?

Following a colourless opening by White, Black has at least equalised. With the text-move, White tries to reintroduce some imbalance into the game, but by allowing Black to obtain a secure passed d-pawn and the potential to mobilise and (eventually) advance his f-, e- and d-pawns, he incurs some positional risk.

Presumably White was banking on being able to mobilise his own queenside pawns, but he is objectively further distant from achieving that aim than Black in the latter's more immediately trenchant, expansionary aims in the centre.

14...♕b6 15.♗c2 ♗b7 16.♘d2 ♖ae8 17.♘e4 ♗d8!?

Objectively 17...♗e7, and if, say, 18.♘g3 ♗c5 19.♗e4 ♗xe4 20.♘xe4 f5 21.♘xc5 ♕xc5, might have improved, since if Black can maintain control of c5, he might better constrain White's queenside pawns, while continuing to play for ...f5 and the eventual mobilisation of his central pawns. That course would have avoided the kind of fuzzy counterplay that White now drums up, based on the light square weakening in Black's camp that now follows.

18.c5 ♕c6 19.f3 ♗e7 20.♖ac1 f5

Black goes all in for a promising, but well nigh incalculable central assault at the cost of an exchange sacrifice.

21.♕c4+ ♔h8 22.♗a4 ♕h6 23.♗xe8 fxe4 24.c6 exf3 25.♖c2

White had no time for 25.cxb7? ♕e3+ 26.♔h1 fxg2+ 27.♔xg2 ♖f2+, and mates; or if 25.gxf3? ♕e3+ 26.♔h1 ♕xf3+ 27.♔g1 ♕e3+ 28.♔h1 ♕e4+ 29.♔g1 ♗g5, and wins.

25...♕e3+?!

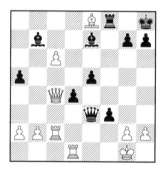

His eyes only on a win, Black spurns draws by repetition available after 25...f2+ 26.♖xf2 ♖xf2, and if 27.cxb7 (or if 27.♔xf2 ♕e3+ 28.♔f1 ♗h4 29.g3 ♕f3+ 30.♔e1 ♗g5 31.cxb7 ♕h1+ 32.♕f1 ♕e4+) 27...♕e3 28.♔h1 ♖xg2 29.♔xg2 (or 29.b8=♕ ♖g1+ 30.♖xg1 ♕f3+ 31.♖g2 ♕d1+) 29...♕e4+ 30.♔f1 ♕f3+ 31.♔e1 ♕e4+ 32.♕e2 ♗h4+ 33.♔d2 ♗g5+ etc.
It seems, however, that White might now have played 26.♖f2! and if 26... fxg2 27.♕e2!, forcing a welcome queen exchange and holding at least. The computer also favours White, after the extraordinary alternative

26...♗a6 27.♕xa6, and if ♗c5 28.♕f1 fxg2 29.♕e1 ♕xe1+ 30.♖xe1 d3 31.c7 ♖xf2 32.c8♕ ♖c2+ 33.♕xc5 ♖xc5. Black also suffers after 26...♗c8 27.♗d7, and if 27...♗xd7 28.cxd7 h6 29.♕d3 ♕xd3 30.♖xd3 ♖d8 31.gxf3 ♖xd7 32.♖e2 ♗f6.

26.♔h1 ♗c8 27.♗d7 f2 28.♖f1

Happily for chess history, the advantage is back clearly with Black, whose powerful pawns and supportive queen can hardly be stopped. After 28.♖cc1 ♗xd7 29.cxd7 d3, and if 30.♖f1 e4 31.♕c8 ♗d8, Black wins.

28...d3 29.♖c3 ♗xd7 30.cxd7 e4 31.♕c8 ♗d8 32.♕c4

Or if 32.♕c5 ♕xc5 33.♖xc5 e3 34.♖e5 e2 35.♖xf2 ♔g8 36.♖e8 e1♕+ 37.♖xe1 ♖xf2 38.♖e8+ ♔f8.

32...♕e1 33.♖c1 d2 34.♕c5 ♖g8 35.♖d1 e3 36.♕c3 ♕xd1 37.♖xd1 e2 0-1

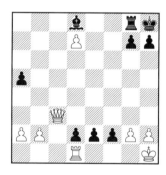

What a remarkable finale! A queen to the good, White cannot defend against Black's simultaneous threats to promote to either of three possible queening squares, d1, e1 or f1.

Mature Romanticism

Adolf Anderssen

2. Adolf Anderssen: in younger years

Such combinative brilliance is rare indeed and it took some time before a worthy successor to Bourdonnais' sparkling attacking style, grounded firmly on the idea of first obtaining control in the centre, eventually emerged. The distinction passed to a young Silesian German, Adolf Anderssen (1818-1879), who made a dashing name for his play through the 1840s in German chess circles, before triumphing in the first ever grand international tournament, at London 1851.

Like Bourdonnais, Anderssen was a great artist of the chessboard, bewitched by the idea of the combination as the ultimate source of mastery and indeed beauty in chess. Neither, however, pursued combinations to the exclusion of soundly-based strategic goals. Their well-honed combinative skills, allied to their exceptionally well-developed positional instincts gave them their cutting edge and set them apart from their peers, not least in especially complex, open and unbalanced play.

Unlike Bourdonnais, however, Anderssen had to adapt his positional/combinative playing style to the demands of a much better informed and more technically proficient, post-1830s chess world. Successful in this, his chess mind proved sufficiently supple to make continuing successful adaptations up to the time of his death. The world's 'champion' by repute from 1851 until his defeat in a match against Paul Morphy in 1858, he regained that reputation on Morphy's effective retirement from chess in the early 1860s.

The late 1830s and 1840s saw considerable change in chess, based on an expansion in the number of chess clubs, chess magazines, mainstream periodical and newspaper columns and instructional books, centred on the main European capitals, especially Berlin, London and Paris, as well as in many of Europe's other large cities. Anderssen himself published a popular collection of superb combinational puzzles, *Aufgaben für Schachspieler*, in 1842, and contributed regularly to the German chess press.

The purely German contribution to this significant expansion in internationally available chess knowledge was considerable. Centred on Berlin, perhaps Germany's greatest achievement, certainly a landmark event, was the publication, in 1843, of the first edition of the *Handbuch des Schachspiels*, which rapidly became the first international openings 'Bible', going through many expanding editions into the early 20ᵗʰ century.

Edited in its first four editions by the Prussian aristocrat, Tassilo von Heydebrand und von der Lasa, the *Handbuch*, often popularly referred to as the *Bilguer*, was a comprehensive and wonderfully judged piece of international openings research, with a large dash of chess history to boot. Von der Lasa, possibly Germany's strongest player in the early 1840s, took over the work after the tragically early death, aged 25, in 1840, of its original editor, Paul Bilguer, whose name was retained on its cover and title page.

Against this background, it might almost have seemed surprising if such a promising player as Anderssen had failed to develop considerable technical as well as purely combinative steel. Although never a professional player, by the end of the 1840s Anderssen had become a many-sided talent and a threat to anyone. Often lauded by later generations mainly for his wonderfully imaginative combinative powers, Andersson's contemporaries also recognised in Anderssen's games a thorough mastery of the manoeuvring arts and closed play.

Many, though certainly not all of Anderssen's most famous combinations occurred in his frequent recorded off-hand 'friendly' games and (non-stakes) matches. As White, he was to hazard only one King's Gambit and no Evans Gambits at all in his (tied) top-class breakthrough match against Daniel Harrwitz, at Breslau 1848, and in winning his most famous event, at London 1851. In these two deadly serious contests, Anderssen relied primarily on hard-hitting positional choices.

At London 1851, Anderssen was particularly clinical against Howard Staunton (1810-1874), the pre-tournament favourite, who was then considered widely to be the world's best player, following his decisive match victory (+11=4-6), against Pierre Saint Amant, at Paris 1844. Anderssen comfortably won their best of seven, third round, knock-out contest (+4-1). He set the tone for the match with a positionally well-controlled win in their first game.

A.Anderssen – H.Staunton

Game 1, Rd 3, London 1851

Sicilian Defence

1.e4 c5 2.d4 cxd4 3.♘f3 e6 4.♘xd4 ♗c5 5.♘c3 a6 6.♗e3 ♗a7 7.♗d3 ♘e7 8.0-0 0-0 9.♕h5 ♘g6 10.e5 ♕c7 11.♖ae1 b5 12.f4 ♗b7 13.♘e4 ♗xe4 14.♗xe4 ♘c6

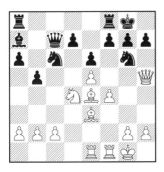

White has achieved an edge and now embarks on a plan to attack on the kingside, by playing g4 (with f5 in the air), and the manoeuvre ♖f3-h3, followed (in the event of ...h6) by g5. Possibly 15.c3, keeping the d-file closed, improves, making it more difficult for Black to open lines and obtain counterplay.

15.♘xc6 dxc6 16.g4 ♖ad8?!
Here Black misses a chance: after 16...♗xe3+ 17.♖xe3 ♕b6, and if 18.♕h3 ♖ad8 (or perhaps first 18...♕c5) 19.♔h1 ♕c5, Black maintains a weather eye on e5 (and inhibits f5), thereby slowing down White's attack sufficiently to establish a rough balance.

17.♔h1 c5 18.♖f3 ♕a5 19.♖ef1 ♕a4?!

Here, too, Black might have put more pressure on White by playing the more critical 19...♕b4, attacking b2. He may have feared the consequences of the complicated line, 20.♗d3, and if 20...c4 21.♖h3 h6 22.♗xg6 fxg6 23.♕xg6 ♗xe3 24.♖xe3 ♕xb2 25.♕xe6+ ♔h8 26.f5, but he might still battle on in this position, by playing the computer suggestion, 26...♕xc2, and if 27.f6 ♖d2 28.fxg7+ ♔xg7 29.♕e7+ ♔g6!.

20.♗d3

White can afford to let his less critical a-pawn fall, as its capture draws Black's queen too far out of play and White's attack crashes through. Black's last practical chance may have been 20...c4, although after 21.♖h3 h6 22.♗xg6 fxg6 23.♕xg6 ♗xe3 24.g5! (the computer again), and if 24...♖xf4 25.♖xf4 ♖d1+ 26.♔g2 ♖g1+ 27.♔f3 ♗xf4 28.♕xe6+ ♔f8 29.g6!, White still most probably wins.

20...♕xa2 21.♖h3 h6 22.g5 ♖xd3

Or if 22...c4 23.gxh6 cxd3 24.hxg7 ♕d5+ 25.♖ff3, forcing 25...♕xf3+, and White wins quickly.

23.cxd3 ♕d5+ 24.♖ff3 ♘e7

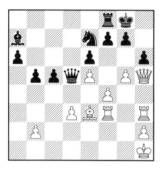

White also remains an exchange ahead with a winning attack after 24...♕xd3 25.gxh6 ♕d1+ 26.♔g2, and now either 26...♕e2+ (or 26...♕c2+) 27.♔g3.

25.gxh6 g6 26.h7+ ♔h8 27.♕g5 ♘f5

Or if 27...f6 28.exf6 ♕xg5 29.fxg5 ♘f5 30.♖f1, threatening ♖c1, and wins.

28.♕f6+ ♘g7 29.f5 ♕b3 30.♗h6 ♕d1+ 31.♔g2 ♕e2+ 32.♖f2 ♕g4+ 33.♖g3 1–0

Playing though such games might lead you to question how far labels such as 'Romantic' might be entirely trustworthy. Right in the middle of what we usually consider to be the Romantic Age we get a game that seems unusually 'modern'. White plays superbly well, but Black, too, after a slightly passive start, reveals an intuitive grasp of the importance of the centre and the development of hard-hitting counterplay.

Apart from a possible slip on White's 15ᵗʰ move, Anderssen's play throughout is exceptionally sound and wholly strategic. His attacking initiative develops in an energetic, correct and gradual way that conforms fully to the needs of the position. Black lost because he made one or two more marginal errors than White. Anderssen's final combinative fireworks work precisely because they are based on a sufficiently critical mass of strategic advantage.

Credit to both players! Yet contrast this heavyweight battle with Anderssen's so-called *Immortal Game*, also played at London 1851, but only as one of a very large number of 'friendly' games that were played 'almost daily' (according to Anderssen's biographer, Hermann Gottschall) between Anderssen and Lionel Kieseritzky, at Simpson's Divan, in downtime from the main tournament, in which Kieseritzky had been defeated by Anderssen (+2=1) in the first knockout round.

It is far from clear how seriously the two protagonists took their friendlier 'contests' but White's final combination in *The Immortal Game*, probably the best known and most re-published in chess history, is still widely held to be emblematic of Anderssen and the early Romantic Age. In his *Manual of Chess*, Emanuel Lasker, an ardent Anderssen fan, considered it 'splendid' but quite rightly cautioned against reading too much into the game's overall course.

A.Anderssen – L.Kieseritzky

'The Immortal Game' London 1851

Up to the diagrammed position, White had outplayed Black. Having sacrificed a minor piece to gain two pawns and a massive lead in development, Anderssen seems on the verge of overwhelming Black's clearly much weakened position.

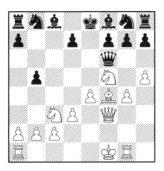

16...♗c5?

And after this move, Black is indeed lost. Black had to try 16...♕c6, and if 17.♘d5 ♘a6, in a last bid to plug some of the awful holes in his position and develop his own pieces.

In a serious tournament game, however, Anderssen surely wouldn't now have wasted much time in replying 17.d4, followed by ♘d5 (or ♗e5), as 17...♗xd4 fails disastrously to 18.♘d5 ♕c6 19.♘c7+ ♔d8 20.♘xd4 ♕c4+ 21.♕d3, and wins. He instead opts for an outrageously speculative (though not wholly unpromising) lunge that he wouldn't have touched in the main tournament.

17.♘d5 ♕xb2 18.♗d6 ♗xg1?

The correct defensive sequence was 18...♕xa1+ 19.♔e2 ♕b2!, and if 20.♔d2 ♗xg1, which might even completely refute White's play.

19.e5 ♕xa1+ 20.♔e2 ♘a6

It is uncertain whether the remaining three of the most famous moves in chess history were actually played out. Some sources indicate that Black resigned and others that Anderssen announced mate. Black is certainly, brilliantly, beautifully bust. After 20...♗a6 21.♘c7+ ♔d8 22.♘xa6 ♕b2 23.♔d2, and if 23...♘c6, defending Black's queen's rook, White plays 24.♗c7+, followed by ♘d6, and mates.

21.♘xg7+ ♔d8 22.♕f6+ ♘xf6 23.♗e7 mate (1-0)

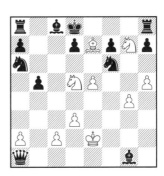

One year later, Anderssen followed this up with his almost equally famous *Evergreen* Game. This was another encounter of a 'lighter' sort, though one which featured a much better contested opening by both players than in the *Immortal* and about which there is no suspicion that it might have been played purely 'for fun'. The final combination in the *Evergreen* is at least as brilliant as in the *Immortal* and certainly sounder throughout.

A.Anderssen – J.Dufresne

'The Evergreen Game', Berlin 1852

Following a sharply contested line of the *Evans Gambit*, Black had just played 18...Rg8, to reach the diagrammed position. Anderssen replied with an exceptionally poisonous first move in what proves to be a brilliant mating combination. It needn't have won. After White's only other try for an advantage, 19.♗e4, however, modern engines indicate that Black might still survive, by playing 19...♕h3 20.g3 ♖xg3+ 21.hxg3 ♕xg3+ 22.♔h1 ♗xf2 23.♗xe7 ♕h3+ 24.♘h2 ♗xe1 25.♖xe1 ♕h4 26.♕d1 ♘xe7, and if 27.♗xb7 ♕xf6.

19.♖ad1 ♕xf3?

Black misses White's point. Black's only correct reply was 19...♕h3!, keeping an eye on d7. Black then defends after 20...♗f1 ♕f5!, and if 21.♗xe7?! ♕xf3! 22.♗c5+ ♔d8 23.♖e7 ♗c8.
Note that, in this line, 20...♕xf3? 21.♖xe7+!, and if 21...♔d8 22.♖exd7+ ♔c8 23.♖d8+! ♖xd8 24.gxf3, again wins for White. After 20...♕f5!, however, both sides may have nothing better than to draw by repetition, after 21.♗d3 ♕h3 (after 21...♕xf6 22.♗xh7, remains unclear) 22.♗f1, and so on.

20.♖xe7+ ♘xe7?!

Permitting a wonderful mate.
Black might prolong the agony, but can't expect to save the endgame after 20...♔d8

21.♖xd7+ ♔c8 22.♖d8+ ♔xd8 (or if 22...♘xd8 23.♕xd7+! ♔xd7 24.♗f5+, and mates on d7) 23.♗e2+ ♘d4 24.♗xf3 ♗xf3 25.g3, and if 25...♗xd1 26.♕xd1

c5 27.cxd4 cxd4 28.♗e7+ ♔c8 29.♕c2+
♔b7 30.♕xh7.

**21.♕xd7+ ♔xd7 22.♗f5+ ♔e8 23.♗d7+
♔f8 24.♗xe7 mate (1-0)**

Yet another picture perfect finish: Anderssen clearly commanded a combinational talent of the very highest order. As the Staunton game indicates, however, Anderssen's genius amounted to very much more than that. Move on a decade, to another of Anderssen's most brilliant games, one that marries a more mature Anderssen's strategic and combinational artistry in a seamlessly transcendent way that still speaks to us powerfully. Every Black move counts in this miniature masterpiece.

J.Rosanes – A.Anderssen

Breslau, 1862

King's Gambit: Falkbeer's Counterattack

**1.e4 e5 2.f4 d5 3.exd5 e4 4.♗b5+ c6
5.dxc6 ♘xc6 6.♘c3 ♘f6 7.♕e2 ♗c5
8.♘xe4 0-0**

Falkbeer's Counterattack had only recently been invented. Its signature third move drives a wedge into White's classic King's Gambit position. Black's awkward e-pawn makes it difficult for White to complete his development and leaves White's erstwhile gambit pawn on f4 looking more a source of long-term self-obstruction and self-weakening than a virulent attacker aimed at undermining Black's early grip on e5.

In this game, White attempts to rid himself of this thorn in his side, by winning Black's e-pawn, but this loses time and is a high-risk plan. Gradually White players began to appreciate that White should rather seek to exchange Black's e-pawn early (e.g. by playing 4.d3). As played, Black already has more than enough piece activity for his pawn. White can't, of course, now allow 9.♘xc5? ♖e8, winning White's queen.

9.♗xc6 bxc6 10.d3 ♖e8 11.♗d2 ♘xe4 12.dxe4 ♗f5 13.e5 ♕b6 14.0-0-0 ♗d4

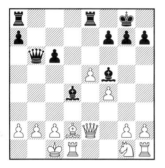

Unable to castle kingside, White was relying on finding safety for his king on the opposite flank. Anderssen's forces, however, flow unerringly into powerful queenside attacking positions. More than likely, Anderssen already envisaged the possibility of a mate on b1. Black's immediate threat to mate on b2, forces White to open the h7-b1 diagonal to the obvious advantage of Black's light square bishop.

15.c3 ♖ab8 16.b3

White again had no choice. Black forces mate after 16.♗e1 ♗e3+. Or, if first, 16.b4 ♕a5 17.♗e1, Black plays 17...♕a3+ 18.♕b2 ♖xb4 19.♕xa3 ♗e3+, followed by 20...♖b1 mate.

16...♖ed8 17.♘f3

White sportingly allows his opponent to play out Black's final combination in its fullest magnificence, with a memorable queen and bishop sacrifice. After 17.cxd4 ♕xd4, threatening mate on a1, Black wins immediately. Black's attack is also decisive after 17.g4 ♕a5, and if 18.♔b2 ♗c5 19.gxf5 ♖xb3+ 20.♔a1 ♖db8 21.♗e1 ♕a3, threatening ...♖b2.

17...♕xb3 18.axb3 ♖xb3 19.♗e1 ♗e3+ 0-1

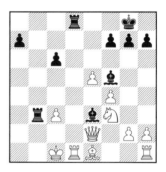

Mate on b1 follows next move: combinative bliss!

The Enigmatic Giant

Paul Morphy

S teinitz was fortunate indeed to be able to draw on the sophisticated mix of the strategic and combinative arts that was increasingly a mark of the maturing Anderssen's game, as well as on the earlier, more purely combinative achievements of Bourdonnais' age. He also drew at least equal inspiration from the example of the great Paul Morphy (1837-1884), though in a more subtly nuanced and fully rounded positional way.

Yet Morphy only graced the chess firmament for a brief few years, winning the first US Championship Congress (New York 1857), followed by a successful tour of Europe (1858-59), from which he

3. Paul Morphy, in 1859

emerged as the world's top player, by general acclamation. Aged only 21, Morphy then promptly retired from all top-class chess, the greatest master of the then prevailing taste for direct cut and thrust in mainly Open Games.

Prodigiously gifted, Morphy conquered the chess world completely in this brief period but departed so abruptly that it caused chess players everywhere to lament the loss of at least another decade or two of what might have been. Morphy's main English language biographer, David Lawson, titled his Morphy opus, *Paul Morphy: The Pride and Sorrow of Chess*, borrowing these tragically apt words from one of Morphy's noted Scottish contemporaries, W.C. Spens.

Shortly after Morphy's death, Steinitz attempted a major analysis of his legacy in an extended essay titled *Paul Morphy and the Play of His Time*, which was published in four parts in the earliest issues of Steinitz's *International Chess Magazine* (January-April, 1885). At the height of his powers and on the verge of his historic first match for the world title against Johannes Zukertort, Steinitz's views command note.

Steinitz first cautions that we should distinguish between Morphy's 'lighter games' and 'more serious contests'. Morphy's chess, he stressed, was conducted at a time when casual contests, simultaneous displays and blindfold exhibitions, a Morphy specialty, still tended to far exceed serious tournament and match play. That Morphy played more of the former sort of chess, generally against clearly weaker opponents, is simply a fact.

Steinitz readily acknowledged that Morphy's combinative brilliance was of the highest order, if most often displayed in these 'lighter' games. Above all, however, he insisted that Morphy's true genius lay mainly in the many 'clear indications in his match style of that steady pressure and studious regard for the balance of position, which requires an almost instinctive judgment in its application, and which has been cultivated and trained to a much higher degree since the Morphy period'.

According to Steinitz, Morphy's intuitively direct, quick-sighted and fundamentally correct playing style was exceptionally forward-looking. He also considered that Morphy simply outshone all of his opponents in his understanding and knowledge of up-to-date opening ideas. Morphy, he stressed, was no reckless romantic, certainly in his 'most serious contests', noting that he rarely gave up 'more than one pawn in the ordinary established gambits', generally preferring 'in the majority of cases' to consume the 'sacrifices [of] his opponents' pawns and pieces'.

In short, Steinitz recognised in Morphy an even more significant transitional figure from older methods of play to a post-romantic 'modernism' than Anderssen. Morphy won all three top-class matches, he played on his European tour: against Harrwitz (+5-2=1), Johann Löwenthal (+9-3=2) and Anderssen (+7-2=2). Morphy's subtly achieved win in the final game of his match against Löwenthal is both technically and tactically arresting.

P.Morphy – J.Löwenthal

14th match game, London 1858

Spanish Opening

1.e4 e5 2.♘f3 ♘c6 3.♗b5 a6 4.♗a4 ♘f6 5.d4 exd4 6.e5 ♘e4 7.0-0 ♘c5 8.♗xc6 dxc6 9.♘xd4 ♘e6

Playing Black, Morphy preferred to seek more dynamic chances by holding back this move. T. Barnes-P.Morphy, London 1858, continued 9...♗e7

10.♘c3 0-0 11.♗e3 f6 (11...♖e8 is a dependable modern alternative), aiming to build on the latent power of Black's two bishops. Löwenthal instead hopes to equalise by following a reasonable, but less trenchant plan of relentless exchanges.

10.♘xe6 ♝xe6 11.♕e2 ♝c5 12.♘c3 ♕e7 13.♘e4 h6 14.♝e3 ♝xe3 15.♕xe3 ♝f5 16.♘g3

Rather than fall in with Black's exchanging plans, Morphy prefers to spice things up by keeping his knight in play, at the cost of a fairly safe gambit. For his pawn, White gains a tempo that can be used to mobilise his potentially threatening e- and f-pawns.

16...♝xc2 17.f4 g6 18.e6

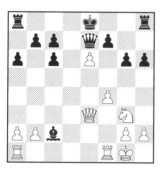

Black can still no doubt defend, but this fine move certainly niggles. Black can't now play either 18...fxe6? 19.♕c3, with a winning queen fork, or 18...0–0–0?,

which allows 19.♖ac1, and if 19...♝d3 20.♕a7 ♕xe6 21.♖cd1, threatening ♖ff3, and White is winning.

18...♝f5 19.♘xf5 gxf5 20.exf7+ ♚xf7 21.♕h3 ♕f6

White's initiative persists, if still slight, and Black must now decide between the slightly passive text or the more active (but perhaps more loosening) 21...♕c5+ 22.♚h1 ♖ae8, or perhaps 21...♚g6 at once, retaining the ...♕c5+ option.

22.♖ae1 ♖he8 23.♖e5!

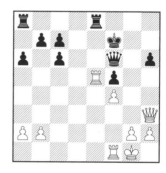

White's command of the e5 outpost may not win but continues to cause practical problems. Black retains his extra, if doubled queen-side pawn, but his king is exposed and his forces are tied down to the defence of his split f- and h-pawns.

23...♚g6 24.♖fe1 ♖xe5 25.♖xe5 ♖d8 26.♕g3+ ♚h7 27.h3 ♖d7 28.♕e3 b6 29.♚h2 c5 30.♕e2 ♕g6?

4. Paul Morphy (l.) v Johann Löwenthal: 1858 match in London

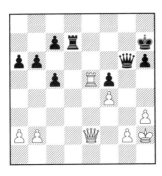

Löwenthal has so far defended well, but here he should have preferred 30...a5, the last move necessary to straighten out and secure his queenside pawns, and if 31.♖e6 ♕d4, obtaining sufficient piece activity to off-set White's pressure on the kingside.

31.♖e6 ♕g7?
Perhaps now fatigued, Black drifts into a position in which he loses by Zugzwang. Instead 31...♕g8, and if 32.♖f6 ♖f7, was absolutely essential.

32.♕h5 ♖d5 33.b3!

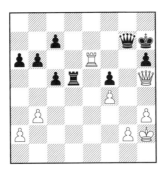

A little bit of Morphy's fabled wizardry! With Black's rook and queen rooted to d5 and g7 (to prevent immediate collapse on f5, g6 or h6), Black must move

one of his queenside pawns. After 33...a5 34.a4, and if 34...b5 35.axb5 a4 36.bxa4 c4 37.♖c6, however, White also wins quickly. As played, Black sheds his a- and f-pawns and goes down in a rook and pawn endgame.

33...b5 34.♖xa6 ♖d6 35.♕xf5+ ♕g6 36.♕xg6+ ♔xg6 37.♖a5 ♖b6 38.g4 c6 39.♔g3 h5 40.♖a7 hxg4 41.hxg4 ♔f6 42.f5 ♔e5 43.♖e7+ ♔d6 44.f6 ♖b8 45.g5 ♖f8 46.♔f4 c4 47.bxc4 bxc4 48.♔f5 c3 49.♖e3 1-0

Morphy's most accomplished adversary, Anderssen, largely shared Steinitz's views about Morphy's all-round playing strength. One year after losing to the American, Anderssen observed in a private letter to von der Lasa, dated 31 December 1859, that not just 'deeper combinations and brighter sparks of genius are at Morphy's disposition than lay within Bourdonnais' grasp, but that in infallible calculation and soundness, he even surpasses the latter'.

Anderssen frankly doubted, at that time, whether anyone could match Morphy, either technically or in his steely 'professionalism'. This latter point might at first seem paradoxical, as Morphy frequently and openly deplored the very thought that chess might be played full-time or even simply for money stakes. Anderssen, however, sensed that the young American actually played as if he were the most consummate 'professional', in the widest sense of the term.

To von der Lasa, Anderssen revealingly confides that Morphy 'treats chess with the earnestness and conscientiousness of an artist. With us, the exertion that a game requires is only a matter of distraction, and lasts only as long as the game gives us pleasure; with him it is a sacred duty [never] a mere pastime ... but always a problem worthy of his steel, always a work of vocation, always as if an act by which he fulfils part of his [life's] mission'.

Anderssen even noted that Morphy's chess 'gave also outwardly such a strict appearance of solemnity, that it took away from it entirely the character of a gay occupation, and it had as far as I am concerned something oppressing, I would almost say strangling. The onlookers were forced to abstain even from the slightest whispering ... to me all the stranger, as I am not aware of having been ever disturbed, during a game ... by any act of conversation'.

Blessed by ample private family means, Morphy never was a chess professional, in any economic sense. He had, however, clearly invested no little time in studying the game. Fully abreast of what was most significant in published theory and developing trends, Morphy continually adjusted his play in accordance with his own changing judgement of the reliability of such knowledge and battled as hard as anyone. Chess at the very top was inexorably becoming much more demanding.

Around 1860, top-class chess still, however, remained almost entirely amateur and organisationally underdeveloped. There were hardly any strong national, let alone international tournaments, and very few high stakes matches. Morphy's 1858-59 tour of the Old World, centred on Paris and London, was a unique phenomenon, only possible because of his outstanding, New World games and reputation. As a full-time mathematics teacher at a Breslau Gymnasium, Anderssen confined almost all of his competitive chess, much of it of the 'lighter' sort, to scholastic vacations.

When Anderssen met Morphy in their match at the very end of 1858, Gottschall notes that Anderssen had been virtually inactive for well over a year. Arriving poorly prepared and relatively rusty, Anderssen also gave away almost two decades to a much younger opponent, who was not just in peak physical condition and playing form, but also thoroughly battle-hardened by almost continual practice against the best players in Paris and London that year. How it showed in the games that they played!

P.Morphy – A.Anderssen

Game 9, Paris 1858

Sicilian Defence

1.e4 c5 2.♘f3 ♘c6 3.d4 cxd4 4.♘xd4 e6 5.♘b5 d6 6.♗f4 e5 7.♗e3 f5?!

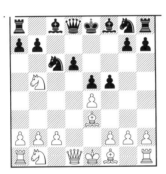

This is a truly reckless move that Anderssen should certainly have reserved for a game of a 'lighter sort'. Black positively encourages White to give up his bishop for the lively attack that follows. Black's erratic choice can perhaps only be explained by Anderssen's growing despair at getting nowhere against Morphy by conventional means.

Even today this is a standard variation. Black has at least several good replies, including 7...a6, which Anderssen had already played in a game against J.Szen, at London 1851, 7...♘f6 and 7...♗e7. Gottschall even suggests that Anderssen played this way without having subjected the line to much, if any in-depth home-preparation - far from professional, even in the mid-19ᵗʰ century!

8.♘1c3 f4

This move fails to equalise but at least has the merit of consistency. White also obtains good chances, however, after 8...a6 9.♘d5, and if 9...axb5 10.♗b6 ♕h4 11.♘c7+ ♔f7 12.♘xa8 ♕xe4+ 13.♕e2.

9.♘d5 fxe3 10.♘bc7+ ♔f7 11.♕f3+!?

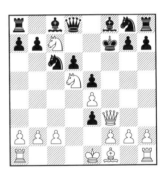

But what's this? After the relatively straightforward 11.♘xa8, and if 11...exf2+ 12.♔xf2 ♕h4+ 13.g3 ♕xe4 14.♗g2 ♕f5+ 15.♔g1, Black struggles to find sufficient compensation for his material deficit. Morphy, it seems, speculates on achieving a win by breathtaking brilliancy.

11...♘f6 12.♗c4 ♘d4

Black's king seems to be in trouble, but with this move and his next, Anderssen successfully complicates.

13.♘xf6+ d5 14.♗xd5+ ♔g6??

This move, however, allows White to regain control completely. Black still fights after: 14...♔e7, and if 15.♕h5 gxf6 16.♕f7+ ♔d6 17.♘xa8 ♘xc2+ 18.♔e2 ♕e7 19.♕xe7+ ♗xe7 20.♖ac1 ♘d4+ 21.♔xe3 ♗d7 22.♖c7 ♖xa8 23.♖xb7 (so far Zukertort), and now 23...♖c8; or 14...♕xd5 15.♘fxd5+ ♘xf3+ 16.gxf3 exf2+ 17.♔xf2, though here White's extra pawn may count more than Black's defensively strong bishop pair.

15.♕h5+ ♔xf6 16.fxe3

Deadly: by opening the f-file, White overwhelms Black's king and wins quickly. It seems that Anderssen had only considered the tempting, but incorrect 16.♕f7+? ♔g5, and if 17.0–0–0 ♔h6 18.♘xa8 ♗e7, threatening ...♖f8, with a fairly safe Black king and reasonably good chances for Black.

16...♘xc2+ 17.♔e2 1–0

Context: this game (and the match, as a whole) may have been dashed off by both players very quickly, as they managed to complete the much lengthier, 10th match game, which took some six hours and was won by Anderssen, later on the same day (27th December). All eleven games of the match were played over only nine days (20-28 December), with the 7th and 8th games also completed on one day (25th December).

It may never be completely understood why Morphy failed to return to top-class chess. A gifted academic, who completed his university law studies, aged 18, three years before he could actually enter professional practice, Morphy had declared before he left for his European chess tour that he wished to pursue a legal career on his return. Despite serious attempts, however, Morphy failed to succeed in law, from which he gradually drifted away just as he had more abruptly ceased to compete in the top-class chess world.

In his *Manual of Chess*, Emanuel Lasker suggests that the savage blow of the US Civil War (1861-65) 'broke the heart and the mind of Morphy' and the Lawson biography amply confirms how much personal turmoil this undoubtedly caused. Morphy, a prominent Southern gentleman, was also a lauded hero of the larger USA because of his remarkable chess exploits. Never a committed Secessionist, far less a soldier, by temperament, he seems to have remained greatly conflicted and quite disengaged throughout these turbulent years.

Deeper psychological issues may also have contributed to a malaise that only worsened after the Civil War. Morphy still struggled to find any professional purpose or fulfilling station in life and soon began a tragic descent into a pronounced reclusive state and confirmed depressive illness. He was, however, able to avoid hospitalisation and, as his family still enjoyed sufficient private means, lived on in reasonable comfort until his death in the family's New Orleans home, cared for by his mother and sister.

Two years before his death, in a letter dated 31 July 1882, Morphy penned the unutterably sad words that, in life, 'I have followed no calling, and have given no cause for a biography. I have received a diploma as a lawyer'. This was in response to a request that he might collaborate in a proposed chapter on his life as a chess champion, in a biography of famous Louisianans. Tragic, indeed!

Revolutionary Change

Wilhelm Steinitz

Although a year older than Morphy, Steinitz had scarcely set out on his own chess career as the American's dazzling few years on the chess stage ended. These two great titans of the game sadly never played against each other. Just as Morphy, who abhorred the very thought of resorting to chess 'professionally', retired from the top-class game, Steinitz decided to commit completely to it, full-time and for the very long-term.

Born into poverty in the Prague ghetto, Steinitz had to endure much tougher financial challenges than Morphy, but he sensed his strength and

5. Wilhelm Steinitz, in later years

was, by all accounts, extraordinarily resilient, resourceful, driven and determined in his attempts to succeed. Recall Anderssen's words, in his letter to von der Lasa, about Morphy's deep sense of chess, as a 'vocation' and 'mission' in life. All through his life, Steinitz shared such commitment and passion.

Steinitz moved from Prague to Vienna in 1857, initially enrolling as a university student. He soon abandoned his studies, however, and at that point turned seriously to chess. By 1861, he was effectively regarded as Austria's 'champion' and chosen to play as Austria's representative, at London 1862. Following that tournament, in which Anderssen and Louis Paulsen placed 1st and 2nd, and Steinitz, on his international debut, finished 6th, he settled in London.

The popularity of chess continued to grow in mid-century. Even more new clubs appeared and this growing popular base enjoyed an ever expanding output of chess books and magazines and dedicated chess columns in newspapers and periodical magazines. Going into the 1860s, fledgling national and regional chess 'federations' also began to flourish, bringing with them increasing numbers of regional, national and international chess tournaments.

In this milieu it became possible, if still only for a hardy few, to derive more secure earnings from chess than in a much more precarious past. Steinitz certainly survived in London, at this time the chess world's largest and most lucrative centre, drawing income variously from stakes games and more serious tournaments and matches, by offering lessons, exhibitions, talks and chess tours and through chess writing.

By 1866, Steinitz had so enhanced his tournament and match playing reputation, that he was able to attract sufficient financial backing to challenge (the still mighty) Anderssen in a high stakes match. He took full advantage of this opportunity, surprising just about everyone, by defeating Anderssen (+8-6), in a hard-fought match that amazingly witnessed no draws. Steinitz eventually broke a lengthy deadlock, only by winning both of the final two match games.

What made the difference? Many things! But we should probably subordinate all points of detail under the overall heading, greater all-round 'professionalism'. Anderssen, the last wholly amateur world number one (by acclaim) was defeated by an antagonist, who was completely immersed in the game. In Steinitz, Anderssen again met an opponent who displayed just as effective a 'professional' edge, as Morphy before him.

Steinitz showed greater determination, stamina and reserves of nervous strength than Anderssen. He also brought a harder-edged work ethic to the board that translated into a complex, flexible and essentially strategically-based playing style more in tune with developing trends. Steinitz's pre-match preparation, overall match strategy and, above all, his drive to experiment judiciously and innovate, gave him a serious edge.

Anderssen faced no standing target. Steinitz darted about. Against Anderssen's favourite Evans Gambit, a fearsome weapon in his hands at the time, Steinitz constantly chose novel ideas that netted him a more than satisfactory 3/6 score. Playing White, he employed a wholly unexpected and deeply strategically-based reinterpretation of the then much neglected Salvio Gambit, with which he completely surprised his opponent, scoring 3/4.

In Game 13, Steinitz also showed that he was more than ready to deal with a switch by Anderssen from his favoured Evans Gambit to a line of the Spanish Opening that had previously scored well for him in his match against Louis Paulsen, at London 1862. Anderssen strained hard to win, but Steinitz's subtle handling of the bishop pair, acting in support of a phalanx of advancing Black pawns on the kingside, held fast and then prevailed when White went wrong.

A.Anderssen – W.Steinitz

Game 13, London 1866

Spanish Opening

1.e4 e5 2.♘f3 ♘c6 3.♗b5 ♘f6

A.Anderssen-W.Steinitz, Vienna 1873, saw Black brilliantly riff on the current game after 3...a6 4.♗a4 ♘f6 5.d3 d6 6.♗xc6+ bxc6 7.h3 g6 8.♘c3 ♗g7 9.♗e3 ♖b8 (to hinder b4) 10.b3 c5 11.♕d2 h6 12.g4 ♘g8 (aiming, via e7-c6, to reach the powerful d4 square) 13.0–0–0 ♘e7 14.♘e2 ♘c6 15.♕c3 ♘d4

obtaining a massive central clamp and control on both flanks.

Nowadays we understand that such slow 'development' may often be justified (generally in closed play), if it leads to significant positional gain. Not so, in the early post-romantic years, when the idea of 'rapid' development largely remained king. This game provided a truly revolutionary lesson in the manoeuvring arts that owe so much to Steinitz, in closed and semi-closed games.

Anderssen went on to suffer one of his most strikingly one-sided losses, after the further moves, 16.♘fg1 0–0 17.♘g3 ♗e6 18.♘1e2 ♕d7 19.♗xd4 cxd4 20.♕b2 a5 21.♔d2 d5 22.f3 ♕e7 23.♖df1

♕b4+ 24.♔d1 a4 25.♖h2 c5 26.♘c1 c4 27.a3 ♕e7 28.b4 c3 29.♕a1, when, with White's queen trapped horrifically on a1, Black's vastly superior kingside forces rapidly overwhelmed White.

4.d3 d6 5.♗xc6+ bxc6 6.h3 g6 7.♘c3 ♗g7

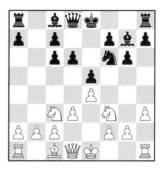

Anderssen often gave up his bishop pair like this, hoping to exploit the relatively fixed nature of Black's centre pawns and press with his knights. He generally sought either to develop queenside play, by playing b4 in response to an early ...c5 (as in this game), or play on the kingside, often involving moves such as, ♘c3/♗e3/♕d2/0-0-0, followed by an eventual g4/h4 pawnstorm.

The first major outing with the ♖b1/b4 plan ended in a win for White: A.Anderssen-L.Paulsen, Match Game 1, London 1862, continued 8.♗e3 0–0 9.♘e2 ♕e7 10.0–0 d5 11.♘g3 ♘e8 12.♖e1 d4 13.♗d2 c5 14.b3 ♘d6 15.♕c1

♗b7 16.♕a3 ♘b5 17.♕a5 a6 18.a4 ♘a7
19.♗c1 ♘c6 20.♕d2 ♘d8 21.a5 ♘e6
22..♗a3 f5 23.♕d1 f4 24.♘f1 ♖f7 25.♘1d2
♘f8 26.♖b1 g5 27.b4 cxb4 28.♖xb4 c5
29.♖b6, with a clear White superiority
on the queenside.

8.0–0 0–0 9.♗g5
Play also went in White's favour, in
Game 7 of the same 1862 match, after
9.♘e2 c5 10.♘g3 ♗b7 11.♖e1 ♘d7 12.♖b1
f5 13.b4 fxe4 14.dxe4 cxb4 15.♖xb4 ♘b6
16.♖b3 ♕e7 17.a4 a5 18.♗e3 ♖a6 19.♕e2
♗c8 20.♖eb1, when Anderssen again
turned his early activity into a winning
advantage.

9...h6 10.♗e3 c5 11.♖b1 ♘e8

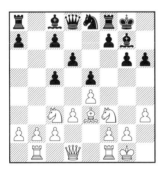

Steinitz, however, believed in the dynamic power of the bishop pair in such
positions. Not fazed by Paulsen's earlier misfortunes against Anderssen, he
was convinced that Black's sound central and potentially mobile kingside
pawns, backed up by Black's bishops,
should offer good prospects.
Here he might also have played 11...
a5, and if 12.a3 ♗e6 13.b4 cxb4 14.axb4
axb4 (the ambitious 14...a4!? might

also be playable) 15.♖xb4 ♕d7 16.♕b1
♕c6, with a rough balance.

12.b4 cxb4 13.♖xb4 c5 14.♖a4
Unfairly criticised by many, this move
is not untypical of Anderssen's maxi-
malist playing style. Anderssen, who
generally out-calculated opponents
en route to victory, targets Black's a-
pawn, reserving the b-file for occupation by his two other major pieces.
Although White's rook eventually runs
into trouble on the a-file, this is not an
unmerited plan.

14...♗d7 15.♖a3 f5
Steinitz activates his kingside pawns,
keeping ...a5-a4 in reserve, with the
idea of pinning down White's rook
on a3. He thereby risks the creation
of potential entry points for White's
queen and a rook (at b7 and c6) and
weakens his a-pawn; he might also
have played 15...♗c6, after which
16.♕d2 ♔h7 17.♖b1 ♘c7 18.♖ab3 f5,
looks rock solid.

16.♕b1 ♔h8 17.♕b7 a5 18.♖b1 a4 19.♕d5

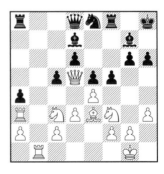

White's rook on a3 looks awkward but

White has designs on Black's a-pawn that might rapidly bring it to life. Black maintains a rough balance but probably no more than that. With the text-move, White signals that he wants more than the likely draw by repetition that would now have transpired after 19.♘h4 ♔h7 20.exf5 gxf5 21.♖b6, and if 21...♖f7 22.♕d5 ♖f8, etc.

19...♕c8 20.♖b6 ♖a7 21.♔h2 f4 22.♗d2 g5 23.♕c4 ♕d8 24.♖b1 ♘f6

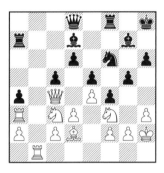

White now unwisely turns down another likely repetition, by playing 25.♘b5, and if 25...♕b6 26.♘c3 etc., but not 26.♖xa4 ♖xa4 27.♕xa4 c4 28.♕a7 (defending f2) 28...♕xa7 29.♘xa7 ♗a4 30.♘e1 ♖a8 31.♖b7 ♗xc2 32.♘xc2 cxd3, followed by ...♘xe4, with advantage to Black. Of course, not 25.♘xa4?, which allows 25...♕c7, followed by ...♖fa8, and Black wins.

25.♔g1 ♘h7 26.♔f1

By now, White really has lost the plot. Black also stands much better after 26.♘b5 ♖b7, and if 27.♖xa4 (or 27.♕xa4 h5 28.♕a6 ♖b6 29.♕a5 g4) 27...h5 28.♖a6 g4 29.hxg4 hxg4 30.♘e1 g3,

when Black's kingside pawns threaten to overwhelm White.

26...h5 27.♘g1 g4 28.hxg4 hxg4 29.f3 ♕h4

And there are certainly no draws now. White has allowed Black's kingside pawns to build up too much attacking momentum. White's king suffocates.

30.♘d1 ♘g5 31.♗e1 ♕h7

This straightforward move is good enough, as the reply it provokes is patently desperate. Black's advantage, however, is such that he might also have won by playing the even more clinicial 31...g3, and if 32.♕d5 ♕h1 33.♕xd6 ♗h3 34.gxh3 ♘xf3.

32.d4 gxf3 33.gxf3 ♘h3 34.♗f2 ♘xg1 35.dxc5 ♕h3+ 36.♔e1 ♘xf3+ 37.♖xf3 ♕xf3 38.♘c3 dxc5 39.♗xc5 ♖c7 40.♘d5 ♖xc5 41.♕xc5 ♕xe4+ 42.♔f2 ♖c8 43.♘c7 ♕e3+ 0–1

Steinitz's fighting spirit and defensive resilience stand out in this game. But what really impresses is the subtle interplay between his pieces and pawns on both flanks. Steinitz lets his pawns take up most of the traction, but his pieces are always well-placed in support. He brought a deeper sense of the cooperative potential of all of the chessboard forces and a new kind of patience to chess. Although old school 'romance' might be lacking, Steinitz could also strike with great combinative force, given the chance.

While Steinitz modelled his earliest (c 1860) playing style on the generally prevailing taste for open combat, largely undertaken 'in front of' pawns, he had soon come to regard that style of play, especially most of the standard kingside gambit openings, with suspicion. He quickly grasped that defenders could avail themselves of far more resources than previously considered possible and that soundly-judged manoeuvres, 'behind' pawns, often led to better founded attacks, including counter-attacks.

Whereas the young Steinitz had earned a dashing reputation for open play, rapid piece development and direct attack, by 1866, he had already moved towards a quite different and more telling playing style, in which he worked his pieces and pawns more judiciously in tandem and slowed play down. The new Steinitz no longer sought to topple kings fast but rather to establish an array of offensive and defensive strong points, from which he might both optimally undermine an opponent's weak points and robustly defend.

By 1885, the mature Steinitz confidently asserted that this new, strategically supple style of play had increasingly become the 'modern' standard. In his essay on Paul Morphy, he noted that it had 'in many respects ... become almost antagonistic to that of the Morphy period', in the sense that 'the assault against the kingside forms the exception [no longer] the rule'. Modern attacks, he maintained, tended 'at the outset' to be more generally 'directed chiefly toward the centre or the queen's wing'.

To illustrate this trend, Steinitz scrutinised tournament winner (and renowned attacking master), Johannes Zukertort's twenty-one wins, at London 1883. In these, he found 'only two ... in which [Zukertort] takes up a kingside attack in the first instance'. Steinitz also characteristically warmed to the 'ingenious' term, 'attacking defence', to describe the kind of counter-attacking style that he was beginning to make his own and used so effectively against Anderssen. He boldly concluded 'that the king is in reality a strong piece', later adding, in his *Modern Chess Instructor* (1889), 'both for the attack and the defence'.

Such novel thoughts first began to stir in Steinitz's mind in his earliest London years. He was particularly impressed, at London 1862, by the pioneering play of Louis Paulsen, a great master of positional manoeuvre, defensive resourcefulness (including the successful acceptance of most kingside gambits) and of a wide range of closed and semi-closed openings. Steinitz (and Paulsen) grasped that successful attacks must be based on a sufficiency of strategic advantages or they might simply rebound. It fell to Steinitz to give much greater voice to such developments than anyone else.

Having established his world-class credentials, by defeating Anderssen, in 1866, Steinitz stood out not just as a player who battled and worked hard, but also as the most successful and daringly innovative player of those years. But his next big innovation must have come to his contemporaries as an incendiary shock. One year after the Anderssen match, Steinitz gave birth to his extraordinary *Steinitz Gambit*, in which White's king embarks on a decidedly murky journey into a central unknown after only five moves.

Stay calm! Steinitz never played such lines without much prior home-preparation. While clear that his king was at risk, Steinitz also reasoned that Black's lone queen might be rapidly driven back, with gain of time, by White's minor pieces. Should White thereafter manage to regain the gambit pawn and exchange queens, White would (in all likelihood) retain an excellent e4/d4 pawn centre, supported by a truly strong king, already well-centralised in an advantageous endgame, as indeed transpired in the gambit's inaugural outing.

With queens on the board, matters are much less clear. Steinitz, however, still trusted in the same pawn structural and development advantages and that his king, behind its strong defensive/offensive phalanx of central and queenside pawns, would be most difficult to hunt down and might even expect to discover distant sanctuary on the queenside. Steinitz also often proved this (theoretically critical) middlegame point, in such fine games as below, against Louis Paulsen.

W.Steinitz – L.Paulsen

Baden-Baden 1870

Steinitz Gambit

1.e4 e5 2.♘c3 ♘c6 3.f4 exf4 4.d4 ♕h4+ 5.♔e2

Paulsen now cautiously advances his d-pawn one square. W.Steinitz-J. Zukertort, London 1872, more ambitiously continued 5...d5 6.exd5 ♗g4+ 7.♘f3 0–0–0 8.dxc6 ♗c5 9.cxb7+ ♔b8 10.♘b5 ♘f6 11.♔d3 (11.c3 may be best) 11...♕h5 12.♔c3 ♗xd4+ (12...a6 may be critical) 13.♘bxd4 ♕c5+ 14.♔b3 ♕b6+ 15.♗b5 ♗xf3 16.♕xf3 ♖xd4 17.♕c6 ♕a5 18.c3 ♖d6 19.♕c4 a6 20.♗a4 ♘d5 21.♔a3 g5 22.b4 ♕b6 23.♕d4 ♕xd4 24.cxd4 ♘b6 25.♗b2 ♘c4+ 26.♔b3

♘xb2 27.♔xb2 ♖xd4 28.♔c3 ♖hd8 29.♖ad1, when, after a wild walk with his king, with his monarch secure, White won the endgame.

Many subsequent games focused on 6...♕e7+ 7.♔f2 ♕h4+, tacitly offering a repetition. W.Steinitz-J.Zukertort, Game 20, World championship, New Orleans 1886, went more trenchantly, 8.g3

8...fxg3+ 9.♔g2 ♘xd4 10.hxg3 ♕g4 11.♕e1+ ♗e7 12.♗d3 ♘f5? (Black traps his own queen; 12...♔f8 was essential) 13.♘f3 ♗d7 14.♗f4 f6 15.♘e4 ♘gh6 (15... ♕g6 16.♘c5) 16.♗xh6 ♘xh6 17.♖xh6 gxh6 18.♘xf6+ ♔f7 19.♘xg4 1–0.

5...d6 6.♘f3 ♗g4 7.♗xf4 0-0-0

Black failed to hold a slightly inferior endgame in the gambit's first outing: W.Steinitz-G.Neumann, Dundee 1867, went 7...♗xf3+ 8.♗xf3 ♘ge7 9.♗e2 0-0-0 10.♗e3 ♕f6+ 11.♔g3 d5 12.♗g4+ ♔b8 13.e5 ♕g6 14.♔f2 h5 15.♗h3 f6 16.exf6 ♕xf6+ 17.♕f3 ♕xf3+ 18.gxf3 g6 19.♘e2 ♘f5? (allowing White to split Black's e-, f- and h-pawns and successfully penetrate in the g-file) 20.♗xf5 gxf5 21.c3 ♗d6 22.♗f4 ♔c8 23.♖hg1 ♔d7 24.♖g7+ ♘e7 25.♖ag1 ♔e6 26.♗xd6 ♖xd6 27.♘f4+ ♔f6 28.♘d3

♖b6 29.b3 ♖h6 30.♘e5 ♖b5 31.a4 ♖a5 32.b4 ♖a6 33.♘d7+ ♔e6 34.♘c5+ 1–0.

8.♔e3 ♕h5 9.♗e2

Black now doubtfully swings his queen to a5, losing tempi. He might, however, have first played 9...♘f6, and only after 10.h3 ♗xf3 11.♗xf3 ♕a5, as in J.Moussard-N.Guliyev, Paris 2015, which is unclear.

Black might also consider 9...g5, and if 10.♘xg5 ♘f6 11.h3 ♗xe2 12.♕xe2 ♕g6, as in J.Barle-L.Portisch, Ljubljana 1975, returning the gambit pawn to create counterplay.

9...♕a5 10.a3 ♗xf3 11.♔xf3 ♕h5+ 12.♔e3 ♕h4 13.b4 g5?

With Black's queen now back on the kingside and White's king close to completing a most secure artificial castling, by playing (via f2, to g1), Black already struggles to find a good plan. The text-move, however, only creates ugly, unforced kingside light square weaknesses and a glaring path of attack for White on the half-open f-file. Black should have preferred the much tougher 13...f5, and if 14.b5 ♘ce7 15.g3 ♕f6.

**14.♗g3 ♕h6 15.b5 ♘ce7 16.♖f1 ♘f6
17.♔f2 ♘g6 18.♔g1 ♕g7**

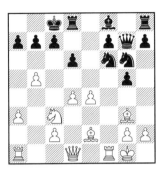

A telling diagram! White may have 'castled' unconventionally, but he also enjoys a wholly conventional set of decisive positional advantages. Black's kingside is riddled with weaknesses. Most of Paulsen's largely impotent pieces, including his queen are stuck in Black's home kingside corner. White dominates in the centre and has already launched a rapid-fire queenside attack that promises success in short order.

19.♕d2 h6 20.a4 ♖g8 21.b6
You can't fault Steinitz's final attack. White sacrifices a pawn and then an exchange to tear open all three queenside files, dominate the h3-c8 diagonal and occupy d5.

**21...axb6 22.♖xf6 ♕xf6 23.♗g4+ ♔b8
24.♘d5 ♕g7 25.a5 f5**
Or if 25...b5 26.a6 and if 26...b6 27.♕c3 c5 28.a7+ ♔b7 29.♗f2, threatening ♕a3 and wins.

26.axb6 cxb6 27.♘xb6 ♘e7

Or 27...fxg4 28.♖a8+ ♔c7 29.♕c3+ ♔xb6 30.♕a5+ ♔c6 31.d5+ ♔d7 32.♕xd8 mate

**28.exf5 ♕f7 29.f6 ♘c6 30.c4 ♘a7
31.♕a2 ♘b5 32.♘d5 ♕xd5 33.cxd5 ♘xd4
34.♕a7+ ♔c7 35.♖c1+ ♘c6 36.♖xc6
mate (1-0).**

Throughout his career, Steinitz maintained faith in his gambit's correctness. He also scored well with it. It should not, however, be overlooked that he essentially dropped it from his top-class repertoire, from around 1886, by which time he considered that it had lost much of its surprise value. Steinitz, certainly in his peak years, rarely let the defence of any mere principle (the White king's uncommon early resilience, in this instance) get in the way of his more practical concern to win chess points.

An early trailblazer in this regard, Steinitz adopted a thoroughly hardheaded, fully professional approach to openings, of a kind that we instantly recognise as today's gold standard. To be successful in the opening demands a constant search for the widest variety of primarily strategic new ideas, a process at which Steinitz excelled. Fully aware that certain ideas might incur extremely high risk, however, he adapted his focus accordingly. Steinitz's 'own' gambit, which he used almost always only when he considered himself better prepared than opponents, certainly fell into this category.

Having defeated Anderssen, at London 1866, Steinitz's next goal was to win a major international tournament. While Steinitz might justifiably claim to be the world's best match player, he couldn't yet be considered the world's number one, without first challenging Anderssen's supremacy in the world's most competitive tournaments. In the 1860s and early 1870s, however, such big international events remained rare and, at first, Steinitz only suffered relative disappointment.

At Paris 1867, Steinitz finished 3rd, behind Ignaz Kolisch and Szymon Winawer. He then took 2nd place, at Dundee 1867, behind Gustav Neumann. Most galling of all was Steinitz's 2nd place, at Baden Baden 1870, behind a resurgent Anderssen, who managed to defeat him in both of their individual games. Thoroughly chastened by this latter result, Steinitz concluded that if he wished to fulfil his ambition to become the world's most acclaimed match and tournament player, he must redouble his efforts at improvement.

Steinitz, at last, won his first international tournament, at London 1872, and then took an outstanding first place, at Vienna 1873, ahead of a truly world-class field that included Anderssen. As Steinitz had also impressively trounced Johannes Zukertort, in a match (+7-1=4), at London 1872, his reputation as the world's absolutely top player undeniably firmed. Following a 7-0 rout, in a match against Joseph Henry Blackburne, at London

1876, Steinitz's match and tournament supremacy could scarcely be questioned.

At this point, Steinitz took a complete break from all top-class tournament competition that lasted six years. During this time, he consolidated an unchallenged reputation as the world's best chess analyst and writer, most particularly in his capacity as editor of Great Britain's foremost chess column, in *The Field* (1873-1882). In these hugely authoritative columns, Steinitz took advantage of an expansive canvas to develop in-depth game analyses, reports and features that set enduringly high standards of internationally recognised excellence.

Steinitz eventually returned to top-class tournament play, at Vienna 1882, where his excellent share of 1st/2nd places, with Winawer, topping yet another stellar field that included his much improved and by then strongest rival, Zukertort (who tied 4th/5th), made it seem as if he had hardly been away from the board at all. Once he had shaken off some early tournament rust, Steinitz's uncanny positional sense, indomitable fighting spirit and extraordinary ability to innovate all showed as brightly as ever.

No one could match Steinitz's originality and depth of preparation, at Vienna 1882. Who else, for example, could either have conceived, let alone dared to hazard Steinitz's new, outwardly shocking anti-French Defence sortie, 1.e4 e6 2.e5!?. At Vienna,

Steinitz nevertheless scored a convincing, +4-1=1, with this line. In fact, Steinitz's single loss only resulted after he failed to convert a clearly winning advantage, following a poorly judged try by Winawer for complete refutation (in their tied, two-game tournament play-off).

This line isn't objectively dangerous for Black but its novelty and Steinitz's thinking behind it confounded opponents. Steinitz never essayed any of his ideas lightly. So what is the point? Steinitz, it seems, anticipated that Black would most likely respond to the line by playing an early ...d6 or ...d5. He then planned to exchange pawns on d6 and seek to control e5 with his pieces,

with the intention of constraining Black's development behind Black's self-blocking pawn on e6 and securing a slight spatial edge.

The line's first outing, W.Steinitz-B.Fleissig, Vienna 1882, which continued 2...d5 3.exd6 ♗xd6 4.d4 ♘e7 5.♗d3 ♘g6 6.♘f3 ♘c6 7.♘c3 ♘b4 8.♗c4 c6 9.♘e4 ♗c7 10.0-0 0-0 11.♖e1, illustrates Steinitz's main aim quite clearly. Having obtained his slight spatial pull, White eventually outplayed his opponent. Next time out, however, White's unusual opening served up something quite extraordinary: an early 'hypermodern' masterpiece, created decades before the term itself even existed, of a most insightful and visionary kind.

W.Steinitz – M.Weiss

Vienna 1882

French Defence

1.e4 e6 2.e5 c5 3.f4 d5 4.exd6 ♗xd6 5.g3 ♗d7

Black sensibly aims to oppose bishops on the long, light diagonal.

A modern player would, however, probably instantly prefer the more natural development, 5...♘c6, and if 6.♗g2 ♘ge7 7.♘f3 0-0 8.0-0 b6 9.♘c3 ♗b7

with ...♕d7 in mind, and absolutely no problems. It is likely that the possibility of such lines soon persuaded Steinitz to revert, as he did, to French Defence main lines.

6.♘f3 ♗c6 7.♗g2 ♘f6 8.0–0 ♘bd7 9.d3 0–0 10.♘bd2 ♘b6?

Impeding Black's b-pawn is, however, a serious strategic error. Weiss may have planned to continue ...♘bd5, followed by ...b5, or considered that if White eventually plays a4, to prevent ...b5, he would gain a strong b4 outpost. Again to the modern eye, Black should instantly grab valuable queenside space, by playing an immediate 10...b5, and if 11.a4 a6, ensuring plenty of scope for potential central and queenside counterplay.

11.♕e2 ♕c7 12.b3 ♗e7 13.♗b2 a5?
And this move is equally bad. After White's powerful reply, Steinitz clamps down hard on all of the key queenside light squares (a4/b5/c4). This makes it extremely difficult for Black ever to achieve ...b5 and break on the queenside. Although already quite cramped, Black might still have tried 13...♖ad8, continuing to cover c4 and hoping to

achieve a simplifying exchange of light square bishops if White should too hurriedly play ♘fe5.

14.a4 ♘bd5 15.♘c4 ♘b4 16.♖ae1 ♘fd5 17.♘fe5 ♗f6 18.♕f2

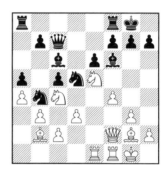

A prophetic diagram! From an 'ugly duckling' start, Steinitz has taken us on a near model 'hypermodern' journey (see Chapter 3), nearly three decades before such novel ideas had even begun to be clearly conceived. White's play is all in accord with Nimzowitsch's much later expressed dictum (see his *My System*) that the centre 'consists of squares ... not pawns [which] must never ... be lost sight of'.

Using 'Nimzowitschian' terms, Steinitz first 'cleared' the centre, by exchanging pawns on d6, aiming to control the critical e5 square with pieces (rather than a conventionally 'occupying' pawn). Steinitz then embarked on a systematic plan of 'overprotecting' e5 to constrain Black: five pieces plus White's f-pawn converged on e5 before that square eventually became ripe for its actual occupation by a knight.

With the centre now under total control,

White threatens to over-run Black's poorly defended kingside, beginning g4-g5. In this concluding phase, he is able to use the critical e5 square as a focal point of continuing control and piece transfer, for which Nimzowitsch later coined the term 'pivot'. Note too, Steinitz's use of a powerful (Richard Réti-like) cross-firing double fianchetto. What an achievement!

18...♗e8 19.g4 ♖d8 20.g5 ♗e7
Faced with a main threat of ♕h4, followed by ♘g4 and ♗e4, Black already looks lost.
White should certainly win after 20... ♗xe5 21.♗xe5 ♕c8 22.f5!

and if 22...♗c6 23.f6 g6 24.♗e4, threatening ♗xg6.

21.♘g4 ♘c6 22.♕h4 ♘d4 23.♗e4 f5

Jettisoning a pawn and the game but Black was now dead lost anyway. No better was either 23...g6 24.♘f6+ ♗xf6 25.gxf6 h5 26.♕g5, or 23...h6 24.♘xh6+ gxh6 25.♕xh6 f5 26.♗xd4 cxd4 27.♕xe6+.
In the remaining moves Black does eventually get round to playing ...b5, albeit much too late and underscoring a salutary lesson in timing.

24.gxf6 ♘xf6 25.♘xf6+ ♗xf6 26.♕xh7+ ♔f7 27.♗g2 ♖g8 28.♘e5+ ♔f8 29.♖f2 b5 30.axb5 ♗xb5 31.♗h3 ♖e8 32.♖e4 ♗c6 33.♖xd4 cxd4 34.♗a3+ ♗e7 35.♗xe6 1-0

Shortly after his success at Vienna 1882, Steinitz was abruptly relieved of his chess column at *The Field*, as a result of the apparent development of a serious (though still somewhat obscure) personal rift with the periodical's owner/editor. Later in that eventful year, Steinitz embarked on what proved to be a highly successful chess tour of the main chess clubs in the USA. On its conclusion, he and his family resolved to quit London to set up new lives in New York.

Before their departure, Steinitz competed in the next big international tournament, at London 1883, where he suffered an unexpected setback. At this event, tournament winner, Zukertort, who scored an exceptional, 22/26, outdistanced Steinitz, who finished 2nd, by a full three points. This outstanding result fully confirmed Zukertort's continuing claim to have matched and perhaps even eclipsed Steinitz's reputational primacy during his long absence from chess. Clamour grew for a deciding championship match.

The players readily achieved backers, who eventually succeeded in bankrolling the first formally recognised professional match for the world championship. The contestants played at three host venues, New York, St Louis and New Orleans, in 1886. The match stakes were set at a record-breaking high of US$2,000 a side. Winner was to be the first player to score 10 wins (draws not counting). Steinitz won comfortably, 10-5 in wins, with five draws.

Aged 49, Steinitz may have been five years older than his opponent but he enjoyed ruder good health. Steinitz's greater capacity for hard work also gave him a decided, chess-technical edge. Zukertort, moreover, suffered from a known tendency to wilt both physically and mentally under prolonged pressure. This proved to be an unfortunate and perhaps even decisive weakness that became manifest towards the end of what must have been the most demanding challenge that either player had ever endured to that date.

Over the board, Steinitz was especially successful in keeping Zukertort's much-feared combinative creativity largely at bay. Much better prepared in the opening, Steinitz dictated the course of most games, generally managing to steer them towards the kinds of closed and semi-closed positions that favoured Steinitz's superior evaluative, planning and manoeuvring strengths. As expected, Steinitz also constantly innovated and simply fought hard, eventually wearing down Zukertort's resistance.

Playing White, Steinitz continually ran poor Zukertort ragged in lines of the latter's favourite Berlin Defence to the Spanish Opening, a battleground that featured in eight match games. In these games, Zukertort faced such an incessant array of testing new ideas that he must surely have regretted his apparent lack of a suitable second-string defence to avoid this torture. Steinitz made a +3 score in these games, with his sole loss coming only through a blunder when he clearly stood well.

Playing Black, Steinitz netted an equally telling 2/3 score against certain lines of the Queen's Gambit favoured by Zukertort that featured an Isolated Queen's Pawn (IQP). In these games, Steinitz took us a long way towards a profoundly modern understanding of how best to directly confront, contain, blockade and eventually neutralise the IQP (of which more later). Game 6 is typical of the kind of consistently draining, ever so slightly strategically superior pummelling that caused Zukertort's eventual collapse.

W.Steinitz – J.Zukertort

Game 6, World Championship, New Orleans 1886

Spanish Opening

1.e4 e5 2.♘f3 ♘c6 3.♗b5 ♘f6 4.0–0 ♘xe4 5.♖e1

Steinitz generally liked to retain his light square bishop in such positions rather than exchange it, such as after 5.d4 ♘d6 6.♗xc6 dxc6 7.dxe5 ♘f5 8.♕xd8+ ♔xd8, entering the robust *Berlin Wall Endgame*, already a known line at this time.

5...♘d6 6.♘xe5 ♘xe5

Steinitz's predilection for the bishops, however, didn't prevent him playing what he later called 'the ordinary continuation': 6...♗e7 7.♗xc6 dxc6 8.♕e2 ♗e6 9.d3 ♘f5 10.♘d2 0–0 11.c3 ♖e8 12.♘e4

and outplaying his opponent in Game 12.

7.♖xe5+ ♗e7 8.♘c3

Steinitz had adopted 8.♗f1, then a novelty, in Game 4, only to blunder and lose from a promising middlegame. He regarded the text-move, another novelty, as an interesting alternative 'experiment'. White plans to develop central and kingside pressure by dropping his bishop to d3, followed by a queen's bishop fianchetto and the rapid deployment of both rooks in the e-file.

8...0–0

Black must now avoid 8...♘xb5? 9.♘d5, and if 9...0–0 10.♘xe7+ ♔h8 11.♕h5 (threatening ♕xh7+, followed by ♖h5 mate) 11...g6 12.♕h6, threatening, ♖h5, which wins quickly. White also wins after 9...♔f8 10.♖xe7 c6 11.♕f3 ♘d6 12.d4, and if 12...cxd5 13.♗g5 ♕xe7 (or if 13...f6 14.♗xf6, or 13...♕a5 14.c3, followed by ♖ae1) 14.♗xe7+ ♔xe7 15.♕xd5.

9.♗d3 ♗f6

Steinitz advocated 9...c6 10.b3 ♘e8, transposing into Game 14, which was drawn.

10.♖e3 g6 11.b3 ♖e8 12.♕f3 ♗g5

After this move, White can offer a

promising 14ᵗʰ move gambit and develops a definite edge. Steinitz preferred 12...♗d4, but the earlier 11...b6, followed by a queenside fianchetto, may offer a more reliable equalising path.

13.♖xe8+ ♘xe8 14.♗b2 c6

Unfortunately Black can't risk 14... ♗xd2 15.♗c4, and if 15...♕f6 16.♕xf6 ♘xf6 17.♘b1 ♗g5 18.f4 ♗h4 19.g3, and wins; or if 15...♘d6 16.♘e4 ♘xc4 17.♘f6+ ♔f8 18.♘xh7+ ♔g8 19.♘f6+ ♔f8 20.bxc4; or 15...d5 16.♘xd5, and if 16...♗e6 17.♖d1.

15.♘c4 ♗c7 16.♕c3 d5 17.♕d4

This important Zwischenzug forces a significant kingside pawn weakness. With a self-blocking pawn on f6, Black will no longer either have the relieving move ...♗f6 available or be able to post a blocking minor piece securely on e6. White can also look forward to playing h4-h5, with a view to inducing further structural weaknesses in the vicinity of Black's king.

17...f6 18.♘g3 ♗e6 19.♖e1 ♘g7 20.h4 ♕d7 21.h5 ♗f7

Steinitz niggles away at Black's g6 point. He also clearly has an eye on an entry by White's queen at h6, either via e3 (as in the game) or after 21...gxh5, by playing 22.♕f4.

22.hxg6 ♗xg6

Zukertort so far defends well. He correctly allows his f- and g-pawns to be split in search of alleviating piece exchanges and to secure a flight square for his king, on f7. Only White stands well after 22...hxg6 23.♕h4, and if 23... ♖e8 24.♖e3, threatening both ♗xf6 and ♕h6.

23.♕e3 ♔f7?

Here, however, Zukertort misses the more accurate 23...♗d6, which threatens ...♖e8, and better contains the White queen. White might still preserve his structural edge and continue to exert pressure, by playing 24.♕f3, but after 24...♖f8, Black is clearly much better placed to resist.

24.♕f4 ♖e8

White also presses after 24...♗xd3 25.cxd3, and if 25...♖f8 26.♘f1 (or possibly 26.♕h4 ♔g8 27.♘f1), planning to activate White's rook along the third rank, via e3, following which the same square can be usefully occupied by White's knight.

25.♖e3 ♘e6

Black's defensive task is no longer straightforward. Ernst Schallopp recommended 25...c5, to exert pressure on e3 and close down the long dark diagonal, by playing ...d4. While this may now be best, White might still try 26.♖f3, in the hope that subsequent ...d4 plans may then offer White opportunities along the c4-g8 diagonal, combined with a possible c3 break.

26.♕g4 ♘f8 27.♘f5 ♗c5

Black offers a pawn to reach an endgame rather than continue to face White's mounting kingside pressure, which will involve such moves as ♖f3 and ♕h4, bearing down on Black's vulnerable f-pawn. Black's queen fatally loses access to d8, after 27...♗d8 28.♘h6+ ♔g7 29.♗f5, and wins.

28.♘h6+ ♔g7 29.♘f5+ ♔f7 30.♘h6+

♔g7 31.♘f5+ ♔f7 32.♘h6+ ♔g7 33.♘f5+ ♔f7 34.♘h6+ ♔g7 35.♗xg6

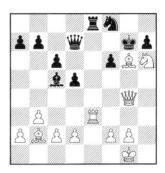

The match rules allowed six repetitions before a draw could be claimed. Having gained clock time, Steinitz now grabs the pawn. He might also have played 35.♕h4, and if 35...♖e6 36.♖g3, threatening both ♘f5+ and ♘g4, but felt no need to risk complications.

35...♕xg4 36.♘xg4 ♖xe3 37.fxe3 ♔xg6 38.♘xf6 ♗b4 39.d3 ♘e6 40.♔f2 h5 41.g4 h4

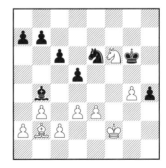

Steinitz hoped for this, correctly assessing that, in due course, White should fairly easily round up and win Black's over-extended h-pawn. Black should perhaps have preferred 41...hxg4, but after 42.♘xg4, and if

42...♔f5 43.♘e5, White still remains favourite to win.

42.♘h5 ♗d6
Black's defences also fail, after 42...♗c5 43.♗e5, and if 43...♘g5 44.♘f4+ ♔h6 45.♘e2 ♘f7 46.♗f4+ ♔g6 47.♘d4 ♗xd4 48.exd4 ♘g5 49.♔g2 h3+ 50.♔f2 b5 51.c3, followed by ♔g3, and wins.

43.♔g2 c5 44.♗f6 ♘g5 45.♗xg5 ♔xg5 46.♔h3 ♗e5 47.♘f4 d4 48.♘e6+ ♔f6 49.exd4 cxd4 50.♘c5 ♔g5 51.♘xb7 ♔f4 52.♘a5 ♗f6 53.♘c6 ♔e3 54.♘xa7 ♔d2 55.♘c6 ♔xc2 56.a4 ♔xd3 57.♘b4+ ♔e2 58.a5 ♗e7 59.♘d5 ♔f3
Or if 59...d3 60.♘f4+ ♔e3 61.♘xd3 ♔xd3 62.a6 ♗c5 63.g5.

60.♘xe7 d3 61.♘d5 1–0

According to Emanuel Lasker, in his justly famous essay on *The Theory of Steinitz*, in his *Manual of Chess*, Steinitz's great strength primarily derived from his thoroughly modern grasp of the underlying 'scientific' basis of planning. Before Steinitz, Lasker maintained, successful plans were thought to evolve principally from a master's 'genius ... or ... creative fancy'. Steinitz insisted that all good plans depended rather on primarily objective factors, brought together in a correct *'valuation'* (Lasker's italics).

That we might win games by developing good plans based on correct valuations is a thought so ingrained in the way we all play nowadays that we risk failing to grasp its substantial mid-19th century novelty and impact. It inspired Steinitz to undertake a fundamental investigation and reappraisal of the great games and understanding of the present and past, in a lifelong struggle to maintain a profoundly innovative mastery sufficient to keep his game freshly incisive throughout his very many years at the top.

Steinitz certainly penetrated the very essence of the game's most elusive secrets much more deeply than contemporaries. In 1875, he wrote revealingly in *The Field* that top players 'are mostly guided ... by certain principles of judgement, which only want expression to be made accessible to the generality of students'. He made it his life's work to grapple with and communicate such judgements, not just to help improve his own game, but also the general level of chess understanding.

Steinitz's views on planning, moreover, implied that successful combinations, too, depend less on inspiration than on objective factors. He argued that combinations are consequently best understood as 'resolutions' in the winning process rather than strokes of genius somehow plucked from thin air. In his essay on Paul Morphy, Steinitz conceived the combination as 'subservient to the delicate shades of difference in the application of position judgement like ... melody ... melted into the harmony and dramatic expression of Richard Wagner's music'.

The mature Steinitz rarely ever, as a result, chased combinations. He rather waited for them to fall into his hands, first seeking to outmanoeuvre opponents and steer games towards concretely advantageous positions in which successful combinations might most naturally arise, when he would pounce. A great admirer of Wagner's revolutionary new music, Steinitz considered that he, too, was re-casting chess in a much grander, modern mould, in which 'the preparation and disposition of forces ... require greater science'.

All such profoundly scientific, empirical and pragmatic attributes set Steinitz apart in all four of his triumphant world championship matches, against Zukertort (1886), Mikhail Chigorin (1889 and 1892) and Isidor Gunsberg (1890-91). Zukertort and Chigorin were both widely considered to be Steinitz's clear superior in the exercise of the dark combinative arts. Yet Steinitz brought off the finest combination played in any of these four world championship matches, against Chigorin.

W.Steinitz – M.Chigorin

Game 4, World Championship, Havana 1892

Spanish Opening

1.e4 e5 2.♘f3 ♘c6 3.♗b5 ♘f6
Chigorin fared badly with this line in the match, scoring only 0.5/3, in Games 2, 4 and 14.
In Game 16, Chigorin switched to 3... a6 4.♗a4 ♘f6 5.d3 ♗c5 6.c3 b5 7.♗c2 d5, leading to a much closer fight, although Steinitz also won that game.

4.d3 d6 5.c3 g6 6.♘bd2
Steinitz first successfully introduced the idea of combining d3/c3 with an early ♘bd2-f1-e3/g3, in Game 1 of his 1876 match, against Blackburne. In Games 16 and 18, of his 1886 match against Zukertort, Steinitz played 6.d4 ♗d7 7.♘bd2 ♗g7 8.dxe5 ♘xe5 9.♘xe5 dxe5 10.♕e2, reaching a position from

which he hoped to make something of the slightly boxed-in placement of Black's king's bishop (behind Black's e5-pawn) and by advancing White's pawns on the kingside.

6...♗g7 7.♘f1 0–0 8.♗a4
Steinitz was the first player to hit on this idea, which plans a future for

White's bishop on c2, in anticipation of the possible Black plan, ...♗d7, followed by ...♘a5, forcing a simplifying bishop exchange. Game 2 had instead gone 8.♘e3 d5 9.♕c2 a6 10.♗a4 dxe4 11.dxe4 ♘d7 12.0-0 ♘c5 13.♗xc6 bxc6 14.♖d1 ♕e7 15.b3, and Black held.

Chigorin now decides on a long-winded manoeuvre aimed at repositioning his king's knight (via d7 and c5) on e6, to be followed either by ...f5 or ...d5. Game 14 saw the more direct 8...d5 9.♕e2 ♕d6, but Steinitz also won that game. Black's simplest reply may be 8...a6, followed eventually by ...b5, returning to more conventional Black play on the queenside.

8...♘d7 9.♘e3 ♘c5 10.♗c2 ♘e6 11.h4!

Steinitz seizes on Black's weak point: without a Black knight on f6, White threatens h5, followed by hxg6, advantageously opening the h-file. In his *International Chess Magazine*, he observed: 'As a rule I am not a dangerous assailant in the early part of the game, but I espied a weakness on the adverse King's wing, and one must not put his fingers into my mouth, even in my old age, or I may bite'. White's flank attack directly cuts across Black's plan to play 11...f5, as after 12.h5, and if 12...f4 13.♘d5 g5 14.h6 ♗h8 15.♗d2, envisaging ♕e2, followed by 0-0-0 and eventually g3, White can then expect to maintain lasting kingside pressure. White also stands well after 11...h6 12.h5, and if 12...♘f4 (or if 12...g5 13.♘f5) 13.hxg6 fxg6 14.g3; while 11...h5 12.g3, and if 12...f5 13.exf5 gxf5 14.♘g5, also leaves White with good prospects.

11...♘e7 12.h5 d5 13.hxg6 fxg6

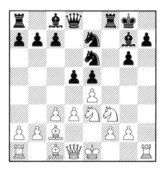

Chigorin keeps the h-file semi-closed and seeks safety for his king on h8. By recapturing this way, however, he allows Steinitz to isolate Black's e-pawn and weaken the central and kingside light squares. But after 13...hxg6, White replies 14.♕e2, followed by ♗d2 and 0-0-0, still with the much better chances.

14.exd5 ♘xd5 15.♘xd5 ♕xd5 16.♗b3 ♕c6 17.♕e2 ♗d7

Chigorin offers his e-pawn in a bid for quick development and counter-attack. Steinitz, however, sticks to his promising plan to castle long and eventually open the position, by playing d4. White also stands well after Chigorin's post-mortem suggestion 17...a5, simply by playing 18.a4.

18.♗e3 ♔h8 19.0–0–0 ♖ae8 20.♕f1!

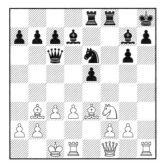

This superb retreat is the game's best move. That White can create serious threats in the centre and on the kingside, with all three of his major pieces 'developed' only on the first rank and no minor piece or pawn placed beyond White's third rank must have surprised many. We are nowadays used to the release of such (modern) Hedgehog Defence-like energy. Back then it was decidedly novel.

In reply, Black fatally allows White to break with d4 immediately. Black also clearly suffers, however, after 20...♘f4 21.d4 (possibly also 21.♘g5, and if 21...h5 22.f3), and if 21...♗g4 22.♘g5 h6 23.d5 ♕f6 24.♘e4 ♕f5 25.♘g3 ♕d7 26.♖d2. Black probably had to try 20...h5, which at least retains a better grip on d4. Even then, however, White's advantage still clearly persists, after 21.♔b1, threatening ♘h4.

20...a5 21.d4 exd4 22.♘xd4 ♗xd4

Black's game now contains too many fragile light square and static pawn weaknesses. Looming problems include such disasters in the half-open h-file as after 22...♘xd4? 23.♖xh7+, and White mates.

23.♖xd4 ♘xd4

Strictly speaking this is an error that leads to a forced mate in six. Chigorin, however, apparently considered that he was dead lost anyway and may have deliberately allowed his opponent to play out the final combination for posterity's sake. If so, we certainly owe him a debt.

Black might still have tried 23...♖e7, and if 24.♖dh4 (24.♕d1, and if 24...♖ff7 25.♗d5 ♕a6 26.♖e4 a4 27.♖e1, may be stronger) 24...♖ff7 25.g3 (threatening 26.♗d4+ ♔g8 27.♕d3, attacking g6, and wins – so far Chigorin) 25...♔g8, intending 26.♕d3 ♕b5 (which Chigorin missed). But even here, scarcely able to move and severely harried by White's menacing forces, Black's chances of survival remain doubtful.

24.♖xh7+ ♔xh7 25.♕h1+ ♔g7 26.♗h6+ ♔f6 27.♕h4+ ♔e5 28.♕xd4+ 1-0

White mates next move. Bravo!

By 1892, Steinitz was acutely aware that his grip on the world title must weaken. In his later fifties, he no longer enjoyed robust good health and required a stick to walk steadily. Mentally alert, but quite worn out by his four recent world championship matches and many literary responsibilities and other engagements, he announced early that year (in his *International Chess Magazine*) that any further 'match between myself and any other master is now almost out of the question, at least for some time to come'.

In 1894, however, Steinitz felt obliged to meet a challenge from a precociously gifted, rapidly rising German star, 25 year-old Emanuel Lasker, who convincingly defeated him. Aged 58, Steinitz was, at last, ripe for overthrow by a worthy successor. In Lasker, Steinitz met such an opponent. Lasker had grown up with and absorbed all of Steinitz's 'modern school' teaching and used his own weapons against him. The age gap, of course, also simply told heavily against an old champion more than twice Lasker's years.

In his *Manual of Chess*, Lasker put his victory into fitting context. Steinitz's unrivalled hegemony, he maintained, rested primarily on the central fact that he could defeat all-comers 'decisively because he was a profound thinker and they were not'. When, however, 'Chess-masters arose who were trained for systematic thinking, who therefore understood ... Steinitz's theory and ... besides had natural talent ... Steinitz was confronted with a task that in his old age he could [no longer] perform'.

In 1894, Lasker was Steinitz's most naturally talented such rival and already a profound Steinitzian thinker. He outsmarted and outfought an old fox, who started their match strongly but whose performance then markedly dipped. In his *Manual of Chess*, Lasker movingly acknowledged how much the chess world owed to Steinitz and added, 'I who vanquished him must see to it that his great achievement, his theories should find justice'. This he achieved quite magnificently in his essay on *The Theory of Steinitz*.

Steinitz had unlocked an enormity of chess truths. Always driven by the power of critical thinking, he brought an objective, science-based order to the problems posed by the game's ever-changing material, time, spatial and structural inter-relationships.

Steinitz's evaluative and planning insights pointed to an enduringly fertile method that continues to resonate. Bear this in mind, while considering an encounter that takes forward a debate about IQP middlegames that Steinitz first raised, in his 1886 world title match, against Zukertort.

Compare this 1896 game with the first game in this chapter and it's plain just how far chess had travelled since the 1830s. It contains all the elements of a modern, top-class, professional clash. The opening is sophisticated. The players' pre-game preparation is knowledge-based, nuanced and precise. The playing mode is objective, evaluative, creative, resourceful and wholly scientific. Steinitz had done most to create this revolutionary new kind of (what we now tend to call) 'classical' chess.

H.Pillsbury – W.Steinitz

St Petersburg 1896

Queen's Gambit Accepted

1.d4 d5 2.c4 e6 3.♘c3 ♘f6 4.♘f3 dxc4 5.e3 c5 6.♗xc4 ♘c6

In *My System*, Aron Nimzowitsch posed the key question about the IQP: 'which predominates, the static weakness or the dynamic strength?'. Steinitz preferred the defence, such as in J.Zukertort-W.Steinitz, Game 9, world championship, Saint Louis 1886, which continued 6...cxd4 7.exd4 ♗e7 8.0-0 0-0 9.♕e2 ♘bd7 10.♗b3 ♘b6 11.♗f4 ♘bd5 12.♗g3 ♕a5 13.♖ac1 ♗d7 14.♘e5 ♖fd8 15.♕f3 ♗e8 16.♖fe1 ♖ac8, achieving rough equality (Steinitz won).

7.0-0 cxd4 8.exd4 ♗e7 9.♗f4

J.Zukertort-W.Steinitz, Game 7, world championship, Saint Louis 1886, had earlier gone 9.a3 0-0 10.♗e3 ♗d7 11.♕d3 ♖c8 12.♖ac1 ♕a5 13.♗a2 ♖fd8 14.♖fe1 ♗e8 15.♗b1 g6 16.♕e2 ♗f8 17.♖ed1 ♗g7 18.♗a2 ♘e7 19.♕d2 ♕a6 20.♗g5 ♘f5 21.g4? (a rather rash choice) 21...♘xd4 22.♘xd4 e5 23.♘d5 ♖xc1 24.♕xc1?! (24.♖xc1 exd4 25.♖e1 improves) 24...exd4 25.♖xd4 ♘xd5 26.♖xd5 ♖xd5 27.♗xd5 ♕e2, with advantage to Black (Steinitz again won).

9...0-0 10.♖c1

J.Zukertort-W.Steinitz, Game 13,

World Championship, New Orleans 1886, led to rough equality after 10.♖e1 ♗d7 11.♕e2 ♕a5 12.♘b5 a6 13.♗c7 b6 14.♘c3 ♖fc8 15.♗f4 b5 16.♗b3 ♕b6 17.♖ed1 ♘a5 18.♗c2 ♘c4, but this time, with some help from his opponent, Zukertort won.

10...♕b6 11.♕d2

Pillsbury attempts to improve on 11.♘b5, with which he had gained an advantage but then lost in a wayward game against Steinitz, at New York 1894, after the somewhat passive retreat 11...♘e8?!. Instead, 11...♘d5, and if 12.♗xd5 ♕xb5, improves.

11...♖d8 12.♖fd1 ♗d7 13.♕e2 ♗e8

Steinitz remains true to the broad outline of his original plan against Zukertort. First, he completes his development and seeks to 'contain' the IQP (Nimzowitsch's term), then manoeuvres to settle a minor piece on d5, to effectively 'blockade' it (also Nimzowitsch). At St Petersburg, Steinitz scored +2-0=1 against Pillsbury's IQP, each game, however, an almighty fight.

In the players' third St Petersburg game, Pillsbury again failed to overcome Steinitz's stubborn defensive resourcefulness, after 13...♖ac8 14.d5 exd5 15.♗xd5 ♔f8 16.♗e3 ♕a5 17.♗b3 ♗e8 18.♘d4 ♘xd4 19.♗xd4 ♗c6 20.♖e1 ♖e8 21.♕d3 ♕g5 22.g3 ♕h5 23.♖e5 ♕h3 24.f3 ♗d6 25.♖xe8+ ♘xe8 26.♗f2 ♖d8 27.♕c4 ♕f5 28.f4 ♖d7 29.♗c2 ♕a5 30.♗xh7?!

which allowed Black to trap this piece, by playing 30...g6, and eventually win in a lengthy and difficult endgame.

14.♗d3 ♖ac8 15.h3 ♘b4 16.♗b1 ♘bd5 17.♗e5 ♗c6 18.♘g5 h6 19.♘ge4 ♘xc3

Chances remain in broad balance. Steinitz now decides to exchange knights on c3 to bring about a c3/d4 pawn structure that Nimzowitsch later termed an 'isolated pawn couple', a temporarily unstable structure (c4 is an especially vulnerable square), which White normally feels impelled to improve by creating so-called 'hanging pawns' (on d4/c4).

Such hanging pawns create different tensions. The pawns themselves may come under strain if the defence can directly confront, constrain and attack them. If left unchallenged, however, the attack often benefits from the hanging pawns' control of the advanced central squares (e5, d5 and c5) and potential to support either a disruptive d5 pawn break or a space-gaining advance by c5.

20.bxc3 ♘xe4 21.♗xe4 ♗xe4 22.♕xe4 ♕c6 23.♕g4 ♗f8 24.c4 f5

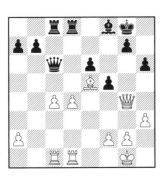

In such mutually tense middlegames, both sides can easily miss chances. Black might have played the more challenging 24...♕a4, and if 25.♕e2 ♗d6 26.♗xd6 ♖xd6, when White's hanging pawns no longer pose any serious threat and Black faces no obvious problems.

25.♕g6 ♕e8 26.♕g3 b6 27.♕b3 ♕c6

28.a4 a5?

Here, however, Steinitz should certainly have preferred ...♗d6 (also good on his last move).

Pillsbury might now have played 29.d5!, and if 29...exd5 30.cxd5 ♕xc1 31.♖xc1 ♖xc1+ 32.♔h2 ♗d6 (or if 32... ♔h7 33.♕xb6 ♖xd5 34.♕e6, followed by ♕xf5+, and f4) 33.f4!, when White's queen dominates. Black's b-pawn is under attack and if Black's bishop vacates d6, White can play d6+, followed by ♕e6, winning Black's f-pawn. Black may then have had no better than to try to hold a difficult endgame, banking on the greater activity of his pieces, after say 29...♕c5, and if 30.♗d4 ♕b4 31.♕xb4 ♗xb4 32.♗xb6 ♖d6 33.♗e3 ♔f7 34.♗f4 ♖dd8 35.dxe6+ ♔xe6.

29.♖c3 ♗d6 30.d5 ♕c7 31.♗xd6

Or if 31.♗d4 ♗b4, and holds.

31...♕xd6 32.♖e3 e5 33.♖b1 e4 34.♖c3

Steinitz no longer has problems. Only White must take care, as Black not only firmly blockades White's d-pawn but also controls the queenside dark squares. Even more significantly,

Black's mobile e- and f-pawns are about to advance. White must avoid 34.♕xb6?, because of 34...♖b8, and Black wins.

34...♕e5 35.♖c2?

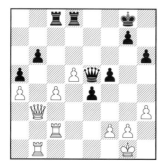

White now squanders a tempo, enabling Black to transfer a rook to g6, which, with ...f4 looming, and given the greater security of Black's king, threatens to develop quickly into a clear kingside advantage.

White had to play 35.♖bc1, and if 35...♖d6 36.c5 bxc5 37.♖xc5 ♖xc5 38.♖xc5, retaining sufficient activity to fight.

35...♖d6 36.♖bc1 f4 37.c5 bxc5 38.♖xc5 ♖xc5 39.♖xc5 f3 40.♕d1?

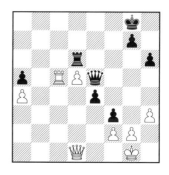

Pillsbury cracks completely. After Black's reply, he is hopelessly lost. His only remaining hope, if slim, was to play 40.♕c3, and seek to hold the dreadfully passive rook and pawn endgame that arises after 40...♕xc3 41.♖xc3 ♖xd5 42.gxf3 exf3 43.♖xf3 ♖d4 44.♖a3 g5.

40...♖g6 41.g4
Or if 41.g3 ♖xg3+ 42.fxg3 ♕xg3+ 43.♔f1 ♕g2+ 44.♔e1 f2+, and wins.

41...e3 42.♕e1
Or 42.♕xf3 e2.

42...e2 43.♖c1 ♕xd5 44.♕c3 ♖c6 0–1

Resolving Classical Tensions

'The theory of Steinitz could be further developed in two directions .... philosophically, as a general theory of the fight ... or with the aim of finding that form of the theory ... most suitable for the practical execution of a chess game'

Richard Réti, *Masters of the Chess Board* (1933)

Réti's famous observation points up a critical difference that lay at the heart of the keen rivalry between two great players, Emanuel Lasker and Siegbert Tarrasch, who together straddled the chess world, from around 1894-1914. Steinitz's magnificent, but huge and often sprawling legacy bequeathed us both a robust scientific approach to chess and a central fighting imperative. The nub of the matter, however, was which comes first: the science or the fight?

World champion throughout these years, Lasker (1868-1941), ultimately won this argument, by convincing us, through his great games and writings, that Steinitz really meant 'neither' but actually 'both'. According to Lasker, Steinitz's complete player requires not just robust knowledge and profoundly objective research skills, but also a completely equal ability to apply such science in a pronounced spirit of creative, pragmatic and passionate combat.

Lasker's towering chess contemporary, Siegbert Tarrasch (1862-1934), sided more with the science. While he never became world champion, Tarrasch was a great teacher (as well as longstanding world number two). A highly accessible communicator, Tarrasch had a passion for the investigation and exposition of the game's more strictly scientific, rules-based essence and (not least) of the theory of the (often sharp) openings that he considered best supported his views.

As theorists and players, both had the highest regard for each other. Tarrasch, however, had one curious blind spot. Perhaps impelled by an occasional surfeit of scientific passion, he sometimes came uncomfortably close to insisting that there must be near absolute 'correctness' in chess, along with singularly 'best' moves. Needless to say, such extreme interpretation of otherwise perfectly valid principle simply grated with Lasker, who, like Steinitz, primarily rejoiced in the game's delightfully vast potential to confound.

In Search of 'Best' Moves

Siegbert Tarrasch

6. Siegbert Tarrasch: circa 1900

The young Tarrasch early on developed a fluent, positionally-based playing style that built on a sure instinct for the exploitation of any available initiative. Its directness and power immediately caught Wilhelm Steinitz's eye. On appraising Tarrasch's game in his first strong international tournament, at Hamburg 1885, the first world champion perceptively noted in his *International Chess Magazine* that the young German 'is evidently a rising star who will most probably develop into one of the first magnitude'.

Aged 23, Tarrasch had just completed his university studies to become a qualified medical practitioner. He had entered the very strong chess field, at Hamburg, without high expectation. To his own and to general surprise, however, Tarrasch competed for top places throughout. He eventually finished in a share of 2ⁿᵈ/6ᵗʰ places, with Blackburne, Englisch, Mason and Weiss, only a half point behind Isidor Gunsberg (12/17), all of these players masters of the very first rank.

In his hugely influential chess autobiography, *Dreihundert Schachpartien* (published 1894), Tarrasch recounts his chess-life story from his earliest years to the mid-1890s. About his Hamburg success, he relates how the news that 'a good chess player might have completed his university studies in a normal timeframe caused widespread astonishment'. Throughout his life, Tarrasch practised medicine and considered himself a primarily amateur player, in the great German tradition most recently and grandly embodied by the late Adolf Anderssen.

Coincidentally, Tarrasch had been a pupil at the Breslau Gymnasium at which Anderssen taught but the two sadly never met or played a game. Tarrasch only began to take up the game seriously in his early teens, when a friend introduced him to chess books, which he devoured. He then advanced to playing in local Breslau coffee shops. There was, however, a wide gulf between that milieu and

Breslau's two or three strongest players, with whom Anderssen mainly played privately at that time.

By 1885, Tarrasch had, of course, not yet developed his fullest powers, but his best games were already marked by a dynamic mix of essentially classical features, for which he soon became famous. He played directly and correctly in the opening, displaying an especial urgency to establish strong pawn centres, backed up by rapidly developed pieces, which he used as a dependably flexible base to promote probing attempts to aggrandise ever more effective, board-wide manoeuvring space.

Steinitz was especially impressed by Tarrasch's finely developed 'power of combination', which he considered 'of the highest type'. At this stage, however, he cautioned 'that his position judgement is not [yet] ripe'. Tarrasch took Steinitz's interest as the encouraging compliment intended. Tarrasch's grand combinative flair and strategic ambition both sparkle brightly, if not entirely without flaw (though he rights himself quickly) in one of his liveliest and most attractive wins, at Hamburg.

F.Riemann – S.Tarrasch

Hamburg 1885

French Defence

1.e4 e6 2.d4 d5 3.♘c3 ♘f6 4.♗g5 ♗e7 5.♗xf6 ♗xf6 6.♘f3 0–0 7.e5 ♗e7 8.♗d3 f6

Black's lively bishop pair, combined with the possibility of combating White's centre, by playing ...f6 and ...c5, are nowadays held to offer Black at least full equality in this very old line. Matters can, however, quickly become tactically murky, such as after, say 8...c5 9.h4, when both sides must continually calculate the correctness of the possibility of the 'Greek Gift' sacrifice, ♗xh7+, followed by ♘g5+.

9.♘e2 c5 10.c3 fxe5 11.dxe5 ♘c6 12.♘g3 ♗d7 **13.♕b1 ♕c7!**

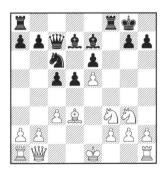

Steinitz and Tarrasch both rightly condemned White's rash 11th and 13th moves, after which White's pawn on e5 becomes critically weak. Riemann may not, however, have anticipated

Black's bold (13th move) refutation which, according to Steinitz required 'high-class' judgment and much 'deep calculation to make sure of [the Black king's] safety'.

Tarrasch fearlessly drops his h-pawn (with check) but wins White's e-pawn and goes on to provide a textbook demonstration of the superiority of concrete counterplay in the centre in response to an unduly speculative attack on the flank.

14.♗xh7+ ♔h8 15.h4

Black's king might seem at risk but White only attacks thin air. Riemann may have intended 15.♕g6, which at first glance seems threatening but which merely backfires after 15...♘xe5 16.♕h5 ♘xf3+ 17.gxf3 ♕f4, intending ...♕h6, in reply to any discovered check by moving White's bishop, with a clear advantage.

15...♘xe5 16.♘g5 c4

With the bit now firmly between Black's teeth, this move is aimed at parrying 17.♗g8, which can now be met by ...♘d3+.

17.♕d1 ♖f6 18.f4 ♘c6 19.♗c2

White also draws blanks after 19.♕h5 ♖h6, and if 20.♘f7+ ♔xh7 21.♘xh6 gxh6 22.♕f7+ ♔h8 23.0–0 ♖g8, when Black's considerable attack only gathers in force.

19...♗e8 20.♘e2 ♗d6?

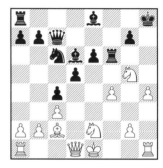

Here, however, apparently in time shortage, Tarrasch misses a chance to bring Black's pressure to boiling point, by playing either 20...♗h5 or 20...♖d8, both of which retain the terrifying prospect of an imminent ...d4 break. Now Black's bishop on d6 gets in the way of such plans, gifting White an effective tempo and scope for counterplay.

21.g3 ♕b6 22.b3 ♗h5 23.bxc4 dxc4 24.♖b1

White can't play 24.♕xd6? ♖d8 25.♕a3 ♕e3, with winning threats for Black. With the text-move, however, White successfully activates his hitherto unemployed queen's rook. This forces Black to sacrifice an exchange to salvage what (if anything) may remain of his earlier, well-crafted attacking momentum.

24...♕c7 25.♘e4 ♖d8 26.♘xf6 gxf6 27.♕c1 ♗c5 28.f5

White might also have played 28.♖b5

and if 28...♘e7 29.♘d4 ♖xd4?! (Black should probably bail out and play 29...♘d5 30.♖xc5 ♕xc5 31.♘xe6 ♕a5 32.♘xd8 ♕xc3+ 33.♕d2 ♕xg3+ 34.♕f2 ♕c3+, forcing a draw.) 30.cxd4 ♕c6 31.♖f1 ♕xb5 32.dxc5 ♕xc5 33.f5 ♕e5+ 34.♔f2 ♘xf5 35.♗xf5 ♕xf5+ 36.♕f4 ♕xf4+ 37.gxf4, with menacing king and rook activity.

28...♕g7 29.♕f4 ♘e5 30.♖f1?

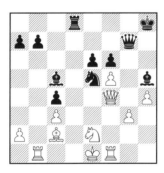

Riemann, who was also severely short of time, misses his only saving resource 30.fxe6, after which Black must realistically abandon any winning thoughts and force the available draw by repetition, by playing 30...♘f3+ 31.♔f1 ♘d2+ 32.♔e1 ♘f3+.

Now White is hopelessly lost.

30...♘d3+ 31.♗xd3 cxd3 32.g4
Or if 32.♘d4 e5 33.♘e6 exf4 34.♘xg7 d2 mate.

32...dxe2 33.gxh5 exf1♕+ 34.♔xf1 ♖d3 35.♕b8+ ♕g8 36.♖xb7 ♖d8 37.♕h2 ♕g4 0–1

In 1887, Tarrasch married and settled in Nuremberg, where he established a medical practice and remained until 1914. The demands of Tarrasch's practice, of course, inevitably constrained his chess activities. In the late-1880s, however, there were still relatively few major international tournaments, so that this didn't perhaps cramp his game as much as it might do nowadays. Despite one or two relative downs, between 1885 and his great breakthrough years (1889-90), Tarrasch soon became Germany's top player.

Ever highly industrious, Tarrasch also found time to study chess deeply and increasingly to write on the game in his leisure hours. While he took pride in his 'amateurism', he nevertheless drew an income from chess writing, tournament winnings, sundry talks and exhibitions that perhaps made him what we might today more properly regard as an active 'semi-professional'. Throughout the year, Tarrasch kept his game in good shape through regular practice in the strong Nuremberg Chess Club.

The years 1889-90, however, propelled Tarrasch to the topmost international rank. At Breslau 1889, Tarrasch became the first German to win a top-class international tournament since Anderssen, at Baden Baden 1870. Scoring 13/17, he outclassed an excellent field, to finish comfortably ahead of second-placed Amos Burn (11.5 points). At Manchester 1890, an even stronger, world class event, Tarrasch then followed this up by scoring a magisterial, 15.5/19, to finish fully three points ahead of second-placed Blackburne.

At a stroke, Tarrasch's reputation soared to such a degree that he became the internationally acclaimed favourite to challenge Steinitz in a world championship match. The members of the wealthy Havana Chess Club, among his most ardent admirers, made him an immediate and financially generous offer to challenge Steinitz for the world title, during the winter of 1890-91. Sadly, this mouth-wateringly attractive contest wasn't to be. Citing constraints on his time due to his busy medical practice, Tarrasch declined.

In *Dreihundert Schachpartien*, Tarrasch confessed that he was both flattered by and sorely tempted to accept the Havana Club's invitation. In his reply to the Club, however, he regretfully declared that he 'could only afford to spend the few summer weeks that every modern person has free from work each year to play in tournaments and matches'. To this he added that 'the quarter of a year' needed to play in such a demanding match might even require him 'to abandon his medical practice'.

Would the young Tarrasch have actually defeated Steinitz at this time? Steinitz went on to defend his title comfortably, against Gunsberg, at New York 1890-91, and then much less assuredly, against (the much tougher) Chigorin, at Havana 1892. Had Steinitz's opponent been Tarrasch, during either of these time slots, lobbing powerful, main line Spanish Openings at the ageing champion rather than Chigorin's string of more speculative Evans' Gambits, who knows what might have been.

While quite unstoppable in most games, at Manchester 1890, Tarrasch, as all winners do in such powerful fields, had to survive one or two insecure moments. Against Emil Schallopp, he first outplayed an opponent, with a dangerous, if occasionally erratic reputation only to stumble in the process of converting his advantage into a win. Steinitz, by now casting an eagle eye on a potential challenger's every move, spotted a deeply hidden refutation of Tarrasch's eventual 'winning' idea, which both sides missed.

E.Schallopp – S.Tarrasch

Manchester 1890

French Defence

1.e4 e6 2.d4 d5 3.♘c3 ♘f6 4.e5 ♘fd7 5.f4 c5 6.dxc5 ♘c6 7.♘f3

White's 6th move, nowadays infrequent, releases the central tension perhaps a little early. Here, however, White might try the livelier 7.a3, and if 7...♗xc5 8.♕g4, which Tarrasch himself successfully championed, in his 1905 match against Frank Marshall.

7...♗xc5 8.♗d3 f6 9.exf6 ♘xf6 10.♕e2 0–0 11.a3 a6 12.♗d2 b5

White's 11th move prevents ...♘b4, followed by ...♘xd3+, eliminating White's attacking light square bishop. But it also allows Black to prepare a promising ...b4 break, which Tarrasch precedes with an original rook manoeuvre to bolster his centre.

13.h3 ♖a7 14.g4 ♖e7 15.♘e5?!

Schallopp begins to show his erratic side. This snatched move simply squanders tempi. White should play the much more natural 15.0–0–0, completing his queenside development.

15...♘d4 16.♕g2 ♘d7 17.♘f3?

According to Tarrasch, in *Dreihundert Schachpartien*, this is the 'decisive error', after which Black wins a pawn. White should now have reconciled himself to playing 17.♘xd7 ♕xd7 18.0–0–0, even if, after 18...a5, threatening ...b4, Black clearly has nothing to fear.

17...♘xf3+ 18.♕xf3 g5!

Tarrasch's 'refutation', if no ordinary one: White's f-pawn falls, but at the cost of creating much open space around Black's king. Tarrasch's judgement is wholly robust, but to retain control in such open positions also often requires excellent nerves.

19.♕g3 ♕c7 20.♘e2 ♗d6 21.0–0–0 ♘c5!?

Here Tarrasch confessed to getting unduly anxious and committing the classically human error of trying to calculate a 'win' out 'perfectly', failing to do so and running short of time. He should have confidently followed through with his initially planned 21... gxf4 22.♕h4 e5 (both ...♘c5 and ...♘e5 are also good), but then he feared that 23.♗f5 might still complicate, even though, after 23...♘c5, Black remains clear favourite to win.

22.♖hf1 ♘b3+?!

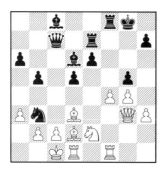

Despite his wobble on the previous move, Black still has a winning advantage, but 22...gxf4, and if 23.♗xf4 ♘xd3+ 24.♖xd3 e5, looks a rather clearer way to proceed.

23.♔b1 ♘xd2+ 24.♖xd2 gxf4 25.♕f3 ♖ef7?
Here, however, Black should certainly have preferred 25...♗b7, threatening the rapid advance of Black's central pawns, with an additional tempo.

26.g5 ♖g7 27.♖g1 ♕f7 28.♘c3 b4 29.axb4 ♗xb4 30.♖dg2 ♕b7?!

Matters have already become a lot more complex than they might have been and Schallopp, to his great credit, keeps finding ways to stay in the game. Tarrasch afterwards suggested the possible improvement 30...♗xc3, and if 31.♗xh7+ (or if 31.bxc3 ♕b7+ 32.♔c1 e5) 31...♔h8 32.♕xc3 f3 33.g6 ♕f6, when 'Black's passed pawns must win in the endgame after a queen exchange'.

31.♘d1 e5 32.g6 h6 33.♖e2 e4?

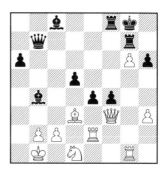

This looks powerful but, with his nerves now shredded, Tarrasch walks into a finely sprung trap. Tarrasch lamented: 'Nothing is so calculated to strain the mind … as putting everything into a search for a solution to a problem and failing to find it'. Black still stands better after 33...♗d6, and if 34.♕h5 f3.

34.♖xe4 dxe4 35.♗c4+ ♔h8 36.♕h5 ♗f5?
And the game now completely turns White's way. Black should have played 36...♗c5, after which best play for both sides may be 37.♕xh6+ ♖h7 38.gxh7

♕xh7 39.♖g8+ ♖xg8 40.♕f6+ ♖g7 (or if 40...♕g7 41.♕h4+) 41.♕d8+, with a draw by repetition. Not, however, 36...♖f6?, which loses to 37.♕xh6+ ♖h7 38.g7+ ♕xg7 39.♕xf6 (Tarrasch).

37.♕xh6+ ♖h7 38.gxh7 ♗xh7 39.♗xa6?

Perhaps fortunately for Tarrasch, Schallopp was now just as exhausted and harried by the clock as a result of his extraordinarily heroic defence. Step forward Steinitz: Schallopp and Tarrasch both appear to have overlooked the surprising resource 39.♘c3!, threatening ♘d5, followed by ♘f4–g6+, which is decisive, such as after 39...e3 40.♘d5 ♗a3 41.♗b3 e2 42.♘xf4, and if 42...e1♕+ 43.♖xe1 ♕g7 44.♕xg7+ ♔xg7 45.♘e6+ ♔h6 46.bxa3, and wins for White.

39...♕e7 40.♕h5?
Now Schallopp implodes. Black wins a piece and the game. White had to play 40.♖g6.

40...f3 41.♖g5 ♕d6 42.♖d5 ♕xa6 43.♖d7 ♕g6 44.♕e5+ ♕f6 45.♕h5 ♕f5 0–1

Tarrasch next returned to top-class chess, at Dresden 1892, where he once again confirmed his world-class reputation, by taking clear first place, scoring 12/16, in the strongest international tournament played that year. At St Petersburg 1893, he then met Chigorin in a magnificent match that finished in an honourable tie, 9-9 in wins (with 4 draws), a contest that in every way compared in quality to the Steinitz-Lasker world title encounter that followed only a few months later.

In these years, Lasker proved far more determined to challenge Steinitz than Tarrasch. Between 1889-90 and 1894, the younger man enjoyed his own, quite separate meteoric rise in tournaments and matches in Europe and the USA. Pausing his mathematics studies, Lasker also played more or less full-time and unhesitatingly grasped his own first chance to wrest Steinitz's title. Lasker's form peaked at just the right time to ensure that he capitalised against the ageing and physically ailing champion. Such is world championship chess!

Back in Germany, Tarrasch still contended that his own long record of success more than matched Lasker's and sniffed a bit. But he had turned down his own earlier chance at the title and could scarcely complain. When, in 1892, Lasker had (not unreasonably) challenged him to a match, Tarrasch had rebuffed him, moreover, on the unduly high-minded grounds that Lasker should first win a major international tournament. As the decade wore on, Lasker's increasingly outstanding results soon completely eclipsed those of everyone else.

In the early to mid-1890s, Steinitz, Tarrasch, Lasker and Chigorin were all generally considered to be in a class of their own. In mid-decade, they were joined for a heady few years by a new American youngster, Harry Nelson Pillsbury, while the ageing Steinitz's powers inevitably waned. By the early 1900s, only Lasker (principally) and Tarrasch reigned supreme by their consistently better results against all-comers and highly admired under-standing of chess.

Despite stylistic differences, all played in the classically modern, dis-tinctively enterprising and concretely analytical manner bequeathed to them largely by Steinitz. Chigorin tended towards a complex improvisatory and combinational playing style. Tarrasch more coolly preferred to dish up his well-principled attacks in a more correctly direct way. Pillsbury leant heavily towards bold confrontational combat. Lasker ploughed a more prag-matically powered path that enigmati-cally borrowed from all styles. All paid due homage to Steinitz.

In an article in *Deutsches Wochen-schach*, written in 1902, Lasker sought to capture Tarrasch's particular con-tribution to the development of this new commonality. Giving due weight to Steinitz, he nonetheless insisted that 'the new school', had not least developed 'so strongly [because of its] acceptance and unconditional applica-tion of Tarrasch's principle of objective critique'. Despite Tarrasch's occasional tendency to overstress the principle of 'correctness' and (singularly) 'best' moves in chess, this was a widely held view.

Virtually all of the rising genera-tion of top players (those born around 1880) drew heavily from *Dreihundert Schachpartien*, which Tarrasch largely conceived as an instructional work, 'especially about the middlegame, al-beit without any rigorously conceived system' and was the kind of magnifi-cent chess autobiography that every-one hoped Steinitz might write but never got round to. Clear, direct and persuasively, but not over-heavily di-dactic in tone, its core is as admirably objective and critical, as Lasker's com-ments suggest that it might be.

Throughout *Dreihundert Schachpar-tien*, Tarrasch's drive to get at the game's fundamental essence and invite well-founded challenge is abundant. As re-gards the Chigorin-Tarrasch, Saint Pe-tersburg match, Tarrasch insightfully guides us through all the games played in a battle between two stylistically op-posite giants that is perhaps best re-membered for the ways in which the players explored many highly original and ingenious ideas, in virtually un-charted territory of the Closed French Defence.

M.Chigorin – S.Tarrasch

Game 4, St Petersburg 1893

French Defence

1.e4 e6 2.♕e2 c5 3.g3 ♘c6 4.♘f3 ♗e7 5.♗g2 d5 6.d3 ♘f6 7.0–0 0–0 8.♘c3

The players have reached a modern King's Indian Attack main line. White now commonly continues 8.e5, and after 8...♘d7 (or 8...♘e8) 9.c4, with chances for both sides. After Chigorin's move, Black can play ...d4, followed by ...e5, reaching a fairly equal, reversed kind of Classical Variation v King's Indian Defence (not yet conceived in the 1890s).

8...a6 9.♗g5 h6!?

Tarrasch criticised this unforced move, considering that it created a target for an eventual White kingside attack. The solid ...d4, followed by ...e5, of course, remains an excellent alternative.

10.♗f4 b5 11.♖fe1 d4 12.♘d1 ♘d7 13.♔h1 ♖e8 14.♖g1 e5 15.♗d2 ♘f8 16.♘e1 ♘e6 17.f4

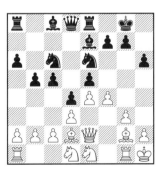

Tarrasch now preferred White, who can hope to hurl his f- g- and h-pawns

forward in a pawn-storm attack. Unduly pessimistic, however, Tarrasch underestimates certain strengths that remain in Black's game: extra space in the centre, imminent queenside counterplay and dogged defensive prospects on the kingside dark squares.

17...♗b7 18.f5 ♘g5 19.♘f2 ♖c8 20.♕h5

Tarrasch also criticised this move, observing that in such positions 'the pawns must first advance to breach openings for supporting pieces'. While admirably thought-provoking, this generalisation may not apply here. At any rate, after Tarrasch's preferred 20.h4 ♘h7 21.♘h3, intending ♗f1, followed by ♕h2 and g4–g5, Black can energetically reply 21...c4, and if 22.♗f1 c3 23.bxc3 dxc3, followed by ...♘d4, with excellent counterplay.

20...♘h7 21.♘f3 c4 22.♗f1 cxd3 23.cxd3 ♘g5 24.♗xg5 ♗xg5 25.♘g4 ♔f8!?

Having obtained a relieving minor piece exchange, Black now embarks on a plan to run his king towards central safety. Black might, however, also have considered 25...♗e3, keeping in play such defensive ideas, as ...f6, and offensive possibilities, such as ...♘b4, and not fearing a minor piece exchange on e3, which would only weaken White's centre.

26.♗e2 ♗f6 27.h4 ♕d6?!

Tarrasch intends to secure his kingside defences, by playing ...♘e7–g8. Now, however, White would clearly stand better, by playing 28.♘xf6 ♕xf6 29.g4 ♔e7 30.g5 hxg5 31.♘xg5!

and if 31...♖h8 32.♘h7 ♕h6 33.f6+ ♔d6 34.♖xg7 ♕xh5 35.♗xh5, when, with no knight on b4, Black's game distinctly lacks prospects.

The computer prefers the immediate 27...♘b4!, and if 28.♘xf6 ♕xf6 29.g4 ♔e7 30.g5 hxg5 31.♘xg5 (or 31.hxg5?! ♕b6!, threatening ...♖h8) 31...♖h8 32.♘h7 ♕h6, which seemingly holds, such as after 33.♕xh6 gxh6 34.f6+ ♔d6 35.♖g7 ♖c7, or 33.f6+ ♔d6 34.♕xh6, which transposes.

28.♘fh2 ♘e7 29.♖af1 ♘g8 30.♗d1 ♖c7

31.♗b3 ♖ec8 32.♘f2 ♗d8

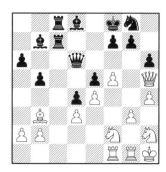

All is not plain sailing for White, who must now retreat his queen before playing g4 (which can't be played immediately because of ...♘f6). Thereafter, according to Tarrasch, Chigorin defaults to the 'strategically correct' plan of advancing White's kingside pawns in front of White's pieces.

33.♕e2 a5 34.♘f3 a4 35.♗d1 ♗c6 36.g4 f6 37.♘h3 ♗e8 38.♕h2 ♗f7 39.a3 ♗b3 40.♘f2 ♗xd1 41.♘xd1 ♖c2 42.♕g3 b4 43.axb4 ♕a6 44.♘f2 ♖xb2 45.g5 hxg5 46.hxg5 ♖cc2 47.♘g4 ♕d6?

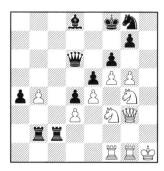

Since move 33, both sides have made cogent progress and this most mutually baffling contest remains in a wholly tense balance. White has developed his kingside attacking potential. Black has consolidated his kingside defences, while simultaneously developing his own counter-attacking potential on the queenside.

Here, however, it seems that instead of passively defending his e-pawn, Black should have offered the sharp gambit 47...a3!, and if 48.gxf6?! (White should probably prefer 48.b5!, and if 48...♖xb5 49.♕h3, with a continuing balance) 48...♗xf6 49.♘fxe5 ♗xe5 50.♕xe5 ♘f6! 51.♘f2 ♕b7 52.♕h2 ♕f7!, with good play for Black, including after 53.♕h8+ ♕g8 54.♕h2 ♕h7!.

7. Tarrasch (l.) v Chigorin: 1893 match in St Petersburg

recapture), by ♖g6, and ♖ag1, with game-winning threats.

49...a3 50.♘xf6 ♕xf6 51.♖g6 a2 52.♖xf6+?

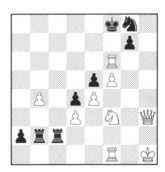

Chigorin now plays quite incorrectly to win Black's queen and completely collapses. White had to be content with the draw by repetition that results after the forcing 52.♘g5 ♔e7 53.♖xf6 ♘xf6 54.♕h8 ♘e8 55.♘e6, and if 55...♖b1 56.♕f8+ ♔d7 57.♕f7+ ♔d6 58.♕f8+, etc.

52...gxf6 53.♖d1

48.gxf6 ♗xf6 49.♕h3?

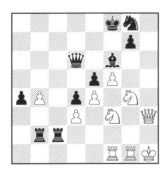

Chigorin goes wrong. He should have first attacked Black's a-pawn, by playing 49.♖a1!, and only after 49...♖xb4 50.♕h3!. With Black's powerful double rook battery on the 7th rank no longer in place, White then threatens ♘xf6, followed (after Black's forced queen

Or if 53.♖g1 ♖b1 54.♕g4 (or 54.♘e1 a1♕ 55.♕g3 ♖xe1) 54...♖xg1+ 55.♕xg1 ♖b2, and wins.

53...♖b1 54.♕f1 ♖cb2 55.♘d2 ♖xd1 56.♕xd1 ♖xd2 57.♕c1 ♖xd3 58.♔g2

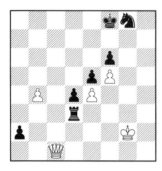

As Black's king can escape to h8 after ♕c8+ and ♕c7+, White has no saving perpetual check and Black's powerful pawns, rook and knight simply mop up.

58...♖c3 59.♕a1
Or if 59.♕b2 ♖c2+ 60.♕xc2 a1♕.

59...♖c2+ 60.♔f3 d3 61.♕d1 ♖b2 62.♕a4 d2 0–1

Not long after Lasker became world champion, Tarrasch headed a further fine field, at Leipzig 1894, to register his fifth top-class tournament win, since 1888. Although Lasker, didn't play at Leipzig, Tarrasch and his supporters could still argue that the older man's exceptional (and quite unmatched) recent top tournament record maintained his reputational edge over the titular champion. Imagine the antici-

pation, therefore, at Hastings 1895, where both Tarrasch and Lasker were to cross swords in their first ever tournament together.

Which one of the two top seeds would dominate, at Hastings? As it turned out, the unexpectedly brilliant Hastings winner, Harry Nelson Pillsbury, and second-placed, Mikhail Chigorin, rather stole their thunder. Lasker finished third, ahead of fourth-placed Tarrasch, with Steinitz in fifth place. The upshot was a further reputational call to arms for the five top Hastings prize-winners to resume battle, at St Petersburg 1895-96.

The St Petersburg tournament was conceived as a magnificently appointed match tournament to be contested by the five greatest players in the world. Sadly, however, once more citing pressures of his medical practice, Tarrasch declined. The remaining four players nevertheless still came together to do battle in six game mini-matches against each other. Notwithstanding Tarrasch's absence, many regard this tournament as the strongest ever held in the 19th century.

This time Lasker dominated. Final results at St Petersburg: Lasker (11.5/18), Steinitz (9.5), Pillsbury (8) and Chigorin (7). At Nuremberg 1896, Lasker then comfortably outdistanced all three of these top players, plus Tarrasch. Through the Moscow winter of 1896-97, Lasker then trounced Steinitz in a return world championship match, to seal his clear world number one status. He followed up these outstanding successes, by taking two further superb tournament firsts, at London 1899 and Paris 1900.

Tarrasch couldn't keep pace. Post-1896, moreover, he went into one of his quieter chess periods. At Vienna 1898, he did, however, manage to secure an epic win in his sole grand tournament outing in the late-1890s. Held in celebration of the Austrian Emperor's 50th Jubilee, this exacting event featured a marathon 36 rounds. In Lasker's absence, Tarrasch and Pillsbury dominated, both scoring 27.5 points, but with Tarrasch edging out Pillsbury (2.5-1.5) in a tie break.

In truth, Tarrasch always prioritised his medical and family responsibilities over the demands of time-consuming tournament and match chess. In *Dreihundert Schachpartien*, he let slip the revealing comment that, in his big breakthrough year (1890), away from the game: 'just as my medical practice grew, so did my family ... and I thereby enjoyed a quite blissful existence'. Through 1888-1897, Tarrasch's family grew to include six children. He delighted in the prosperous, cultured and respectable life as a German doctor and family head.

In these years, Tarrasch also simply devoted much of his time to lectures and copious chess writing, in all of which he exuded a deep understanding of what were emerging ever more clearly as the three main elements in chess, *Force*, *Time* and *Space*, including their highly complex inter-dependence *cum* inter-changeability. As Tarrasch later summed up, in his best-selling, *The Game of Chess*, published in 1933, towards very the end of his life, 'Time can be changed into Space or Force, or *vice versa*'. His books are chock-full of the clearest advice.

Ever practical, Tarrasch stressed that, in chess, 'you must not *lose* a single move [and that] in the Opening every tempo must, whenever possible, be utilised for the development, so that the essential pawns are moved with all speed, and the minor pieces developed'. Above all, he held that the timely and 'systematic utilisation of Space, or ... disposition of the pieces, is the most important factor ... and, within certain limits, even more important than Force ... often a win is obtained because one player forces a decisively better position by a sacrifice'.

Tarrasch had a special regard for *Time* and *Space* and gave us a whole string of the earliest model examples of what we now take for granted can be achieved if an opponent plays without due care to timely development and the maintenance of sufficient space in which to generate counterplay. At Vienna 1898, poor Carl Walbrodt plays much too passively, allowing Tarrasch to dominate space and squeeze him relentlessly all over the board, eventually converting this domination into a decisive material advantage.

S.Tarrasch – C.Walbrodt

Vienna, 1898

Queen's Gambit

1.d4 d5 2.c4 e6 3.♘c3 ♘f6 4.♘f3 ♗e7 5.♗f4 c6 6.e3 ♘bd7 7.h3 ♘f8?!

This rather artificial manoeuvre allows White to establish a queenside and central dark square clamp that promises a long-term space advantage. Black should have preferred the already known and reliable 7...0–0.

8.c5 ♘g6 9.♗h2 ♕a5

White maintains the integrity of his queenside pawns after 9...b6 10.b4, and if 10...a5 11.a3, so Black tries to complicate. White's clever reply, however, shows that White can still achieve b4 and a3 anyway.

10.a3 ♘e4 11.♗d3 ♘xc3 12.♕d2 ♘h4 13.♘xh4 ♗xh4 14.b4 ♕d8 15.♕xc3 0–0 16.0–0 ♕d7 17.♕c2

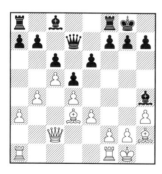

White should probably have preferred a4, intending b5, followed by ♖fb1 (threatening a5–a6), in an attempt to dominate the queenside completely.

Tarrasch instead judged that he had already achieved enough on the queenside and that the time had come to launch a kingside attack. He noted that such attacks tended to cause 'the most acute and severe problems'. The downside is that Black might eventually achieve some diversionary play in the a-file, as happens.

17...f5 18.♔h1 ♗d8 19.♗e5 ♗c7 20.f4 ♗xe5 21.fxe5 ♕e7 22.g4 g6 23.♖f4

Tarrasch plans to continue his attack by moving his queen and queen's rook to the g-file, followed by an exchange of pawns on f5, at a moment when Black must either recapture with his e-pawn (leaving White with a strong, protected passed e-pawn) or concede the open g-file to White's major pieces. Black, however, also gets in ...a5, which proves to be more than an irritant.

23...♗d7 24.♖g1 ♔h8 25.♕g2 a5 26.♗b1

axb4 27.axb4 ♖a4 28.gxf5 exf5

Here, 28...gxf5, might also have been possible, combining the blocking resource ...♗e8–g6, with continual attacks on White's b-pawn. According to Tarrasch (but without detailed analysis), White can then strongly continue with the manoeuvre, ♖f3–g3, and if ...♗e8–g6, ♖g5, followed by h4–h5. Matters, however, may not be quite as straightforward as that.

29.♕d2 ♖g8 30.♕e1 ♗e6 31.h4 ♖aa8 32.♖ff1 ♖g7 33.♖g2 ♖ag8 34.♖h2 ♕d7?

After this move, however, Black's game notably deteriorates. Rather than go into passive mode, Black had to try 34...g5, after which Tarrasch gave 35.♗xf5 ♗xf5 36.♖xf5 gxh4 37.♖f6, but appears to have missed 37...♖g3, threatening ...♕g7, with excellent counterplay. Note, too, that after 35.♗d3 gxh4 36.♕xh4 ♕xh4 37.♖xh4 ♖g3, and if 38.♗xf5 ♗xf5 39.♖xf5 ♖g1+, Black forces a draw by repetition.

35.♗d3 ♖a8 36.♕g3 ♕e7 37.♖g1 ♖ag8 38.♖hg2 ♖f8 39.♕f4 ♖fg8 40.♕h6

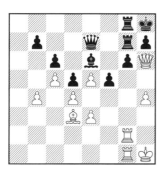

With the kingside dark squares now firmly under control and all of Black's pieces in severely constricted holding positions, Tarrasch begins to wind up the pressure faultlessly. White first plays his rook/g2 to g5, and king, to f4, in preparation for a game-winning h5 pawn break.

40...♗d7 41.♔h2 ♗e6 42.♖g5 ♗d7 43.♔g3 ♗e8 44.♔f4 ♗d7 45.h5 ♗e8 46.hxg6 ♗xg6 47.♗e2

The mundane 47.♗xf5, and if 47...♕f7 48.♖1g4, apparently also wins. Tarrasch, however, sticks to his original intention to play the elegant ♗h5, after which Black can only expect, at length, to lose material anyway, even after 47...♕e6 48.♗h5, and if 48...♗f7 49.♕xe6 ♗xe6 50.♖xg7 ♖xg7 51.♖a1, when Black's b-, f- and h-pawn weaknesses and absence of activity (combined with the possibility of a b5 pawn break), add up to a winning advantage.

47...♕d8 48.♗h5 ♗xh5 49.♕xh5 ♖xg5 50.♖xg5 ♖xg5 51.♕xg5 ♕f8

The game might have more instructively concluded 51...♕xg5+ 52.♔xg5

♔g7 53.♔xf5 ♔f7 54.♔g5 ♔g7 55.e6!, and if 55...♔f8 56.♔h6 ♔e7 57.♔xh7 ♔xe6 58.♔g6 ♔e7 59.♔f5 ♔f7 60.♔e5 ♔e7 61.b5! ♔d7 62.bxc6+ bxc6 63.♔f6 ♔d8 64.♔e6 ♔c7 65.♔e7 ♔b7 66.♔d7, and wins, due to White's clever use of the opposition and delightful 55th and 61st move pawn breaks.

52.e6 1-0

After a few years' hiatus, the Lasker-Tarrasch rivalry began to pick-up again in the early 1900s. First, Tarrasch returned from a lengthy absence from top-class chess, at Monte Carlo 1902 and 1903. Four years on from Vienna 1898, his lack of practice showed in a modest share of 5th/7th places (in 1902). In 1903, however, he won outright. Following his victory, at Paris 1900, Lasker also absented himself, until returning, at Cambridge Springs 1904, where he finished second, behind Frank Marshall.

These returns to the board coincided with growing clamour for the world champion once again to defend his title. In 1904, Tarrasch and Lasker duly opened match negotiations that were widely welcomed. In his early 40s, Tarrasch was perhaps past his absolute best but, still the natural challenger, he fully believed in his chances. In January 1905, however, Tarrasch suffered a serious leg injury, due to a fall on ice, and the players' agreement, although highly advanced, sadly collapsed.

Tarrasch had asked for a lengthy, one year's match postponement because of his injury. Lasker, who stood to lose financially, flatly declined. A mooted match between Lasker and Geza Maroczy then also fell through, it seems largely because Maroczy couldn't meet Lasker's financial demands. Tarrasch's repute as 'true' challenger nevertheless persisted, especially after he drubbed Marshall in a match (+8-1=8), at Nuremberg 1905. The parties eventually faced off, only in 1908, in the match of the decade.

Excitement ran high. At Ostend 1907, Tarrasch had topped a six player, four game mini-match tournament ahead of three of his closest rivals, C. Schlechter, Marshall and D. Janowski. He then rather grandiosely announced in the tournament book that, having played in fourteen top-class tournaments and finished first in seven of them, he would only in future play in matches, first up, he hoped, against Lasker. Meanwhile Lasker had also defeated Marshall (+8-0=7), in a one-sided title defence, at New York 1907.

After intense negotiations, the long-awaited Lasker-Tarrasch showdown finally took place, at Düsseldorf and Munich. Lasker won decisively (+8-3=5). Tarrasch maintained that he obtained many near winning advantages in several of his lost or drawn games. In truth, Lasker simply made much more of his own advantages, while Tarrasch, who made too many serious slips, found himself regularly out-played by the more pragmatic, quick-witted and endlessly resourceful champion.

Tarrasch (46) may, of course, have left his challenge a little late on age grounds. That apart, the match was lost by a player, who tended towards an ultimately unattainable ideal of 'correctness' and who seemed, as a result, psychologically prone to allowing his errors to prey a little too much on his mind. Tarrasch, moreover, faced the world's most perennially unflappable opponent, as well as its greatest fighter. Lasker simply saw error as an occasionally unavoidable part of an inherently difficult game.

In *Gesunder Menschenverstand im Schach* (1925), Lasker later mused that Tarrasch's chess-thought world 'was built on the foundations of the definite article ... of '*the* correct move but seldom of *a* correct move ... *the* best move but never *a* best move'. Lasker believed in *good* moves, of course, and in the formidable Tarrasch's over the board ability to find them much more often than not. Given the chance, Tarrasch could overwhelm anyone, as in Lasker's first loss in their match.

Em.Lasker – S.Tarrasch

Game 3, World Championship, Düsseldorf 1908

Spanish Opening

1.e4 e5 2.♘f3 ♘c6 3.♗b5 a6 4.♗a4 ♘f6 5.0–0 ♗e7 6.♖e1 b5 7.♗b3 d6 8.c3 ♘a5 9.♗c2 c5 10.d4 ♕c7 11.♘bd2 ♘c6 12.h3 0–0 13.♘f1

The players reach a modern main line position by an old-fashioned route. We more commonly see 9...0–0 10 h3 c5 11 d4 ♕c7 12 ♘bd2 ♘c6, nowadays. The line has, however, since rather fallen out of favour, due to the squeeze play that White can now begin to exert after 13.d5 ♘d8 14.a4, or if 13...♘a5 14.b3. Lasker's quasi-gambit alternative is no longer considered to cause Black any real problems.

13...cxd4 14.cxd4 ♘xd4 15.♘xd4 exd4

16.♘g3

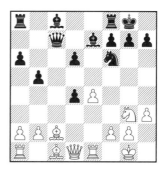

Tarrasch's active reply to this move equalises. After the manoeuvre ...♘d7, followed by ...♗f6, Black rapidly develops all of his forces and targets White's slightly uncomfortable e-pawn. In Game 5, Lasker switched to 16.♗g5, although after 16...h6 17.♗h4 ♛b6 18.♛d3, Tarrasch again had objectively little to fear but defended indifferently and lost.

16...♘d7 17.♗b3 ♛b6 18.♘f5 ♗f6 19.♗f4 ♘e5 20.♗d5 ♖a7 21.♛b3?

Lasker considered that he lost this game because he chased 'tempting attacking prospects' that proved completely unfounded. Tarrasch, he wrote, now 'held on to the gambit pawn securely'. Lasker should have preferred 21.♘xd4, and if 21...♘c4 22.♘e2 ♘xb2 23.♛d2, when White can expect to regain his pawn and maintain a continuing balance.

21...♖c7 22.g4 g6 23.♘h6+ ♔g7 24.g5 ♗d8 25.♛g3 f6

Reality hits home with this accurately timed counter-punch that exposes the fragility of White's grip on the kingside dark squares. White has no real attack and is about to be unceremoniously pushed back on the kingside. Black obtains a clear advantage, after 26.gxf6+ ♖xf6, and if 27.♔h1 ♗e6. White loses at once, after 26.h4? fxg5 27.hxg5 ♖xf4

28.♛xf4 ♗xg5, gaining a winning material plus.

26.♘f5+ ♔h8

Perhaps Lasker had hoped for 26...gxf5?, after which he can play 27.gxf6+ ♔h8 28.♗h6

and if 28...♖ff7 29.♗xf7 ♖xf7 30.♗g7+ ♔g8 31.♗h6+, with a draw in hand. After the much better text-move, however, White's knight must retreat and White's prospects become even grimmer.

27.♘h4 fxg5 28.♗xg5

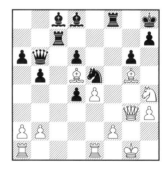

White's retreat has turned into a rout. After this move, White's f-pawn becomes fatally weak. Black must also win, however, after 28.♗xe5+ dxe5 29.♘f3 g4, and if 30.♘xe5 gxh3 31.♖ac1 ♛f6.

28...♗xg5 29.♕xg5 d3 30.♔h1 ♖c2 31.♖e3 ♖fxf2 32.♘g2 d2 33.♖g1 ♖c1 34.♕e7 ♖xg1+ 35.♔xg1 d1♕+ 36.♔xf2 ♕f3+ 37.♔e1 ♕a5+

Although Tarrasch overlooks the immediately overwhelming 37...♘d3+ 38.♔d2 ♕a5+ 39.♔xd3 ♕d1 mate, it scarcely matters now. White is hopelessly lost.

38.♖c3 ♗xh3 39.♕xd6 ♕axc3+ 40.bxc3 ♕xc3+ 41.♔e2 ♕c2+ 42.♔e3 ♕d3+ 43.♔f4 g5+ 44.♔xg5 ♘f7+ 0–1

After losing to Lasker, any remaining hope that Tarrasch might still have entertained about winning the world title effectively ended. He remained a player of the very highest class up to the Great War years, and, in 1911, tied a notable match (+3-3=11), against rising Austrian star, Carl Schlechter. As Tarrasch neared 50, however, younger players increasingly caught up and overtook him, foremost among them, the extraordinarily gifted Cuban champion, José Raúl Capablanca.

Unsurprisingly Tarrasch remained as prolific as ever with his wonderfully eloquent chess pen. In 1909, *Dreihundert Schachpartien* went into a second successful edition. Then in 1912, Tarrasch published a second outstanding book, *Die Moderne Schachpartie*, which he subtitled, *A Critical Study of 224 Classical Games with special regard to Opening Theory*. This deeply researched and well-considered work addressed the key advances in chess theory made since around 1900.

Die Moderne Schachpartie delivers an exceptionally fine state of the art tour to all of the main openings played in that classical era. A 'must read' for all serious players, it provided a first-class complement to *Dreihundert Schachpartien*, which, moreover, benefited by the wide scope it gave, not just to Tarrasch's own games, but also to those of all other great masters. Although neither book was translated into English, both must have been devoured by a huge international audience in the original German.

Tarrasch's best writing is peppered with excellent opening, middlegame and endgame advice. He had a talent for the communication of highly memorable hints and maxims. If occasionally over-dogmatic, he was nonetheless consistently clear and fully open to debate. His guiding spirit is perhaps best summed up in the concluding words to a lecture given to the Cologne chess club, in 1907: 'I don't wish to bring you 'truths', rather what I consider to be 'true' on the basis of the experiences I have gained over the last quarter of a century'.

I take this quote from Wolfgang Kamm's definitive (2004) biography, *Siegbert Tarrasch: Leben und Werk*. Kamm also provides an outline of the substance of that lecture. The main distillations of Tarrasch's hard-won experiential truths, on which he enlarged in this lecture:

♟ Every Opening tempo should either develop a piece or a central pawn

♟ With the Attack, doubled, isolated, even doubled-isolated pawns are rarely as 'weak' as they are frequently thought to be

♟ Backward pawns on open files can quickly become vulnerable

♟ Avoid the creation of 'holes' that can be exploited by occupying forces without fear of capture by defending pawns

♟ Middlegame Attacks should be directed against an opponent's weak points

♟ There are no sidelines, only one move is 'right'

♟ The main chess struggle is generally fought in the centre

♟ In many cases the key battle is for control of the e5 square

♟ In the Opening, and if the bishops remain undeveloped, the respective moves, d3 and ...d6, should generally be avoided

♟ With the exception of mate, no move can avoid making some weakness

♟ Don't attack at will but only where an opponent demonstrates a weakness, albeit sometimes very slight

♟ There is no fundamental difference between 'closed' and 'open' positions, as just one move might fundamentally reverse such matters

♟ Chess theory ebbs and flows unceasingly, with new judgements possible not just slowly but frequently overnight

In all of the above, Tarrasch's points always aim to strike a 'right' note, in a bid to express his take on classical values. Taken as a whole, with the possible exception of his singular fixation on the absolute existence of 'right' moves, they provide much more food for thought than mere dogma. In 1909, a little known German chess writer bestowed on Tarrasch the not undeserved title, *Preaceptor Germaniae*, which Tarrasch acknowledged with creditable blushes.

Tarrasch famously ends the *Preface* in *The Game of Chess* with the passionate words: 'I have always a slight feeling of pity for the man who has no knowledge of chess, just as I would pity the man who has remained ignorant of love. Chess, like love, like music, has the power to make men happy.' Tarrasch saw romance and great beauty in chess. One of his most cherished games was his wonderfully lyrical win, against Nimzowitsch, at St Petersburg 1914, which earned the second brilliancy prize.

A.Nimzowitsch – S.Tarrasch

St Petersburg 1914

Queen's Gambit

1.d4 d5 2.♘f3 c5 3.c4 e6 4.e3 ♘f6 5.♗d3 ♘c6 6.0–0 ♗d6 7.b3 0–0 8.♗b2 b6 9.♘bd2

In the tournament book, Tarrasch preferred 9.♘c3. Black's knight on c6, he explained, 'is a little better placed than White's on d2, as [the latter] has no move and makes little impact in the centre'. This comment really only splits hairs. Curiously, at Hamburg 1910, in a game between the same two players, with colours reserved, Tarrasch played 9.♘c3, and actually lost!

9...♗b7 10.♖c1 ♕e7 11.cxd5 exd5 12.♘h4?

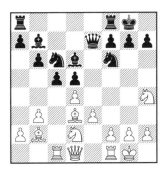

This move, however, squanders tempi and really is bad. After Black's reply (correctly covering f5), White all too ambitiously hopes to exploit (potential) attacking chances along the long dark square diagonal, forgetting that Black also has moves. After the more natural 12.dxc5 bxc5 13.♖e1, followed

perhaps by a3 and ♕c2, both sides have prospects, in a tense standoff between Black's hanging c- and d-pawns and White's probing pieces.

12...g6 13.♘hf3 ♖ad8 14.dxc5 bxc5

Black has now achieved hanging c- and d-pawns with a time bonus, for which Black's slight weakness along the long dark square diagonal offers no great gain for White. Growing in confidence, Tarrasch now states: 'Black has two hanging pawns, which are generally held to be weak but which I consider strong … Black commands the centre and has a distinct advantage'.

15.♗b5 ♘e4 16.♗xc6 ♗xc6 17.♕c2

Tempi count: if White were again to move, he could exchange knights on e4, followed, after …dxe4, by playing ♘d2, splitting Black's central pawns, with chances for both sides. With the move, however, Black now cuts completely across such plans. Note, too, that after 17.b4 ♗b5, and if 18.bxc5 ♘xc5, followed by ...♘d3, is also better for Black.

17...♘xd2 18.♘xd2 d4!

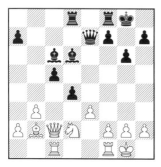

This is an early example of a fine breakthrough motif by Black's (dynamically supported) hanging pawns that has since become 'standard'. Black threatens devastating bishop sacrifices, whose impact White now either badly miscalculates or simply misjudges. White should now play 19.e4, and if 19...♖fe8 20.♖fe1, blocking the a8–h1 diagonal, when Black retains some advantage but White battles on.

19.exd4 ♗xh2+ 20.♔xh2 ♕h4+ 21.♔g1 ♗xg2

Black's double bishop sacrifice is lethal. If Nimzowitsch thought his next move might hold, he is rapidly confounded. Black also wins by force, after 22.♔xg2 ♕g4+ 23.♔h1 ♖d5, and

if 24.♕xc5 ♕h5+ 25.♔g1 ♖g5+ 26.♕xg5 ♕xg5+ 27.♔h1 ♕xd2.

22.f3 ♖fe8 23.♘e4

Or if 23.♖fe1 ♖xe1+ 24.♖xe1 ♕xe1+ 25.♔xg2 ♕e2+, followed by ...♖d5, and wins.

23...♕h1+ 24.♔f2 ♗xf1 25.d5

White finally clears the long dark diagonal but can't exploit it.

After 25.♖xf1 ♕h2+, however, White loses his queen. Black now sets up the final combination with a very fine introductory quiet move.

25...f5 26.♕c3 ♕g2+ 27.♔e3 ♖xe4+ 28.fxe4 f4+

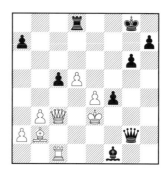

Tarrasch misses the quickest mating finish, 28...♕g3+ 29.♔d2 ♕f2+ 30.♔d1 ♕e2 mate. The actual conclusion, however, is an equal delight.

29.♔xf4 ♖f8+ 30.♔e5 ♕h2+ 31.♔e6 ♖e8+ 32.♔d7 ♗b5 mate (0-1)

Chess as a Principled Fight
Emanuel Lasker

You have to stand back a bit to understand such a complex figure as Lasker. That he was the world's strongest player, from around 1894 until the Great War years, and possessed by far the most pragmatic approach to chess at that time, has already been made clear in the discussion about his rivalry with Tarrasch. Lasker certainly retained a much healthier scepticism than Tarrasch about the role played by generalised principles, maxims or rules, in winning games.

Lasker didn't decry such abstractions. He merely approached them all with an open mind and a clear sense of balance. To Lasker, the chessboard struggle itself was paramount. All chess knowledge derived from that source and its further development depended on constant review of its outcomes. In the heat of battle, the strongest players always treat acquired knowledge with due caution, attuned to expect to have to grapple with a legion of well-nigh inevitable and surprising new thoughts and exceptions.

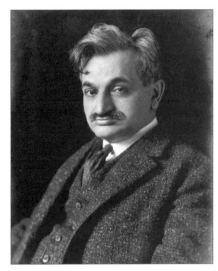

8. Emanuel Lasker, in mid-1920s

Yet, while Lasker maintained this firm conviction throughout his life, he nevertheless acknowledged and taught that there was one special type of rule that merited quite exceptional attention. This was what he called, in his essay on *The Theory of Steinitz*, 'the rules of Steinitz' (sometimes Steinitz's 'method'), whose primary injunction was that the serious player should always search for the most accurate 'valuation' they are capable of, to inform planning.

Lasker argued that Steinitz's 'rules' carry an unusually timeless weight that derives from Steinitz's intrinsically philosophical insistence that the central point to grasp about chess is that all games begin in a broad state of 'balance'. Once clearly understood, this way of thinking impels players to focus as much on the idea of good decision-making as on the application of acquired knowledge. Both play a significant role in any top player's skills-set.

This starting point led Steinitz to conceive attacks based on accumulating a sufficiency of small advantages and aimed at exploiting an opponent's weak points. Conversely, it implied that the defence should concern itself with the protection of weak points, economy of defensive means and well-founded counterattack. The very young Lasker bought completely into this new way of thinking, which only gradually went mainstream as the 19th century drew to its close.

In his *Manual of Chess*, Lasker later ventured a number of interesting 'Criticisms' and 'Additions' to Steinitz's theories. Principal among these: an elaboration of best means of *Co-operation* of the chessboard forces; a *Principle of Justice* that implies that actual error attracts due retribution in chess; and a sense of *Proportionality* that must attach to any given disposition of force. Lasker passionately advised students to think critically from first principles and took obvious delight in cautioning against all received wisdom.

Having won the German 'master' title, in 1889, Lasker grew rapidly in strength, gaining clear match wins, against von Bardeleben, Mieses, Bird (twice) and Blackburne, and then two stunning tournament victories, at London 1892 and New York 1893, in the latter scoring 13/14. Increasingly a full-time professional through these years, Lasker very rarely lost games or even looked uncomfortable as he racked up points against all but Steinitz, Tarrasch and Chigorin (whom he had not yet met).

Aged 58 and ailing, Steinitz surely wasn't surprised to lose his title to such an obviously gifted, worthy and (perhaps decisively) very much younger, 25 year-old opponent. Despite a spirited 3-3 start to the match, Steinitz's form suddenly nosedived, allowing Lasker to score five successive wins, after which the match (to ten wins, with draws not counting) was effectively over. Having both absorbed and applied Steinitz's own modern methods against him, Lasker duly saw the match out (+10-5=4).

Em.Lasker – W.Steinitz

Game 11, World Championship 1894

Queen's Gambit

1.d4 d5 2.c4 e6 3.♘c3 ♘f6 4.♘f3 ♗e7 5.e3 0–0 6.♗d3 c5

Such Semi-Tarrasch lines (as we now know them), in which White plays a restrained e3 and Black responds with a direct attempt at freeing his game, by playing ...c5, were regarded by Tarrasch himself as entirely correct for both sides. They have a rich history that goes back (at least) to the Saint

Amant-Staunton match (Paris 1843) and remain subtly demanding.

7.dxc5 dxc4 8.♗xc4 ♕xd1+ 9.♔xd1 ♘c6
Steinitz often combined this move and ...♗d7, against various lines of the Queen's Gambit. Black can also opt for a queenside fianchetto (with Black's knight on d7), as in S.Bogdanovich-A. Korobov, Kiev 2013, which continued 9...♗xc5 10.♔e2 a6 11.♗d3 ♗e7 12.♖d1 b5 13.a3 ♗b7 14.b4 ♘bd7, with chances for both sides.

10.a3 ♗xc5 11.b4 ♗b6

Lasker has invited a queenless middle-game, in which White's (centralised) king is likely to stand well in any eventual endgame. White also enjoys a little more space and slightly the more active piece development. Black's game, however, remains solid and he can certainly hope to achieve full equality, as long as he continues to develop actively. Steinitz, alas, soon begins to drift all too passively.

Curiously Steinitz was guilty of similar passivity, in Game 19, in which he tried 11...♖d8+ 12.♔e2 ♗f8 13.♗b2

♗d7 (13...b6 14.♖hd1 ♗b7, seems simpler) 14.♖hd1 ♖ac8 15.♗b3 ♘e7 16.♘d4 ♘g6 17.♖d2, when, while Black's game remains defensible, the position is certainly rather easier for White to play. Lasker won, to secure his tenth win and the title.

12.♔e2 ♗d7 13.♗b3 ♖ac8 14..♗b2 a5?

After this somewhat impetuous and patently risky thrust, Black definitely stands worse. White now gains valuable additional queenside space and serious dark square prospects (along the a3–f8 diagonal and against Black's a-pawn). Steinitz's lapse is all the more surprising as he might instead have played the natural developing alternative, 14...♖fd8, and if 15.♖hd1 ♘e7 16.♖ac1 a6 17.♘e5 ♗e8 18.♖xd8 ♗xd8, still with perfectly robust defensive prospects.

15.b5 ♘e7 16.♘e5 ♗e8 17.a4 ♗c7 18.♘c4 ♗d7 19.♖ac1
Correctly taking his time, White threatens ♗a3, followed by b6, winning material. Black just about survives, after the less patient 19.b6, and

if 19...♗d8 20.♞xa5 ♗xb6 21.♞xb7 ♖b8 22.♞d6 ♗xe3.

19...♞ed5 20.♞xd5 ♞xd5 21.♞e5 ♗xe5
Black must concede the bishop pair on an open board, in which all of White's pieces actively combine with menace. He would certainly be lost, after 21...♗e8? 22.♞d3, and if 22...f5 23.♗a3 ♖f6 24.♖c2, with winning threats in the c-file.

22.♗xe5 f6 23.e4
Here, there was a strong case for 23.♗d4, threatening e4, and if 23... f5 24.♖hd1, when White maintains steady, if not yet winning pressure. Lasker's sharper choice, by changing the nature of the endgame, aims for more, but may be a little too greedy.

23...fxe5 24.exd5 ♔f7 25.♖hd1 ♔e7?

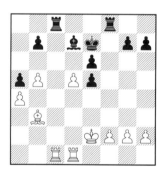

Steinitz, however, fails to spot his sole defensive resource, 25...♖xc1, and if 26.♖xc1 ♖c8, when the various pawn or bishop and pawn endgames arising, after 27.♖xc8 ♗xc8 28.♔d3 (or 28.d6 ♔e8) 28...♔e7, and if 29.b6 ♔d6 30.dxe6 ♗xe6 31.♗xe6 ♔xe6 32.♔e4 g6,

seem to be drawn. Nor is it clear in this line whether White can make any tangible progress, after 27.♖d1 ♔e7, and if 28.♖d3 (28.d6+ ♔f6) 28...e4 29.♖g3 g6. After four consecutive Steinitz losses (in Games 7-10), perhaps Lasker simply got lucky.

26.d6+ ♔f6
Or if 26...♔f7 27.♖c7 ♖xc7 28.dxc7 ♔e7 29.b6, and there is no defence to the manoeuvre ♗c2-e4 (forcing ...♗c8), followed by ♖b1-b5.

27.♔e3 ♖xc1 28.♖xc1 ♖c8 29.♖xc8 ♗xc8 30.♗c2 ♔f7

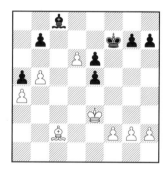

As White can now get his bishop to e4, before Black's king can threaten White's d-pawn, such as after 30...g6 31.♗e4 ♔f7 32.♔d3 ♔e8 33.♔c4 ♔d7 (33...b6 34.♗c6+) 34.♔c5, followed by ♔b6, this bishop and pawn endgame is hopeless.

31.♗xh7 g6 32.♗e4 ♔f6
Or if 32...♔g7 33.♗xe5 ♗d7 (or 33... ♔xh7 34.♔f6) 34.h4 b6 35.h5 ♔xh7 36.♔f6, followed by ♔e7, and wins.

33.g4 g5 34.♔f3 ♔f7 35.♗e4 ♔e8 36.h4

Creating a second passed pawn and now clearly decisive.

36...♔d7 37.h5 ♔e8 38.♔e3 1–0

From relatively impoverished, but well educated north German Jewish roots, Lasker moved, as a promising mathematics student, to late-1880s' Berlin. An even more gifted chess player, Lasker soon also found that he might draw an income through play in the city's lively chess cafés. When, in mid-1891, he was offered a lucrative opportunity to run the 'chess pavilion', at what was to become a highly successful 'German Exhibition', in London, for much of the rest of that year, he put his mathematics studies on hold.

Unlike Tarrasch, Lasker saw no objection to the life of a chess professional, as long as it paid well. As it turned out, Lasker enjoyed a lifelong ability to flit from one to another in a string of profitable professions. A talented mathematician, as well as a world-beating chess player, Lasker developed into a wide-ranging freelance intellectual and writer, who published works on philosophy and on the theory of games, as well as on sundry other subjects, including, of course, much on chess.

Lasker's chess skills alone gave him a dependable earning power, well into the 1930s. His extraordinarily early elevation, aged just 25, to world champion, conferred such a financial premium on his chess talents that, from 1894 onwards, he probably spent rather more of his time in chess than previously planned. In addition to his many subsequent top tournament outings, in these years, Lasker also successfully defended his title, for the first time, in 1896-97, against Steinitz.

Through the 1890s, Lasker devoted most of his energy to consolidating his world number one status in chess. In addition to his top-class matches and tournaments, he greatly expanded his chess journalism, lecturing and exhibition activities, both in Europe and in the USA. Along the way, Lasker nonetheless still found time to keep in touch with his university studies. Early in 1900, he eventually secured his doctorate in mathematics, from Erlangen University.

During the spring of 1895, Lasker delivered a series of twelve lectures, in London, which he eventually issued in his first chess book, *Common Sense in Chess*, published in the following year. Lasker's book characteristically opens with the firm assertion that the game's 'primary characteristic seems to be – what human nature mostly delights in – a fight … but a fight within which the scientific, the artistic, the purely intellectual element holds undivided sway [and] becomes a harmonious whole'.

Lasker then proceeds to 'endeavour to describe' what he believes to be the essentially pragmatic underpinnings of a well-played game of chess. Using a wide range of opening, middlegame, endgame and complete game examples, he conveys his 'common sense' view of how best to bring optimum pressure to bear upon 'questions at issue'. Cautioning that hard work is essential, his voice is distinctive, but his analyses and prescriptions also unmistakably draw deeply from Steinitz's thought world.

Sadly, the 60 year-old, ex-world champion, was clearly no match for Lasker, when they again met to contest their second title match, at Moscow 1896-97. Lasker simply overwhelmed his opponent, scoring +10-2=5. The age gap and the older man's even worse physical shape and staying power, than in 1894, ensured that this was a one-sided contest. Steinitz retained

a profound chess understanding, of course, but could no longer sustain the quality of his play, as in his prime.

It speaks volumes that no other player dared challenge Lasker, at that time. He would have been odds-on favourite to defeat anyone. While Steinitz began most games well enough and conceived some excellent plans, his timing and especially his tactics frequently failed at later moments. With his Steinitz-inspired, 'common sense' chess sparking at full power throughout, Lasker could mostly afford to manoeuvre patiently until a tiring Steinitz momentarily let his guard down, as in Game 2 in their match.

Em.Lasker – W.Steinitz

Game 2, World Championship, Moscow 1896

Spanish Opening

1.e4 e5 2.♘f3 ♘c6 3.♗b5 ♗c5 4.c3 ♘ge7 5.0–0

Steinitz adopts an old line that dates back, at least, to the early 1840s, and perhaps surprised Lasker, who now avoids the sharpest reply, 5.d4, and if 5...exd4 6.cxd4 ♗b4+ 7.♗d2 ♗xd2+ 8.♕xd2. Having assessed this line at home, however, he employed it, in Game 4, which continued 8...d5 9.exd5 ♘xd5 10.♗xc6+ bxc6 11.0–0 0–0–0 12.♘c3, with easier play for White (who won). Bobby Fischer later championed the more critical 8...a6!. M.Tal-R.Fischer,

Curaçao 1962, then continued 9.♗a4 d5 10.exd5 ♕xd5 11.♘c3 ♕e6+ 12.♔f1 ♕c4+ 13.♔g1 0–0 14.d5 ♘a7 15.♖e1 ♘f5 16.h3 ♘b5, with an eventual draw. Fischer's 14ᵗʰ move, however, was his real improvement on (the doubtful) 14...♖d8?! 15.♕e1 ♗g4 16.♗b3 ♕f4 17.dxc6 ♗xf3 18.♕xe7 ♗xc6, played in Alekhine-Bogoljubow, St Petersburg 1913 (although Black won).

5...♘g6

Steinitz chooses slow play. White now obtains a strong (e4/d4) pawn centre.

Black banks on retaining sufficient central space, to complete his development and gradually develop queenside and central counterplay. Fischer preferred the active 5...♗b6 6.d4 exd4 7.cxd4 d5, as in L.Evans-R.Fischer, Buenos Aires 1960, which continued 8.exd5 ♘xd5 9.♖e1+ ♗e6 10.♘e5 ♘de7 11.♗e3 0-0 12.♗xc6 ♘xc6 13.♘xc6 bxc6 14.♘c3 ♕f6 15.♕a4 ♗d5, with compensation for Black's broken queenside pawns (the game was drawn).

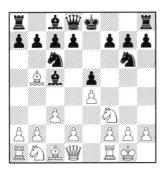

6.d4 exd4 7.cxd4 ♗b6 8.♘c3 0-0 9.a4 a6 10.♗c4 h6 11.h3 d6 12.♗e3 ♘ce7 13.♖e1 c6 14.♕b3 ♗c7 15.♘d2 ♖b8 16.♖ac1 b5 17.axb5 axb5 18.♗d3 ♔h8

While White may still stand objectively better, one nevertheless has to admire the way in which Steinitz methodically manoeuvres towards his positional goals. Black may suffer some cramp but remains solid. Now, having already made some queenside ground, Black plans to break, with ...f5, aiming to exchange pawns on e4 and secure prospects on the central light squares (especially d5) and in the half-open f-file.

19.♘e2 f5 20.exf5 ♗xf5 21.♗xf5 ♖xf5 22.♘g3 ♖f8 23.♕e6

In the absence of clearly forcing tactics, such games of essentially strategic manoeuvre can be wearingly difficult for both sides. Has Black fully equalised? Does White still have an edge and, if so, critically how does he hang on to it? Lasker now offers a queen exchange, no doubt hoping to make further progress in the e-file and on the queenside, without queens on the board.

23...♕c8 24.♕xc8 ♖fxc8 25.♘b3 ♔g8 26.♘e4 ♔f7 27.g3 ♔e8 28.♖e2 ♔d7 29.♖ce1 ♗b6?

Steinitz blinks first. Lasker has cleverly manoeuvred his forces to set up subtly veiled threats in the e-file that Steinitz

9. Steinitz (l.) v Lasker: world championship match 1894

either now overlooks or miscalculates. White's reply to the text-move, is thoroughly poisonous. Steinitz should have played 29...♖f8, and if 30.♗f4 ♖f5 31.h4 ♖bf8 32.♗e3 ♘d5, which still seems solid.

30.♗f4 ♗c7?!

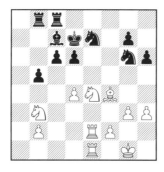

Black may have intended 30...♘xf4?, but overlooked 31.♘f6+, and if 31... gxf6 (or if 31...♔d8 32.♖xe7, winning material) 32.♖xe7+ ♔d8 33.♖e8+ ♔c7 34.♖1e7 mate. Steinitz also clearly disliked 30...♘f5, which allows 31.♗xd6, and if 31...♘xd6 32.♘xd6 ♘f4 33.♖e7+

♔xd6   34.gxf4   ♖c7, when White still remains favourite to win, by continuing 35.♖7e6+ ♔d7 36.♖g6, and if 36...♖f8 (or 36... ♖g8 37.f5, threatening f6) 37.♖xg7+ ♔d6 38.♖g6+ ♔d5 39.♖xh6 (or 39.♖ee6).

31.h4 h5

Not now 31...♘f5?, allowing 32.♘ec5+!, and mates.

32.♗g5 ♗d8

Black can no longer secure a knight on f5, and his game collapses. After 32... ♘f5, White has the crushing 33.g4!, and if 33... hxg4 34.h5 ♘f8 35.♘g3!, and wins, as Black's knight cannot move from f5, without allowing ♖e7+; or if 34...♘gh4 35.♗xh4 ♘xh4 36.♘f6+, and mates. White also wins quickly, after 32...♖e8 33.g4 hxg4 34.h5 ♘f8 35.♘ec5+ dxc5 36.♘xc5+ ♔c8 37.♖xe7.

33.g4 hxg4 34.h5 ♘f8 35.♘ec5+ dxc5 36.♘xc5+ ♔d6 1–0

White mates in five: 37.♗f4+ ♔d5 38.♖e5+ ♔c4 (or if 38...♔xd4 39.♖1e4 mate) 39.♖c1+ ♔xd4 (or 39...♔b4 40.♗d2 mate) 40.♖c3, followed by ♘b3 mate.

The sheer scale of Lasker's dominance, in these years, was breathtaking. He saw out the 1890s, with a searing, +19-1=7, at London 1899 (Steinitz's last tournament); and saw in the 1900s, with an even more remarkable, +14-1=1, at Paris 1900. None of his serious rivals could keep pace with him. Pillsbury perhaps pushed him hardest but not even he could match the depth and consistency of Lasker's powerful all-round game, which was a notch or two above that of allcomers.

What was his secret? None perhaps really, other than that he fought at the board much harder than most; and that he possessed exceptional powers of deeply penetrative calculation; which, allied to his *common sense* gift for accurate valuation and imaginative plans, enabled him to keep game after game going until (mostly) his opponents first cracked. Lasker prized known paths but never slavishly, at all times ready to depart from them. He was quite simply the most formidably masterful and unruffled fighting machine of those times.

In his thought-provoking, *Die hypermoderne Schachpartie* (1925), Savielly Tartakower drew on Friedrich Nietzsche's philosophy to help explain Lasker's spell. Lasker, he maintained, 'insisted on the power of the "will" ... time and again finding moves and plans of such mysterious energy, uncanny correctness and profound inspiration, as to astonish the chess world'. To many, Lasker certainly seemed to play chess like a kind of Nietzschean 'Superman', with an unusually heady regularity, well into the 1920s.

Lasker's win, with Black, against Chigorin, at London 1899, is a good example of Lasker's accomplished, deeply strategic and profoundly correct style of play that virtually all of his opponents routinely found so difficult to deal with. Lasker, as ever, fights hard, but in a rigorously disciplined way, at all times subservient to the underlying flow of the game. Lasker's well-conceived manoeuvres gain ever more advantage as his opponent's mis-steps multiply. Black's final combination crushes all resistance.

There are indications that Lasker prepared rather cleverly for this game. In this tournament, Chigorin was almost certain to adopt his then perennial favourite (2.♕e2) against the French Defence, which Lasker probably adopted because of that. Lasker would appear to have developed an interesting idea that enabled him to steer play into a reversed version of a Vienna Opening, in which Black might expect to obtain a pair of useful bishops and an early grip on d4, which determined the longer-term course of the game.

M.Chigorin – Em.Lasker

London 1899

French Defence

1.e4 e6 2.♕e2 ♘c6 3.♘c3
Chigorin often went his own way in the opening. He was perfectly aware that by playing this move (and closing off the option of c3), he might lose control of the d4 square, but he had ideas of his own about how to play such positions. The more flexible 3.♘f3 is more popular nowadays.

3...e5 4.g3 ♘f6 5.♗g2 ♗c5 6.d3 d6 7.♗g5 h6 8.♗xf6 ♕xf6 9.♘d5 ♕d8 10.c3
Having (deliberately) conceded the bishop pair (Chigorin liked knights), White has gained time and hopes to make something of his flexible and potentially space-gaining pawns in the middlegame. Black's bishop pair and sound pawns, however, fully compensate.

10...♘e7 11.♘xe7 ♕xe7 12.0-0-0 ♗d7 13.f4 0-0-0 14.♘f3 ♗b6 15.♖hf1

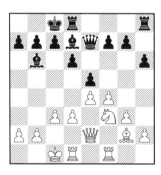

White would like to advance his d-pawn, possibly preceded by ♖he1, but he must always take into account that Black might then swap pawns on f4, followed by ...g5, with open lines for his bishops and counterplay. Chigorin's 'mysterious' rook move perhaps envisages the fuzzy possibility, 15...exf4 16.gxf4 g5 17.♘d4.

15...f6 16.♔b1 ♖he8 17.f5
White, who now completely rules out ...exf4, still hopes to get in d4, but that still isn't easy to achieve without putting his e- and f-pawns at significant risk.

17...♗a4 18.♖c1 ♔b8 19.♘d2 a6
Black retains his bishop pair, making it as difficult as possible for White to make central progress without permitting counterplay. In the much longer-run, Black can also hope that his bishops might eventually support the gradual advance of his queenside pawns, although his light square bishop would be best placed for that purpose on the f7 square.

20.♗f3 ♗a7 21.h4?
After this doubtful thrust, Black hits on a very clever manoeuvre that regroups his rooks on more effective files and allows his light square bishop to reach f7, all without allowing White time to get in an effective d4. White

should have preferred the immediate 21.♘c4, and if 21...♖c8!? (21...♖h8, and if 22.♘e3 h5, looks more tense) 22.♘e3 ♖ed8 23.♕d2 ♗e8 24.d4, when play still remains in rough balance.

21...♖c8 22.♘c4 ♖ed8 23.♘e3 ♗e8 24.♖fd1 ♗f7 25.c4?

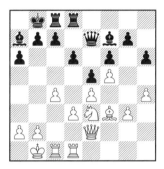

After this second unhappy pawn push, which weakens the central dark squares and allows Black, with his reply, to take control of d5, White can scarcely hope any longer to get in d4, and his game deteriorates. Instead 25.d4?! exd4 26.cxd4 d5!, is no better. White should, however, have played 25.♘d5, and if 25...♕e8 26.d4 c6 27.♘b4 exd4 28.cxd4, which would have kept Black's advantage (after 28... c5) to a playable minimum.

25...c6 26.♖c2 ♗d4 27.♖dc1 ♕c7 28.♘d1 ♕a5 29.♘c3?!

The queenless endgame, after 29.♕d2 ♕xd2 30.♖xd2 b5, might have offered better defensive chances. With or without queens, however, it is no fun to defend such lifeless positions. Black dominates the centre and queenside

and his lively bishops, supported by gradually advancing queenside pawns and active rooks, contain much menace.

29...b5 30.b3 ♖d7 31.cxb5?!

With this and his next move, Chigorin prefers to go down fighting rather than passively wait for Black to pile on ever-escalating pressure, such as after 31.♗h5 ♗g8, and if 32.♕f3 ♕b4 33.♘e2 ♗c5 34.♘c3 ♖b7.

31...axb5 32.♘d5 ♔b7 33.g4 ♖dd8 34.♘e7 ♗xb3!

The powerful, counter-sacrificial refutation of White's play: White's reply is forced, or if 35.♘xc6 ♖xc6 36.♖xc6 ♕b4 37.♖6c2 (or 37.♖1c2 ♗xc2+ 38.♔xc2 ♕b2+, winning) 37...♗xa2+ 38.♔xa2 ♕a4+, and mates next move.

35.♘xc8 ♖xc8 36.♕d2

Bereft of queenside space and any vestige of counterplay, White can no longer defend his numerous weak points. Black's bishop on b3 is clearly immune from capture, and if 36.♖d2 ♗f7 37.♖cc2 ♖a8 38.♖b2 b4!, with ...b3, additionally in the attacking mix, Black must win quickly.

36...♕a3 37.♖h1 ♖a8 38.♖h2 ♗xa2+
White has done what he can to defend laterally but Black's bishop now insists on its capture, winning at once.

39.♖xa2 ♕b3+ 40.♔c1
Or if 40.♖b2 ♗xb2 41.♕xb2 ♕xd3+, and wins.

40...♖xa2 41.♕xa2 ♗e3+ 42.♕d2 ♕xd3
0–1

Between Paris 1900 and his next top-class outing, at Cambridge Springs 1904, Lasker continued to undertake numerous tours and other engagements but concentrated mainly on seeking a switch from full-time chess to academia. Based in Manchester, where he obtained a temporary assistant mathematics lectureship, throughout most of 1901-02, Lasker then moved to New York, where he remained until 1907, initially in the hope of finding a permanent professorial post in the USA.

Lasker's academic ambitions eventually hit buffers. It is, however, hard to imagine that, as a full-time mathematics professor, he might long have remained world chess champion. While he played a significant mathematical role in the development of the so-called 'Lasker-Noether Theorem', in the early 1900s, Lasker never lost his even more primal urge to play chess. Lasker's interest in academia, moreover, appears to have been motivated at least as much by his dissatisfaction with the game's financial rewards as a pure love of maths.

Lasker craved financial security. Like Steinitz before him, Lasker also frequently bemoaned the prevailing amateur ethos that inhibited the fullest flowering of professional chess. As world champion, Lasker could generally negotiate relatively high fees. He was, however, frequently unhappy to find that his negotiations in such matters often attracted undue criticism, even in the USA, where he had expected to encounter a much more enlightened approach. Lasker's biographer, Jan Hannak, suggests that this was already a sore point by the time of the Cambridge Springs tournament.

Lasker didn't play at his best, at Cambridge Springs, finishing in a share of 2ⁿᵈ/3ʳᵈ places, with David Janowski, on 11/15, both well behind US champion, Frank Marshall, on an outstanding, 13 points. Distinctly tournament rusty and still uncertain about his future, either in or out of the game, Lasker certainly hadn't failed abjectly. In those days, however, great champions were more or less expected to dominate every event they played in. At Cambridge Springs, Marshall had completely eclipsed the rest of an excellent field.

Black against Janowski, Lasker's last round, 'no holds barred',

Cambridge Springs slugfest was an epic must-win battle for the world champion. One point ahead in the tournament table, Janowski needed only to draw to secure outright second place. As if to give some credence to a later (quite misguided) contention by Réti, in *Masters of the Chessboard*, to the effect that Lasker often chose 'deliberately bad' moves to wrong-foot opponents, the world champion chose a highly reckless 7th move, following a very sharp opening choice.

Contra Réti, it might be said in Lasker's defence that he probably wasn't aware that this move was quite as bad as we now believe it to be (with much hindsight). He was, however, certainly playing provocatively, with a calculated gambler's eye to its (hoped for) psychological impact on a player renowned for the attack but often uncomfortable when required to defend. True to form, Janowski replied with his own provocation, so that he might do the attacking.

Both sides got what they wanted: Janowski, an attack, albeit somewhat speculative; Lasker, a double-edged defensive battle, in which he might hope to outplay his opponent. Lasker prevailed, however, only because he out-manoeuvred and out-calculated his opponent at one or two absolutely key turning points. The game, though complex, at one stage ran completely away from him and he was fleetingly lost. Janowski, however, by then couldn't cope and went into extraordinary freefall.

D.Janowski – Em.Lasker

Cambridge Springs 1904

Four Knights Game

1.e4 e5 2.♘f3 ♘c6 3.♘c3 ♘f6 4.♗b5 ♗c5 5.♘xe5 ♘xe5 6.d4 ♗d6 7.f4

White can avoid the complications, by playing 7.dxe5 ♗xe5 8.0–0 or earlier 5.0–0, but the text-move is perfectly good and certainly critical.

7...♘g6?!

There is still 21st century interest in this double-edged line but the two main alternatives, 7...♘c6 8.e5 ♗b4, and 7...♘eg4 8.e5 ♗b4, are now known to be better than Lasker's choice. Black aims, in all three of these lines, to give back one of his knights in return for White's 'extra' pawn, to secure king safety, adequate central space and the easy development of his remaining forces.

8.e5 c6!?

The main downside to Lasker's 7th move is that after 8...♗b4 9.exf6 ♕xf6 10.0–0, White is now likely to gain a valuable tempo for the attack, by playing an early f5. E.Barbosa-A.Abdel Elah, Albena 2014, then continued 10... ♗xc3 11.bxc3 0-0 12.f5 ♘e7 13.♕h5, with powerful kingside threats.

9.♗c4!?

If White wished to retreat this bishop, it would have been objectively better (certainly safer) placed on either d3 or a4. On c4, it permits Black to gain a tempo by playing ...d5.

Tarrasch's sacrificial suggestion, 9.exd6, and if 9...cxb5 10.♕e2+ ♔f8 11.f5 ♘h4 12.0-0 may, however, amount to a complete refutation. P.Leonhardt-R.Spielmann, 14th match game, Munich 1906, then concluded 12...h6 13.♘xb5 g6?! (or if 13...b6 14.g3!) 14.fxg6 fxg6 15.♘c7 ♖b8 16.♕g4 1-0. R.Teichmann-W.Napier, 6th match game, Glasgow 1905, had earlier varied 11...b4 12.♘b5 ♘d5 13.fxg6 hxg6 14.0-0 ♕h4 15.g3 ♕h5, when Black held on to draw, but only with a huge slice of luck.

9...♗c7　10.exf6　♕xf6　11.0-0　d5 12.♗xd5!?

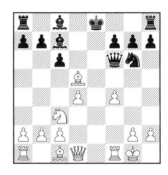

Janowski no doubt had this ingenious, if highly speculative (borderline dubious) sacrifice in mind at move 9. Given that he only needed to draw to finish ahead of Lasker and take outright second place in the tournament, it certainly takes the breath away that he actually played like this.

12...cxd5 13.♘xd5 ♕d6 14.♕e2+ ♘e7
White has a clear lead in development and two powerful pawns for the sacrificed bishop, while the awkward position of Black's knight on g6 is a continuing matter of concern for Black. If, instead of retaining castling rights, Black played 14...♔f8, White might reply 15.♘xc7 ♕xc7 16.f5, and if 16...♘h4 17.f6, with continuing pressure.

15.♖e1 ♗d8!?
Black preserves his bishops and continues to retain castling options. His best move might, however, have been 15...♗e6, and if 16.♕b5+ ♔f8 17.♘xe7 ♕xe7, which seems to hold safely; even after the plausible 18.d5 (or if 18.♕xb7 ♕d8, with ...♗d5 looming) 18...♕d7 19.♕b4+ (or 19.♕c5+ ♗d6) 19...♗d6

20.dxe6, which fails to 20...♗xb4 21.exd7 ♗xe1.

Black also successfully defends, in this line, after 16.♘xe7 ♔xe7, and if 17.f5? ♕xh2+ 18.♔f1 ♕h1+ 19.♔f2 ♕h4+ 20.♔f1 ♗g3.

16.c4 f6!?

Black operates in severely cramped space and this cautious attempt to obtain a secure square for his king on f7 is quite understandable. Perhaps 16... ♗e6, and if 17.♘xe7 ♗xe7 18.d5 ♗d7 (or perhaps 18...♗f5, and if 19.g4 ♗d7) might have been a little better, or possibly 16...♔f8, and if 17.♗d2 a5.

17.♗d2 a5 18.♕h5+ g6

Matters are becoming completely obscure. After 18...♔f8, White probably retains at least sufficient dynamic compensation for his sacrificed bishop but perhaps no more than that, such as after 19.f5 ♗d7, and if 20.♘xe7 ♗xe7 21.♖e4 ♗c6 22.d5 ♗e8 23.♕e2 ♕d7, with continuing challenges for both sides.

19.c5 ♕a6?

This move, however, is certainly bad.

Lasker should have played the much tougher 19...♕c6, and if 20.♘xe7 ♗xe7 21.♕e2 ♕d7 22.d5 ♔f7 23.♕c4 ♗d8 24.♖e3 ♔g7 25.♖ae1 ♕f7. As foreseen by Janowski, Black must avoid 21... ♕c7?, in this line, due to the very dangerous reply 22.f5!, threatening ♗f4, followed by d5.

20.♕h6 ♗e6 21.♘xf6+?

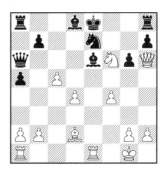

Janowski returns the error. White had two almost certainly winning alternatives: either 21.♕g7, and if 21...♗xd5 (or if 21...♖f8 22.♘b6 ♖f7 23.♕h8+ ♖f8 24.♕xh7) 22.♕xh8+ ♔d7 23.♕xh7, with a clear positional and material advantage; or 21.♘xe7 ♗xe7 22.d5, and if 22...0–0–0 23.♖xe6 ♗xc5+ 24.♔h1 ♕c4 25.♕g7 ♖hg8 (or if 25...♗xd5 26.♗xa5) 26.♕xf6 ♗d4 27.♕e7, which is just as alarming.

21...♔f7 22.♘e4 ♘f5 23.♕h3 ♗e7 24.♗c3 ♗d5?!

In the heat of this tremendously complex battle, Lasker again slips badly. Black should have safeguarded the position of his knight on f5, by playing 24...h5.

25.g4 ♘h4 26.♘d6+ ♔f8 27.♖xe7?!

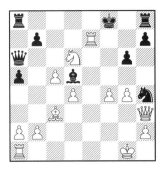

Janowski envisages an extraordinary, but perhaps no better than a quixotic queen sacrifice. White might instead have continued to maintain roughly equal chances, by playing 27.♔f2, and if 27...♗xd6 28.cxd6 g5 29.♖e5 (or if 29.fxg5 ♘g6) 29...♕xd6 30.fxg5 ♘g6.

27...♘f3+ 28.♕xf3

It is, however, now too late for 28.♔f2 ♔xe7, and if 29.♕h6 ♖ag8.

28...♗xf3 29.♖f7+?

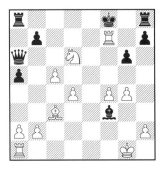

And this move loses. Surprisingly, while White only has a minor piece for his queen, he might still battle, by playing 29.♖ae1, and if 29...♗d5 (not 29...♗xg4? 30.d5) 30.f5!, which threat-

ens f6, followed by ♖e8+, and mates. Black's rooks play little or no real part in the struggle and Black is caught in a punishing bind. Black can apparently hold, but no longer achieve any advantage.

One computer-aided piece of fantasy then runs 30...♖d8 31.♗d2 h5 32.♖e8+ ♖xe8 33.♖xe8+ ♔g7 34.f6+ ♔xf6 35.g5+ ♔g7 36.♖e7+, drawing by repetition. Another possibility goes 30...♕c6 31.f6 h5 32.f7 ♕a4 33.g5 ♕xa2 34.♖xb7 ♗xb7 35.d5!, which forces Black to bail out by playing 35...♕a4 36.♖e8+ ♕xe8 37.fxe8♕+ ♖xe8 38.♗xh8 ♗xd5. Black also gets nowhere, after 30...h5 31.f6, and if 31...♕c6 32.f7 ♕a4 33.g5 ♕c2 34.♖7e2 ♕d3 35.♖e3 ♕a6 36.♖e7 ♕d3 37.♖d7.

29...♔g8 30.d5 ♗xd5 31.♖g7+ ♔f8 32.♖e1 ♕c6

Now, however, White's forces have lost all coordination, so that by threatening to capture White's c-pawn, followed, after its defence, by the manoeuvre ...♖d8 and ...♖xd6, Black wins by force.

33.b4 ♖d8 34.♗d4 ♖xd6 35.cxd6 ♗h1 0–1

Or if 36.♖e2 ♕c1+ 37.♔f2 ♕xf4+ 38.♔e1 ♕xd4, and wins.

During 1904, with his hopes of a professorship fading, Lasker obtained backing for a new venture, *Lasker's Chess Magazine*. As a writer, Lasker was quite the equal of Steinitz and Tarrasch, and his magazine, which ran until 1909, gave him a platform that allowed him to range widely over all sorts of issues about chess. During these years, Lasker also worked on his first philosophical work, *Kampf* (in English *Struggle*), which was published in the same year (2007) that he trounced Frank Marshall (+8-0=7), in his only world title defence, in a decade.

The Lasker-Marshall match, which was hosted in New York, while Lasker still lived in the USA, was eagerly awaited. Outside of the USA, however, the public's enthusiasm was tempered by a clear perception that Tarrasch should have been in Marshall's place. The US champion was a worthy opponent but a rather better tournament than match player. Tarrasch, moreover, had already trounced him, in their 1905 match. But the Lasker-Marshall match, at least signalled Lasker's return to top-class chess, after only two major outings (in 1904 and 1900), in the last seven years.

After the Marshall match, the chess world continued to clamour for the true showdown. Lasker moved back to Europe, later in 1907, where moves then gathered apace to get the two old German rivals back to the board. After lengthy negotiations, a Lasker-Tarrasch title match at last materialised, at Düsseldorf and Munich 1908. In a truly tense and much more internationally eye-catching contest than against Marshall, Lasker eventually ran out winner by a comfortable margin (+8-3=5).

For a while, Tarrasch seemed loath to accept that his defeat might have settled anything. Aged 46, however, any realistic hopes that Tarrasch might still have entertained of launching any future title challenge had been effectively dashed. The players' personal relations had been greatly strained in the run-up to the match, both by Tarrasch's often outrageously expressed sense of prickly self-worth and by the extremely tough hand Lasker played in the financial negotiations. Thankfully these two great players eventually reconciled.

Lasker simply outplayed his older rival, displaying an edge in virtually all aspects of the game, including attack and defence. Above all, Lasker calculated much more deeply and clearly than Tarrasch, an aspect of the latter's game that Capablanca, quoted in the *Evening Post* (New York), in 1916, considered a definite weakness. And this, moreover, against an opponent, described by the same Capablanca, in an interview in *El Grafico* (Buenos Aires), in 1939, as 'a man of a thousand resources at the chessboard', was a severe handicap.

Playing Black, Tarrasch found life especially hard against Lasker, whose +5-1=2, in these games virtually decided the match. Lasker's success had less to do with raw power than with his ability to develop good middlegame plans on the back of sound opening choices. Rather than seek to overrun defences, by employing sharp, theoretical lines, Lasker tended to use the advantage of the move to tease out promisingly playable middlegames, often in less-analysed sidelines.

This strategy worked especially well when Tarrasch switched from defending against Lasker's Spanish Opening (in Games 1, 3 and 5) to playing the McCutcheon Variation of the French Defence (in Games 7, 9 and 11). Rather than react by playing the most critical move (5.e5), Lasker blithely essayed the innocuous 5.♗d3 (twice), before turning, at least, to the rather more challenging 5.exd5. Tarrasch lost his way in these less worked out sidelines, losing twice and gaining only one draw.

Em.Lasker – S.Tarrasch

Game 11, World Championship, Munich 1908

French Defence

1.e4 e6 2.d4 d5 3.♘c3 ♘f6 4.♗g5 ♗b4 5.exd5 ♕xd5 6.♘f3

This perhaps unexpected move tempts Black into an over-sharp response (6...c5) that allows White to exchange favourably on f6. Safer is 6...♘e4, and if 7.♗d2 ♗xc3 8.bxc3 b6, keeping play closed. Em.Lasker-E.Znosko Borovsky, St Petersburg 1909, later went 8...♘xd2 9.♕xd2 ♘d7 10.♗d3 c5 11.c4 ♕d6 12.c3 b6 13.0–0 ♗b7 14.♕e3 0–0 15.♖ad1 ♖ad8 16.♖fe1, with a useful central pawn mass (White won). Em.Lasker-F.Marshall, Game 11, world championship 1907, which Tarrasch would certainly have known of, had earlier gone 6.♗xf6 gxf6 7.♕d2 ♗xc3 (7...♕a5 may be best) 8.♕xc3 ♘c6 9.♘f3, when White's better pawns and freer development offer an edge (Lasker again won).

6...c5 7.♗xf6 gxf6
So far, play remains in known 1900s' theory. Tarrasch's post-game comments, however, suggest that he was already beginning to doubt the wisdom of his 6th move, during the game. That Tarrasch's king is somewhat vulnerable because of Black's broken kingside pawns is not the main issue. As play is unavoidably becoming open in the centre, White's slight lead in development is of more significant weight.

Lasker knew what he was doing. White's initiative persists, even after 7...♗xc3+ (breaking up White's queenside pawns) 8.bxc3 gxf6, as in Em.Lasker-W.Shipley, New York 1911, an eventually drawn simultaneous exhibition game (though against a strong opponent), which continued 9.♗e2 ♘c6 10.0–0 ♗d7 11.c4 ♕d6 12.c3 0–0–0 13.♖b1 ♔b8 14.♕b3 ♗c8 15.♖fd1, with continuing pressure for White.

8.♕d2 ♗xc3 9.♕xc3 ♘d7

Tarrasch now considered his game difficult. He surely knew of the (eventually drawn) game, P.Leonhardt-M. Vidmar, Nuremberg 1906, which continued 9...♕e4+ 10.♗e2 ♗d7 11.dxc5 ♗b5 12.0–0–0 ♕f4+ 13.♕d2 ♕xd2+ 14.♔xd2 ♗xe2 15.♔xe2 ♘a6 16.c6 bxc6 17.♖d6, at which point White has an endgame edge. Was he caught out? At any rate, he now takes a high-risk decision to keep queens on the board.

Well ahead in the match, and with the more comfortable position, Lasker reacts cautiously. In different circumstances, he might now have played the livelier (and perhaps very much stronger) 10.0–0–0, and if 10...♕xa2 11.dxc5 ♕a1+ 12.♔d2 ♕a4 13.♘d4, threatening ♗b5.

10.♖d1 ♖g8 11.dxc5 ♕xc5

Still behind in development and with his king unsafe, Tarrasch continues to faces difficult decisions on virtually every move.

White is clearly better after 11...♕e4+?! 12.♗e2 ♖xg2, because of the excellent reply 13.♔f1!, and if 13...♖g7 14.♗b5 a6 15.♖d4 ♕f5 16.♗a4 e5 17.♖h4 (with ♖g1 also available), when White completely dominates on the kingside (and elsewhere) and must surely win.

12.♕d2 ♕b6 13.c3 a6?

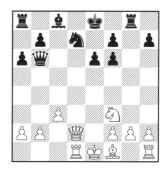

To maintain maximum pressure, White should probably have preferred either 13.a4 or 13.g3.

Tarrasch now misses a possible saving chance. Black hadn't time for the preparatory text-move. Though tricky to judge, Black really had no option other than to play 13...♘c5!, immediately, and if 14.♗b5+ ♔f8! (not 14...♔e7?! 15.♘d4!, and if 15...♖d8 16.♕e3 e5 17.f4, with an attack) 15.♕h6+?! ♔e7 16.♕xh7 ♗d7 17.♗xd7 ♖xg2!, with dangerous counter-threats.

14.♕c2 f5 15.g3 ♘c5 16.♗g2 ♕c7 17.♕e2

17...b5

Black's lost tempo counts. This ambitious thrust on the queenside may be consistent but only creates further targets for White. White's advantage may, however, already have reached decisive proportions.

Black clearly also suffers after 17...♗d7

18.0–0 0–0–0 19.♘e5, and if 19...♗a4 20.b3 f6 21.♘d3 ♗b5 22.c4 ♗d7 23.♘xc5 ♕xc5 24.♖d3, with a crushing grip in the centre and likely game-winning threats.

18.0–0 ♗b7 19.c4

The inevitable happens. With Black's b-pawn under attack, Black has no good move. He can scarcely risk exchanging pawns on c4, as this would only enable White's forces to swarm all over Black's shattered kingside and exposed king, via the queenside. As played, Black succumbs to a deadly penetration by White's queen to h6.

19...b4 20.♕d2 ♖b8 21.♕h6 ♗xf3 22.♗xf3 ♕e5 23.♖fe1 ♕xb2 24.♕f4

Black has maintained material parity but only at ruinous positional cost. With Black's distant queen no longer able to help out in defence, White is

poised to exploit the now quite fatally weak c6 and d6 squares, followed shortly by mate.

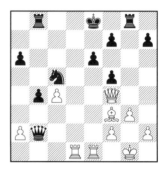

24...♖c8 25.♕d6 f6 26.♗h5+ ♖g6 27.♗xg6+ hxg6 28.♖xe6+ 1–0

Following the Tarrasch match, Lasker began to experience tougher challenges from a younger generation. Lasker's most dangerous, emerging European rival, Akiba Rubinstein, initially impressed by sharing, 1st/2nd places, with the world champion, at St Petersburg 1909, (and defeating him in their individual encounter). In 1911, José Raúl Capablanca, then burst on to the scene, wresting a fine 1st place, at San Sebastian, with the loss of only one game, against 2nd/3rd placed Rubinstein.

Had Lasker faced either of these two players in the run-up to 1914, he would probably have been favourite. Rubinstein and Capablanca, however, both had a game that might easily have caused an upset. Neither match happened. As actually transpired, Lasker twice successfully defended his title, in 1910, before either Rubinstein or Capablanca had established sufficient bargaining power: first against the redoubtable Viennese player, Carl Schlechter, and then against David Janowski.

The Schlechter match was a curious affair. Six years younger than Lasker, Schlechter was a formidable opponent, who rarely ever lost games. Largely due to his unfortunate reputation as a player, however, who took too many draws, he lacked generous backers. Originally intended on a grand scale, as in the Lasker-Tarrasch match, where the winner had to win eight games (draws not counting), the Schlechter challenge had to be drastically scaled back, eventually to the best of only ten games.

Much still remains obscure about this match, not least why Lasker should have agreed to put his title at stake in such a short sprint. More crucial, however, is whether the match rules required Schlechter to win by a two point margin, to gain the title. We simply don't know. Lasker won Game 10, a great, if far from flawless battle, to tie (+1-1=8) and retain his crown. Some argue that Schlechter only needed a draw in Game 10, to become champion, but felt morally obliged to play to win, as a point of 'honour'.

Lasker's next, but much less fancied challenger, Janowski, had the complete support of an extremely wealthy sponsor, who backed his favourite on the grander, Lasker-Tarrasch match basis.

Lasker, however, brusquely brushed Janowski aside, winning by an absolutely thumping margin (+8-0=3). How must Schlechter have felt at that moment? His one big chance had brought him so close to the title. Janowski had totally flopped. Chess history inexorably moved onward.

Only months before the lights went out in Europe, with the outbreak of the Great War (1914-18), Lasker crowned a magisterial two decades as world champion, by winning a fabulously strong tournament, at St Petersburg. Lasker (13.5/18) thrillingly edged Capablanca (13), into second place, with relative newcomer, Alexander Alekhine (10), a distant third. To win this event, Lasker had to claw back a 1.5 point deficit carried forward from the preliminary part of the tournament. He scored 7/8 in those final rounds, two points more than Capablanca, an extraordinary achievement.

Lasker's sensational win against Capablanca, at St Petersburg 1914, with only three rounds remaining, summed up and signed off an era. After St Petersburg, it was clear that these two stood head and shoulders above all others and that Capablanca was Lasker's likeliest successor. In this must-win game, Lasker strained every last sinew to teach the young Cuban a profound lesson in the correctly applied classical arts; delivered spiced and enhanced by Lasker's incomparable ability to play superb chess in an unabashed spirit of 'struggle'.

Em.Lasker – J.R.Capablanca

St Petersburg 1914

Spanish Opening

1.e4 e5 2.♘f3 ♘c6 3.♗b5 a6 4.♗xc6 dxc6 5.d4 exd4 6.♕xd4 ♕xd4 7.♘xd4 ♗d6

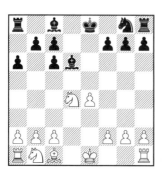

Modern players generally prefer 7...♗d7, followed by 0-0-0, more flexibly locating Black's king on the queenside. Capablanca's plan to castle kingside is a solid, but (at least initially) more purely defensive idea. Playing Black, Lasker had successfully adopted the same plan, against Alekhine, in the previous round.

8.♘c3 ♘e7

Capablanca must surely have been wondering what Lasker had in mind. The epic Alekhine-Lasker game had gone 8...f6 9.♗e3 ♘e7 10.0-0-0 0-0 11.♘b3 ♘g6 12.♗c5 ♗f4+ 13.♔b1 ♖e8 14.♖he1 b6 15.♗e3 ♗e5 16.♗d4 ♘h4 17.♖g1 ♗e6 18.f4 ♗d6 19.♗f2 ♘g6 20.f5 ♗xb3 21.axb3 ♘f8 22.♗xb6 ♗xh2 23.♖h1 cxb6 24.♖xh2 b5, when, having fully equalised, Black eventually managed to outplay his opponent after an exhausting 89 moves.

9.0-0 0-0 10.f4 ♖e8 11.♘b3 f6 12.f5!

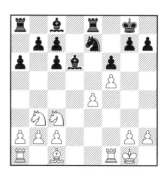

Lasker had successfully adopted this constraining motif (also played in the Alekhine game) in several of his best games in this line in the past. Capablanca afterwards claimed that the idea hadn't fazed him, but it certainly contains more than a little poison. By targeting e6, White restricts Black's light square bishop and kingside pawns. Longer-term, White envisages the advance of his g- and h-pawns to gain space and open lines on the kingside.

12...b6 13.♗f4 ♗b7?

After this move, White stands markedly better. Capablanca confessed that in his rush to develop his light square bishop he had simply overlooked Lasker's clever reply. By exchanging bishops on d6 and (almost counter-intuitively) straightening out Black's doubled c-pawns, White now gains the chance to post a very strong knight at e6.

Lasker had expected 13...♗xf4 14.♖xf4 c5 15.♖d1 ♗b7, and if 16.♖f2 ♖ad8 17.♖xd8 ♖xd8 18.♖d2 ♖xd2 19.♘xd2, which he considered offered White a slight pull, due to his still threatening 4-3 kingside pawn majority. Capablanca seems to have shared this concern during play but he objectively had nothing better.

14.♗xd6 cxd6 15.♘d4 ♖ad8

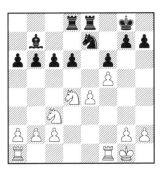

A difficult decision: Capablanca allows White's knight to occupy e6, in the hope that he might rapidly complete his remaining development and eject it later. After 15...♗c8 (the only way to contest e6 directly), White can exert lasting pressure on Black's game, by playing 16.♖ad1, and if 16...♗d7 (or if 16...c5 17.♘b3 ♖d8 18.♖d2 ♗b7 19.♖fd1) 17.♘f3 d5 18.g4 h5 19.h3.

16.♘e6 ♖d7 17.♖ad1 ♘c8

White's rooks now successfully tie down Black's forces to the defence of d6. Capablanca later suggested (the perhaps not completely convincing)

17...c5, and if 18.♘d5 ♗xd5 19.exd5 b5, followed by ...♘c8–b6–c4 (or perhaps via d7) to land on e5. White might also try 18.♖f3 and if, say 18...♔f7 (but not 18...♘c6? 19.♖fd3) 19.♔f2 g6 20.♖h3 ♖h8 21.g4 h5 22.♘f4, with continuing pressure.

18.♖f2 b5 19.♖fd2 ♖de7 20.b4 ♔f7 21.a3 ♗a8?

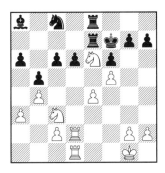

This understandable bid for much-needed counterplay based on opening the a-file completely backfires. Black perhaps had to play the radical 21...♖xe6 22.fxe6+ ♖xe6, gaining a pawn and practical compensation for the exchange, if far from yet guaranteed holding chances.

22.♔f2 ♖a7 23.g4 h6 24.♖d3 a5 25.h4 axb4 26.axb4 ♖ae7

Capablanca despairingly accepts that he cannot achieve anything on the a-file. Black's knight and bishop lack all activity and, given the imminence of a powerful White breakthrough on the kingside (by playing g5), it is also already too late to expect much relief by any exchange sacrifice on e6.

27.♔f3 ♖g8 28.♔f4 g6 29.♖g3 g5+

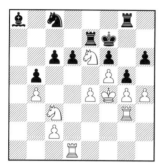

Black must now surely be lost. Rather than wait for g5, such as after 29...♗b7 30.g5, and if 30...fxg5+ 31.hxg5 h5 32.♖f3, followed by ♔g3, Capablanca takes the bull by the horns and tries to block it. Sadly, however, this only allows White to break through in the h-file. Réti gave 29...gxf5 30.exf5 d5 31.♘e2, and if 31...♘d6 32.♘2d4 ♘e4 33.♖a3, when White wins in the a-file so assiduously opened by Black.

30.♔f3 ♘b6

Or if 30...gxh4 31.♖h3 ♖h8 32.♖xh4 ♖a7 33.♘e2 ♖a3+ 34.♔f2, threatening ♖dh1, and wins.

31.hxg5 hxg5 32.♖h3 ♖d7

Or 32...♘c4 33.♖h7+ ♔e8 34.♖a1, dominating both the a- and h-files and winning instantly.

33.♔g3 ♔e8 34.♖dh1 ♗b7 35.e5

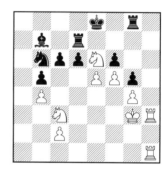

White's most elegant conclusion: if 35...fxe5 36.♘e4 ♘d5 37.♖h7 ♗c8 38.♖h8, and wins.

Clearing the e4 square for White's final piece to join the attack undermines all further hope of resistance.

35...dxe5 36.♘e4 ♘d5 37.♘6c5 ♗c8 38.♘xd7 ♗xd7 39.♖h7 ♖f8 40.♖a1 ♔d8 41.♖a8+ ♗c8 42.♘c5 1-0

Hypermodern Ideas and the Maturing Mainstream

'It is incorrect to speak of a hypermodern school. For the only thing ['hypermoderns'] have in common is that they are all pioneers who want to develop still further the laws of chess strategy, of which Steinitz laid the foundations'

Richard Réti, *Masters of the Chess Board* (1933)

With Aron Nimzowitsch (1886-1935) and Richard Réti (1889-1929) in the vanguard, the so-called 'hypermoderns' rebelled against what they considered to be an increasingly arid pre-Great War classical consensus. They developed entirely new *Flank Openings*, *Indian Defences* and other rich, asymmetric ways of playing White and Black, all primarily based on the notion that to control key central squares, without immediately rushing to occupy them, offered a valid alternative to more conventional (1.e4 and 1.d4) openings.

This 'rebelliousness', however, should be judged in context. In intent, Nimzowitsch and Réti both remained firmly Steinitzian, aiming to modify and extend the existing order, not to usurp it. In his *Manual of Chess*, Emanuel Lasker, for one, warmly acknowledged the value of their ideas, which 'quickened the imagination ... taught us to suspect mechanical chess ... insisted on the high value of the central pawns [and] warned against their premature advance'.

Lasker, who adapted well to these new trends remained a significant mainstream figure well into the 1920s and 1930s. The third and fourth world champions, José Raúl Capablanca (1888-1942) and Alexander Alekhine (1892-1946), however, drove the game forward even more decisively than either Lasker, or anyone else, through those decades. Stark stylistic opposites, these two great players, in their different ways, best merged the new with the old nostrums.

Capablanca, world champion from 1921-27, raised the principle of economy of means and technical precision to heights of exceptional artistry. Alekhine, who reigned from 1927-35 and 1937-46, was a gloriously dynamic, restlessly innovative, combinative genius. Sparks flew in the great world championship match that these two contested, while both in their prime. The mainstream markedly matured through these inter-War decades.

New 'System'

Aron Nimzowitsch

As a young man before the Great War, Nimzowitsch was already on a mission. In a sharply drafted article in the *Wiener Schachzeitung* (October 1913), he baldly asserted: 'no-one has ever made any attempt to explore and formulate the laws of chess strategy. Tarrasch's "decrees" really cannot claim to be such'. Nimzowitsch discerned numerous inadequacies in the conventionally classical mode of play that Tarrasch so eloquently and effectively propounded.

10. Aron Nimzowitsch, in mid-1910s

Nimzowitsch had a point. The younger generation increasingly strained to break free of the most constraining of the conventionally classical opening and middlegame boundaries. The prevalence of far too many all too 'correctly' played (all too often drawn), 1.e4 e5 or 1.d4 d5 games, threatened to become stifling. As yet, no top player had made any all-encompassing statement about the 'principles' that might govern change in a post-classical future.

Out of this mix, Nimzowitsch eventually gave us *My System*. First published in 1925, *My System* is a highly original work that had been very many years in the making. Unlike Tarrasch's *Dreihundert Schachpartien* and *Die Moderne Schachpartie*, both essentially highly instructively annotated games collections, Nimzowitsch instructs through the medium of a manual that sets out to confront the truths behind the game's major *elements* and *position play* much more directly.

In *My System*, Nimzowitsch succeeds in delivering a series of finely observed and often highly original essays on each of his *elements* and also on *position play*. He says much that is new but also builds on the past, with a huge nod to the revolutionary Steinitz. In so doing, he also duly acknowledges the often considerable contributions made by other great players, including (frequently) Tarrasch.

In the context of its time, *My System* is a tour de force, a successful, post-classical reset, of which even Tarrasch took note. Nimzowitsch shortly followed it up with another fine book, *Chess Praxis*, an annotated collection of his 109 best and most exemplary games. Together both books offer a wealth of insightful exposition of the new paths that the game was beginning to take in a post-classical era.

Whether Nimzowitsch created a 'system', of a practically applicable kind is moot. What cannot be denied, however, is that he set about his task with admirably 'systematic' ambition. Advocating in his *School of Chess Excellence (Vol 3)*, that his turn of the 21st century pupils should all be 'familiar with Nimzowitsch's ideas', top grandmaster coach, Mark Dvoretsky, rated *My System*, 'among the books devoted to positional play ... simply the best'.

Among *My System's* most memorable sections are those on what Nimzowitsch called *restraint*, *blockade*, and *over-protection*. He mapped out the circumstances in which each of these stratagems might best apply, noting historical anticipations. Nimzowitsch indicated that an *over-protection* strategy, for example, tends to work best: in support of an advanced, central strong point that can be occupied (often by a powerful knight) and exploited as a pivot to switch attacks to the flanks (see Steinitz-Weiss, Vienna 1882).

Nimzowitsch also considered Steinitz to be a significant pioneer in the development of early forms of *restraint* and *blockading* ideas, especially when facing an IQP (see Pillsbury-Steinitz, St Petersburg 1895). As ever, taking such discussion much further, he then hit on one of his most profound and most historically fruitful contentions: while 'restraint is conceivable without the presence of enemy doubled pawns ... a really complete restraint, which extends over large tracts of the board and makes it difficult for the opponent to breathe, is only possible when the opponent labours under the disadvantage of a doubled pawn'.

This single insight both explained and underpinned the developing rationale for such openings as the *French: Winawer Variation* (often internationally referred to as *Nimzowitsch's Variation*), characterised by doubled White pawns on c2/c3, and (especially) many lines of the *Nimzo-Indian Defence*, with doubled White pawns on c3/c4, in which Nimzowitsch achieved many remarkable *restraint* and *blockade* successes that remain exemplary. One of the very best of these is Nimzowitsch's magical win, at Dresden 1926, against Paul Johner.

In this game, Black sets up a typically powerful blockading pawn triangle (e5/d6/c5), to which he later adds a queenside blockading (b6/a5) pawn extension. The constraining pressure Black exerts on White's centre and queenside is palpable and prevents any hope of White achieving anything in those parts of the board. Play then turns to the kingside, where both sides have chances. After one or two serious White misjudgements, Black crashes through on that flank.

P. Johner – A.Nimzowitsch

Dresden 1926

Nimzo-Indian Defence

1.d4 ♘f6 2.c4 e6 3.♘c3 ♗b4 4.e3 0-0
Nimzowitsch's strategic conception later helped inspire Hübner's Variation: 4...c5 5.♗d3 ♘c6 6.♘f3 ♗xc3+ 7.bxc3 d6, after which 8.0-0 0-0 9.♘d2, leads back into the game continuation; while 9.e4 e5 10.d5 ♘e7, leads to another main line.

The sharp 8.e4 e5 9.d5 ♘e7 10.♘h4, is best met by 10...h6 11.f4 ♘g6, a Nimzowitschian 'prophylactic' that maintains the blockading pawn on e5 and stiffens Black's grip on the kingside. B.Spassky-R.Fischer, Game 5, World Championship, Reykjavik 1972, then famously continued 12.♘xg6 fxg6 13.fxe5 dxe5 14.♗e3 b6 15.0-0 0-0 16.a4 a5 17.♖b1 ♗d7 18.♖b2 ♖b8 19.♖bf2 ♕e7, leading to at least full equality (Black won).

5.♗d3 c5 6.♘f3 ♘c6 7.0-0 ♗xc3 8.bxc3 d6 9.♘d2 b6 10.♘b3
Against 10.f4, Nimzowitsch intended 10...e5 (also good on Black's 9th move), and if 11.fxe5 dxe5 12.d5 ♘a5 13.♘b3 ♘b7 14.e4 ♘e8, which he considered quite solid.

10...e5 11.f4 e4
Not Black's only possibility, but by establishing a disruptive Black pawn in the heart of White's centre, Black throws some doubt on White's previ-

ous move. Nimzowitsch's notes now start to reflect increasing confidence about Black's prospects.

12.♗e2 ♕d7 13.h3 ♘e7 14.♕e1?
This move is a definite error, allowing Black to completely clamp down on White's kingside with his next three moves. Instead Nimzowitsch suggests 14.♗d2 ♘f5 15.♕e1 g6, and if 16.g4 ♘g7 17.♕h4 ♘fe8 18.a4 f5 19.g5, which he considers 'difficult to assess'.

But not 14.g4?! h5, and if 15.g5 ♕xh3 16.gxf6 ♕g3+, when Black can either draw or press for more by playing 17.♔h1 ♕h4+ 18.♔g1 ♗h3 19.♕e1 ♕xf6, and if 20.♖f2 ♘f5.

14...h5 15.♗d2 ♕f5 16.♔h2 ♕h7!

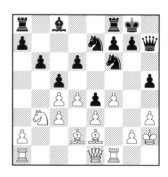

The Black queen's novel switch to the unexpectedly powerful h7 square combines well with Black's pawn on h5, both to prevent White from playing g4 (to challenge for critical kingside space), and to prepare serious break-through threats in the g- and h-files. White daren't now play 17.♕h4 ♘f5, and if 18.♕g5 h4, which loses control of g3 and, after a subsequent …♗e6, leads to positions in which White's queen is in severe danger of being trapped.

White's game is also fast becoming stat-ic elsewhere on the board. Black's pawn on e4 completely locks down White's centre, while White's doubled c-pawns present a sorry picture of self-blocking immobility that severely constrains the coordination of his own forces. White finally faces the chilling prospect of confronting two finely placed knights (on f5 and f6), both offering a frighten-ing array of additional combinative op-tions.

17.a4 ♘f5 18.g3 a5 19.♖g1 ♘h6 20.♗f1 ♗d7 21.♗c1 ♖ac8 22.d5 ♔h8 23.♘d2 ♖g8 24.♗g2 g5 25.♘f1

White defends g3 and hopes to involve his queen's rook in defence along the second rank. By this stage, however, White's king now operates behind ex-tremely restricted lines and is likely to be attacked without mercy.

White's game also folds after 25.fxg5 ♖xg5, and if 26.♖f1 ♗f5 27.♖f4 ♖cg8 28.♘f1, when Black can play 28…♘d7, followed by …♘e5, with overwhelming threats against White's chronically weak (c4/d3/f3/g4) interior light squares.

25…♖g7 26.♖a2 ♘f5 27.♗h1 ♖cg8 28.♕d1 gxf4 29.exf4 ♗c8 30.♕b3 ♗a6 31.♖e2

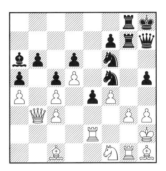

White makes a last ditch, but tacti-cally flawed bid to obtain counter-play against e4. Black either mates or wins White's queen, however, af-ter 31.♗d2 ♖g6, and if 32.♗e1 ♘g4+ 33.hxg4 hxg4+ 34.♔g2 ♗xc4 35.♕xc4 e3 (Nimzowitsch).

31…♘h4 32.♖e3
Or if 32.♘d2 ♗c8 33.♘xe4 ♕f5, and if 34.♘f2 ♕xh3+ 35.♘xh3 ♘g4 mate.

32…♗c8 33.♕c2 ♗xh3 34.♗xe4
Or 34.♔xh3 ♕f5+ 35.♔h2 ♘g4+ 36.♔h3 ♘f2+ 37.♔h2 ♕h3 mate.

34…♗f5 35.♗xf5 ♘xf5 36.♖e2 h4 37.♖gg2 hxg3+ 38.♔g1 ♕h3 39.♘e3 ♘h4 40.♔f1 ♖e8 0–1

The Power of the Kingside Fianchetto
Richard Réti

Richard Réti's greatest contribution to chess was to give us *Réti's Opening* and much of the fundamental thinking that underpins the wide range of *Réti-English* systems, to which this eventually led. Réti's key insight was to grasp that the combination of a kingside fianchetto, and the moves, ♘f3 and c4, offered White excellent prospects of playing to control the central light squares (especially d5).

In his most famous book, *Masters of the Chess Board*, Réti explained that by targeting the d5 strong point, White can hope to establish a central grip, as promising as any likely to arise from any of the

11. Richard Réti: circa early to mid 1920s

main, classically-inspired (1.e4 or 1.d4) openings: only 'without fixing the middle pawns too soon'. Such well-founded innovation proved not just exciting but also strategically hard-hitting and rapidly entered the mainstream.

Réti maintained that what he called his 'system of opening' was 'a definite opening system', that is, one that truly aims 'to turn the opening advantage to account'. Inspired by his many early successes, few offered any more than briefly lingering dissent at such claims. Many rather followed his lead. Soon there was a vast, new surge in discernibly subtle and nuanced *Flank Openings*, though this term took many more years before entering popular use.

Like Nimzowitsch, Réti's desire to seek new paths emerged from a deep sense of the game's potential for change and extension. Their hard work and wealth of invention served as the basis for a wholly beneficial critique and enrichment of the classical mainstream. Not merely 'rebels', they were both driven by rigorously objective principles, whose outcomes proved as fruitful as any *obiter dicta* pronounced by that recognised sage of conventional 'classicism', Tarrasch.

These two great players, moreover, remained scrupulously independent-minded and sometimes disagreed. Réti, for example, expressed scepticism about Nimzowitsch's experiments with 'reversed' forms of the *Nimzo-Indian* or *Queen's*

Indian Defences, as he appears to have regarded the attempt to control e5, in such lines (based on a queenside fianchetto), to tend more to pure equality than his fianchetto-based assaults on d5, launched from the opposite flank.

According to Réti, 'to derive an advantage from the opening move, one must play with a system which does not allow the second player to bring about a closed position without disadvantage in space, nor to place irremovable bulwarks in the centre'. With some justification, not least by results and take-up by peers, Réti considered his *Réti-English* systems better met that requirement than Nimzow-itsch's 'reversed' *Indian* defences (themselves still also lively today).

In a similar way, Réti tended to reject any suggestion that that his flank systems might be best understood as 'reversed' forms of *King's Indian Defence*, an opening in whose parallel, early development he was also a significant advocate from Black's side. While certain lines can, of course, assume such a character, if both players are willing to play that way, *Réti-English* systems, properly taken as a whole, offer much more diverse, dynamic, direct and distinctive White options.

Réti's new opening made its most dramatic, early appearance, at Carlsbad 1923, against Akiba Rubinstein. This wonderfully conceived, model demonstration of many of the opening's most enduring strengths was followed, at New York 1924, by two further outstanding achievements, against Capablanca and Bogoljubow, justly described by Alekhine, in the tournament book, as respectively 'sensational' and 'epochal'.

R.Réti – A.Rubinstein

Carlsbad 1923

Réti's Opening

1.♘f3 d5
After 1...♘f6 2.c4 g6, Reti pioneered the outflanking idea, 3.b4. R.Réti-J.R.Capablanca, New York 1924, then continued 3...♗g7 4.♗b2 0-0 5.g3 b6 6.♗g2 ♗b7 7.0-0 d6 8.d3 ♘bd7 9.♘bd2 e5 10.♕c2 ♖e8 11.♖fd1 a5 12.a3 h6 13.♘f1 c5 14.b5 ♘f8 15.e3 ♕c7 16.d4 ♗e4 17.♕c3 exd4 18.exd4 ♘6d7?! (Black targets a poisoned pawn on c4; 18...♘e6 was much better) 19.♕d2 cxd4

20.♗xd4 ♕xc4 21.♗xg7 ♔xg7 22.♕b2+ ♔g8 23.♖xd6 ♕c5 24.♖ad1 ♖a7 25.♘e3 ♕h5 26.♘d4 ♗xg2 27.♔xg2 ♕e5 28.♘c4 ♕c5 29.♘c6 ♖c7 30.♘e3 ♘e5 31.♖1d5 1-0.

2.g3
An early form of *Réti v Slav* debate arose, in R.Réti-E.Bogoljubow, New York 1924, which went 2.c4 e6 3.g3 ♘f6 4.♗g2 ♗d6 5.0-0 0-0 6.b3 ♖e8 7.♗b2

♘bd7 8.d4 (targeting e5) 8...c6 9.♘bd2 ♘e4 10.♘xe4 dxe4 11.♘e5 f5 12.f3 (Black's poor 9th and 10th moves lost tempi and over-extended Black's centre pawns, prompting their energetic undermining) 12...exf3 13.♗xf3 ♕c7 14.♘xd7 ♗xd7 15.e4 e5 16.c5 ♗f8 17.♕c2 exd4 18.exf5 ♖ad8 19.♗h5 ♖e5 20.♗xd4 ♖xf5 (White now wins with study-like brilliance; 20...♖d5 21.♕c4 ♔h8, would only prolong Black's agony)

21.♖xf5 ♗xf5 22.♕xf5 ♖xd4 23.♖f1 ♖d8 24.♗f7+ ♔h8 25.♗e8 1–0.

2...♘f6 3.♗g2 g6 4.c4 d4 5.d3 ♗g7 6.b4 0–0 7.♘bd2 c5

Faced with novel problems, Rubinstein opts to allow White to undermine his d–pawn, in the hope of maintaining equality by directly confronting the gradual advance of White's centre pawns. Ever since this game, however, Black players have been wary of drifting into such positions as the White pawn mass often contains real potential.

Nowadays if Black opts for a ...d4 defence, he or she usually seeks to maintain a pawn on that square, such as here, by playing 7...♘fd7, followed by ...e5, or by preventing White's undermining b4, by playing an earlier ...a5.

8.♘b3 cxb4 9.♗b2 ♘c6 10.♘bxd4 ♘xd4 11.♗xd4 b6 12.a3 ♗b7 13.♗b2 bxa3 14.♖xa3 ♕c7 15.♕a1

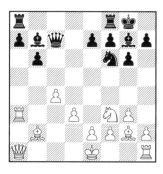

Réti has achieved just about all White might hope for from the opening. He exerts powerful cross-fire pressure on both long diagonals and will soon be able to consider how best to edge forward his central pawns. Meanwhile, White also bears down menacingly on the a- and b-files, consigning any hope that Black might securely advance his passed, but backward a-pawn to the very long-term.

Note that White's queen finds itself on an unusually splendid square in the very corner of the board, adding to the attack both on the queenside and in the centre. In such positions, Réti all but invented this strikingly powerful (♕a1) stratagem, whose raw correctness has bestowed upon it an exciting, almost totemic appeal that still resonates.

15...♘e8 16.♗xg7 ♘xg7 17.0–0 ♘e6 18.♖b1 ♗c6 19.d4 ♗e4 20.♖d1 a5
Black's a-pawn has advanced but remains immobile. White's plan to play d5 and land his knight on the advanced c6 outpost is much more alarming.

21.d5 ♘c5 22.♘d4 ♗xg2 23.♔xg2 ♖fd8 24.♘c6 ♖d6 25.♖e3 ♖e8 26.♕e5
Aided by his now quite tangible control of central space, White attacks Black's e-pawn, leaving Black with a difficult choice between 26...e6 (accepting an unpalatable self-pin) and the actual text-move (which weakens key central light squares).

26...f6 27.♕b2 e5 28.♕b5 ♔f7 29.♖b1 ♘d7 30.f3 ♖c8 31.♖d3 e4!?
Justifiably concerned about the wholly passive nature of his position, Black makes a gambit bid for freedom. He can't safely play either 31...♘b8?, which allows 32.c5, and wins, or 31...♘c5?! 32.♕xb6, and if 32...♘xd3 33.exd3 ♕xb6 (or if 33...♖xc6 34.dxc6 ♕xc6 35.♕xa5) 34.♖xb6 ♔f8 35.♖a6.
He might, however, still have shifted his king to and fro and, after the consolidating reply 32.e4, waited to see whether and how White might eventually seek to achieve a favourable kingside breakthrough.

32.fxe4 ♘e5?

Clearly Black's intent, but a move that loses. Black had to play 32...♖e8, sit back and stubbornly continue to exert pressure on White's extra, furthest advanced e-pawn.

33.♕xb6 ♘xc6
Black perhaps missed White's crushing reply, after which he faces only a range of completely lost rook and pawn endgames. After 33...♘xd3 34.exd3, however, Black will be completely unable to hold back White's overwhelmingly powerful central pawn mass.

34.c5 ♖d7 35.dxc6 ♖xd3 36.♕xc7+ ♖xc7 37.exd3 ♖xc6 38.♖b7+ ♔e8 39.d4 ♖a6 40.♖b6 ♖a8
Black loses a decisive second pawn. But Black is also quite lost after 40...♖xb6 41.cxb6, and if 41...♔d7 42.e5, winning the pawn race.

41.♖xf6 a4 42.♖f2 a3 43.♖a2 ♔d7 44.d5 g5 45.♔f3 ♖a4 46.♔e3 h5 47.h4 gxh4 48.gxh4 ♔e7 49.♔f4 ♔d7 50.♔f5 1–0

Virtuosic Technique and Positional Insight
José Raúl Capablanca

It is all too easy to be swept away by su-
perlatives in regard to Capablanca, to
whom, at his best, winning at chess seemed
almost effortless. A prodigy, like Morphy,
he learned to play, aged four, and quickly
developed a comparably precocious, natural flair for the game. His family took sensible steps to prevent any neglect of his
wider education. Even so, by the age of 13,
he comfortably defeated Juan Corzo, Cuba's
national champion, in a fully competitive
(though non-title) match, which caught
early international attention.

Born into a prosperous Havana family, Capablanca was packed off, in 1904, to
learn English and complete his secondary

12. José Raúl Capablanca: in late 1910s

schooling, in New York. His longer-term goal was to enter Columbia University
to study chemical engineering. Not long after travelling to the US, however, Capablanca discovered the Manhattan Chess Club, where, as an exceptionally gifted
16 year-old, he was talent-spotted by Emanuel Lasker, who attested to his great
promise, in *Lasker's Chess Magazine* (February 1905).

While Capablanca initially stuck to his academic brief, he gradually succumbed to the allure of the game at which he excelled completely. In 1910, he
eventually abandoned his engineering studies, after only two years at Columbia.
Early in 1909, already an established (US-based) star, he had defeated US champion, Frank Marshall, in a match, by the wholly one-sided margin (+8-1=14),
thereby confirming his reputation as world-class.

Early in 1911, Capablanca made an even grander statement on his first chess
trip to Europe. At San Sebastian, an event in which all of the world's top players
competed, except Lasker, Capablanca finished first (on 9.5/15), a half-point ahead
of Rubinstein and Vidmar, who tied for 2nd/3rd places. Later that year, Capablanca
issued a formal world title challenge to Lasker. This was eventually declined, in
favour of a challenge by Rubinstein.

Rubinstein's light shone with exceptional brightness, in 1912, with four firsts, at San Sebastian, Pistyan, the Russian national tournament, at Vilnius, and Breslau (this shared). While Capablanca committed to a new venture, *Capablanca-Magazine*, he hardly played any serious chess that year. By repute, Capablanca only clearly edged ahead of Rubinstein, at St Petersburg 1914, where he finished emphatic runner-up to first-placed Lasker. The Great War then intervened, postponing everything.

In an article in *Munsey's Magazine* (October 1916), Capablanca attributed the lion's share of his 'precocious start in chess … to a mastery of the principles of the game, born of what I often felt to be a peculiar intuition'. This intuitive feel for the right move in virtually any position allowed Capablanca, throughout most of his career, to assess positions with lightning speed and accuracy, as if shrouded by an aura of near complete invincibility denied all others.

In *Masters of the Chess Board*, Réti observed that Capablanca played chess as if it were 'his native language [in which] grammar is an unnecessary crutch … replaced by [his] feeling for the language [and] the rich experience stored in [his] subconscious mind'. He added approvingly that Capablanca's possession of this Morphy-like gift, also ensured that he frequently 'succeeded in pointing out the exaggeration in many of the old rules'.

Capablanca's genius almost always drove him down uncannily 'correct' paths. He belonged to no school, eschewed dogma and followed his own rules. Untouched by preconceptions, his moves simply 'worked' much more often than not. Put an early foot wrong against the 25 year-old Capablanca, nearing his absolute peak, and you, too, might quickly find yourself on the wrong side of a blistering first brilliancy prize-winning game, as Ossip Bernstein discovered, at St Petersburg.

J.R.Capablanca – O.Bernstein

St Petersburg 1914

Queen's Gambit Declined

1.d4 d5 2.♘f3 ♘f6 3.c4 e6 4.♘c3 ♘bd7 5.♗g5 ♗e7 6.e3 c6 7.♗d3 dxc4 8.♗xc4 b5 9.♗d3 a6 10.e4

Bernstein had favoured this defence for at least a decade but hadn't previously encountered Capablanca's critical 10th move. White immediately threatens e5, followed by ♘ce4, with significant pressure on the central dark squares. F.Marshall-Em.Lasker, played four rounds earlier at St Petersburg, went 10.0–0 c5 11.♕e2 0–0 12.♖ad1 c4 13.♗b1 ♘d5 14.♗xe7 ♕xe7 15.e4, and was eventually drawn.

Capablanca didn't now consider Bernstein's temporary gambit reply to be 'wholly correct'. But he also generally doubted the strategic validity of Black's highly ambitious attempt to mix (Meran-like) queenside counter-attack with (Queen's Gambit Declined-like) solidity. Black might still, however, have played the more conventionally thematic, 10...c5, or 10...h6, and if 11.♗h4 0-0, and just battled.

10...e5 11.dxe5 ♘g4 12.♗f4 ♗c5 13.0-0 ♕c7?!

Black may have intended 13...♕e7, missing the force of 14.e6!, and if 14...fxe6 (14...♕xe6? 15.e5, threatening ♘e4, is crushing) 15.e5 0-0 16.♗g3, with much the better game for White. This may nevertheless have been a better practical try, since now, while Black will regain the gambit pawn, it comes at disastrous cost in position and time.

14.♖c1 f6 15.♗g3 fxe5 16.b4!

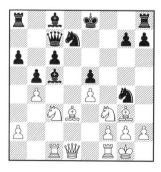

Nemesis strikes. White had clearly been angling for this thrust, which would also have been strong against either knight recapture on e5 on the

previous move. White now seriously undermines Black's grip on the d5, c6 and b5 squares. Black's retreat is forced. After 16...♗xb4 (or if 16...♗e7 17.♘d4)17.♘d5 ♕d6 18.♘xb4 ♕xb4 19.♖xc6, and if 19...0-0 20.♗c2, White has overwhelming attacking threats; while 16...♗d6 allows the same winning reply, only without complications.

16...♗a7 17.♗xb5 axb5 18.♘xb5 ♕d8 19.♘d6+ ♔f8 20.♖xc6

For a bishop, White has three good pawns and every prospect of netting even more material or mating Black's king. All of White's pieces are poised for attack. Black's king looks decidedly defenceless.

20...♘b6 21.♗h4 ♕d7

Black obtains no respite after 21...♘f6 22.♕b3, and if 22...♕e7 23.♘g5 h6 (or 23...♗d7 24.♘f5 ♗xf5 25.exf5, followed by ♘e6+) 24.♘xc8 ♖xc8 25.♘e6+ ♔g8 26.♖xc8+ ♘xc8 27.♖c1, threatening ♖c7.

22.♘xc8 ♕xc6

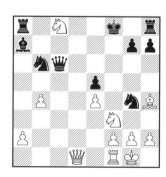

Or if 22...♕xd1 23.♖xd1 ♖xc8 24.♖xc8+ ♘xc8 25.♖d8+, and wins.

Capablanca now concludes brilliantly. He and his contemporaries, however, appear to have overlooked the arguably even more effective engine solution: 23.♗e7+ ♔f7 (or if 23...♔g8 24.♕d8+ ♔f7 25.♘g5+ ♔g6 26.♕xh8) 24.♘g5+ ♔g6 25.♕xg4 (Capablanca may have seen this) 25...♕xc8 26.♘e6+ ♔f7 27.♕xg7+ ♔xe6 28.♖d1! (I forgive him, however, if he missed this devilishly quiet move), with forced mate in three.

23.♕d8+ ♕e8 24.♗e7+ ♔f7 25.♘d6+ ♔g6 26.♘h4+ ♔h5

Or if 26...♔h6 27.♘df5+ ♔h5 28.♘g3+ ♔h6 29.♗g5 mate.

27.♘xe8 ♖xd8 28.♘xg7+ ♔h6 29.♘gf5+ ♔h5 30.h3!

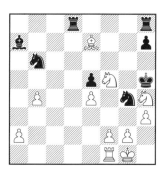

I do, however, rather like Capablanca's more human solution! A rook down and without queens on the board, White still threatens mate, by capturing Black's knight, followed by f3+, and either g3 or g4. Black has no good knight move: if 30...♘h6 31.♘g3 mate, or if 30...♘xf2 31.♖xf2, threatening g4 mate.

Surprisingly Black must return his extra rook, remaining three clear pawns down, with his king still stuck in a treacherous swamp on the kingside. Black's only attempt to avoid this outcome, 30...♖dg8, fails to the wonderful 31.♘g3+ ♔h6 32.♖c1! (threatening ♖c6+)

and if 32...♖c8 33.♘gf5+ ♔h5 34.hxg4+ ♔xg4 35.f3+ ♔h5 (or if 35...♔f4 36.g3 mate) 36.g4 mate. White also wins in this line after 32...♔g7 33.♘hf5+ ♔f7 34.♖c7, or 32...♘c8 33.♘hf5+ ♔g6 34.hxg4.

30...♘c8 31.hxg4+ ♔xg4 32.♗xd8 ♖xd8 33.g3 ♖d2

Black might have spared himself the rest. Even after 33...♔h3, White plays 34.♘f3, followed by ♖e1 and ♔f1–e2, winning quickly.

34.♔g2 ♖e2 35.a4 ♘b6 36.♘e3+ ♔h5 37.a5 ♘d7 38.♘hf5 ♘f6 39.b5 ♗d4 40.♔f3 ♖a2 41.a6 ♗a7 42.♖c1 ♖b2 43.g4+ ♔g6 44.♖c7 ♖xf2+ 45.♔xf2 ♘xg4+ 46.♔f3 1–0

Virtuoso performances like this linger long in the memory. In *Masters of the Chess Board*, however, Réti hints that something more uniquely profound lay beneath all the surface bravura. Clearer on this in his earlier (1921) book, *Modern Ideas in Chess*, Réti reveals that he had early on found something mysterious in the young Capablanca's game, which helped Réti, himself, begin seriously to question 'the wisdom of the old principle [that] in the opening every move should develop another piece'.

Réti argued that 'contrary to all the masters of that period' (around 1914), Capablanca 'had for some time ceased to adhere to that principle'. The young Cuban rather displayed an instinctive urgency in the development of his plans, in which 'every move not demanded by that plan amounts to loss of time'. Capablanca, it seemed, instinctively shied away from all old-style rules, seeking instead to base his powerful 'schemes' purely on any given position's essential 'elements'.

Capablanca's ability to override any received wisdom inspired many. Réti, for one, firmly concluded henceforth that 'chess principles … can be viewed … only as maxims'. The distinction between 'principles' and 'maxims' had, of course, lain at the heart of many a lively debate between Tarrasch and Lasker. By 1914, however, a shift towards an increasingly healthy scepticism about the role played by any overarching edifice of absolute 'givens' was rapidly beginning to kick in.

Capablanca was certainly leaving the conventionally classical chess mind-set of a Siegbert Tarrasch behind. His play was more akin to that of the down-to-earth, doyen of struggle, Emanuel Lasker, but even more forward-looking, flexible and universal in character, in ways that were hard to define. 'Hypermoderns', such as a Nimzowitsch or Réti, could clearly tune into it. In Capablanca's expert hands, it enabled him to produce the most technically virtuosic and artistically executed plans, time and again.

If we could more clearly analyse, define and market the elements that underlay Capablanca's ultimately intuitive genius, we might help fashion a few more world champions. We certainly can't do that easily (nor could he). But his example remains. Capablanca could rely on his extraordinarily fluent chess instincts like no other, as exemplified by his masterly defence against Frank Marshall, in a most famous game, played in the Manhattan Chess Club International, in 1918.

Caught out completely in the opening, Capablanca had to play at his most resourceful, first-principled best, to steer his way through unexpectedly novel complications against a most dangerous and especially well-prepared opponent. Marshall famously unleashed his still enduringly robust *Spanish:Marshall Attack*, in its first ever top-class outing. Where others might have floundered, Capablanca, who was also a first-class fighter when roused, revealed that he felt only challenge.

J.R.Capablanca – F.Marshall

New York 1918

Spanish: Marshall Attack

1.e4 e5 2.♘f3 ♘c6 3.♗b5 a6 4.♗a4 ♘f6 5.0–0 ♗e7 6.♖e1 b5 7.♗b3 0–0 8.c3 d5 9.exd5 ♘xd5 10.♘xe5 ♘xe5 11.♖xe5 ♘f6

The modern main line, 11...c6 12.d4 ♗d6, with the idea of playing ...♕h4, to provoke an enduring kingside light square weakening (after the reply g3), has since largely superseded Marshall's original, more direct attacking idea. With a powerful knight on d5 and the prospect of rapidly developing his light square bishop, followed by ...♖ae8, Black retains more controlled, long-term positional compensation for the gambit pawn.

12.♖e1 ♗d6 13.h3 ♘g4 14.♕f3

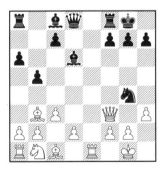

Marshall's 13th move is risky but nonetheless challenging. Black's last chance to seek more controlled positional compensation for the gambit pawn lay in 13...♗b7.

Play now becomes obscure and predominantly tactical. Not now 14.hxg4?

♕h4, when Black's attack rages, such as after 15.♕f3 ♗h2+ 16.♔f1 ♗xg4

and if 17.♕e4 ♗f4 18.g3 ♕h2 19.gxf4 ♗h3+ 20.♔e2 ♖ae8, and Black wins.

Capablanca already understood that he had been caught in a prepared line but remained intuitively certain that, as he had made no 'mistake', his game must be wholly defensible. Instead of the text-move, he noted that he might also have safely played 14.d4, and after 14...♘xf2 15.♕f3!, transposing back into the game continuation.

14...♕h4 15.d4

Retaining his nerve, Capablanca resolved to hold firm to two key thematic ideas: that his queen was best placed on f3 (both for attack and defence); and that it was especially important to maintain pressure on Black's weakest structural point (f7) with his queen and light square bishop. For the rest, all was to be concrete calculation.

Black now commits himself to a wholly sacrificial path. After the plausible alternative 15...h5 16.♗e3, White retains his extra pawn and can look forward to completing his queenside development without any real difficulty.

15...♘xf2 16.♖e2 ♗g4

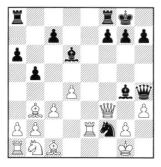

Black gives up two minor pieces for a rook, hoping to drive White's king into dangerously open central terrain. Black's knight can't retreat: after 16...♘g4, White's best reply, apparently first noticed by John Grefe, only in the 1970s, is the surprising 17.g3!, and if 17...♕xh3 18.♕xa8, when White's queen can return to g2 quite safely. White also clearly stands better after either 16...♗xh3 17.gxh3, and if 17...♘xh3+ 18.♔g2 (or 18.♔f1), or 16...♘xh3+ 17.gxh3 ♗xh3 18.♖e4, forcing an almost certainly game-winning queen exchange.

After the text-move, White must avoid 17.♕xf2?, which allows 17...♗g3 18.♕f1 ♗xe2 19.♕xe2 ♖ae8, and Black wins.

17.hxg4 ♗h2+
Or if 17...♗g3 18.♖xf2 ♕h2+ 19.♔f1 ♕h1+ 20.♔e2, which transposes.

18.♔f1 ♗g3

White's king must run and White's queen's rook, knight and bishop, remain rooted to their starting squares. Unfortunately for Marshall, White still has a promising plan to send his king towards a potentially safe haven on d3, followed by the eventual activation of his pieces on the queenside. White's king also escapes after 18...♘h1 19.♘d2, and if 19...♘g3+ 20.♔e1 ♘xe2+ 21.♔xe2 ♖ae8+ 22.♔d3 ♕e1 23.♘e4, when White will eventually unravel.

19.♖xf2 ♕h1+ 20.♔e2 ♗xf2

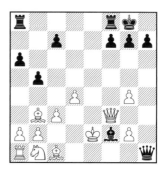

This is another cold-blooded moment. After 20...♕xc1, White plays 21.♕xg3 ♕xb2+ 22.♘d2 ♖ae8+ 23.♔d3, and if 23...b4 24.♕xc7 ♖c8 (or if 24...♕xa1 25.cxb4 ♖d8 26.♗xf7+ ♔h8 27.♖f4) 25.♗xf7+ ♔h8 26.♗e6, and wins. Note how Black's persistent Achilles Heel on f7 plays a critical part in this and several subsequent variations.

21.♗d2 ♗h4 22.♕h3 ♖ae8+ 23.♔d3 ♕f1+ 24.♔c2 ♗f2
Try as he might, Black just can't prevent his opponent from gradually wriggling his king into complete safe-

ty and developing his queenside. After 24...♕f2, White has 25.♕f3, and if 25...♖e2 (or if 25...♕g1 26.a4) 26.♕xf2 ♖xf2 27.♗d5 ♖d8 28.♗f3 ♖f1 29.b4, with the idea of a4.

25.♕f3 ♕g1

Black just doesn't have sufficient firepower to cause problems. After 25...♖e2, the computer clamours for 26.a4!, and if 26...b4 27.♖a2!, threatening both ♗c4 and cxb4, with a winning advantage.

26.♗d5 c5 27.dxc5 ♗xc5 28.b4 ♗d6 29.a4

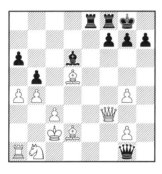

White's rook now enters the fray, followed shortly by the release of White's undeveloped knight from its lengthy (b1) gaol-term. Black's chances of survival are quite dismal.

29...a5 30.axb5 axb4 31.♖a6 bxc3 32.♘xc3 ♗b4

Black aims to swap bishop for knight, gifting White a powerful bishop pair, and soon collapses. But even after, say 32...♗e5, and if 33.b6 ♕c5 34.b7 ♕c7, White establishes a powerful rook on a8, and must still win.

33.b6 ♗xc3 34.♗xc3 h6 35.b7 ♖e3 36.♗xf7+ 1-0

Based in the New World, Capablanca had the good fortune to avoid the worst miseries of the Great War, which hit Lasker and the other Central European masters hardest, perhaps most lamentably, Carl Schlechter, who failed to survive the ordeal. In 1913, however, the Cuban matador had perhaps already enjoyed an even larger slice of good luck: Capablanca's native Cuba, increasingly cognisant of his cosmopolitan ease and budding world chess champion's celebrity, recruited him into its diplomatic service.

Capablanca's diplomatic status freed him from any ultimate dependency on a wholly 'professional' chess career. Part of a mutually advantageous arrangement that continued well into the 1930s, it allowed him to combine a role as a prominent state representative with ample free time made available to pursue his glittering chess career. Capablanca's first major diplomatic posting was to St Petersburg, late in 1913, where he certainly had the opportunity both to prepare for and compete in the great St Petersburg tournament.

As a chess player, of course, Capablanca's reaction to the outbreak of war must have been one of concern. At St. Petersburg 1914, he had emphatically stamped his claim to be considered Lasker's likeliest heir. Aged 25,

Capablanca had every expectation that he would soon play a title match. In 1894, Lasker had also been 25 years old, when he first won the world title. The Great War, which threatened to rob Capablanca of some of his very best years, caused an abrupt rupture.

During the war years, Capablanca nonetheless stoically consolidated and, indeed, greatly enhanced his reputation, by winning four strong New York tournaments (in 1914, 1915, 1916 and 1918). Capablanca scored a superb, 11/11, 13/14, 14/17 and 10.5/12, in these events, suffering only one loss, against Oscar Chajes (in 1916). At Havana 1919, Capablanca then crushed Boris Kostic in a match (5-0), shortly followed by a crushing 1ˢᵗ place (on 10.5/11), at the so-called 'Victory' tournament, at Hastings, later that year.

As the world gradually began to confront the devastation of the war years, not even Lasker himself (who turned 50, in 1918) believed he could any longer resist Capablanca in a title match. Life in Central Europe remained in chaos and the chess world itself had moved on. Rubinstein, who had suffered especially badly during the war, never fully recovered the form of his greatest pre-war years. Everyone waited for the only apparently sensible outcome: would a Lasker-Capablanca match, however, actually happen?

It almost didn't! The players eventually met, at Havana 1921. But only after Lasker had announced that he would prefer to renounce his title in

Capablanca's favour without a contest. Although Capablanca and others thankfully persuaded him otherwise, they couldn't budge his wish to be considered the 'challenger'. The 'champion' lost this somewhat strange title 'defence' (-4=10+0), at a point when, denied a request to transfer what might still have been up to a maximum of a further ten games to a cooler US location, he simply 'resigned'.

After some 27 years as champion and faced with his obvious successor, Lasker's heart no longer seemed to be in playing yet one more battle for a title that he had held far longer than anyone might ever do in the future. When he came to the board, however, the old lion nonetheless still competed at strength. Despite the odd circumstances, Lasker bowed out with a dignity befitting a player who had dominated chess for an era. Capablanca had to play at his best to defeat him.

In his book on the match, Lasker likened Capablanca's 'soul [to] that of a mathematician'. He saw in Capablanca a consummate 'practitioner', whose great strength lay in his ability to act 'in accordance with the logic of [a] position's permanent character'. Lasker maintained that Capablanca, 'cannot be intimidated by unsound or suspicious sacrifices. If he has enough time to think, he studies his opponent's move closely and without mercy lays bare its weaknesses'. Words that strangely recall Adolf Anderssen's on Paul Morphy!

Lasker also pointed to one possible weak point. He considered that 'Capablanca likes neither complications nor taking chances ... to know in advance where he is headed ... as though he distrusted Anderssen's and Chigorin's [highly combinative] style, or even hated and perhaps feared it'. But that prescient insight was for the future. For the present, Capablanca was simply the world's best player by a distance. In Game 3, the best played in their match, Capablanca went +3 ahead against Lasker, a critical turning point.

J.R.Capablanca – Em.Lasker

Game 11, World Championship, Havana 1921

Queen's Gambit Declined

1.d4 d5 2.♘f3 e6 3.c4 ♘f6 4.♗g5 ♘bd7 5.e3 ♗e7 6.♘c3 0–0 7.♖c1 ♖e8

This move may be solid enough and still gets trotted out occasionally. Capablanca championed the livelier try for equality: 7...c6, and if 8.♗d3 dxc4 9.♗xc4 ♘d5 10.♗xe7 ♕xe7 11.0–0 (Alekhine and Capablanca drew eight games, with 11.♘e4, in their 1927 world championship match) 11...♘xc3 12.♖xc3 e5.

8.♕c2 c6 9.♗d3 dxc4 10.♗xc4 ♘d5 11.♗xe7 ♖xe7

more conventional 11...♕xe7, and if 12.0–0 ♘xc3 13.♕xc3 e5, or possibly ...b6, followed by ...♗b7, retaining options of a c5 break.

12.0–0 ♘f8 13.♖fd1 ♗d7 14.e4 ♘b6

Perhaps Black should have swapped knights to try to free up a little more manoeuvring space. Lasker, however, may have been deliberately playing to complicate.

15.♗f1 ♖c8 16.b4 ♗e8 17.♕b3 ♖ec7 18.a4 ♘g6 19.a5 ♘d7 20.e5

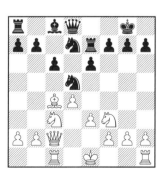

Lasker now provocatively rejects the

Cramped for space, Lasker confronts

an opponent, who knows how to set about its exploitation. White's pincer-like, b4/a5 pawns severely squeeze Black's queenside and Capablanca will soon land a powerful knight on d6, while all but preventing any potentially freeing ...c5 break. Capablanca already considered that, 'sooner or later', Black would have to resort to a bid for freedom that would probably only prove to be weakening.

20...b6 21.♘e4 ♖b8 22.♕c3 ♘f4 23.♘d6 ♘d5 24.♕a3 f6 25.♘xe8

While it may seem counter-intuitive to abandon d6, this is an excellent reply to Black's 24ᵗʰ move. With this and his next two moves, White weakens Black's kingside pawns and creates attacking potential for his more active forces in the centre and on both flanks.

25...♕xe8 26.exf6 gxf6 27.b5

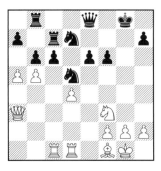

White aims to open the a- and c-files and isolate Black's b-pawn. Black must go along with this plan, or else choose the immediately destabilising alternative, 27...cxb5 28.♖xc7 ♘xc7 29.♕d6, and if 29...♕d8 30.♖c1 ♖c8

31.axb6 axb6 32.♘d2, which is clearly much worse.

27...♖bc8 28.bxc6 ♖xc6 29.♖xc6 ♖xc6 30.axb6 axb6 31.♖e1 ♕c8 32.♘d2 ♘f8 33.♘e4 ♕d8 34.h4

This is the kind of position that Capablanca aimed to bring about after Black's 24ᵗʰ move. Black lacks counterplay. His pawns are all far less secure than White's and he is likely to struggle to cover White's many potential entry points, in the a-, c- and g-files and on the 6ᵗʰ, 7ᵗʰ and 8ᵗʰ ranks. Black retains a 'good' knight on d5, but White soon manages to exchange it, adding to Black's woes on the light squares. Capablanca now secures g5 for White's knight, should Black ever play ...f5.

34...♖c7 35.♕b3 ♖g7 36.g3 ♖a7 37.♗c4 ♖a5 38.♘c3 ♘xc3 39.♕xc3 ♔f7 40.♕e3 ♕d6 41.♕e4 ♖a4

Having exchanged Black's more active knight, White retains the much more threatening minor piece and clear winning chances. Now, however, Black is certainly lost. He had to play 41...♖a7, and if 42.d5 e5, although, even then, White can still increase pressure, beginning with moves, such as ♗b3, ♔g2 and h5.

42.♕b7+ ♔g6

Black also loses after 42...♔g8 43.♕c8, threatening e6, and if 43...♔f7 44.d5 e5 45.♗b5 ♖a7 46.♖c1 ♔g7 47.♕g4+. Black's game is too full of holes to hope for salvation. Capablanca might now have despatched his opponent immediately, by playing 43.h5+ ♔h6 44.♕f7!, and if 44...♕d8 (or if 44...e5 45.dxe5 fxe5 46.♖c1, threatening ♗b5) 45.♗d3 ♖xd4 46.♖xe6, and wins.

43.♕c8 ♕b4 44.♖c1 ♕e7 45.♗d3+ ♔h6 46.♖c7 ♖a1+ 47.♔g2 ♕d6 48.♕xf8+ 1–0
A delightful, alternative game-winning flourish: White mates next move.

Between winning the world title, in 1921, and losing it, to Alekhine, at Buenos Aires 1927, Capablanca perhaps restricted his tournament appearances a little more than was wise for the maintenance of his fullest powers. He started in full vigour, at London 1922,

scoring an undefeated 13/15, ahead of Alekhine (11.5), but only returned to the board, at New York 1924, where he finished in a slightly disappointing 2nd place (on 14.5/20), fully 1.5 points behind his resurgent, old adversary, Lasker.

Bogojubow (15.5/20) and, once again, Lasker (14) relegated Capablanca (13.5) into an even more unaccustomed 3rd place, at Moscow 1925. The world champion then won comfortably in a relatively minor event, at Lake Hopatcong 1926, before again recovering his fullest powers, to outclass an outstanding, six-player field, at New York 1927. In a highly testing, four game mini-match format, against five of his greatest rivals, Capablanca scored a magnificent, 14/20, ahead of Alekhine (11.5), Nimzowitsch (10.5), Vidmar (10), Spielmann (8) and Marshall (6).

The relative ease of Capablanca's New York victory may, however, have helped lull the champion into a false sense of security about his upcoming title defence. While Alekhine had already secured Capablanca's prior agreement to meet him in that match, the New York tournament inevitably came to be widely regarded as a kind of ultimate challengers' test. Nimzowitsch also had a potential challenger's interest, though he neither had Alekhine's chess pedigree nor the finance in place.

Just before the New York tournament, Capablanca had also shown clear signs of undue complacency about his Buenos Aires chances, in a *New York Times* article. While lauding Alekhine's possession of 'the most marvellous chess memory that ever existed [and] best-rounded game among the masters', Capablanca then unfortunately added, 'that he has not the proper temperament for match play [nor] the proper combative spirit [and] is extremely nervous ... which should act to his detriment in a ... protracted struggle'.

Such comments might have been better left unsaid, or, at least, expressed with greater tact than seemed to be within the supremely confident champion's possession. At any rate, at New York 1927, Capablanca must surely have known that he was almost bound to face an unusually 'nervous' Alekhine. The challenger participated under a heavy psychological burden. To maintain a potential champion's credibility, Alekhine either effectively had to finish first or, at worst, in outright second place, behind only Capablanca, should he win.

Alekhine's temperament, combativeness and nerves all did, indeed, show signs of unusual strain, at New York. Noticeably more tentative in his play and more attentive than usual to his ongoing tournament progress, Alekhine had to battle hard to achieve his goal. Against Capablanca, he shared three cagey draws, but lost their first game, completely outplayed by the world champion, who, perhaps sensing his opponent's vulnerability, played unusually sharply.

If this win was a rout, it was nevertheless quite brilliantly executed by Black. Alekhine, perhaps taken aback by Capablanca's adoption of an unexpectedly double-edged strategy, reacted impulsively. Capablanca's cool refutation hit hard. Alekhine's notes in the tournament book balance due praise for his opponent and objective self-criticism. Looking forward to Buenos Aires, however, New York scarcely mattered. Some months later, a transformed Alekhine soon won the much bigger prize.

A.Alekhine – J.R.Capablanca

New York 1927

Queen's Indian Defence

1.d4 ♘f6 2.c4 e6 3.♘f3 b6 4.g3 ♗b7 5.♗g2 c5

This ambitious move, in place of the solid 6...♗e7, was quite topical at the time. Alekhine chooses the critical reply, leading to Modern Benoni-like structures of a type that had scarcely yet been tested. Also interesting is 6.0-0, leading after 6...cxd4 7.♕xd4, into modern Hedgehog paths.

6.d5 exd5 7.♘h4 g6 8.♘c3 ♗g7 9.0–0 0–0

F.Sämisch-P.Romanovsky, Moscow 1925, a game that Capablanca would certainly have been aware of, as he had also played in that tournament, had gone 9...d6 10.cxd5 0–0 11.e4, leading to a standard type of Modern Benoni that Capablanca probably judged quite playable for Black. Capablanca, however, later advocated 10.♗g5, as a likely improvement.

10.♗f4 d6 11.cxd5

Alekhine, too, opts for standard paths. After 11.♘xd5, aiming to maintain a piece on d5 and keep the d-file half-open, Black probably equalises fully, by playing 11...♘xd5 12.♗xd5 ♗xd5 13.♕xd5 ♘a6, and if 14.♕d2 (or if 14.♗xd6 ♖e8 15.♕d2 ♗e5) 14...♖e8 15.♖ad1 ♕e7 16.e3 ♖ad8.

11...♘h5 12.♗d2 ♘d7 13.f4?!

Alekhine, however, now starts to overplay his hand. In his book on the tournament, he severely criticised this and his next move, as an ill-judged attempt to overrun Black on the kingside.

White should instead prefer the more natural 13.e4, which raises the possibility of ♘f5, and keeps play in keen balance. White has a strong pawn centre. Black keeps it in check by the exertion of pressure along the long dark diagonal and in the e-file (with control of e5 a key focus).

13...a6 14.♗f3?!

White continues with his plan to drive Black's knight back to f6, followed by the advance of his g- and f-pawns. After 14.e4 b5, Black mobilises his queenside pawns, without any real challenge. The constraining, 14.a4, might instead have been better.

14...♘hf6 15.a4 c4!

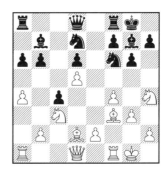

Not one to miss such a glorious attacking opportunity, Capablanca hits back hard on the queenside: Black threatens both ...♘c5 and ...b5, seizing the advantage. Alekhine now confessed to complete pessimism about his kingside prospects. He might, however, have tried to mitigate the worst of Black's developing pressure, by playing 16.b3 (or perhaps b4).

16.♗e3 ♕c7 17.g4 ♘c5 18.g5 ♘fd7 19.f5 ♖fe8 20.♗f4 ♗e5

Having instead ploughed on with the extremely doubtful advance of his f- and g-pawns, Alekhine has only succeeded in creating further central and kingside weaknesses, while simultaneously losing ground on the queenside. Black controls b3, threatens ... b5 and maintains an iron grip on the pivotal e5 square and play in the half-open e-file. The vast open spaces that White has created behind his far-flung g- and f-pawns are also about to tell savagely against him.

21.♗g4 ♘b3 22.fxg6 hxg6 23.♖b1 ♗xc3 White's d-pawn now falls and the win becomes clear. In severe time trouble, Alekhine confessed that he only played on (certainly from move 33), driven by a purely reactive, à *tempo* momentum.

24.bxc3 ♕c5+ 25.e3 ♘e5 26.♗f3 ♘d3 27.♔h1 ♗xd5 28.♖xb3 ♘xf4 29.♖b1 ♖xe3 30.♘g2 ♖xf3 31.♖xf3 ♘xg2 32.♔xg2 ♖e8 33.♔f1 ♗xf3 34.♕xf3 ♕xg5 35.♖e1 ♖xe1+ 36.♔xe1 ♕g1+ 37.♔d2 ♕xh2+

38.♔c1 ♕e5 39.♔b2 ♔g7 40.♕f2 b5 41.♕b6 bxa4 42.♕xa6 ♕e2+ 0-1

Capablanca went into the 1927 Alekhine match perhaps only as marginal favourite. Since 1921, Alekhine had played far more successful top-class chess than Capablanca and worked much harder on his game. As a result, Alekhine believed in his chances and battled with an unexpected intensity. Gradually worn down by his opponent's tenacity and generally fine play, Capablanca eventually succumbed in a punishingly protracted encounter, 6-3, in wins, with 25 draws.

Capablanca was shocked by his Buenos Aires failure but took it with initial good grace. Sadly, however, the remainder of the ex-champion's chess career was virtually all to be played out in the shadow of his increasingly all-consuming desire to obtain the title re-match that never took place. As the years rolled by, Capablanca gradually took to speaking as if he had only 'lent his' title to Alekhine, which didn't help. Alekhine, in fact, fully merited a true champion's reputation, well into the 1930s, by his consistently world-class results.

Mind you, during those years, Capablanca enjoyed near universal acknowledgement, as Alekhine's paramount rival. The outstanding quality of Capablanca's own, 1928-1931 tournament performances made this crystal clear. In October 1928, Capablanca issued an open title challenge that he never withdrew. After 1931, partly in reaction to his frustration at getting nowhere with his title ambitions, he took a three year break from the game. By the late-1930s, the chess world had changed

Why was there really no Alekhine-Capablanca re-match? At root lay irreconcilable disagreements that went back to the strict terms of the so-called London Rules. All but dictated by Capablanca, at London 1922 (though top players there agreed to them), these required Capablanca's challenger to guarantee a prize fund of $10,000 (plus all costs). This was an enormous sum for the time, perhaps equivalent to up to around $250,000 in today's money, and much higher than ever before.

Alekhine had had to move mountains to obtain such Buenos Aires backing and required (not unfairly) that any Capablanca re-match meet the same terms. Not even a Capablanca, however, could obtain easy access to such funds. Cue many a battle between the two (and/or intermediaries) over interminable points of detail that went nowhere. For all other challengers, Alekhine considered (not unwisely) that the London Rules left room for negotiation around what the market might actually bear.

The 1929 Wall Street Crash and resultant Great Depression only further deepened Capablanca's financial woes. As the US dollar depreciated, Alekhine (again, not unfairly) insisted

that, in Capablanca's case, the $10,000 stipulation should be measured by its true 1922 value (in gold). Capablanca's supporters argued that Alekhine was being deliberately obstructive. Alekhine, however, always insisted that he needed cast-iron guarantees on the finance.

Through the 1930s, both players themselves became ever more acrimonious and distrustful. They began to avoid each other completely or even speak. We may never fully get to the bottom of the causes of this disastrous breakdown. That it got in the way of what would have been a desirable showdown that should probably have taken place sometime in the early 1930s, is a sad loss. Now, who would have dared to call that one!

Alekhine defended his title twice, against Effim Bogoljubow (1929 and 1934), and then in a third match, which he unexpectedly lost, against Max Euwe (1935). Although the ebullient Bogoljubow's optimistic playing style packed real attacking punch, he was no truly sustained match for Alekhine or Capablanca. Bogoljubow did, however, take outstanding 1st prizes at Moscow 1925 and Bad Kissingen 1928, in the run-up to his 1929 title challenge.

While Bogoljubow comfortably outdistanced Capablanca, both at Moscow and Bad Kissingen, he lost both of their individual games. Capablanca's win, at Bad Kissingen, was achieved in an especially memorable endgame. Chances were more or less dead level out of a fairly colourless opening. Bogoljubow, however, then got far too excited about his kingside

prospects. Capablanca hit back on the queenside with well-crafted force and an elegant mate in the centre.

E.Bogoljubow – J.R.Capablanca

Bad Kissingen 1928

Queen's Indian Defence

1.d4 ♘f6 2.c4 e6 3.♘f3 b6 4.♘c3 ♗b7 5.♗g5 ♗e7 6.e3 ♘e4 7.♗xe7 ♕xe7 8.♘xe4 ♗xe4 9.♘d2 ♗b7 10.♗e2 ♕g5 11.♗f3 ♗xf3 12.♕xf3 ♘c6 13.♕g3

As Bogoljubow led the tournament by 1.5 points (ahead of Capablanca) when this game was played, legend has it that he was more than happy to exchange queens and agree a quick draw. Whether true or not, after a colourless opening, neither side has the slightest weakness, material is much reduced and an early hand-shake would have surprised no one.

13...♕xg3 14.hxg3 ♔e7 15.g4 h6 16.a3?!

Black is now able to speculate on a clever idea to create play in the b-file. Steinitz warned about making unnec-

essary pawn moves that might create weaknesses (here on b3). Boguljubow should have preferred the immediate 16.♔e2, and if 16...a6 17.♘e4.

16...a6 17.♔e2 ♖hb8 18.♘e4!?

Bogoljubow seems driven to attempt to create play on the kingside. If White purely wished to maintain the balance, perhaps simplest was 18.b3, and if 18... b5 19.c5 b4 (or 19...d6 20.♖ac1) 20.a4, preventing any a- or b-file line opening completely.

18...b5 19.c5 d5 20.cxd6+ cxd6 21.f4?!

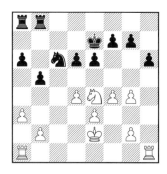

This and White's next move continue kingside action but risk losing control in the c-file. The draw was still likely, after 21.♖ac1, and if 21...♖c8

(but not 21...♔d7? 22.g5!, achieving a true kingside advantage) 22.♖c3 ♘a5 23.♖hc1.

21...♖c8 22.f5 ♘a5 23.♔d3!?

Black's increasing queenside piece activity is beginning to become uncomfortable, though White may still play the more active 23.♖ac1, and if 23...♘b3 24.♖xc8 ♖xc8 25.fxe6 fxe6 26.g5, and probably hold.

23...♘c4 24.♖ab1?!

Black is now clearly better, White should have preferred 24.b3, and if 24...d5 25.♘c5 ♘e5+ 26.dxe5 ♖xc5 27.♖hc1 ♖ac8 28.♖xc5 ♖xc5.

24...d5 25.♘c3?!

Black now gains complete superiority in the c-file and White's game further deteriorates. Better was 25.♘c5, although Black can then still maintain pressure, by continuing 25...e5.

25...♖c6 26.fxe6 fxe6 27.g5

White still hopes for kingside play but Black can just take this pawn. Unfortunately it is probably also too late to hope to contest the c-file, by playing 27.♖hc1 ♖ac8 28.♖c2, as after 28...♔f7, and if 29.♖bc1 ♔g6, Black's king heads for White's vulnerable g-pawn.

27...hxg5 28.♖h5 ♔f6 29.♖h3 ♖ac8 30.♘a2 a5

Black controls play on all fronts. White can no longer prevent Black's rooks from decisive penetration in the c-file and is soon lost.

31.♖f3+ ♔g6 32.g4 ♘d6 33.♘c3 b4 34.axb4 axb4 35.♘d1

Or if 35.♘a2 ♘e4 36.♘xb4 ♖c4 37.♘a2 ♖c2, threatening mate on d2, and wins.

35...♖c2 36.♖f2 b3 37.♖a1 ♘e4 38.♖e2 ♖8c6 39.♖b1

White has no better move and is now caught in a mating net. White can neither allow 39.♘c3 ♖6xc3+ 40.bxc3 ♖xc3 mate, nor move his rook from the first rank, because of the reply ...♖c1, and wins.

39...e5 40.♖a1

Or if 40.dxe5 ♖6c4 (threatening ...♘c5 mate) 41.♖xc2 ♖xc2, followed by ...♖d2 mate.

40...♖6c4 41.♖a5 ♘c5+ 0–1

Mate follows, after either recapture, by playing ...e4.

Chess as Unstoppable Force
Alexander Alekhine

13. *Alexander Alekhine: mid-1920s*

Alekhine's best chess was visceral. Rather like Lasker, Alekhine played in a style that was primarily concrete, analytically alert, combinative and extraordinarily resourceful. Like Lasker, he also always fought hard, with a shared taste for occasional, well-calculated risk-taking. Alekhine worked much harder than Lasker on his openings and embraced a much wider opening repertoire. In this, he was more fully in accord with the newly emerging hypermodern spirit bestirring the game, as the Great War years loomed.

Going into the 1920s, such attributes provided a sound basis for Alekhine's game and for his ultimate goal of successfully challenging for Capablanca's world title. However, he was well aware that he didn't yet possess Capablanca's near instantaneous powers of accurate positional judgment. On his exit from Russia, in 1921, he immediately set to work on improving not just his all-round skills, but also especially that critical element of positional judgment in his game that he deemed most deficient.

Fortunately hard work was a habit that came quite easily to Alekhine. Born into a minor aristocratic Russian family, he enjoyed a relatively comfortable childhood and adolescence, but while he learned to play the game, aged seven, he was no chess prodigy. Throughout his life, success in chess came to Alekhine more by dint of continual practice, disciplined theoretical research and a profound ability to reflect wisely on his game rather than through any innately Capablanca-like, intuitive process.

Well supported and exposed to a wide range of national and international competitive challenges in his teens and very earliest twenties, Alekhine made rapid progress. By early 1914, aged only 21, he had earned the right to play in the great St Petersburg tournament, where he surprise everybody by taking outright 3ʳᵈ place. By then it was clear that Russia had a potential world champion in its ranks, with even more promise than the already established, Rubinstein, or rival newcomer, Nimzowitsch.

As war broke out, Alekhine was declared winner, half-way through an abbreviated tournament, at Mannheim. Following brief incarceration in a German prison, he later served as a medical orderly in the Russian ranks, suffering shell-shock and lengthy hospitalisation. After the 1917 October Revolution, Alekhine lost his 'bourgeois' inheritance but he and other Russian chess players somehow survived the chaotic revolutionary and Civil War years. In 1920, he won the first Soviet Chess Championship. In 1921, with his newly-wed, Swiss journalist wife, he obtained a permit to travel to Europe.

Aged 29, and eventually domiciled in France, Alekhine was determined to re-ignite his 1914 fire to seek to challenge for the world title. He threw himself almost immediately into tournament chess, taking three outright 1st places that year, at Triberg, Budapest and The Hague, without loss of a game. What a calling card! The overall quality of his play at least matched that of his many defeated top-class opponents, among them Bogoljubow (twice) and Rubinstein (strikingly).

A.Alekhine – A.Rubinstein

The Hague 1921

Queen's Gambit Declined

1.d4 d5 2.♘f3 e6 3.c4 a6 4.c5
Rubinstein had recently been successfully experimenting with 3...a6, a flexible move that fits in with many lines of the *Queen's Gambit Declined* and *Accepted*. In the 21st century, Magnus Carlsen has successfully championed its close relation (3...♘f6 4.♘c3 a6), which has very old antecedents, including P.Saint Amant-H.Staunton, 15th match game, Paris 1843. That game continued 5.c5 ♗e7 6.♗g5 0–0 7.e3 b6 8.b4 ♗b7, with chances for both sides (Black won).
In his book, *My Best Games of Chess (1908-1923)*, Alekhine suggests that 4.cxd5,

leading to an Exchange Variation, in which ...a6 might be deemed (very) slightly out of place, may be the line's critical test. He believed, however, that Rubinstein would be well-prepared for that and decided to seek new paths. Unknown to Alekhine, Rubinstein had devised an original plan in reply to Alekhine's (Saint Amant-like) attempt to gain early ground on the queenside.

4...♘c6 5.♗f4 ♘ge7 6.♘c3 ♘g6 7.♗e3
Departing from Staunton's solid 4...♘f6, Rubinstein planned to strike back in the centre, by playing ...e5. He hadn't, however, foreseen Alekhine's

critically concrete 7th move, which, while it temporarily blocks White's own e-pawn, more importantly constrains Black's e-pawn. Both players were now out of their 'books'. Black now logically takes time out to break White's grip on c5 (à la Staunton).

7...b6 8.cxb6 cxb6 9.h4!

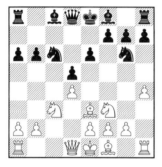

Highly original: White's excellent plan to rush his h-pawn to h6, to gain kingside space and weaken Black's dark squares, rings alarm bells. Rubinstein should now certainly have blocked this by playing the forthright 9...h5, and if 10.♗g5 f6 11.♕c2 ♔f7 12.♗d2 ♗b7, against which Alekhine intended 13.e3, followed by a3 and ♗d3, with perhaps still a very slight edge.

9...♗d6 10.h5 ♘ge7 11.h6 g6
Rubinstein perhaps hadn't fully grasped how difficult his game might become in the next few moves, after White establishes his dark square bishop, on f6. White also stands well after the equally unattractive, 11... gxh6 12.♗xh6 ♘f5 13.♗g5, and if 13...f6 14.♗c1 (possibly also 14.♗d2) 14...♗b7

15.e3, due to the broken nature of Black's kingside pawns.

12.♗g5 0–0 13.♗f6 b5 14.e3 ♗d7 15.♗d3 ♖c8 16.a4
White's unshakeable dark square bind on the kingside spoils White for choice. With this well-timed, second undermining pawn thrust, White coaxes Black into a reply on the queenside that helps White's knight relocate to a strong post. Both 16.0–0 and 16.♘e5 were also promising.

16...b4 17.♘e2 ♕b6 18.♘c1 ♖c7 19.♘b3 ♘a5 20.♘c5

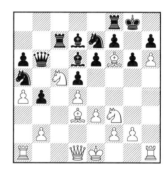

This fine move only underlines Black's chronic dark square problems. After 20...♗xc5 21.dxc5 ♕xc5 22.♗d4 ♕c6 23.♘e5 ♕d6 24.♘g4, and if 24...f5 25.♗e5 ♕b6 26.♘f6+, White's dark square advantage assumes winning proportions. Black perhaps had to try the wholly passive 20...♗c8, but after 21.♗g7, and if 21...♖e8 (or if 21...♖d8 22.♖c1) 22.♘e5 ♘f5 23.♘g4, White's tangible pressure persists.

20...♘c4 21.♗xc4 dxc4 22.♘e5 ♗xe5

23.♗xe7 ♗d6

Black prolongs the game by giving up an exchange but his hopes of a draw remain doubtful. The alternative, 23…♖e8 24.dxe5 ♖xe7 25.♘e4, and if 25…♕c6 26.♕f3 f5 27.exf6 ♖f7 28.♕f4 c3 29.bxc3 bxc3 30.0–0, is however, no better.

24.♗xf8 ♗xf8 25.♘xd7 ♖xd7 26.a5 ♕c6 27.♕f3 ♖d5 28.♖c1 ♕c7 29.♕e2 c3 30.bxc3 bxc3

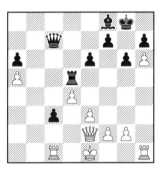

White can now block this pawn and tie up Black's bishop in its passive defence. Perhaps 30…♖xa5 offered better practical chances. Even then, however, White can activate his c-pawn and still hope to win, by playing 31.c4, and if 31…b3 32.♕d3 b2 33.♖b1 ♗b4+ 34.♔f1 ♖a1 35.c5.

31.♕xa6 ♖xa5 32.♕d3 ♗a3

Or if 32…♖a3 33.♔e2, threatening ♖a1.

33.♖c2 ♗b2 34.♔e2 ♕c6 35.f3 f5 36.♖b1 ♕d6

Or 36…♕d5 37.♔f2, threatening ♖xc3, and wins.

37.♕c4 ♔f7 38.♕c8 ♕a6+

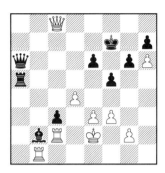

Black must exchange queens or his open king will soon find itself in a mating net. White's pawn on h6 is a key attacking asset in such lines.

39.♕xa6 ♖xa6 40.e4 g5 41.♔d3 ♔g6 42.d5

Without queens, the win is straightforward. The further advance of White's d-pawn decides quickly.

42…fxe4+ 43.fxe4 exd5 44.exd5 ♖a4 45.♖d1 ♔xh6 46.d6 ♔h5 47.d7 ♖a8 48.♔e4 ♖d8 49.♔f5 ♔h4 50.♖h1+ 1–0

In 1922, Alekhine's results were slightly more variable. He nevertheless performed more than sufficiently well to underscore his growing reputation as second only in class to Capablanca. Bogoljubow (at Bad Pistyan) and Rubinstein (at Vienna) took fine first places ahead of him, but they couldn't match Alekhine's consistency. Shortly after finishing second to Capablanca (but ahead of both Bogoljubow and Rubinstein), at London 1922, Alekhine finished 1st, at Hastings (heading Bogoljubow and Rubinstein yet again).

At London 1922, Capablanca was in a class of his own, both on the board and just as imperiously off it. He scored a magnificent, 13/15, in the tournament itself, finishing 1.5 points ahead of Alekhine. Early in the event, he grandly invited all of its top participants to share a glass of fine champagne with him, at a plush London hotel, so that he might obtain their agreement to the so-called 'London Rules', which he, alone, had drawn up, to govern any future world title challenges.

In his wonderful book of chess reminiscences, *Goldene Schachzeiten*, Milan Vidmar, who finished 3rd, at London, provides an excellent eye witness account of what happened. Nothing had been discussed in advance with any of the parties, yet they all added their signatures to the 'London Rules', without demur. Had they any real choice? The champion, as ever, held virtually all the negotiating cards: 'we all lifted our glasses and drank to his good health – a new chapter in chess history had opened'.

Vidmar recalls that he only very slowly grasped the enormity of what he and the others (Alekhine, Bogoljubow, Maroczy, Réti and Tartakower) had actually signed. Not even he, an extremely successful industrial engineer, could conceive of being able to raise the colossal $10,000 purse (including all costs and expenses) required by the

'London Rules'. At a stroke, it effectively destroyed Rubinstein's still serious dream of a title challenge, as well as the longer-term hopes of most others.

Vidmar concedes that all of the signatories were wholly at one with Capablanca, when he argued that it was, at last, high time that the economics of top-class professional chess should be improved markedly. The memory of Steinitz's appalling descent into poverty in his last several years still stood as a terrible reminder of the game's regrettably fragile, reward to risk ratio, even at the utmost pinnacle. Yet the new threshold had been set at an extraordinary height. Would it work?

Really only Alekhine still dreamt. He was, however, under no illusion about the scale of the task that now lay ahead of him. From then on, it was clear that he would have to battle not only to maintain and enhance his reputation as Capablanca's natural challenger, but also to demonstrate to potential backers, from whom he required an extraordinary sum, that he had the capacity to prevail against an apparently well-nigh invincible chess automaton.

Alekhine knuckled down to hard work with conviction and energy. He later wrote a fine book, *On the Road to the World Championship (1923-27)* that covered the most critical years in an epic personal quest that saw him criss-cross Europe, the USA and Latin America. In 1926, he was finally able to persuade the Argentinean government to finance his title challenge, at Buenos Aires. Back in 1922, he was still taking stock of preliminary options.

An important element in Alekhine's long chess march was literary. In *My Best Games of Chess (1908-1923)*, Alekhine presented the chess world with a deeply annotated games collection that has 'world-class' stamped all over it. This was one of the first chess books that I ever bought and it remains riveting. Alekhine not only played the most exciting, combinative chess but annotated all of the key points in these games in crystal clear prose and with incisive analytical precision.

Alekhine's brilliant win against Bogoljubow, at Hastings 1922, a game that, in his own judgement, contained one of his two greatest combinations, inspired widespread international admiration. Bogoljubow certainly played the opening far too meekly, allowing Alekhine to entangle him with too much early positional rope. But the sustained power of Alekhine's beautifully quiet and subtly flowing combinational *dénouement* never fails to set chess pulses racing.

E.Bogoljubow – A.Alekhine

Hastings 1922

Dutch Defence

1.d4 f5 2.c4 ♘f6 3.g3 e6 4.♗g2 ♗b4+ 5.♗d2 ♗xd2+ 6.♘xd2 ♘c6 7.♘gf3

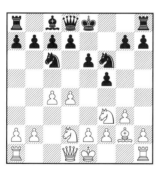

Alekhine frequently exchanged his dark square bishop, in the Dutch, as he felt that it had 'a very limited range of action in this opening'. In reply, he generally advised White to recapture with his queen, followed by ♘c3. With a knight on d2, White's best course is probably to seek to disrupt Black's centre, either by playing the immediate 7.d5, or perhaps the same break at his 10th move.

7...0–0 8.0–0 d6 9.♕b3 ♔h8 10.♕c3 e5 11.e3

With this and his next two pawn moves, White continues to avoid direct challenge, allowing Black to secure a solid (...d6/...e5/...f5) pawn centre and fully equalise.

White might still try for mutually complex chances, by playing 11.d5, and if 11...♘e7 12.e4, or safely exchange pawns on e5 and seek to contest the open d-file.

11...a5 12.b3 ♕e8 13.a3 ♕h5 14.h4

As played, Black has made more progress than White and is poised to play ...e4, gaining tangible additional central space. At last, White begins to wake up. Bogoljubow's robust h-pawn advance may weaken g4. In return, however, it secures a good post for White's knight on g5.

14...♘g4 15.♘g5 ♗d7 16.f3?

This second pawn move, however, seriously compromises White's kingside pawns and is wholly misjudged. Whatever came over Boguljubow? It was still possible to play 16.dxe5, and if 16...dxe5 17.b4, with continuing chances for both sides. From now on, only Black can press (in all board sectors) and completely dominates.

16...♘f6 17.f4

A highly unpleasant consequence of the pawn-structural problems caused by White's previous move: in trying to straighten out his kingside pawns,

Bogoljubow permanently weakens g4 and loses control in the centre. White's game, however, is lifeless. Black remains in complete command, even after, say 17.dxe5 dxe5 18.b4 h6 19.♘h3 ♖ae8, not least due to the long-term vulnerability of White's quite ugly (backward) g-pawn.

17...e4 18.♖fd1 h6 19.♘h3 d5

Black not only controls the centre, but can also expect to make serious inroads on the queenside light squares and (ultimately) on White's chronically weakened kingside. White can't even hope to close down the queenside, by playing 20.c5, when Black still wins the battle for the queenside light squares, by playing 20...a4, and if 21.bxa4 (or 21.b4 ♘a7) 21...♕g6 22.♘f1 ♘a5 23.♖db1 ♗xa4.

20.♘f1 ♘e7 21.a4 ♘c6 22.♖d2 ♘b4 23.♗h1 ♕e8 24.♖g2

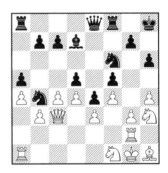

Bogoljubow offers a rather desperate queenside gambit: he apparently still hoped that he might eventually get in g4, aiming to hit at Black's cramping e-pawn. Realistically, however, by this

stage, White's game is simply a wreck. No better was 24.c5 ♕g6, and if 25.♖g2 ♖a6 26.♘f2 ♖c6 27.♕d2 ♖c8, followed by …b6, Black will powerfully open either the c-file (after an exchange of pawns on b6) or the b-file (after …bxc5).

24…dxc4 25.bxc4 ♗xa4 26.♘f2 ♗d7 27.♘d2 b5!

In full combinational flow, Alekhine now gives Bogoljubow no chance. No mere hanging on to an extra pawn for Alekhine, who instead resumes what he called 'the struggle for the central squares' and initiates a hard-hitting sequence of strategically well-founded tactics.

28.♘d1 ♘d3 29.♖xa5

White has no escape. After 29.cxb5 ♗xb5 30.♖xa5 ♘d5 31.♕a3 ♖xa5 32.♕xa5 ♕c6, Black's queen and/or rook decisively penetrate. Black must also win material, due to the perilously trapped nature of White's queen, after 30.♕xc7 ♘d5 31.♕d6 ♘5b4, threatening …♖f6.

29…b4 30.♖xa8

Or if 30.♕a1 ♖xa5 31.♕xa5 ♕a8 32.♕xa8 ♖xa8, and Black's rook wins.

30…bxc3 31.♖xe8 c2!

The poetry continues. Black drops a second rook (with check) but his pawn queens.

32.♖xf8+ ♔h7 33.♘f2 c1♕+ 34.♘f1 ♘e1!
Once again, deeply aesthetic: Black threatens to deliver a smothered mate (on f3), which forces the win of White's c-pawn.

35.♖h2 ♕xc4 36.♖b8 ♗b5 37.♖xb5
White must now give up even more material, or allow 37.♘d2 ♕c1, and if 38.♖xb5 ♘f3+, and mates. With his remaining pieces all in a futile jumble on the kingside, White might already resign with a clear conscience.

37…♕xb5 38.g4 ♘f3+ 39.♗xf3 exf3 40.gxf5 ♕e2!
Many roads now win for Black. Alekhine's is consistent and pleasing. As White would now lose instantly, after either 41.♘h3 ♘e4, or 41.♖h3 ♘g4, Bogoljubow's only remaining

alternative is to stall for a few more moves before having to play (a clearly losing) e4, succumbing to Zugzwang.

41.d5 ♔g8 42.h5 ♔h7 43.e4 ♘xe4 44.♘xe4 ♕xe4 45.d6 cxd6 46.f6 gxf6 47.♖d2 ♕e2

One final delicacy: White must accept Black's queen offer, leading to a trivially won king and pawn endgame.

48.♖xe2 fxe2 49.♔f2 exf1♕+ 50.♔xf1 ♔g7 51.♔f2 ♔f7 52.♔e3 ♔e6 53.♔e4 d5+ 0–1

From 1923-1926, the overall quality and consistency of Alekhine's tournament performances continued to maintain his status as Capablanca's natural challenger. Midway through 1923, however, ex-world champion, Emanuel Lasker, who many thought had retired after losing his title to Capablanca, unexpectedly returned to the board, to cause a complication. At Maehrisch Ostrau 1923, Lasker trounced an exceptionally strong field, taking 1st place, with a score of 16/20. All still feared him.

In the very first sentence of *On the Road to the World Championship*, Alekhine duly acknowledged, that 'in 1924 the question of my involvement in competition for the World Championship was still something of an open one'. At New York 1924, Lasker had occasioned total consternation. In a fabulous repeat of his outstanding success, at St Petersburg 1914, Lasker took

1st place, at New York (on 16/20), ahead of Capablanca (14.5) and Alekhine (12), in an uncanny echo of the same top three standings, at St Petersburg.

Perhaps fortunately for Alekhine, Lasker didn't challenge Capablanca to a title match. Nor did he show any apparent wish to do so. Following his fine, 2nd place, at Moscow 1925, once again ahead of Capablanca, Lasker, now in his mid-fifties, 'retired' once more. It seems likely that Lasker would have accepted an invitation to play, at New York 1927, but none was forthcoming. Apparently he and the New York organisers had personal issues and negotiations collapsed.

In 1924, Alekhine recognised that the logic of a possible Lasker title challenge was highly persuasive. Even more significantly, he retained sufficient objectivity to accept that Capablanca's game still remained 'unquestionably superior' to his own. Rather than rush matters, Alekhine renewed efforts to seek further self-improvement. Even as 1925 wore on, a year of outstanding performance, he still only allowed himself to believe that any challenge that he might then make would certainly be competitive credible.

Alekhine's complete dominance, at Baden-Baden 1925, where he finished (16/20) well ahead of a world class field, marked a significant turning point. After Baden-Baden, Alekhine at last considered himself to be 'fully the equal of the world champion', but still with two small caveats. He considered that his play sometimes exhibited a 'perhaps excessively dogmatic' element and that he must further improve his command of 'the transition from the middlegame into the most favourable possible endgame'.

In this assessment, Alekhine perhaps underplays those dynamic elements in his game that even Capablanca might have feared at that point.

These include his zeal in the search for challengingly new and more varied methods of play in the opening, highly imaginative combinative skills and unremitting readiness to fight. At Baden Baden, where he displayed all of these qualities, an undefeated Alekhine achieved the second of what he considered to be his greatest combinations, against Richard Réti.

R.Réti – A.Alekhine

Baden-Baden 1925

Reversed Alekhine's Defence

1.g3 e5 2.♘f3 e4 3.♘d4 d5 4.d3 exd3 5.♕xd3 ♘f6 6.♗g2 ♗b4+ 7.♗d2 ♗xd2+ 8.♘xd2 0–0 9.c4

Among several potential Black improvements against his opponent's experimental opening, Alekhine particularly recommended, 3...c5 4.♘b3 c4 5.♘d4 ♗c5, and if 6.c3 ♘c6, with equality. He argued that, here, White gains little by having g3 as his 'extra' move (over a conventionally played Alekhine's Defence), as it effectively rules out the natural challenge by the e-pawn (here, playing White, 6.e3).

As matters now stand, after an exchange of pawns on d5, White can hope to gain tangible additional queenside and central space and has come out of the opening with a pull.

9...♘a6 10.cxd5 ♘b4 11.♕c4 ♘bxd5 12.♘2b3 c6 13.0–0 ♖e8 14.♖fd1 ♗g4

15.♖d2 ♕c8 16.♘c5 ♗h3 17.♗f3

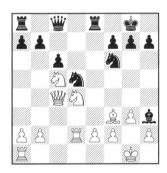

Still under some slight pressure, Alekhine would now have settled for the draw by repetition that Réti eventually avoids, by retreating his bishop to a (slightly) poorer post on his 20th move.

White correctly avoids exchanging bishops, as this only allows Black active prospects on the kingside light squares. White certainly daren't play 17.♗xh3 ♕xh3 18.♘xb7?, when

Alekhine gives 18...♘g4 19.♘f3 ♘de3, and if 20.♕xf7+ ♔h8 21.♘h4 ♖f8, and Black wins.

17...♗g4 18.♗g2 ♗h3 19.♗f3 ♗g4 20.♗h1 h5!

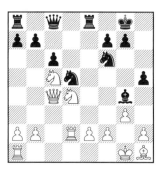

This accurate possibility is what all the fuss was about. Black plans ...h4, followed by ...hxg3, weakening White's kingside pawns and providing a point of potential counterattack (g3). Without this resource, Black's game risks descent into dangerous central and queenside passivity. Still nevertheless with an objectively slight pull, White launches a menacing minority attack on the queenside.

21.b4 a6 22.♖c1 h4 23.a4 hxg3 24.hxg3 ♕c7 25.b5?
While strategically desirable, this move is tactically flawed. Réti clearly didn't anticipate the power of Black's excellent 26th move. White's correct strategy was to combine the minority attack with a central attack, based on playing e4 either now or possibly earlier. Alekhine thought that his game remained sufficiently robust, after

25.e4 ♘b6, and if 26.♕b3 ♘bd7. Now, however, only Black presses.

25...axb5 26.axb5 ♖e3!

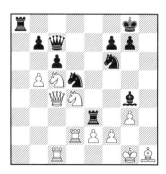

A magnificent resource: Black's rook cannot be captured, because of ...♕g3+, followed by ♘xe3, and mates; Black also threatens ...♖xg3+, and wins.

After Réti's reply, White might already be lost. White should instead have played 27.♗f3!, and if 27...♗xf3 28.exf3 cxb5 29.♘xb5 ♕a5! (Alekhine) 30.♖xd5 ♖e1+ 31.♖xe1 ♕xe1+ 32.♔g2 ♘xd5 33.♕xd5 ♖a1 34.♕d8+, forcing a repetition.

Alekhine also suggested 27.♔h2, and if 27...♖aa3 (or 27...♗h5, and if 28.fxe3 ♘g4+ 29.♔h3 ♘dxe3, followed by ...♘f2+) 28.♘cb3 ♕e5 29.bxc6 bxc6, to which the computer adds 30.fxe3 ♕h5+ 31.♔g1 ♕h3 32.♗xd5 ♘xd5 33.♕xc6 ♕xg3+ 34.♔h1!, and holds.

27.♘f3 cxb5 28.♕xb5 ♘c3
Now with something to bite on, Alekhine's ambition irresistibly soars. By accurately forcing White to capture his b-pawn, Black sets up a brilliant fi-

nale. White can't allow 29.♕c4 b5!, and Black wins.

29.♕xb7 ♕xb7 30.♘xb7 ♘xe2+ 31.♔h2 ♘e4!

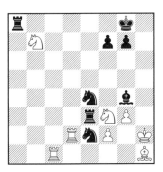

Alekhine now drily observed that this gloriously nonchalant knight move marked: 'The beginning of a new combination … aiming, after a series of twelve practically forced moves, at the capture of White's exposed knight at b7'. In passing, note that after 32.fxe3? ♘xd2, Black wins an exchange.

32.♖c4 ♘xf2!

Avoiding both 32…♘xd2 33.♘xd2, and 32…♗xf3 33.♖xe4, when White holds.

33.♗g2 ♗e6!

Black now frees g4, for a crushing knight check.

34.♖cc2 ♘g4+ 35.♔h3 ♘e5+ 36.♔h2 ♖xf3

Black can't recapture this rook without loss of a minor piece. By vacating e3, Black also sets up a path for his knight (on e6) to embark on a most wonderfully conceived final flourish.

37.♖xe2 ♘g4+ 38.♔h3 ♘e3+ 39.♔h2 ♘xc2 40.♗xf3 ♘d4 0–1

Or if 41.♖f2 ♘xf3+ 42.♖xf3 ♗d5

and wins. What a skewer!

In the years leading up to Buenos Aires, Alekhine worked just as hard off the board as on it. As his playing strength soared, Alekhine also increasingly cultivated an easy cosmopolitan urbanity that quite matched that of his Cuban diplomat *cum* world champion rival. Alekhine's outstanding world record breaking blindfold simultaneous displays, especially at New York 1924 and Paris 1925, added greatly to his popularity. Later in 1925, building on his pre-1914 Russian legal diploma, he added a doctorate in French law.

Alekhine also continued to work hard on his outstanding chess books. In early 1925, he published *The Book Of The New York 1924 International Chess Tournament*, in which he annotated every game played in penetrating detail. Capablanca himself rated the book's quality highly. Alekhine later observed that its writing hugely benefited his own game, not least because of the valuable opportunity it afforded for close study of the ways in which Capablanca and Lasker approached chess.

Between late March 1927 and the start of the Buenos Aires match, in September that year, Alekhine also somehow found time to draft an equally splendid book on the games of the New York 1927 tournament, which was eventually published (in German), early in 1928. The final published work contains an intimate and insightful introduction in the form of an extended essay that expands on the tournament's significance 'as a prologue to the world championship match'. It was, no doubt, finalised only after Alekhine had won, at Buenos Aires.

In this essay, Alekhine maintained that he had detected a recent mini-crisis in Capablanca's play that was leading him away from the assured positional and tactical grandeur of his youth towards an over-reliance on technique and intuition. In consequence, he determined to play ultra-solid chess against the champion, to keep playing while broadly balanced chances remained on the board and to 'check most thoroughly every one of

[Capablanca's] tactical ideas, as it was [not] to be precluded that there would be no detectable "hole"'.

Alekhine had apparently come to 'the rather paradoxical conviction that the tactician in Capablanca was much inferior to the strategist at that time' and that he should therefore, on no account, force play in the opening and middlegame. Out went undue opening experiment. In came a near continuous series of ultra-orthodox Queen's Gambits (with both colours), a match strategy that enabled the challenger 'in no small measure [to] exploit Capablanca's tactical omissions [in] Games 1, 11, 21 and 34'.

Shortly before Buenos Aires, Alekhine comfortably won a warm-up tournament (on 8/9), at Kecskemet. His subsequent match strategy surprised many but it proved extraordinarily successful. As the match was to be decided by the first player to reach six wins (draws not counting), the four games mentioned above made a major impact on the outcome. Let Game 21, which extended Alekhine's lead, to 4-2 (in wins), tell its story.

J.R.Capablanca – A.Alekhine

Game 21, World Championship, Buenos Aires 1927

Queen's Gambit Declined

1.d4 d5 2.c4 e6 3.♘c3 ♘f6 4.♗g5 ♘bd7 5.e3 ♗e7 6.♘f3 0–0 7.♖c1 a6

Alekhine had specially prepared this line (still a stubborn choice) and the Cambridge Springs Defence for use in the match. He considered Capablanca's reply 'tame' and 'virtually refuted (as a winning attempt)' by Black's 10th move, in this game. Capablanca switched to the more critical, 8.cxd5 exd5 9.♗d3, in Games 23, 25 and 27 (all drawn).

8.a3 h6 9.♗h4 dxc4 10.♗xc4 b5

Alekhine had instead played 10...b6, in Games 13, 15, 17 and 19, achieving draws in each. The more active text-move improves Black's chances.

11.♗e2 ♗b7 12.0-0

Black has no problems after his dynamic reply to this move. White's only blocking attempt, 12.b4, however, allows 12...a5! (discovered in home analysis), which promises plenty of counterplay, such as after 13.♕b3 axb4 14.axb4 ♘d5 15.♗xe7 ♕xe7, and if 16.0-0 (or if 16.♗xb5 ♖fb8) 16...♘xb4 17.♖b1 ♘d5 18.♘xb5 ♖fb8.

12...c5 13.dxc5 ♘xc5 14.♘d4

Alekhine also dismissed the tactical flurry, 14.♗xf6 ♗xf6 15.♘xb5 ♕xd1 16.♖fxd1 ♘b3, and if 17.♖c7 ♗xf3 18.♗xf3 axb5 19.♗xa8 ♖xa8, leading to positions in which White may risk serious discomfort on the queenside light squares.

14...♖c8 15.b4 ♘cd7 16.♗g3

Black's game is already a little easier to play than White's, due to White's continuing, if objectively still only very

14. Alekhine (l.) v Capablanca: World Championship match 1927

slight, light square unease. There is, however, certainly no need yet for panic.

16...♘b6 17.♕b3 ♘fd5 18.♗f3 ♖c4 19.♘e4 ♕c8 20.♖xc4?!

So far, Capablanca has conducted the defence well. Here, however, rather than lightly abandon control of c4, Alekhine recommended 20.♕b1. Black then scarcely achieves anything, after 20...♖d8 (or 20...♕a8 21.♘d2) 21.♘d2 ♖xc1 22.♖xc1 ♕a8. Capablanca may have wished to avoid the complications, after 20...♖xc1 21.♖xc1 ♘c4 22.a4 (more active than 22.♗d6), and if 22...bxa4 23.♗e2 ♘db6 24.f3 a3, but White seems to be fine.

20...♘xc4 21.♖c1 ♕a8 22.♘c3?

This is much worse: Capablanca falls in surprisingly meekly with Black's design on control of c4 and d5. White had to risk 22.♘c5, after which Alekhine gives 22...♗xc5 23.bxc5 ♖c8 24.♗e2 ♖xc5 25.♗xc4 ♕c8, 'winning a pawn'. In this line, however, White clearly improves, by playing 24.e4!, and if 24...♘f6 25.a4 ♖xc5 26.♕b4!, with good practical chances.

22...♖c8 23.♘xd5 ♗xd5 24.♗xd5 ♕xd5 25.a4 ♗f6 26.♘f3 ♗b2!

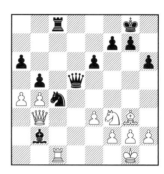

Black prepares ...e5-e4, 'without restricting the activity of the bishop' (Alekhine). Black's entrenched grip on d5 and c4 and control in the d-file provide a firm basis for the final attack. Black would now win, after 27.♖d1 ♘xe3 (Alekhine's 27...bxa4 28.♕xa4 ♘b6 29.♖xd5 ♘xa4, is also strong), and if 28.♖xd5 ♖c1+ 29.♖d1 ♖xd1+ 30.♕xd1 ♘xd1. Alekhine also gave 27.♖b1 ♘a3, and if 28.♕xb2 (or 28.♕xd5 exd5 29.♖d1 bxa4) 28...♘xb1 29.♕xb1 ♕b3 30.♕f1 bxa4, winning.

27.♖e1 ♖d8 28.axb5 axb5 29.h3 e5 30.♖b1

Unable to drum up any counterplay, Capablanca opts for a quick execution rather than linger on in hopeless endgame passivity, after either 30.e4 ♕d3, and if 31.♕xd3 ♖xd3 32.♖b1 ♗c3, followed by ...f6, or 30.♕c2 ♕d3, and if 31.♕xd3 ♖xd3 32.♔f1 e4 33.♔e2 f6.

30...e4 31.♘d4

Or if 31.♘h2 ♕d3 32.♖xb2 ♕xb3 33.♖xb3 ♖d1+ 34.♘f1 ♘d2 35.♖a3

♘xf1, followed by ...♘xe3+, and wins (Alekhine); neither can White expect to defend for long, in this line, after 32.♕a2 ♗f6, and if 33.♘g4 ♗c3. After 31.♘e1 ♕d2, Alekhine gives 32.♕c2 ♕xc2 33.♘xc2 ♖d2, and if 34.♘e1 ♘a3, and wins.

31...♗xd4 32.♖d1 ♘xe3 0–1
Or if 33.♕xd5 ♖xd5 34.fxe3 ♗xe3+.

After Buenos Aires, Alekhine took a year's rest. Refreshed, he then embarked on what was to become a sustained period of exceptional chess excellence that lasted from 1929 until the eve of his third world title defence, against Max Euwe, in 1935. During these years, Alekhine won two world title matches and nine tournaments (one of them shared), with only one 2nd placed finish in a tenth tournament. Alekhine also scored outstandingly well, on top board for France, in four of FIDE's new International Team Tournaments.

Excluding the two world title matches, Alekhine lost only five games in tournament and team events during this run (a whopping 81% success rate). At San Remo 1930, he achieved an extraordinary, 14/15, ahead of a glittering cast. At Bled 1931, he scored 20.5/26, playing equally dazzling chess against an even more select top-class ensemble. While he didn't play Capablanca, this was nonetheless the performance of a great champion.

How did he do this? Alekhine primarily considered himself as an artist, who delighted in the often combinative realisation of great beauty in chess. Universal in style, he relished logical games of manoeuvre, the pursuit of the initiative, the thrill of the attack and counter-attack and even games of mere stubborn defence. But perhaps crucially, Alekhine had mastered the art of seeking concrete solutions to openings problems, backed up by constant home preparation, much better than most.

In his book, *Alexander Alekhine*, Alexander Kotov employs a striking phrase to describe Alekhine's stylistic ideal: 'creativity from the very first move'. Against Alekhine, opponents always had to be ready for early surprises, in the sure knowledge that they were informed by a mass of hard work on background ideas, including typical middlegame and endgame transitions. Alekhine was in the vanguard of the further development of such intensely analytical methods of play and home preparation, in those inter-war years.

Such traits were not lost on Max Euwe, whose biographer, Alexander Münninghof, writes that Euwe and his second, Hans Kmoch, early on concluded 'that the main reason why the world champion outplayed his opponents so effortlessly was his greater knowledge of the opening'. In consequence, they adjusted Euwe's 1935 title match preparations to include an in-depth study of 'a few openings (those that Alekhine liked to play and which suited Euwe)'. In these, however, they observed that 'the number of "key positions" to be studied was vast'.

Euwe's ability to trade opening blows against Alekhine successfully certainly contributed to Euwe's unexpected match victory and where Euwe showed the way, others followed. The professional, Alekhine, regained his title from his essentially amateur opponent, in the players' 1937 re-match. Now aged 45, however, and beset by several, much younger, fitter and equally knowledgeable rivals, Alekhine was no longer secure in his primacy. World War II saved Alekhine from any

immediate title challenge but left him increasingly only champion by default.

At Zürich 1934, still in his absolute pomp, Alekhine scored his only ever career win against Emanuel Lasker. That remarkable survivor, then in his mid-sixties and playing for a third time out of retirement remained a threat to anyone. Lasker plays an excellent (12ᵗʰ move) innovation. Alekhine, however, better understands the resulting types of middlegame and pounces on an inadequate, 17ᵗʰ move. Two years later, Salo Flohr demonstrated the efficacy of Lasker's chosen plan, on the back of some excellent home preparation - a sign of the times.

A.Alekhine – Em.Lasker

Zürich, 1934

Queen's Gambit Declined

1.d4 d5 2.c4 e6 3.♘c3 ♘f6 4.♘f3 ♗e7 5.♗g5 ♘bd7 6.e3 0–0 7.♖c1 c6 8.♗d3 dxc4 9.♗xc4 ♘d5 10.♗xe7 ♕xe7 11.♘e4

W.Steinitz-Em.Lasker, Game 5, world championship 1894, had gone, 11.e4!?

♘f4!? 12.g3 ♘g6 13.0–0 ♖d8 14.♕e2 b5 15.♗b3 ♗b7 16.♕e3 a6, with an eventual draw. 1930s theory preferred either 11.0–0 or Alekhine's choice. According to Alekhine, both moves offer White 'an advantage in space [without] worry about a possible loss'.

11...♘5f6 12.♘g3 e5

Alekhine considered this 'an interesting attempt by Lasker to solve swiftly the problem of the queen's bishop'.

At Buenos Aires 1927, Alekhine and Capablanca contested seven hard-fought draws, after 12...♕b4+ 13.♕d2

♕xd2+ 14.♔xd2. Both options remain viable, even today.

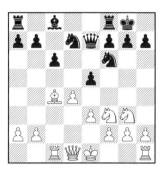

13.0–0 exd4 14.♘f5

White retains more tension after the probably more critical challenge, 14.exd4, which opens the e-file and leads to mutually sharp play in an IQP middlegame, such as after 14...♘b6 15.♖e1 ♕d6 16.♗b3 ♘bd5 (perhaps preceded by ...a5).

14...♕d8 15.♘3xd4

Given Flohr's excellent discovery on Black's 17th move, it may be that White's only way to try to make any real headway in this line, is to play 15.♘5xd4, and if 15...♘b6 16.♗b3 ♗g4 17.♕c2.

15...♘e5 16.♗b3 ♗xf5 17.♘xf5 ♕b6?

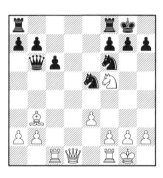

Flohr showed that Black equalises completely, after the correct response, 17...g6!, as in M.Euwe-S.Flohr, Nottingham 1936, which continued 18.♕d4 ♕xd4 19.♘xd4, and was soon drawn. Black also equalises, after either 18.♘d6 ♕e7, or 18.♕d6 ♖e8. Lasker, alas, sends his queen on an ill-advised journey that only vacates swathes of alarmingly vulnerable central and kingside space for the White hordes.

18.♕d6 ♘ed7

After 18...♘g6, White plays 19.♘h6+, an ugly blow that ruinously ruptures Black's kingside pawns.

19.♖fd1 ♖ad8

With no Black queen at hand, defence is difficult. After the immediate 19...g6, a weakening move that Black would prefer to avoid, White creates havoc on the dark squares, by playing 20.♘h6+ ♔g7 21.♕f4, and if 21...♖ae8?! 22.♖xd7! ♘xd7 23.♘xf7 ♘f6 24.♕h6+, and wins.

20.♕g3 g6 21.♕g5 ♔h8?!

With Black's queen still out of touch on the faraway queenside, Lasker may not have relished the thought of entering the wholly unenviable endgame that arises after 21...♕b5 22.♘h6+ (or 22.♗xf7+ ♖xf7 23.♘h6+ ♔f8 24.♘xf7, which transposes) 22...♔g7 23.♕xb5 cxb5 24.♘xf7 ♖xf7 25.♗xf7 ♔xf7 26.♖c7, and if 26...b6 27.♖xa7, but he had nothing better. His kingside and central defences are now hopelessly outgunned in short order.

22.♘d6 ♔g7 23.e4

White threatens not only to play e5, followed by decisively doubling rooks in the d-file, but also raises the deadly prospect of an attacking rook switch, via c3-h3.

23...♘g8 24.♖d3 f6

White threatened to win by doubling rooks in the d-file, followed either by ♘f5+ or ♘xf7. Powerless to prevent that course, Lasker generously invites his opponent to finish him off by delivering a spectacular mate. White also mates grandly, after 24...h6 25.♘f5+ ♔h7 26.♘xh6, and if 26...f6 27.♘f5! fxg5 28.♖h3+.

25.♘f5+ ♔h8 26.♕xg6 1–0

Or if 26...hxg6 27.♖h3+, and mates.

Soviet Dynamics

'No, chess has not changed, it has not become different. This is all fairy tales ... It is only ... that the initial information is now easier to obtain ... the process of analysis has remained the same. A chess player should himself analyse ... nothing can replace analysis'

Mikhail Botvinnik, quoted by Genna Sosonko in *Russian Silhouettes* (2009)

Mikhail Botvinnik (1911-1995), world champion from 1948-57, 1958-1960 and 1961-1963, threw a long shadow across much of the twentieth century. His words above, spoken in 1994, encapsulate the chess credo that became central to his long-lived success ever since he began his rise to the top in the 1930s. There are no 'fairy tales'! Analysis – do it! Botvinnik doesn't just speak to past but also future generations, including the computer age.

By the 1930s, Botvinnik's generation enjoyed access to a substantial and growing body of games and analyses, stretching far back into the Victorian era. Virtually all of the game's modern range of openings had already been invented. But there remained vast scope for much further research, discovery and practical test, in whose vanguard Botvinnik led with boundless energy, investigative talent and ambition of steel.

Botvinnik's talents were innate but his steel also owed much to the state he grew up in. The young USSR early on decided to finance structures able to support widespread workers' participation in chess and a small elite group of generously supported semi- or full-time professionals. Botvinnik spearheaded that elite, which came to be loosely described as a 'Soviet School' and whose leading members all took a lead from Botvinnik's earliest inspirational successes and dynamism.

While Chapter 4 focuses mainly on Botvinnik, it also accords due recognition to the stylistically unique contributions made by the 7th -10th world champions, Vassily Smyslov, Mikhail Tal, Tigran Petrosian and Boris Spassky, who all grew up in the Soviet era and embraced its dynamic tradition. It begins, however, with a section on the 5th world champion, Max Euwe, whose influence on dynamic developments and on Botvinnik himself were substantial.

Thoroughgoing Hard Work and Exacting Logic
Max Euwe

Born in 1901, and around a decade or so younger than virtually all of the leading lights of the 1920s, the young and highly talented Dutchman, Max Euwe, grew up with and readily absorbed the new asymmetric chess spirit and its myriad new openings and middlegame notions. After opening with a King's Indian Defence (at Amsterdam 1923), the spirited youngster engagingly insisted that while 'Lasker calls this move [g6] an exaggeration ... I am not sure why ... I don't think that the weakening of the kingside is very significant'.

Quick to this new world's starting blocks, Euwe simply took as a given that chess could be played in all sorts of ways. Mere handles, 'classical', 'hypermodern' or otherwise, hardly mattered. The point was to understand and make the widest range of plausible systems actually work. That put an increasingly high premium on openings theoretical investigation in a demanding search to discover the often deeply hidden threads of logic that underpinned successful planning.

As his chess matured, Euwe became especially adept in the application of such demanding research skills. By 1934-35, when he successfully challenged and subsequently defeated Alekhine to gain the world title, Euwe had become renowned for his command of the widest range of openings systems and his equally uncommon ability to stick to logical paths in a game, no matter the complications. Off the board, Euwe also possessed excellent nerves and trained hard in the gym to maintain peak physical condition.

A true amateur, Euwe's title win was all the more impressive because of that. Through the early 1920s, as he made an early international impact, Euwe stuck to his university studies and eventually earned a doctorate. Shortly thereafter he became a full-time maths teacher, in a leading girls' school, in Amsterdam. Married in 1926, and soon with a young family, it speaks much for his sense of self-disciplined order that he also continued to excel in the chess world.

Nonetheless there probably never was a more reluctant world title challenger than Euwe. Especially as an amateur, he feared that he lacked sufficient hard-wrought, top-class experience. Fortunately Euwe's ever-improving tournament and match outings, contested almost wholly during academic vacations, convinced key supporters that he might realistically mount a challenge, in 1934-35, against an Alekhine now in his early mid-forties. Nine years' Alekhine's junior, Euwe had arrived at many a chess player's mid-thirties peak.

According to Euwe's biographer, Alexander Münninghoff, Euwe's persuader in chief was his friend and main second in the 1935 match, Hans Kmoch. Together they embarked on a rigorous chess and sports training programme that, against most neutrals' expectations, paid dividends. With the sole exception of a series of reverses with the French Defence, early in

15. *Max Euwe (l.), Vassily Smyslov, Paul Keres, Mikhail Botvinnik and Samuel Reshevsky: World championship, The Hague 1948*

the match, Euwe's openings and his subsequent ability to keep to hard-hitting, well-prepared middlegame paths, caused Alekhine significant problems.

Moreover, as the match took place in the Netherlands, Euwe had the fans on his side. Determined that the match should provide a propaganda coup for Dutch chess, Euwe ensured that the games were staged in many different venues throughout Holland, including Game 9, held in the Assembly Hall of the school which employed him as a teacher. While it all looked bleak after Euwe's early calamities with the French Defence, the local hero eventually clawed back a three point deficit to win (+9-8=13), by a one point margin.

Münninghoff recounts that Euwe played purely for the honour and even had to forgo his normal teaching salary during the period of leave he negotiated to play the match. Alekhine pocketed the entire prize fund (10,000 Guilders, worth around 100,000 Euros today). Following a few weeks rest, Euwe returned full-time to the class room. As world champion, Euwe played three international tournaments, before Alekhine regained the title, in their 1937 re-match, triggered by a clause in the 1935 match contract.

Alekhine's decisive result in the 1937 re-match (+10-4=11) should not detract from Euwe's thoroughly deserved 1935 triumph. Alekhine may not have been at his absolute best, in 1935, but he most certainly didn't underestimate a younger opponent who had stung him more than once in the past, including in an exceptionally tight, eight game training match, in 1926-27, which ended, +3-2=5, in Alekhine's favour. In 1935, a dominant Euwe eventually wore even Alekhine down. Game 26 was both dramatic and pivotal.

M.Euwe – A.Alekhine

Game 26, World Championship, Zandvoort 1935

Dutch Defence

1.d4 e6 2.c4 f5 3.g3 ♗b4+ 4.♗d2 ♗e7 5.♗g2 ♘f6 6.♘c3 0–0 7.♘f3 ♘e4 8.0–0 b6

Earlier in the match, Alekhine mainly played Slav or Grünfeld Defences. With the match level after Game 23, however, Alekhine seemed stung into provocative action. Alekhine's adoption of the ambitious, but strategically (slightly) risky Dutch Defence (Alekhine's own oft-stated view) certainly met that bill but was nonetheless rather a gamble.

The line Alekhine adopts, moreover, cedes early space, as he had already experienced, after 8...♗f6, in the eventually drawn (though rather chaotically played) 24th match game. Having lost Game 25, however, in a race to the best of 30 match games, Alekhine perhaps felt that he had to risk all to retain his title.

9.♕c2 ♗b7 10.♘e5 ♘xc3 11.♗xc3 ♗xg2 12.♔xg2 ♕c8 13.d5

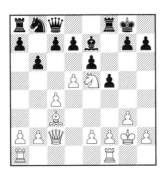

Already, at least, a little better, Euwe stakes a long-term claim to extra space in the centre. In reply, Black establishes a reasonably solid ...d6/ ...e5/ ...f5 pawn centre that White now gradually seeks to undermine. Black still faces the problem of how best to find play for his somewhat passively placed queenside forces.

13...d6 14.♘d3 e5 15.♔h1

White might already have played 15.f4, and if 15...e4 16.♘f2, keeping open the possibility of a g4 break, while retaining the idea of White's knight reaching e3 (via d1), as played.

15...c6 16.♕b3 ♔h8

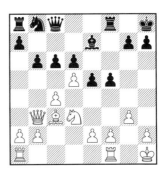

Euwe, however, had been speculating on the possibility of achieving a c5 break, which would work, for example, even after 16...♘a6 17.c5, and if 17... ♘xc5 (or 17...bxc5 18.♘xe5) 18.♘xc5 bxc5 19.dxc6+ ♔h8 20.♕d5. By tucking his king into the corner, Alekhine avoids this. But he might also have tried 16...c5, and if 17.f4 e4 18.♘e1 ♘d7 19.♘g2 ♗f6, gaining a move on his defence in the game.

17.f4 e4 18.♘b4 c5 19.♘c2 ♘d7 20.♘e3 ♗f6 21.♘xf5

Euwe's pulse must have been racing. With this move, he offers his knight for three advanced and connected central pawns and attacking prospects (albeit unclear). Alekhine, too, had seen this coming but no doubt felt that must play like this. He will certainly have foreseen that he might still fight back on the kingside after his 23rd and 24th moves.

21...♗xc3 22.♘xd6 ♕b8 23.♘xe4 ♗f6 24.♘d2 g5 25.e4 gxf4 26.gxf4 ♗d4 27.e5 ♕e8 28.e6 ♖g8 29.♘f3?!

Moves 21-28 seem more or less forced for both sides. White's chances lie mainly in the rapid advance of his passed d- and e-pawns, in a bid to force Black's pieces into back rank impotence. Alekhine, however, has, indeed, managed to conjure up much

needed kingside space and counter-attacking prospects. Note that after 29.exd7? ♕e2!, Black stands well.

White's most accurate continuation, however, was the post-game discovery 29.♕h3 (!-Euwe), and if 29...♘f6 30.♘f3 ♗xb2 31.♖ae1, when (if still tricky) White clearly continues to press. Playing this way rules out any danger in the g-file and retains a powerful platform for White's knight on g5, together providing a highly advantageous base for the further advance of White's e- and/or d-pawns.

29...♕g6 30.♖g1 ♗xg1 31.♖xg1 ♕f6!?

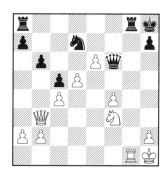

Alekhine, however, misses a big saving chance. By now, both sides were running into serious time trouble and the pressure, in front of a partisan crowd, must have been immense. Alekhine holds easily after 31...♕f5, and if 32.exd7 (or if 32.♘g5 h6!) 32...♖xg1+ 33.♔xg1 ♕xd7 34.♔f2, with equality (Euwe).

32.♘g5 ♖g7?!

A second Alekhine slip: Black might still have played 32...♖g6, and if

33.exd7 ♕xf4 34.♕c3+ ♔g8 35.♕e1 ♖xg5 36.♕e8+ ♔g7 37.♖xg5+ ♕xg5 38.♕xa8 ♕c1+, with a draw by perpetual check. Not, however, 32...h6? 33.exd7 hxg5 34.♕h3+ ♔g7 35.♖xg5+, and White wins.

33.exd7 ♖xd7 34.♕e3 ♖e7 35.♘e6 ♖f8 36.♕e5 ♕xe5 37.fxe5 ♖f5

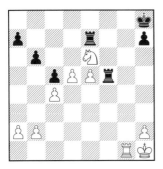

Matters are no longer quite so straightforward for Black, who might also have sought to hold by playing 37...♖xe6 38.dxe6 ♖f5 39.♖e1 ♔g7, although, even here, White might still try 40.♖e3, and if 40...♔f8 41.♖a3.

38.♖e1 h6?
This move, however, is simply a blunder, after which Black is dead lost. Black might still have transposed into the rook and pawn endgame in the

previous note, by exchanging on e6. He might also have played 38...♔g8, after which Euwe intended 39.♖g1+ ♔h8 40.♖g5

and if 40...♖xg5? 41.♘xg5 ♔g7 42.d6!, and wins. In this line, however, Black should play 40...♖f2, after which White can reply 41.h4, and perhaps still hope to make progress.

39.♘d8 ♖f2
Black can't, of course, capture White's e-pawn, as this loses a rook (due to a winning ♘f7+ fork). Without this possibility, however, Black's hapless rook (e7) cannot avoid being corralled by White's knight, rook and pawns (as occurs).

40.e6 ♖d2 41.♘c6 ♖e8 42.e7 b5 43.♘d8 ♔g7 44.♘b7 ♔f6 45.♖e6+ ♔g5 46.♘d6 ♖xe7 47.♘e4+ 1–0

Towards New Methods of Systematic Preparation
Mikhail Botvinnik

16. *Mikhail Botvinnik: 1936*

A precocious youth, though not a chess prodigy, Botvinnik made his earliest international impact by defeating Capablanca in a simultaneous display given by the world champion, at Leningrad 1925. Within two years, he was already strong enough to qualify for a place in the 1927 USSR Championship, held in Moscow, where he finished 5th/6th equal. By 1933, he had two national championships under his belt and was considered the best Soviet player by a distance.

During these years, Botvinnik also worked diligently at his school and university studies and, not unlike Euwe, was keen to pursue a successful career outside chess. In 1931, Botvinnik graduated as a fully qualified electrical engineer and entered a post-graduate study programme. From 1933, however, his studies slowed. In that year, the regime singled him out to receive full and formidable backing in an attempt to develop him into a player of absolute world class.

Botvinnik's first major assignment was to contest a match against the Czech player, Salo Flohr (1908-1983), who was at that time considered the most promising young talent in Europe and a potential world championship candidate. Botvinnik passed this stiffest of tests with flying colours, tying 6-6, in a match played in major public venues, in Moscow and Leningrad, before very large crowds. Three years Flohr's junior, this result augured well for Botvinnik's longer-term prospects.

Botvinnik later recalled that this match marked 'the birth' of what he called 'the new method of preparation'. The method required generous amounts of freed-up time and financial resource and evolved through the 1930s; he first wrote at length about the essentially finished product, in 1941. For the Flohr match, the state put Botvinnik up in a rest home and provided two first-class seconds, Abram Model and Slava Ragozin, both well-known to Botvinnik and all three from Leningrad.

Based on an analysis of Flohr's available games, together the team made a deep study of Flohr's playing style and especially his openings. They fashioned a comprehensive match plan that was based largely on deeply researched openings analyses. The plan stuttered at first but was ultimately vindicated by the final outcome. Botvinnik went two down after losses in Games 1 and 6. However, he managed to draw level with two exceptionally fine wins, in Games 9 and 10, which owed much to his well-conceived openings.

This match is best remembered for those two Botvinnik wins. In Game 9, Botvinnik essayed a big improvement on his disappointing play (in Game 1), on the White side of a Caro-Kann: Panov Attack. With Black, in Game 10, Botvinnik caught Flohr out in a fighting Stonewall Dutch that he understood well but Flohr hadn't yet met in top-class contests. In that game, Botvinnik and his seconds guessed that Flohr might react passively against an unfamiliar line that demands trenchant responses and were proved right.

Botvinnik's openings research was deeply systemic. His overriding ambition was to get as close to the heart of the perennial problem that confronts all players with an eye on the greatest of prizes: how best to derive and develop good plans from richly sound opening systems. Botvinnik didn't seek traps, although if he spotted concrete refutations, he would, of course, play them. He rather aimed to master the art of spotting the widest range of promising openings transitions into dynamically challenging middlegames.

Botvinnik's method certainly owed a dynamic debt to his exiled countryman, Alekhine. Aided by the state, however, Botvinnik added robust teamwork to Alekhine's pioneering openings investigative, but largely lone genius. Through the 1930s, support teams, seconds, coaches and training partners began to assume a greater prominence at the very top in chess than ever before. With the help of his team, Botvinnik spotted an excellent 10ᵗʰ move novelty to gain his first win, in Game 9, of the Salo Flohr match.

M.Botvinnik – S.Flohr

Game 9, Leningrad 1933

Caro Kann: Panov Attack

1.e4 c6 2.d4 d5 3.exd5 cxd5 4.c4 ♘f6 5.♘c3 ♘c6 6.♗g5

Botvinnik had prepared this edgy 6th move for the Flohr match. It contains both tactical and positional bite and leads to an immediate sharpening of the opening battle. Its main point is to deter solid ...e6 responses; after 6... e6?!, White can play 7.c5!

establishing an unshakeable queenside bridge-head (on c5) that can be firmly supported by the further advance of White's a- and b-pawns. Black then lacks clear-cut central and kingside counterplay, while White's queenside pressure persists. Botvinnik-H.Kmoch, Leningrad 1934, later continued 7... ♗e7 8.♗b5 0-0 9.♘f3 ♘e4 10.♗xe7 ♘xe7 11.♖c1 ♘g6 12.0-0 ♗d7 13.♗d3 f5 14.b4 ♗e8?! (White retains an edge after 14...b6 15.♘e2, but 'doing nothing' on the queenside leads to even worse.) 15.g3 ♖c8 16.♖e1 ♕f6 17.a3 ♘e7 18.♘e5 ♕h6 19.f3 ♘f2 20.♕e2 ♘h3+ 21.♔g2 g5 22.♘b5 ♗xb5 23.♗xb5 ♖f6 24.♗d7 ♖d8 25.b5 ♕h5 26.c6 ♖h6 27.♔h1 1-0.

6...dxc4

This is a critical reply, certainly much better than the pawn grabbing alternative 6...♕b6?! 7.cxd5 ♕xb2?, which was dramatically refuted, in M.Botvinnik-R.Spielmann, Moscow 1935, after 8.♖c1! ♘b4 9.♘a4 ♕xa2 10.♗c4 ♗g4 11.♘f3 ♗xf3 12.gxf3 1-0. White can now either advance his d-pawn (as in the game) or venture the equally critical gambit alternative 7.♗xc4 (not then tested).

7.d5 ♘e5

Both this move and 7...♘a5, remain interesting. After the latter knight move, existing 1930s theory (probably accepted by both players) considered White better, by continuing 8.♘f3.

8.♕d4 ♘d3+?!

Owing to the strength of Botvinnik's 10th move, this reply has since virtually disappeared from practice. Towards the end of the 20ᵗʰ century, however, attention turned towards the almost certainly better, if unclear 8...h6.

9.♗xd3 cxd3 10.♘f3!

This is a huge improvement on Botvinnik's play, in Game 1, which had gone 10.♗xf6 exf6 11.♕xd3 ♗d6 12.♘ge2 0–0 13.0–0 ♖e8, when Flohr's active bishops eventually triumphed over White's knights. White's IQP may seem strong but Flohr easily contained it and gradually began to steal ever more squares on both flanks. The text-move, which rightly ignores Black's (lame-duck) d-pawn in favour of rapid development, puts much more pressure on Black.

It is questionable, in fact, whether Black can now satisfactorily defend. After 10...e6, Botvinnik intended 11.♗xf6 ♕xf6 12.♕xd3, with a development plus. S.Furman-B.Naglis, Moscow 1970, instead went crushingly 11.0–0–0 ♗e7 12.♖he1 0–0 13.♖xd3 exd5 14.♖xe7 ♕xe7 15.♘xd5, and wins. Black's chances seem equally bleak after 10...h6 (or 10...♗f5 11.0–0) 11.♗f4, and if 11...g5 12.♗e5 ♗g7 13.♕xd3.

Flohr rather desperately opts for a line in which his 'fighting' king might survive in the middle of the board.

10...g6 11.♗xf6 exf6 12.0–0 ♕b6
According to Botvinnik, Black is already quite lost. In his notes, he gives the line 12...♗e7 13.♖ad1 0–0 14.♖xd3, and if 14...♗f5 15.♖d2 ♗d6 16.g4 ♗c8 17.♘e4, and wins.

13.♖fe1+ ♔d8 14.♕h4!

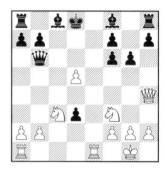

White still needn't sweep up Black's d-pawn. After the text-move, White threatens to overwhelm Black, by playing ♘e5, such as after: either 14...♗d7 15.♘e5, and if 15...♗e8 16.♘c4 ♕a6 17.d6; 14...♗e7 15.d6 (15.♖ad1 and if 15...g5 16.♕e4, is also strong), and if 15...♕xd6 16.♖ad1 ♗d7 17.♖e3; or 14...♗g7 15.♘e5 ♖f8 16.♕xh7 (Botvinnik).

14...g5 15.♕h5 ♗d6
Black has only avoided the calamitous outcomes given in the previous note by creating further weaknesses and must now lose material.
After 15...♕c7 16.♘e4, matters might even be worse.

16.♕xf7 ♖f8 17.♕xh7 g4 18.♘d2 ♕c7 19.♕h6!

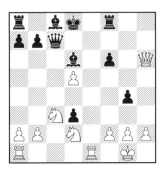

White decisively keep queens on the board. Already a pawn down and with a weakling on d3 that can be picked off virtually at will, Black has no chance. Black's king, moreover, still has scant cover, while his undeveloped queen's rook and bishop merely spectate.

19...♕f7 20.♘c4 ♗e5 21.♘xe5

Botvinnik satisfies himself with a straightforward endgame win. Tarrasch later pointed out the even stronger 21.♘b5!.

21...fxe5 22.♕g5+ ♕e7 23.♕xe5 ♕xe5 24.♖xe5 ♗f5 25.♖f1 ♔d7 26.f3 b5 27.fxg4 ♗xg4 28.h3 b4 29.♘e4 ♖xf1+

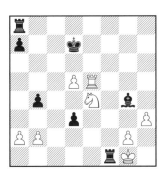

Two pawns ahead and with a well-supported, advanced (and rapidly advancing) passed d-pawn, White now wins quickly. Black's d-pawn remains completely stranded and poses no threat at all. After 29...♗e2, Botvinnik gives 30.♖xf8 ♖xf8 31.d6, and if 31...♖f1+ 32.♔h2 ♖d1 33.♖e7+ ♔c6 (or 33...♔d8 34.♘c5) 34.d7 ♔c7 35.♘c5, and wins.

30.♔xf1 ♖f8+ 31.♔e1 ♗f5 32.g4 ♗g6 33.♖e6 1–0

Following the Flohr match, Botvinnik further added to his reputation, by winning a tournament that mainly consisted of the best Soviet masters, at Leningrad 1934. Euwe, who also played (but purely for training purposes, in the run-up to his 1935 world title match) finished mid-table. Botvinnik then obtained permission to play in his first foreign tournament, at Hastings 1934-35, where he finished in a tie, with Lilienthal (5/9), behind Euwe, Flohr and Sir George Thomas (6.5) and Capablanca (5.5).

Despite his perhaps very slight Hastings blip, Botvinnik had long since been able to count on the crucial support of Nikolai Krylenko, supreme architect and policy overlord of all aspects of the internal and external policy aims of Soviet chess, since the early 1920s. By 1931, Krylenko had become People's Commissar of Justice and State Prosecutor General and was one of the most powerful (and feared) men in the land. Krylenko now ensured that Botvinnik would obtain the chance to shine in two grand Moscow Internationals, in 1935 and 1936.

Botvinnik triumphed, at Moscow 1935, scoring 13/19, and tying for 1st/2nd places, with Flohr (13/19), ahead of Lasker (12) and Capablanca (11.5); for which an exultant state gifted him a car and almost doubled his postgraduate engineering grant. Capablanca (13/18) won outright, at Moscow 1936, but Botvinnik's clear 2nd place (12), amply confirmed that he belonged with the best. Shortly after, at Nottingham 1936, Botvinnik and Capablanca then shared 1st/2nd places (10/14), ahead of Euwe, Reshevsky and Fine (9.5), Alekhine (9) and Flohr and Lasker (8.5).

In recognition of his Nottingham success, Botvinnik received the prestigious, Soviet Order of the Badge of Honour. Still just 25 years old, Botvinnik had climbed high in the consciousness of the Communist Party and the public widely. The first Soviet citizen to demonstrate that the world's first Leninist-Socialist state could produce excellence in an intellectual sports endeavour equal to anything in the West, Botvinnik was an iconic state asset. The quality of Botvinnik's chess now fully reflected a budding world champion's potential.

At Nottingham, Botvinnik collected a best game prize for his powerful demolition of Milan Vidmar's defences, in an IQP Queen's Gambit. Botvinnik had developed a deep understanding of the finer points in the handling of such IQP games, which he often reached from lines of the Caro Kann: Panov Attack, as well as the Queen's Gambit. Above all, he prized the IQP's considerable cramping effect, in the middlegame, in which, as against Vidmar, he repeatedly outplayed opponents before they could benefit from the IQP's longer-term structural downsides.

Now in his early fifties, Vidmar no longer played with the full vigour of his youth but remained, in Botvinnik's words, 'a remarkably strong practical player'. Due to his demanding business and academic responsibilities, Vidmar had never studied chess as much as his fully or even semi-professional peers. This proved an especially weighty handicap in the ever-increasingly knowledge-rich chess of the 1930s, not least against such well-versed and hard working young talents, as Botvinnik.

Vidmar does, indeed, handle the defence quite inexactly at certain key moments. As a result, Botvinnik skilfully banks various small advantages on his way to a wonderfully harmonious final assault. While certain of Botvinnik's early observations on the course of this game might be occasionally very slightly challengeable, there is no doubting his markedly superior, overall understanding, in what is as highly instructive a game, as it is satisfyingly very well-played.

M.Botvinnik – M.Vidmar

Nottingham 1936

Queen's Gambit

1.c4 e6 2.♘f3 d5 3.d4 ♘f6 4.♗g5 ♗e7 5.♘c3 0–0 6.e3 ♘bd7 7.♗d3 c5

Other alternatives include 7...dxc4 8.♗xc4 c5, and if 9.0–0 a6 10.a4 b6 11.♕e2 ♗b7, which was played successfully by Rubinstein but less so by Bent Larsen, in games played respectively, in Berlin 1926, and Biel 1976, against P. Johner and T. Petrosian.

8.0–0 cxd4 9.exd4 dxc4 10.♗xc4 ♘b6

'The inadequate professional knowledge of my venerable opponent begins to show', writes Botvinnik, who preferred the 'more precise [10...a6] to provoke the reply 11.a4, which would have given Black the b4 square'. All well and good but Black's 10th move reveals designs on control of d5 and perhaps isn't all that bad.

11.♗b3 ♗d7 12.♕d3 ♘bd5?!

On stronger ground here, Botvinnik insightfully suggests that 'Black should strive for simplification [and] for this it was more useful to play 12...♘fd5'. Black does, indeed, suffer in this game, by allowing White's forces to develop actively without real challenge. Simply occupying d5, on its own, is rarely ever a complete plan in such positions.

Mystifyingly, however, Botvinnik doesn't cite, Em.Lasker-W.Steinitz, Game 15, world championship 1894, which continued 12...♖c8 13.♘e5 ♗c6 14.♘xc6 ♖xc6 15.♖fd1 ♘fd5 16.♗xe7 ♘xe7 17.♗c2 ♘g6!? (17...g6 looks simpler) 18.♕f3 ♘d5 19.♗e4

Black then over-stretched, by playing 19...♘xc3!? 20.bxc3 ♖b6 21.c4, with a definite edge for White (who won). He might, however, instead have tried 19...♘gf4 20.♘xd5 ♘xd5, and if 21.♖ac1 ♕b6, with chances for both sides.

Both Botvinnik and Lasker played at Nottingham but they don't seem to have shared even a few passing words about the merits of Steinitz's method. A historic chance missed? The young Michael Adams's interpretation, in

F.Manca-M.Adams, Arnhem 1988, which saw 12...♗c6 13.♖ad1 ♖c8 14.♘e5 ♗d5 15.♘xd5 ♘fxd5 16.♗xe7 ♕xe7 17.f4 g6, with a definite edge for Black (who won), is also noteworthy.

13.♘e5 ♗c6 14.♖ad1 ♘b4 15.♕h3 ♗d5 16.♘xd5 ♘bxd5?

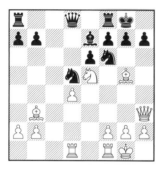

Vidmar incautiously gifts White a golden opportunity to advance his f-pawn and open up a dangerous attacking path in the f-file. Black should still play 16...♘fxd5, even if White then continues to press, by playing 17.♗xe7, and if 17...♕xe7 18.a3 ♘c6 19.♗xd5 exd5 20.♘xc6 bxc6 21.♖fe1, due to his better developed pieces and Black's targetable backward c-pawn.

17.f4 ♖c8
The blocking attempt 17...g6, loses an exchange, after 18.♗h6, and if 18... ♖e8 19.♗a4. White might even have more, by playing 19.f5!, and if 19...exf5 20.♖xf5 ♕c8 (or 20...gxf5 21.♕xf5 ♘h5 22.♗c2 ♘df6 23.♕g5+ ♔h8 24.♘xf7 mate) 21.♖df1 gxf5 22.♖xf5 ♘f4 23.♕g3+ ♘g6 24.♘xg6 hxg6 25.♕xg6+, and mates. White also emerges ma-

terial ahead, after 17...♘e4 18.♘xf7!, and if 18...♔xf7 (or 18...♖xf7 19.♕xe6) 19.♖de1! (Botvinnik).

18.f5 exf5?!
Vidmar now unwittingly sets up White's final, winning combination. He perhaps had to try 18...♕d6, and if 19.fxe6 ♕xe6 20.♕d3, hoping to hang on grimly. After 19...fxe6 20.♘c4, and if 20...♕a6 (or 20...♕d7 21.♖fe1) 21.♖de1!, White probably wins, such as after 21... ♖xc4 22.♖xe6 ♕b5 23.a4 ♕b4 24.♖xe7 ♕xe7 25.♗xc4, with an extra pawn.

19.♖xf5 ♕d6

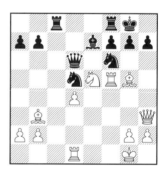

Due to the vulnerability of Black's rook (on c8), White now wins quickly. Even after 19...♖c7 20.♖df1!

threatening ♘xf7, however, Black surely loses anyway. Botvinnik gave

two plausible winning lines: (a) 20...
♘b6 21.♕h4 (threatening ♖xf6), and if
21...♘bd5 22.♘xf7 ♖xf7 23.♗xd5 ♘xd5
24.♖xf7 ♗xg5 25.♕xg5!, and wins; and
(b) 20...a6 21.♘xf7, and if 21...♖xf7
22.♗xd5 ♘xd5 23.♖xf7 ♗xg5 24.♕e6!.

20.♘xf7 ♖xf7

Or if 20...♔xf7 21.♗xd5+, and wins.

21.♗xf6 ♗xf6

Or 21...♘xf6 22.♖xf6 ♗xf6 23.♕xc8+.

22.♖xd5 ♕c6 23.♖d6 ♕e8 24.♖d7 1-0

After Nottingham 1936, Botvinnik
took time out to complete and defend
his post-graduate candidate's thesis.
Although successful in this, his decision caused him to miss out on playing in the 1937 USSR Championship,
which led to a political caution. The
state's chess functionaries made it
abundantly clear to Botvinnik that he
must put chess first, for the USSR.
Botvinnik was far from averse to 'putting chess first' but he never lost the
strong secondary desire to make a separate mark in engineering.

As a kind of public penance for his
absence from the 1937 championship,
Botvinnik was required to contest a
somewhat contrived 'play-off' match
against its winner, Grigory Levenfish.
Then in his late 40s, Levenfish, the
strongest of the older Russian masters
and a worthy opponent, shocked everyone by 'retaining' his title after tying

the match (+5-5=3). Botvinnik, whose
main focus was on battles with the international elite and, privately, didn't
really see the competitive point of the
match, complained of 'poor form'.

Following this curious interlude,
normal international chess service
resumed, at the AVRO tournament,
early in 1938. Conceived by the Dutch
Radio Company as a 'candidates' tournament, it brought the eight strongest
players in the world together, ostensibly to decide Alekhine's world title
challenger. A major fly in that oint-
ment, however, lay in Alekhine's point
blank refusal to accept any challenge
not of his own choice. During a post-
tournament meeting with Botvinnik
and Flohr (as a witness), he seems to
have agreed to an eventual Botvinnik
challenge, subject to the arrangement
of finance.

Full results at AVRO 1938 were:
Keres and Fine (8.5); Botvinnik (7.5);
Euwe, Alekhine and Reshevsky (7);
Capablanca (6); Flohr (4.5). Although
Botvinnik finished in third place, he
defeated both Alekhine and Capablanca quite brilliantly and was widely
regarded as Alekhine's most dangerous threat. The Estonian, Paul Keres
(1916-1975), and the American, Reuben
Fine (1914-1993), had near equivalent
popular support but lacked access to
the levels of finance likely to be available to a fully Soviet backed challenge
by Botvinnik.

The outbreak of World War II (1939-
45) shattered all dreams. Paul Keres, for

one, suffered regime-change thrice. Following the Nazi-Soviet Pact (August 1939), the three Baltic States were incorporated into the USSR. Overnight officially 'Soviet', Keres played both in the 1940 USSR championship and in the subsequent 1941 Absolute Match-Tournament. In June 1941, Germany then invaded its erstwhile USSR ally and 'freed' the three Baltic States. Keres lost his 'Soviet' designation, only to regain it on the USSR's reincorporation of the three Baltic states, at the end of the War.

Keres's initial 'Soviet' years also raised a problem that was quite as tricky to solve as it was unexpected. The USSR now had two budding world champions. As Botvinnik put it, 'the question to be settled [in 1940-41] was essentially this: which of the two Soviet players – Keres or Botvinnik – should represent the Soviet Union in the battle for the World Championship'. The matter became critical after the disappointing results by both clear favourites, in the 1940 USSR Championship, whose top six were: Lilienthal and Bondarevsky (13.5/20), Smyslov (13), Keres (12), Botvinnik and Boleslavsky (11.5).

This outcome led directly to the 1941 Absolute Match-Tournament, which required those top six, 1940 Championship finishers to meet in an all-play-all, four game match-tournament. In this extremely demanding contest, ostensibly only for the 1941 USSR Championship, although much more was really at stake, Botvinnik defeated all five of his opponents in their four game matches and decisively solved the Keres 'problem'. Final scores were: Botvinnik (13.5/20), Keres (11), Smyslov (10), Boleslavsky (9), Lilienthal (8.5) and Bondarevsky (8).

Botvinnik's by now routinely applied training methods gave him an edge over most opponents. At least as naturally gifted as any of his rivals, he also gained much by working closely with his excellent (long crucially salaried) grandmaster trainer and coach, Slava Ragozin. Players like Alekhine, Keres, Fine and the rest, still worked largely on their own, perhaps contracting occasional seconds but with no comparable access to the invaluable services of such dedicated 'Ragozins'.

Botvinnik and Ragozin together closely analysed opponents' games, deeply prepared openings and tested ideas in many privately-played training games. They concerned themselves with physical as well as mental fitness, drawing up practical programmes to work on both. Botvinnik, moreover, took particular care to analyse his own games deeply and draw critical conclusions about his own strengths and weaknesses, not just those of his peers. The team got just about everything right in Botvinnik's critical, Absolute Match-Tournament win against Keres.

P.Keres – M.Botvinnik

Absolute USSR Championship, Leningrad 1941

Nimzo-Indian Defence

1.d4 ♘f6 2.c4 e6 3.♘c3 ♗b4 4.♕c2 d5 5.cxd5 exd5 6.♗g5 h6 7.♗h4 c5

In his book *One Hundred Selected Games*, Botvinnik relates that he conjured up this (excellent) move, in A.Kotov-M. Botvinnik, Moscow 1940, which continued 7...c5 8.e3 cxd4 9.exd4 ♘c6 10.♗b5 0–0 11.♘ge2 ♕b6 12.♕d3 ♗xc3+ 13.bxc3 ♘e4 14.0–0 ♗f5, with pleasant play for Black and an eventual draw. A few rounds later, Vladas Mikenas provocatively essayed 8.0-0-0, and defeated him. Keres now unwisely copies Mikenas.

8.0-0-0 ♗xc3!

A rude awakening: Botvinnik energetically seeks to tear open the c-file and attack White's king fast. V.Mikenas-M. Botvinnik, Moscow 1940, had instead gone far less urgently, 8...0–0 9.dxc5 ♗xc3 10.♕xc3 g5 11.♗g3 ♘e4 12.♕a3 ♗e6 13.f3 ♘xg3 14.hxg3 ♕f6 15.e3 ♖c8 16.♔b1 ♘d7 17.♘e2 ♖xc5 18.♘d4 a6

19.♗b5 (19.♗d3, and if 19...♖ac8 20.g4 ♘e5 21.♖c1, is also promising) 19...♖ac8 20.♗xd7 ♗xd7 21.g4, with a White pull. After the text and Black's next two moves, White lacks sufficient time to be able both to tuck his king into safety on a1 and to take up (Mikenas-like) fight in the centre. According to Botvinnik, Black's improvement is so strong as to require White to rein in all ambition and scramble for equality (at best), by playing 9.♗xf6, and if 9... ♕xf6 10.♕xc3 ♘c6 11.♘f3.

9.♕xc3 g5 10.♗g3 cxd4

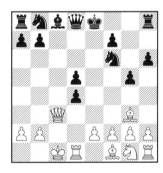

White obtains no respite. After opening the c-file, Black only needs to get in ...♗f5, to cut off the White king's only possible escape route to the corner, via b1.

11.♕xd4 ♘c6 12.♕a4

White has no better move. White's exposed king is about to take a battering by Black's rapidly developing queen-side forces, come what may. White is also clearly in trouble, after: either 12.♕e3+ ♗e6, and if 13.♘f3 0–0 14.♘d4 ♕b6 15.♔b1 ♖ac8; or 12.♕d3 ♗e6 13.h4 (or 13.♘f3 0–0) 13...♘e4.

12...♗f5 13.e3

White desperately hopes to neutralise Black's light square diagonal pressure, by exchanging bishops on d3. Sadly, however, he really needs to develop all of his kingside pieces but hasn't the time. Black must also prevail quickly, after either 13.♘f3 0–0, or 13.f3 ♕b6, and if 14.e4 dxe4 15.♔b1 0–0.

13...♖c8 14.♗d3

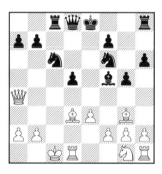

After 14.♘e2, Botvinnik gives 14...a6, and if 15.♘c3 b5 16.♕xa6 b4 17.♗b5 ♗d7, and wins; 14...0–0, and if 15.♘c3 ♘e4, may even be stronger.

14...♕d7 15.♔b1 ♗xd3+ 16.♖xd3 ♕f5 17.e4

By discarding this pawn, White at last manages to get his king to a1. By now, however, White's game has so deterio-rated that he can no longer realistically

expect to postpone complete catas-trophe on his stricken queenside for many more moves.

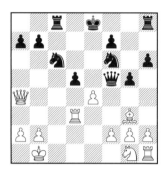

17...♘xe4 18.♔a1 0–0 19.♖d1 b5 20.♕xb5 ♘d4 21.♕d3 ♘c2+ 22.♔b1 ♘b4 0–1

The harrowing war years were a time of basic survival. As Germany launched its attack on the USSR, Botvinnik was granted permission to accom-pany his wife, Gayane, a dancer with the Kirov Opera and Ballet Theatre, in the company's evacuation from Leningrad to Perm (then Molotov). In Perm, Botvinnik was engaged by the Ural Energy Organisation, as an elec-trical engineer and research scientist. Botvinnik relished this new job oppor-tunity. The Party, of course, insisted that he must also work hard at chess.

Botvinnik succeeded in both fields. Following his success in the 1941 Abso-lute Match-Tournament, he took fur-ther 1ˢᵗ places, at Sverdlosk and in the Moscow championship, both in 1943, and in the 1944 and 1945 USSR cham-pionships. After the War, with his sky-high reputation still internationally intact, Botvinnik reached final agreement to meet Alekhine in a title match, scheduled for London. In extremely poor health, however, and subsisting in poverty, in Lisbon, Alekhine died suddenly, early in 1946, taking his title with him.

Alekhine's unfortunate death raised numerous questions. In his absence, who should hold the title (interim or otherwise)? If not Botvinnik, should it be Max Euwe, Alekhine's immediate world title predecessor? What about others, notably Fine, Reshevsky and Keres? Was the old, somewhat discredited system for deciding a challenger, in which the title-holder possessed considerable sway, in need of overhaul and, if so, by whom? Should FIDE step in, bearing in mind that the USSR wasn't even a member?

It took time to unravel all this. The earliest and most creditable step was taken by Euwe, who immediately ruled out any option that declared him world champion. The Netherlands instead organised a post-war 'super' tournament, at Groningen 1946, in which Botvinnik (14.5/19) again triumphed, ahead of Euwe (14) and Smyslov (12.5). Throughout 1946, the idea of a 'super' Match-Tournament, to decide the vacant world crown, to be followed by a fairer, regular (FIDE) world championship qualifying cycle, gathered widespread support.

At Moscow, later in 1946, Botvinnik scored, +1=1, against Reshevsky, in a historic USA-USSR match, won by the USSR (12.5-7.5). This was the two countries' first 'face to face' encounter. In 1945, the USSR had previously defeated the USA (15.5-4.5), but in a 'radio' match. Botvinnik judged Reshevsky to be 'a striking and original player [who] calculated variations excellently and had an extraordinary positional understanding'. Alas, he also suffered, 'from an incurable form of time-trouble'.

S.Reshevsky – M.Botvinnik

USSR-USA, Moscow 1946

French Defence

1.e4 e6 2.d4 d5 3.♘c3 ♗b4 4.e5 c5 5.a3 ♗a5 6.♕g4 ♘e7 7.dxc5 ♗xc3+ 8.bxc3 ♘d7 9.♕xg7

Botvinnik preferred 9.♘f3, calling this move 'routine'. White now wins both Black's g- and h-pawns but drops his e-pawn, after which Botvinnik possesses a promising mass of potentially mobile pawns in the centre. That said, matters remain quite double-edged. Both sides were already out of 1940s theory.

The modern main line, also known then, begins with 6.b4.

9...♖g8 10.♕xh7 ♘xe5 11.♗e2 ♕a5 12.♗d2 ♕xc5 13.♘f3 ♘xf3+ 14.♗xf3 e5 15.♗h5?

This move meets with a staggeringly powerful reply. Reshevsky may only have reckoned on 15...♗e6. Black needn't, however, concern himself with the defence of his f-pawn. He can gambit his f-pawn and develop a lively attack. White should instead have completed his kingside development, by playing 15.0-0 (not mentioned by Botvinnik), which remains challenging for both sides.

15...♗f5 16.♗xf7+

Although White can capture this pawn with check and force Black's king to seek sanctuary in the centre, Black stands well. Black's connected rooks rapidly embarrass White's over-extended forces, which can't get at Black's king on d7. Black also stands well, after 16.♕xf7+ ♔d7, threatening both ...♖af8 and ...♖xg2.

16...♔d7 17.♕h6 ♖xg2 18.♖f1 ♕b6?!

Here, however, Botvinnik blinks. He confessed to missing the rather more

effective 18...♕c4!, and if 19.♖b1 ♕e4+, with continuing pressure for Black.

19.♕xb6 axb6 20.0-0-0

This temporary gambit offers White his best hope of achieving an active defence. Although nominally a pawn to the good, White's broken pawns provide Black with tempting targets; Black's strong central pawns also control all the key squares along Black's fifth rank.

20...♖xa3 21.♔b2 ♖a4 22.♗e3

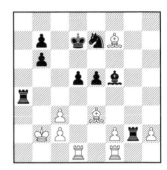

Reshevsky now correctly decides to jettison his loose h-pawn, to activate a rook on the g-file. Together with White's double attack against b6 and d5, this perceptibly strengthens White's game.

22...♗e6 23.♗xe6+ ♔xe6 24.♗xb6 ♖xh2 25.♖g1 ♖h6 26.♖g7 ♖g6 27.♖h7 ♘f5

Botvinnik offers an enterprising gambit in an attempt to maintain, at least, a minimal edge, but it shouldn't have worked. After 27...♖c4, however, Black may have nothing objectively better than accepting the repetition, 28.♗d8, and if 28...♘c6 29.♗b6.

28.♖xb7 ♘d6 29.♔b3 ♖a8 30.♖c7 ♖b8 31.♖c6 ♔d7 32.♖c7+ ♔e6 33.♖c6 ♖b7
Botvinnik hopes to make something of the rather awkward position of White's king's rook and bishop rather than re-peat the position, by playing 33...♔d7. With both sides now in serious time trouble, Reshevsky, at first, defends well.

34.c4 dxc4+?!

After this move, however, only White's game improves. Black should have played 34...d4, after which the forcing 35.♖h1 (not 35.c5 ♔d5!), and if 35...♔d7 36.♖c7+ ♖xc7 37.♖h7+ ♔c6 38.♗xc7, re-mains dead level (Botvinnik).

35.♔b4 ♔e7
Not 35...♔d7? 36.♔c5, and White wins. Now White's most accurate continua-tion is 36.♖d5, after which 36...♖f6 seems sufficient to hold. Reshevsky's reply, no doubt time-shortage in-duced, is still good. Crucially, however, having played it, he failed to press his

clock. Also in severe time-trouble and somewhat non-plussed, Botvinnik re-lates that he then 'did nothing'.

With only seconds to go, Reshevsky suddenly noticed his error, but then, 'had to make his remaining moves [to move 40] instantly.' Botvinnik mused plaintively that 'in a normal tourna-ment game I would have immediately told my opponent to press his clock ... but in a team competition?'

36.♔a5 ♔d7 37.♖xc4 ♖e6 38.♔a6 ♖b8 39.♖c7+ ♔e8 40.♔a7 ♖d8 41.♖h1?

These last moves were played in an inexact blur: Black missed 37...♖g1!, winning an exchange; White missed 38.♗c5, securing a pull. Much worse, Reshevsky, who 'had not been writ-ing down his moves and [was] afraid of overstepping the time limit [still played] instantly', and catastrophically blunders. After the correct 41.♔a6, White would retain his extra pawn, though Black can no doubt still hold, with due care.

41...♘b5+ 42.♔b7 ♘xc7 43.♗xc7 ♖d4!
This was Botvinnik's (only) clearly

winning sealed move: Black threatens ...♖c4, when, with his rooks dominant along Black's 5th rank and White's distant king cut off from any purposeful route back to help defend White's pawns, Black achieves sufficient space in which to manoeuvre and eventually suffocate White.

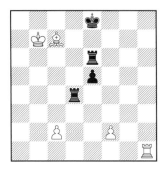

44.c3 ♖c4 45.♗a5 ♔d7 46.♖h8 ♖f6

'A clever manoeuvre found during our night time analysis. White's king, bishop and c-pawn are passive, and now his rook will occupy a bad position' (Botvinnik).

47.♖d8+ ♔e7 48.♖d2 ♖d6 49.♖a2 ♔d7 50.♖b2 ♖c5 51.♗b6

White's forces have completely run out of moves and his c-pawn drops, while his king still remains helplessly adrift on the queenside. If instead 51.♗b4 ♖c7+, Black mates in five.

51...♖xc3 52.♖b4 ♔e6 53.♖b2 ♖dd3 54.♖a2 ♖d7+ 55.♔a6 ♖b3 56.♗e3 ♖d6+ 57.♔a5 ♖d8 58.♔a6 ♖xe3 0–1

Immediately after the 1946 USSR-USA match, five of the six strongest players in the world (Botvinnik, Euwe, Keres, Reshevsky and Smyslov) sat down, in Moscow, to thrash out a gentleman's agreement for what was to become the 1948 Match-Tournament for the World Championship, at The Hague and Moscow. The sixth player, Reuben Fine, had had to rush back to the USA, but left a proxy with Reshevsky. In his compelling autobiography, *Achieving the Aim*, Botvinnik provides a detailed account of what went on at that meeting and over the next, far from untroubled year.

There was, first of all, absolutely no disagreement about the envisaged six participants. Nor did these players have any significant difficulty in agreeing either to the match-tournament format or to the two joint venues. FIDE had already also strongly declared itself in favour of such a solution and scheduled that it should take a final decision, at its 1947 Congress. After a few months, however, it became clear that there might be a huge problem brewing in the upper reaches of the Soviet Communist Party, from whom there had been nothing other than worrying silence.

When the Party at last spoke, it almost derailed all plans by quite unrealistically demanding that the event (whose format it accepted) must be held only in Moscow. Botvinnik reports that this somewhat clumsy diplomatic *faux pas* even drove him to consider whether to abandon chess and turn completely to engineering. Whatever internal wrangling then took place, however, the Party eventually accepted that the players' wholly sensible gentleman's agreement must be honoured in full. Moreover, burying a longstanding distaste for FIDE, the USSR even finally deigned to join it.

Psychologically reinvigorated, Botvinnik warmed up for the 1948 Match-Tournament, by taking 1st place in a strong international tournament, at Moscow 1947, his seventh successive top-class tournament 1st, since winning the 1941 Absolute Match-Tournament. The 1948 World Championship Match-Tournament proved to be his eighth successive such triumph. Winning all four of his mini-matches, Botvinnik deservedly achieved the 'Aim' referred to in the title of his autobiography by a significant margin: Botvinnik (14/20); Smyslov (11); Reshevsky and Keres (10.5); Euwe (4).

Note that the tournament was reduced from six to five players. Fine had just quit chess to embark on a career in psychoanalysis. Note, too, that Botvinnik fully grasped the scale of the huge debt that he owed to the USSR, which had long generously backed him, in the hope that he might eventually triumph at this level. In *Russian Silhouettes*, Genna Sosonko quotes Botvinnik as saying, 'In life I was fortunate. As a rule, my personal interests coincided with public interests'. We shouldn't, however, underestimate just how hard Botvinnik simply worked for his laurels.

By 1948, the quality of Botvinnik's all-round game and his recent record was pre-eminent. The range and depth of his openings understanding especially impressed. In *Achieving the Aim*, Botvinnik confided that he had 'succeeded in working out a method in which the *opening innovation* was hidden far into the middlegame ... had a positional justification ... no refutation in the ordinary sense ... so my opening systems lived for years bringing success in tournament after tournament'.

Botvinnik's discovery of the wealth of promising opportunities, arising after White's 15th move, in the second of his two wins, against Euwe, is a case in point. Given their respective tournament places, it may come as a surprise to learn that Botvinnik considered that his games against Euwe were of the utmost importance. Prior to the Match-Tournament, Botvinnik hadn't ever won against him. Defeating Euwe, therefore, came as a huge psychological release. Botvinnik even judged his second win, against Euwe, his 'best' in the tournament.

M.Botvinnik – M.Euwe

World championship Match-Tournament, Moscow 1948

Qeen's Gambit: Meran Defence

1.d4 d5 2.♘f3 ♘f6 3.c4 e6 4.♘c3 c6 5.e3 ♘bd7 6.♗d3 dxc4 7.♗xc4 b5 8.♗d3 a6 9.e4

White rushes forward his central pawns, while Black plays for rapid queenside development, space and counterplay, creating a richly dynamic imbalance. The ambitious Meran Defence owes its main (1920s) counter-attacking roots to Rubinstein's genius.

9...c5 10.e5

With White's 10th and 11th moves, Botvinnik opts for Blumenfeld's Variation, which, as in this game, often leads to the exchange of both of White's centre pawns. Reynolds' Variation (10.d5), brings about a quite different central tension, in which, at least, one of White's e- and d-pawns tends to remain in powerful action.

10...cxd4 11.♘xb5 axb5

Both sides remain true to their home preparations. Playing Black, Botvinnik later favoured Sozin's alternative (11...♘xe5), only to abandon the idea, following a painful loss against Reshevsky, in the USSR v USA match, at Moscow 1955, in the still critical line, 12.♘xe5 axb5 13.♕f3.

12.exf6 ♕b6

Vishy Anand much later breathed convincing new life into what was then a somewhat neglected sideline, 12...gxf6 13.0–0 ♕b6 14.♕e2 ♗b7, in his 2008 world title match, against V. Kramnik.

13.fxg7 ♗xg7 14.0–0 ♘c5

Euwe follows conventional theory, which prized the bishop pair. Unknown to Euwe, however, Botvinnik had long discovered a promising new White counter, based on maintaining a tight constraint on the central dark squares (especially e5). Botvinnik was convinced that the new plan's effectiveness could not be 'hindered' by any routine exchange of knight for bishop at d3; and that the idea also held water, after 14...0–0 15.♖e1, and if 15...♗b7 16.♗f4. Botvinnik (and team) had already worked through the new plan's main ideas after the secret training game, M.Botvinnik-V.Ragozin, Moscow 1939, which continued 14...♗a6 15.b4 0–0 16.♖e1 ♗b7 17.♗f4 (a recurring motif) 17...f5?! 18.a4 bxa4 19.♘c4 ♗d5?! 20.♗xd5 exd5 21.♖e7 ♖f7 22.♖xf7 ♔xf7 23.♕d3!, when, facing a defence riddled with weakness, White soon won. Botvinnik relished the opportunity to put the new plan into effect for the first time in a tournament game.

15.♗f4 ♗b7 16.♖e1 ♖d8

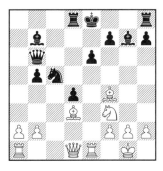

Faced with White's plan to play ♗e5 and exchange dark square bishops, Black has no straightforward task. With those bishops gone, the dark square insecurity around Black's king becomes palpable and his broken kingside offers vulnerabilities ripe for attack. Euwe resolves to reinforce his central and kingside command, by manoeuvring this rook to d5.

After 16...♘xd3 17.♕xd3, Botvinnik gave 17...♗xf3 (or if 17...♕c6 18.♖ac1 ♕d5 19.♗e5 f6 20.♗d6) 18.♕xf3 0–0 19.♕g4, with an edge. L.Szabo-J.Foltys, Budapest 1948, later went 19.♖ac1 ♖ac8 (or if 19...♖xa2?! 20.♕g3! ♔h8 21.♗c7 ♕b7 22.♗e5) 20.♕g3 ♔h8 21.h4 ♖fe8 22.h5 h6 23.♗e5 f6 24.♗f4 e5 25.♕g6, with a powerful attack (White won).

Paul Schmidt suggested 16...♗d5 17.♗e5 ♗xe5 18.♘xe5 ♖g8, which Botvinnik considered risky, possibly after either 19.g3, or Euwe's recommendation 19.♗f1. Black can't seek to castle into safety on the kingside, as after 16...0-0?, White plays 17.♗xh7+ ♔xh7 18.♘g5+, and if 18...♔g6 19.♕g5 f5 20.♕g3, with a winning attack.

17.♖c1 ♖d5 18.♗e5 ♗xe5

Black's game has fast become surprisingly lifeless. White's iron grip on the dark squares prevents any realistic hope that Black's e- and f-pawns might suddenly spring into life, while at the same time ensuring that White's pieces continue to enjoy the availability of e5, as an attacking pivot.

Black also suffers after 18...0–0 19.♗xg7 ♔xg7 20.♘e5

threatening ♖xc5, followed by ♕g4+

and ♕h5, and if 20...♘xd3 21.♕xd3 ♔h8 22.♕f3 f6 23.♕f4!, threatening ♘g6+, and soon leading either to mate or decisive material gain (Botvinnik); or, if in this line, 21...f6 22.♖c7+! ♕xc7 23.♕g3+, followed by a knight check, winning Black's queen.

19.♖xe5 ♖xe5 20.♘xe5 ♘xd3 21.♕xd3 f6

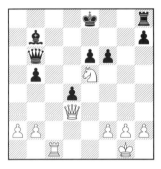

Poor Euwe had no doubt spotted his opponent's fine sacrificial reply. He was, however, completely defenceless. White's queen cannot be diverted from its crushing route to g7, after which Black's kingside collapses. White also wins quickly after 21...b4 22.♕g3, and

if 22...♕d6 23.♕g7 ♖f8 24.♘g4 ♔e7 (or if 24...♕f4 25.♖c4) 25.♕f6+ ♔e8 26.♕g5 f5 27.♘f6+ ♔f7 28.♘xh7.

22.♕g3 fxe5 23.♕g7 ♖f8 24.♖c7 ♕xc7
White's total seventh rank domination and variously threatened mates force Black either to give up his queen or allow the satisfyingly aesthetic conclusion, 24...♕d6 25.♖xb7, and if 25...d3 26.♖a7 ♕d8 27.♕xh7, threatening ♕g6+.

25.♕xc7 ♗d5 26.♕xe5 d3 27.♕e3
White mops up not just Black's pawn on e5 but also his more critical d-pawn; or, if Black wishes to hold on to the latter, a whole bishop.

27...♗c4 28.b3 ♖f7 29.f3 ♖d7 30.♕d2 e5 31.bxc4 bxc4 32.♔f2 ♔f7
Or if 32...c3 33.♕xc3 d2 34.♕c8+ ♔e7 35.♕xd7+ ♔xd7 36.♔e2, and wins.

33.♔e3 ♔e6 34.♕b4 ♖c7 35.♔d2 ♖c6 36.a4 1–0

Grandmaster of Logic and Harmony
Vassily Smyslov

I n *Half a Century of Chess*, Botvinnik wrote that winning the world title met 'the goal set by Krylenko in the 1920s [and] opened a new era of supremacy in the world of the Soviet chess school, which was to continue for almost a quarter of century'. Following a show trial and extorted 'confessions' of a kind not unknown to him, as a prominent, ex-dispenser of Stalinist justice, Nikolai Krylenko may have been 'eliminated', in July 1938; his chess dream child, however, continued to thrive far beyond his own brutal 'purge' from the Party.

17. *Vassily Smyslov, Amsterdam interzonal 1964*

Following a 1925 Party decree that re-quired 'physical education [to become] an integral part of general political and cultur-al upbringing and education', Krylenko rapidly embarked upon a widespread ex-tension in the game's reach and state infrastructure. By the late 1930s, organised chess in the USSR far surpassed that of any other country, whether measured by numbers of players, elite playing strength or opportunities to play in USSR-wide palaces and houses of culture. Chess teaching was proficient and widespread.

Vassily Smyslov (1921-2010), the first budding world champion to develop from an early age within this system, made his first major (1938) breakthroughs by becoming USSR Junior champion and tying for the Moscow Championship. Outstanding results in the 1940 USSR Championship and in the following year's Absolute Match-Tournament duly confirmed his world-class. Smyslov fortu-nately survived the war years, with his chess talent still buoyant. By 1948, he was widely regarded as world number two, behind only Botvinnik.

Botvinnik likened Smyslov's naturally fluent playing style to Capablanca's. Both had what he called a formidably reliable 'move searching algorithm' that was ultimately intuitive in character and exceptionally valuable in 'original' positions as well as in endgames. Between 1953 and 1958, Botvinnik considered Smyslov to be practically 'unbeatable'. They tied their first world title match (12-12), in 1954.

Smyslov decisively won their second (12.5-9.5), only to lose in a stipulated 'return' match (12.5-10.5).

In his *125 Selected Games*, Smyslov relates that he devoted ten thoroughly exhausting years (1948-58) to his battle for the world title. Pipped by David Bronstein, at the first Candidates' tournament (Budapest 1950), he missed out in his first bid to challenge Botvinnik. At Moscow 1951, Botvinnik and Bronstein tied (12-12), with the champion retaining the title. After much further effort and a splendid resurgence in form, Smyslov then decisively won both of the next two Candidates' tournaments to set up 1954 and 1957 challenges.

In his quest for the title, Smyslov judged that his central challenge lay in seeking to match Botvinnik's formidable 'theoretical preparation'. By dint of extraordinarily hard work, Smyslov considered that he largely achieved this. In accordance with his more dispassionate temperament, however, he maintained that he prepared less 'single-mindedly for [the] specific opponent', preferring to dwell less on 'psychology' than to aim 'for a broad and objective evaluation of the position'.

Fundamentally artistic in temperament, Smyslov inclined to a lifelong aesthetic ideal that conceived of chess, as he wrote in *125 Selected Games*, as 'a search for truth, and victory a demonstration of its rightness'. Reflecting on his tied (1954) title match, however, Smyslov felt driven to conclude that he must also draw more ruthlessly from Botvinnik's steelier, game-winning focus. To defeat Botvinnik, he would require not just great artistry but also 'exceptional will-to-win ... utmost composure and energy'.

In 1957, Smyslov successfully moved his game up that crucial gear, to play at his most powerful, as well as harmonious best, to win the world title. Smyslov refused to be moved, for example, by an exceptionally audacious opening challenge, in Game 12, eventually spotting a hidden weak point in Botvinnik's plans. Smyslov thereafter displayed masterly endgame technique and an artistry that characterised not just his victory in this game but also in the match overall.

V.Smyslov – M.Botvinnik

Game 12, World Championship, Moscow 1957

Modern Defence

1.e4 c5 2.♘f3 g6 3.c4 ♗g7 4.d4 d6 5.♘c3 ♘c6 6.♗e3 ♗g4

Botvinnik had defended against lines of The Sicilian Defence: Richter Rauzer Attack, in Games 2, 4 and 8. This quite novel switch came as a surprise. Black might remain in a main line of an Accelerated Dragon Sicilian, by playing 6...cxd4 7.♘xd4 ♞f6. Botvinnik, however, was determined to pursue a speculative gambit that proves more doubtful than apparently expected.

7.dxc5 dxc5 8.♕xd8+ ♖xd8 9.♗xc5

Out of theory since move 6, Smyslov realised that Botvinnik must have prepared this line in depth. He nevertheless grabs Black's pawn, trusting in the logical basis of his own game. Clear that Black's idea involved an early battle for control of d4, he argued: 'What is important is not just that White wins a pawn, but that he eliminates Black's control' of that pivotal point.

9...♗xc3+ 10.bxc3 ♞f6

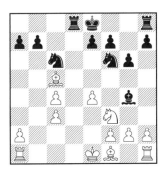

White has an extra pawn and two bishops but his queenside pawns are seriously split and Black's lively pieces look threatening. White can't now play, either 11.♘d2 ♖xd2 12.♔xd2 ♞xe4+, or 11.♗d4 ♞xd4, and if 12.♘xd4 ♞xe4 13.f3 ♞xc3, when Black wins. But he does have a third, and much stronger reply, which Botvinnik may simply have misjudged in his preparation.

11.♘d4 ♞xe4 12.♘xc6 bxc6 13.♗xa7 ♗f5 14.f3 ♞d6

Had Botvinnik realised that he might have to defend this position, he wouldn't have chosen this line. As a result of his powerful 11th move, White has managed to exchange knights on c6 and win Black's a-pawn. Facing two strong bishops and a fast advancing a-pawn, Black is clearly in trouble. White is also much better after 14...♞xc3 15.a4, and if 15...♖d7 16.♗b6 0–0 17.a5.

15.a4 ♖a8 16.♗b6 0–0 17.c5 ♞c8 18.g4 ♗e6 19.a5 ♞xb6

Completely pinned down on the queenside, Botvinnik nonetheless battles as ingeniously as he possibly can. White only fleetingly obtains two passed a- and b-pawns, but even the inevitable return of one of these pawns scarcely diminishes White's already near-winning momentum.

20.cxb6 ♖fb8 21.♗d3?!

This proves to be good enough, due to the critically ongoing strength of White's far-advanced b-pawn and much the more active king.

Here, however, Smyslov notes that he missed the more accurate and immediately decisive conclusion: 21.♔f2 ♖xb6 22.axb6 ♖xa1 23.b7 ♖b1 24.♗a6, and if 24...♖b2+ 25.♔e3 ♔f8 26.♖d1 ♔e8 27.♖d4 c5 28.♖b4, and wins.

21...♖xb6 22.axb6 ♖xa1+ 23.♔d2 ♖a2+
Or if 23...♖xh1 24.b7 ♖xh2+ 25.♗e2, and White crushingly queens.

24.♔e3 ♗c8 25.♖d1 ♖b2 26.♗c4 ♔g7 27.♖d8 ♗e6
Or 27...♗b7 28.♖d7 ♖xb6 29.♖xe7, followed by ♖xf7+, and wins.

28.♗xe6 fxe6 29.♖b8 e5
White can now play c4–c5, thereby securing White's pawn on b6 and releasing White's rook to reach d8. From there, it cuts off Black's king from the queenside and the win is certain. White 'must', however, also win 'thanks to his passed pawn', after the alternative 29...♔f6 30.♔d4 (30.b7, and if 30...♔e5 31.h4, may be even better) 30...♖b5 31.f4 (Smyslov).

30.c4 ♔f7 31.c5 ♔e6 32.♖d8

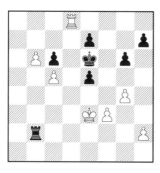

Black's rook and king are defensively stymied:
(a) by the threat of b7-b8=♕ (if Black's rook moves from the b-file); and
(b) by the loss of Black's c-pawn (if Black's king moves to the f-file). As a result, Smyslov's king and rook can now combine to force a marvellous win: firstly, by ejecting Black's rook from the b-file; and secondly, by then manoeuvring White's rook to the a-file (or d-file) and eventually behind White's b-pawn.
At that point, White will threaten b7-b8=♕. Black's rook will be forced into a purely passive blocking role (on b8). White's king will be free to embark on a decisive, final central infiltration that forces a transition into a variety of winning king and pawn endgames.

32...g5 33.h3 ♖b1 34.♔d2 ♖b5 35.♔d3 ♖b1 36.♔c4 ♖c1+
First step completed: Black must vacate the b-file due to the threat of ♖d3–b3.

37.♔b4 ♖b1+ 38.♔a4 ♖a1+ 39.♔b4 ♖b1+ 40.♔a3 ♖a1+ 41.♔b2 ♖a5 42.♖d3 ♖a8 43.♔b3 ♖a5 1–0
Black doesn't wait for the completion of Step two. White has various ways to win: for example, by playing 44.♔b4 threatening ♖a3, and if 44...♖a8 (or 44...♖b5+ 45.♔a4) 45.♖b3 ♖b8 (or 45...♔d7/ d5 46.b7 ♖b8 47.♔a5) 46.♔c4 ♖b7 47.♖d3 ♖b8 48.♖a3 ♖d8 49.b7 ♖b8 50.♖b3 ♔d7 (or 50...h6 51.♖b4) 51.♔d3 ♔c7 52.♔e4 ♖xb7 53.♖xb7+ ♔xb7 54.♔f5, winning all king and pawn endgames.

Rapid-Fire Brilliance

Mikhail Tal

Mikhail Tal (1936-1992) was one of the game's most dazzlingly successful early developers. In 1957, he became the youngest USSR champion. In 1960, he defeated Botvinnik (+6-2=13) to become the youngest ever world champion. For much of his life, however, Tal sadly suffered chronic ill-health, originating in early kidney disease. Partly as a result, in 1961, he rather less happily became the youngest ever ex-world champion, losing to Botvinnik (+10-5=6) in their auto-matically triggered return match.

Though Tal thereafter continued to play at an exceptionally high level, well into the 1980s, his persistent health problems, aggravated by an increasingly complicating set of dependencies on prescribed medicines, alcohol and tobacco, helped prevent him from ever again becoming a world title challenger. A not in-frequent visitor to hospital wards and operating theatres, Tal bore such obstacles stoically, one of the most outgoing and friendliest of top players, often seen with a very large smile on his face.

A largely untamed spirit, Tal loved the attack, combination and sacrifice. Blessed from a very young age with lightning fast analytical and decision-taking skills, he generally headed directly for highly complex positions that played to his rapid-fire calculating strengths. Some discerned an undue recklessness in his play, even occasional outright unsoundness, but you couldn't argue with the young Tal's electrifying ge-nius and outstanding re-sults. Tal regularly found brilliant solutions to prob-lems, where others failed simply to cope.

Tal put great store on what he called, in a 1960

18. Bobby Fischer v Mikhail Tal: Leipzig Olympiad 1960

interview with Peter Clarke, the 'subjective or perhaps psychological element in chess [that] exists over and above the objective aspect'. He had a particular admiration for the way his idols, Lasker and Alekhine, aspired to a kind of total chess, fired up not just by science, but also subjective factors, such as psychology and fight. All three of these great players took chess theory seriously, of course, but they also simply summoned up their fullest powers, when faced by an actual opponent.

In the young Tal's case, this interest in the 'subjective' was occasionally dismissed as somehow lightweight. The plain fact, however, is that Tal always worked much harder on the game than most such criticisms gave him credit for. Frankly, without hard work, Tal would never have become world champion. Tal's main goal was generally always only to achieve that happy balance (familiar to us all) between in-depth study and 'trying to preserve a clear head' for the post opening phase in games.

The 'clear head' words are Tal's, from the concluding press conference to his triumphant 1960 world title match. Tal explained that he and his team had, of course, also conventionally 'tried to discover the vulnerable points' in his opponent's game. In this, too, they had no little success, already setting the tone for the way that the 1960 match eventually played out, with an explosive Tal win, which featured a powerful new 12th move, in the very first match game.

Genna Sosonko takes up the story in *Russian Silhouettes*. Tal's life-long second and friend, Alexander Koblenz, it seems, 'accidentally hit upon the variation … communicated to Tal only half an hour before' Game 1 began. 'Crawling on all fours among the theoretical bulletins laid out on the carpet of his hotel room [Koblenz] found it by chance, and Tal employed it brilliantly'. Perhaps not quite the more calmly reflective discovery in the classically austere Botvinnik tradition, but it certainly worked!

M.Tal – M.Botvinnik

Game 1, World Championship, Moscow 1960

French Defence

1.e4 e6 2.d4 d5 3.♘c3 ♗b4 4.e5 c5 5.a3 ♗xc3+ 6.bxc3 ♕c7 7.♕g4 f5 8.♕g3 ♘e7
Quite a provocation against one of the world's sharpest tacticians: Black allows White's queen to lay waste to his kingside in return for the opportunity to destroy White's centre. As ever, well-prepared, however, Botvinnik had a surprise 11th move in mind.

9.♕xg7 ♖g8 10.♕xh7 cxd4 11.♔d1

This was hottest theory. White's king often finds sanctuary, on d1, in such lines. In this position, the move had first been played, in S.Gligoric-T. Petrosian, Candidates' 1959, which continued 11...♘bc6 12.♘f3 ♘xe5 13.♗g5 ♘5g6 14.♗xe7 ♘xe7 15.cxd4 ♗d7 16.♗d3, with an edge for White (Black held). Botvinnik diverges.

11...♗d7 12.♕h5+

Botvinnik's novelty may have been aimed principally at dissuading 12.♘f3, after which Black can play 12...♕xc3, and if 13.♖b1 ♗a4

with queenside counterplay.
Black's game also seems good, after 12.♘e2 ♗a4, and if 13.♕h5+ ♔d7!. Tal, however, inserts a clever queen check that asks a searching question. Should

Black block or play 12...♔d8, giving up castling rights?
Botvinnik blocks, but the resulting complications seem to favour White. In Game 12 of the players' 1961 return match, Botvinnik fared much better, by playing 12...♔d8, with his pieces rather better co-ordinated than in 1960. Play then continued 13.♘f3 (13. ♘e2, 13.♖b1 and 13.cxd4, also merit attention) 13...♕xc3 14.♖a2 ♘bc6, with at least equality (Tal won).

12...♘g6 13.♘e2 d3

A critical moment: Black must make something happen quickly or White will consolidate. Botvinnik opts for a highly speculative gambit to open the a4–d1 diagonal. This idea, however, only serves to strengthen White's centre, without achieving its main objective, to get at White's king. It is, however, far from clear, whether Black has any significantly better course.
Botvinnik may have rejected 13...dxc3 14.♘f4 ♔f7, because of the dangerous attacking reply 15.♗d3, and if 15...♕xe5 16.g4 ♘c6 17.gxf5 exf5 18.♖b1 b6 19.♖b5 ♘ce7 20.♖e1, with mounting

pressure on Black. White also stands well, after 13...♗a4 14.♘f4, and if 14...♕xc3 15.♖a2, forcing the awkward 15...♔f7. After 13...♘c6 14.cxd4 0-0-0, Black's king is safe, but he remains two pawns down without counterplay.

14.cxd3 ♗a4+ 15.♔e1 ♕xe5

After this recapture, Black remains a pawn down with a vulnerable king and dreadfully weakened central dark squares. Botvinnik's prospects, however, would scarcely have been better, after 15...♗b5 16.♔d2, and if 16...♕xe5 17.f4 ♕f6 18.♖b1, while 16.♗d2, and if 16...♗xd3 17.♘d4 ♕xe5+ 18.♔d1, also comes strongly into consideration.

16.♗g5 ♘c6 17.d4 ♕c7 18.h4 e5 19.♖h3

In his attacking element, Tal shifts his king's rook rapidly to e3, adding fuel to his growing fire in the e-file, which Botvinnik now rather forlornly allows White to open. Had Black kept the e-

file closed, by playing 19...e4, however, he would have remained in a near certainly fatal, long-run bind, such as after 20.♘f4, and if 20...♕f7 21.♖b1 b6 22.♘xg6 ♖xg6 23.♗a6 ♔d7 24.♕e2.

19...♕f7 20.dxe5 ♘cxe5 21.♖e3 ♔d7 22.♖b1 b6 23.♘f4 ♖ae8 24.♖b4

Tal doesn't let up. White's second lateral rook development (via b4 to d4) creates a complete central clamp and directly threatens Black's increasingly vulnerable d-pawn.

24...♗c6 25.♕d1 ♘xf4 26.♖xf4 ♘g6 27.♖d4 ♖xe3+

White now overpowers d5, and wins an exchange. Black might have tried 27...♔c7, but after 28.♗a6, and if 28...f4 29.♖xe8 ♖xe8+ 30.♔f1, his chances of defence seem unlikely.

28.fxe3 ♔c7 29.c4 dxc4 30.♗xc4 ♕g7 31.♗xg8 ♕xg8 32.h5 1-0

Pom Pom Pom Pounce

Tigran Petrosian

The mysterious chess playing style of Tigran Petrosian (1929-1984), is often thought hard to pin down. His first English language chess biographer, Peter Clarke, opted for 'Master of Defence'. Ray Keene and Julian Simpole, in *Petrosian vs the Elite*, settled on 'Master of Manoeuvre'. Mikhail Botvinnik was most taken by Petrosian's profoundly prophylactic *cum* combinative genius. Boris Spassky likened Petrosian to 'a very nice cat', which, after sidling gently along, 'pom pom pom', suddenly pounces.

Spassky's playful graphic is drawn from a fascinating 1970 interview, conducted by Ray Keene and David Levy,

19. Tigran Petrosian: 1962

and reproduced in their book, *Siegen Olympiad*. Spassky, who wrested the world title from Petrosian, in 1969, having previously lost to him, in 1966, considered his great rival's elusive approach to chess to be quite different from the likes of Botvinnik, Bobby Fischer and himself, who were all more conventionally 'primitive ... have an idea, make a plan and [go] boom boom boom', all-out for victory, at once.

In an earlier interview, conducted shortly after Petrosian defeated him to win the world title, at Moscow 1963, Botvinnik remarked (not dissimilarly) that Petrosian had mastered a style that was 'concerned most of all about safety and of depriving his opponent of ways to attack'. In *Achieving the Aim*, Botvinnik drew even closer attention to the extraordinary ease with which Petrosian seemed able to create 'positions where events develop as though in slow motion [against which] attacking forces advance only slowly [and] get stuck in [a] swamp'.

In an interview in *Sovetsky Sport*, conducted shortly after his first, 1966 match, against Spassky, Petrosian tacitly accepted all of the above. In his own words, he considered that, by nature and in chess, he was 'naturally cautious [and] altogether dislike[d] situations which involve risk'. Aware, however, that he also possessed exceptional 'combinational' gifts, he conceded (gently) that it was perhaps this very 'tactical mastery which makes me refrain from many combinations, since I find refutations for my opponent'.

Petrosian grew up in deprived, though secure family circumstances. The war years were harsh, but his extraordinarily rapid rise as a young chess player both helped him survive and embark on an entirely new and more commodious life. Although he only learned how to play chess, aged 12, his playing ability became so rapidly apparent that he was soon talent-spotted and eventually encouraged to move to Moscow, in 1950, already considered one of the USSR's brightest prospects.

Petrosian's journey through the 1950s to a world championship challenge, however, was far from easy. Competition for top spot was unsurprisingly fierce. David Bronstein's star first shone brightly, followed by that of mid-1950s colossus, Smyslov. Mikhail Tal's blazing chess comet then shot briefly through the sky. Soviet also-rans, in those years, included such giants, as Paul Keres, Boris Spassky, Viktor Korchnoi, Effim Geller and many other, scarcely less minor talents.

By dint of sheer perseverance, however, Petrosian gradually homed in on his goal. The fabulously strong USSR Championships, then doubled as a Zonal qualifier, every third year and it speaks for Petrosian's promise that he finished sufficiently well in these punishing events, to qualify for all four Interzonals and subsequent (1953, 1956, 1959 and 1962) Candidates' tournaments. Petrosian placed consecutively 5th, equal 3rd, outright 3rd and then 1st, in these latter events, en route winning two USSR championships, in 1959 and 1961.

The worst criticism levelled at Petrosian, during those years, was that excessive caution often led him to coast (especially in qualifiers) and to take far too many short draws. Though there was some truth in that accusation, the short draw was an unusually widespread international blight, at that time. Petrosian (17.5/27) only just managed to win, at Curaçao 1962, ahead of Geller and Keres, 17; Fischer 14, Korchnoi 13.5; Benko 12; Filip 7; Tal 7/21. One year later, Petrosian comfortably defeated Botvinnik (+5-2=15).

From the start of their 1963 match, a well-prepared and thoroughly determined Petrosian was more than up for Botvinnik. Despite a nervous loss in Game 1, Petrosian soon drew level, by winning Game 5, probably his best in the contest. Thereafter he soon settled into a winning stride that proved too much for the defending champion. While the age gap mattered, Petrosian also simply outplayed Botvinnik, who found it hard to land telling blows against an opponent who played almost continually without weakness.

T.Petrosian – M.Botvinnik

Game 5, World Championship, Moscow 1963

Grünfeld Defence

1.c4 g6 2.d4 ♘f6 3.♘c3 d5 4.♘f3 ♗g7 5.e3 0–0 6.♗e2 dxc4

Botvinnik diverges from what Petrosian called the 'recommended' route to equality (6...e6), as in A.Sokolsky-M.Botvinnik, Leningrad 1938, which had gone 7.0-0 b6 8.cxd5 exd5 9.b3, achieving little (Black won). Petrosian had, in fact, prepared the more ambitious, 9.b4, recently played in V.Simagin-D.Osmanagic, Sarajevo 1963, which continued 9...c6 10.a4 ♖e8 11.♗a3, with a slight spatial edge on the queenside.

7.♗xc4 c5 8.d5 e6

Perhaps surprised by Petrosian's choice of opening, Botvinnik heads for exchanges and a simplified endgame, in which, however, White has the better pawn structure. If Black wishes to maintain a more complex middlegame tension, he can choose from a wide range of acceptable alternatives, including 8...♘bd7, 8...♘e8, followed by ...♘d6, and 8...♗g4.

9.dxe6 ♕xd1+ 10.♔xd1 ♗xe6 11.♗xe6 fxe6 12.♔e2

Petrosian had considered this position beforehand, judging that White had a slight pull and might press. White can expect to establish one of his knights powerfully on e4 and, in the very long-term, hope to make ground by advancing his healthily connected 4-3 kingside pawn majority. As a first step, Petrosian plans to exchange one pair of rooks and edge forward his a- and b-pawns in a bid to contain Black's 3-2 majority of pawns on the queenside.

12...♘c6 13.♖d1 ♖ad8 14.♖xd8 ♖xd8 15.♘g5 ♖e8 16.♘ge4 ♘xe4 17.♘xe4 b6 18.♖b1

White's pressure intensifies. He aims to control the c4 and b5 light squares, by establishing pawns on a4 and b3,

supported by ♗d2 and ♖c1. White will
then generally welcome any exchange
of his bishop for Black's knight, as his
remaining, well-centralised knight (on
e4) will continue to dominate. Black
must also worry about possible b4
breaks and longer-term prospects of
a breakthrough by White's rook in the
c-file.

18...♘b4 19.♗d2 ♘d5

Not 19...♘xa2, allowing 20.♖a1 ♘b4
21.♗xb4 cxb4 22.♖xa7 ♗xb2 23.♖b7,
when Black's pawn on b4 is a clear liability rather than strength.

20.a4 ♖c8 21.b3 ♗f8 22.♖c1 ♗e7 23.b4!

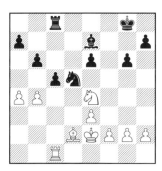

With this very fine move, albeit near
impossible to analyse precisely,
Petrosian takes advantage of White's
temporary pin in the c-file, to force
either the 'actual' isolation of Black's
c-pawn (after an exchange on c5) or its
'artificial' isolation, as in the game (after 23...c4 24.b5). In both cases, Black's
c-pawn, while passed, is likely to
come under serious long-term attack,
should it advance (if it doesn't, White
will control the c4 square).

23...c4 24.b5 ♔f7?

Given the tension and perhaps also
looming time pressure, Botvinnik
slips. Black must now almost certainly
lose his c-pawn to Petrosian's intended: ♗c3, followed eventually by ♘d2,
g3, and e4, dislodging Black's defending knight, on d5. Petrosian had instead expected the much better, 24...
♗a3 25.♖c2 c3 26.♗xc3 ♗b4 27.♔d2
♖c4 28.♗xb4 ♖xe4 29.♗d6 ♖xa4, which
restricts any White pull to a minimum
(Petrosian intended to continue 30.f3).

**25.♗c3 ♗a3 26.♖c2 ♘xc3+ 27.♖xc3 ♗b4
28.♖c2 ♔e7**

White also wins Black's c-pawn after
28...e5 29.♘d2, and if 29...c3 30.♘e4
♔e6 31.♔d3 ♖d8+ 32.♔c4 ♗a5 33.♘xc3
♗xc3 34.♔xc3 ♖d1.

29.♘d2 c3

Or if 29...♗xd2 30.♔xd2 ♖d8+ 31.♔c3.

30.♘e4 ♗a5 31.♔d3 ♖d8+ 32.♔c4 ♖d1

Or 32...♖d2 33.♔b3.

33.♘xc3 ♖h1?

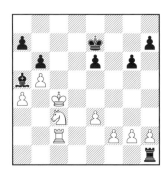

'Now Black's position becomes completely lost' (Petrosian). Under intense pressure, Botvinnik opts to regain his pawn but fatally abandons the centre. Black had to exchange minor pieces and hope that his rook's activity might still offer drawing chances, a pawn down in a rook and pawn endgame.

34.♘e4 ♖xh2 35.♔d4 ♔d7

White's king, knight and rook rapidly threaten to overwhelm the Black king in the centre. Black's bishop and rook are complete bystanders. White wins even more quickly after 35... ♖xg2 36.♖c7+ ♔d8 37.♖xh7, followed by ♔e5.

36.g3 ♗b4 37.♔e5 ♖h5+ 38.♔f6 ♗e7+ 39.♔g7

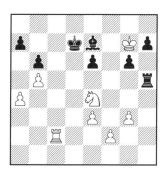

Black has managed to scramble his rook and bishop into positions that create a semblance of defence but, in fact, they (and Black's unfortunate king) remain effectively movebound. Tied to the defence of Black's g- and h-pawns by White's powerfully placed king, Black's rook cannot hope to budge White's well-placed and increasingly threatening knight, such

as, for example, after 39...♖e5 40.♖c4, and if 40...♖h5 41.♖d4+ ♔e8 42.g4, followed by g5.

39...e5 40.♖c6 ♖h1 41.♔f7

This strong move was sealed. White threatens ♖e6, dislodging Black's bishop and leading quickly to decisive material gain.

41...♖a1 42.♖e6 ♗d8

Black's king, rook and bishop fail to coordinate. Black loses immediately after either 42...♗b4 43.♖xe5, and if 43...♖xa4 44.♘f6+ ♔d6 45.♖d5+ ♔c7 46.♖d4, or 42...♗c5 43.♖xe5, and if 43...♖xa4 44.♘xc5+.

43.♖d6+ ♔c8 44.♔e8 ♗c7 45.♖c6 ♖d1

Black's rook must rush back to the d-file to prevent White's forces from rounding up Black's king and bishop, but it can't also secure his kingside pawns. If, however, 45...♖xa4 46.♘g5 ♔b7 47.♘e6 ♗b8 48.♘d8+ ♔a8 49.♖c8, and wins. Or if 45...♔b7 46.♘g5, threatening both ♘e6 and ♘xh7.

46.♘g5 ♖d8+ 47.♔f7 ♖d7+ 48.♔g8 1–0

When pressed in his 1966 *Sovetsky Sport* interview to reveal what he most valued in chess, Petrosian unhesitatingly replied: 'Logic! ... I like only those games where I have played in accordance with the demands of the position ... logical, "correct" play'. But wherein lay this 'logic'? One further piece of the mysterious Petrosian puzzle must now be put in its place. Ever since, as a youngster, he actually kept a much thumbed copy of *Chess Praxis* under his pillow, Petrosian constantly drew on the magnificent thought world of Nimzowitsch.

Petrosian's veneration of Nimzowitsch was no passing whim. In 1979, he provided an extended, highly personal preface to a new, Russian edition of *Chess Praxis*, whose warmth is sincere and transparent. 'Each time I look through *Chess Praxis*', he maintained, 'I discover as though anew those sayings of Nimzowitsch, which ... lay at the basis of my chess philosophy [including] thoughts ... as though addressed to chess "artists" [and] a more generous scattering of "directions" for chess "scientists"'.

After giving many highly practical examples of such 'thoughts' and 'directions', Petrosian concludes by firmly advising any aspiring player 'to compile a little notebook of Nimzowitsch's sayings ... and during the analysis of games by other strong players to glance at it frequently. Then many of the moves, plans and ideas of grandmasters will become understandable [which] in turn will broaden your understanding ... and ... make you a stronger player'.

Petrosian and, indeed, Nimzowitsch's 'logical' thought world is alive with a richly modern and diverse mix of often conflicting, even contradictory ways of thinking, whose outcomes don't always resolve. The honest answer to the game's toughest questions, such as, say whether the IQP is a liability or asset, is, as a close reading of Petrosian or Nimzowitsch indicates, essentially twofold: first, build up your own take on the best available, top-level judgements (always, of course, in continuing flux); then judge for yourself.

At his peak, Petrosian, who gained the nickname 'Iron' precisely because of this profoundly independent intellectual resilience, raised the process of settling on such personalised judgements to a level of dependability that few others could match. Neither Botvinnik (in 1963) nor Spassky (in 1966) could either conclusively breach his defences or repel his most furious attacks. Few could act, for example, on the demands of a position as well as Petrosian, in Game 7, of his 1966 title defence, in which Spassky essayed an old Petrosian favourite, with completely disastrous results.

Spassky's main vulnerability in the 1966 match lay in the opening. With White, other than in Game 7, Spassky made relatively little headway, against Petrosian's Caro Kann, French and Sicilian Defences. Playing Black, Spassky lost two crushing games in main lines of the King's Indian and Nimzo-Indian Defences. Petrosian's tight winning margin (+4-3=17) belied the fact that, by Game 22, he had already gained the minimum 12 points necessary to retain his title.

B.Spassky – T.Petrosian

Game 7, World Championship, Moscow 1966

Torre Attack

1.d4 ♘f6 2.♘f3 e6 3.♗g5 d5 4.♘bd2 ♗e7 5.e3 ♘bd7 6.♗d3 c5 7.c3 b6

Petrosian deliberately avoids the (up till then) routine 7...0–0, after which Petrosian had himself championed the promising attacking line 8.♘e5, and if 8...♘xe5 9.dxe5 ♘d7 10.♗f4. The well-known game, T.Petrosian-V. Liublinsky, Moscow 1949, had then gone 10...f5 11.h4 c4 12.♗c2 b5 13.♘f3 ♘c5 14.g4, leading to double-edged play (White won), while the solid 14.♘d4, also looks good.

8.0–0 ♗b7 9.♘e5 ♘xe5 10.dxe5 ♘d7 11.♗f4?!

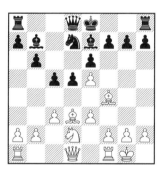

With no Black king on the kingside, the ♘e5 attacking plan simply falls flat. In the comfort of his study, Petrosian had come to realise that Black might safely castle queenside (in such positions) and launch his own kingside counterattack. Black might already even consider 11...g5 12.♗g3 h5, as in

Z.Klaric-E.Geller, Sochi 1977, which continued 13.f4 h4 14.♗e1 gxf4 15.exf4 ♕c7 16.♕g4 0–0–0 17.♕h3 ♖dg8, with good prospects. White perhaps had no better than 11.♗xe7 ♕xe7 12.f4, although after 12...f6 (or first 12...0-0-0), Black has good play.

11...♕c7 12.♘f3 h6 13.b4 g5

With his 13th move, an evidently dazed Spassky throws a rather desperate gambit at Black's queenside. As Petrosian's queenside defences are virtually impregnable, however, Black can ignore it and get on with his more threatening kingside designs. The rapid advance of Black's g- and h-pawns now threatens to trap White's dark square bishop, leaving White with little alternative other than to create a further target for Black, by advancing his h-pawn.

14.♗g3 h5 15.h4 gxh4 16.♗f4 0–0–0 17.a4?!

White continues to throw his queenside pawns forward, more in hope than conviction of success. Black, indeed, now clamps down powerfully on that flank, adding to his equally obvious superiority on the kingside. White might then still hope to control d4, but alone that offers little. White's pawn on e5 also remains dreadfully weak.

Black also enjoys a clear advantage, however, even after the slightly more fluid 17.bxc5 ♘xc5, and if 18.♘d4 ♖dg8, much, in fact, as played in the game. White can't then go pawn grabbing: after 19.♘b5? ♕d7 20.♘xa7+ ♔b8 21.♘b5 d4, and if 22.f3 h3 23.g3 h4 24.g4 dxe3, for example, White's kingside lies completely in shreds.

17...c4 18.♗e2 a6 19.♔h1 ♖dg8 20.♖g1 ♖g4 21.♕d2 ♖hg8 22.a5 b5 23.♖ad1 ♗f8 24.♘h2

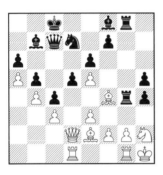

Strategically quite lost, Spassky brings matters to a tactical head. By 'forcing' Petrosian to 'sacrifice' an exchange that he had every intention of playing, however, he enables Black to transform his doubled h-pawns into a deadly, g- and h-pawn attacking duo and win White's e-pawn. Had White done 'nothing', Black would have instead continued to pile up almost certainly winning pressure on e5, with moves, such as ...♖8g6, ...♗g7, and, if need be, ...♕d8 (and possibly even ...♕h8).

24...♘xe5 25.♘xg4 hxg4 26.e4
Black's bristling pawns and complete

spatial dominance pose insuperable problems. White is clearly in imminent danger of being squeezed to death. Keeping queens on the board is no palliative. Black also mops up in the endgame after 26.♕d4 ♗g7, and if 27.♕c5 ♕xc5 28.bxc5 ♘g6 29.♗xg4 ♘xf4 30.exf4 ♗xc3.

26...♗d6 27.♕e3 ♘d7 28.♗xd6 ♕xd6 29.♖d4

Black's irresistible pressure also persists after 29.f4 f5 30.exf5 exf5 31.♖ge1 ♘f6, and, if, say, 32.♔g1 ♖e8 33.♕d4 h3 34.gxh3 (or 34.g3 ♖e4 35.♕f2 ♕e7) 34...♘e4 35.♗f1 ♕xf4 36.♕e3 ♕c7 37.hxg4 ♖h8 38.♖e2 f4, with an overwhelming attack.

29...e5 30.♖d2 f5 31.exd5
Or if 31.exf5 ♕f6, followed by ...♕xf5.

31...f4 32.♕e4 ♘f6 33.♕f5+ ♔b8 34.f3
Black threatened ...♗c8, followed by ...h3, with a winning breakthrough.

34...♗c8 35.♕b1 g3 36.♖e1 h3
The same breakthrough, however, also wins here.

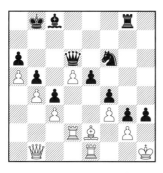

37.♗f1 ♖h8 38.gxh3 ♗xh3 39.♔g1 ♗xf1 40.♔xf1 e4 41.♕d1

After 41.fxe4 f3, Black soon mates.

41...♘g4 42.fxg4

Or 42.fxe4 ♘e3+, and wins.

42...f3 43.♖g2 fxg2+ 0–1

Classically Direct Attack

Boris Spassky

Attack came naturally to Boris Spassky (b 1937). Aged 14, determined to enhance his attacking powers, he switched from his earliest trainer, Vladimir Zak, to one of the great grandmasters of attack, Alexander Tolush. In a fascinating biographical foreword to Bernard Cafferty's, *Spassky's 100 Best Games*, Spassky confided to Leonard Barden that switching to Tolush, 'a brilliant player who loved to sacrifice pieces', coincided with his own growing sense that 'chess has something extra besides sound strategy – attacks, sacrifices, creative ideas'.

Already universally well-grounded, Spassky began to develop an increasingly acute awareness of the most promising moments in games when it might pay to embrace complications. Tolush relished such opportunities. Spassky learned much about daring and calibration of risk. Such play mightily stretched players, while simultaneously offering the exciting prospect of pulling off marvellous wins. To Spassky, risk was an irrevocable part of the game. Best to confront it, head on!

Note, however, that Spassky's attacks generally tended towards the more disciplined, essentially sounder positional edge of the stylistic spectrum than the edgier attacks of a Mikhail Tal, in which raw tactics and psychology often figured with greater prominence. As he enhanced his attacking skills, Spassky never lost sights of his classical roots. The mature Spassky rarely attempted to force matters early, but rather to develop soundly, saving his main effort for big decisions, made at the most complex of middlegame moments.

Through the mid-1950s, Spassky's promise was rated exceptionally highly. World junior champion (1955), he was the youngest player to qualify for the Amsterdam Candidates' tournament (1956). There he tied for 3rd/7th places, with Bronstein, Geller, Petrosian and Szabo (all on 9.5/18), behind Smyslov (11.5) and Keres (10). Disaster, however, befell him, at the USSR Championship (1958), where he suffered a catastrophic last round loss, against Tal, that kept him out of the 1959-1962 world title events.

Spassky eventually managed to retrieve his world-class momentum, largely as a result of resolving a number of challenging personal and competitive problems. By the end of 1961, he had dissolved his difficult first marriage, engaged an outstanding new coach (Igor Bondarevsky) and won his first USSR Championship. To Leonard Barden, he also revealed that he had fully recharged his attacking batteries, in a series of training sessions with Konstantin Klaman, 'a highly original and daring player', who taught him 'a lot about complicated sacrificial attacks'.

Spassky didn't look back. In 1964, he won a specially organised USSR 'Zonal Tournament of Seven', to qualify to play at that year's Amsterdam Interzonal, where he finished in 4th place. That result secured him a

20. Boris Spassky: IBM Amsterdam tournament 1973

place in the 1965 Candidates' match series. In this new KO match format, Spassky impressively despatched Keres (+4-2=4), Geller (+3=5) and Tal (+4-1=5), to set up his first (1966) world title challenge against Petrosian. Although unsuccessful, he nevertheless learned much from this loss and very quickly bounced back.

Shortly after the 1966 title match, Spassky's scored a momentous, undefeated 1st place, in the 2nd Piatigorsky Tournament, at Santa Monica 1966, in which Petrosian slumped. Spassky triumphed as if he were the world champion: Spassky (11.5/18), Fischer (11), Larsen (10), Portisch and Unzicker (9.5), Petrosian and Reshevsky (9), Najdorf (8), Ivkov (6.5), and Donner (6). This outcome strongly suggested that the main reputational battle of the remainder of the 1960s was likely to be between the clear first and second prize-winners in this magnificent field.

The Soviets had long feared the young Bobby Fischer's world title potential. Tal, Petrosian and one or two others had managed to keep him at bay from the late-1950s. Now it was Spassky's turn to lead in that task. The two had shared 1st/2nd places, at Mar del Plata 1960, where Spassky defeated Fischer (with a little good fortune) in their individual game. At Santa Monica, where the two next met, Spassky scored a wholly merited second win against the American and, of course, won the tournament. Their second Santa Monica game was a draw.

Spassky's Santa Monica win against Fischer was both powerfully and impressively played. Spassky chose one of the most highly principled lines against Fischer's Grünfeld Defence. Played well, such ambitious, space-gaining lines are likely to test the mettle of even the world's absolute best. Igor Zaitsev, in 64, noted: 'as usual [Spassky] does not try to decide the course of the game in the opening, a harmonious development and a strong centre being quite adequate'. Fischer blinks first.

B.Spassky – R.Fischer

2nd Piatigorsky-Cup, Santa Monica 1966

Grünfeld Defence

1.d4 ♘f6 2.c4 g6 3.♘c3 d5 4.cxd5 ♘xd5 5.e4 ♘xc3 6.bxc3 ♗g7 7.♗c4 c5 8.♘e2 ♘c6 9.♗e3 0-0 10.0-0 ♕c7 11.♖c1 ♖d8 12.♕e1

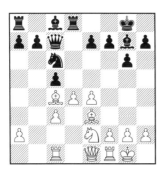

B.Spassky-R.Fischer, Olympiad, Siegen 1970, later varied 12.h3 b6 13.f4 e6 14.♕e1 ♘a5 15.♗d3 f5 16.g4 fxe4 17.♗xe4 ♗b7 18.♘g3 ♘c4 19.♗xb7 ♕xb7 20.♗f2 ♕c6 21.♕e2 cxd4 22.cxd4 b5 23.♘e4, offering a pawn for compensating central and kingside complications, in which Fischer eventually went wrong and again lost.

12...e6 13.f4 ♘a5 14.♗d3 f5 15.♖d1
As in their later game, at Siegen, Spassky keeps the centre fluid, leaving his opponent guessing about future White plans. The alternative, 15.e5 b6, all too readily accommodates Black's desire to establish a firm grip on the central light squares.

15...b6 16.♕f2 cxd4 17.♗xd4 ♗xd4

This exchange weakens Black's grip on significant dark squares, but it could scarcely have been avoided. Similar positions might also arise after 17... ♗b7 18.♗xg7 ♕xg7 19.♘d4, and if 19... ♕f7 20.♗c2.

18.cxd4 ♗b7 19.♘g3 ♕f7?!

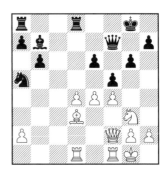

Black should have preferred 19...♕g7, and if 20.♗c2 (threatening d5) 20... fxe4 21.♘xe4 ♖ac8 22.♘g5 ♗d5 23.♖fe1 ♕f6, which may wholly equalise. With Black's queen on f7, White now breaks in the centre, to secure a persistent initiative. White also stands better, after 19...fxe4 20.♘xe4, with White's knight on an ideal post, from which it exerts pressure on Black's g5 and f6 dark squares.

20.d5 fxe4 21.dxe6 ♕xe6 22.f5
This second (and complementary) thrust forces Black on to the defensive. Black's king would now be

fatally exposed after 22...gxf5 23.♘xf5 (threatening ♕g3+, and wins), and if, say 23...♖e8 24.♗b5 e3 (or 24...♗c6) 25.♕b2 ♕e5 26.♘h6+ ♔g7 27.♖f7+ ♔xh6 28.♖d6+, creating a mating net.

22...♕f7 23.♗xe4 ♖xd1 24.♖xd1 ♖f8 25.♗b1 ♕f6 26.♕c2 ♔h8

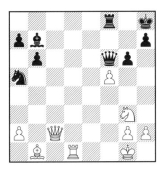

All of White's pieces point threateningly towards Black's kingside, while Black's poorly placed knight remains out of play, with no easy way to retrieve it. After 26...♖c8 27.♕d2, and if 27...♘c4 28.♕d7, forcing 28...♕c6, White can simply exchange queens and win Black's g-pawn.

27.fxg6 hxg6 28.♕d2?!
Here Spassky slips. After 28.♘h5!, and if 28...♗e4 29.♕e2 gxh5 30.♗xe4, White secures excellent chances to press in a threatening middlegame. With queen and rooks on the board, Black's knight looks even more despairingly stranded than in the various endgames (if still somewhat in White's favour) that Fischer is now able to reach.

28...♔g7 29.♖f1 ♕e7 30.♕d4+ ♖f6 31.♘e4 ♗xe4 32.♗xe4 ♕c5 33.♕xc5 ♖xf1+

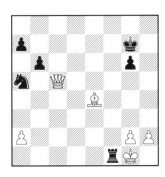

Fischer has survived the worst. White, however, retains the more threatening, long range minor piece, able both to support: the possible creation of an outside passed pawn on the kingside; and White's rook and king in possible attacks against Black's isolated a- and c-pawns. Also possible was 33...bxc5, and if 34.♖xf6 ♔xf6 35.h4 ♘c4 36.♔f2 ♘d6, with his knight better centralised. White might, however, prefer 34.♖c1, and if 34...c4 35.♖c3, to keep rooks on the board.

34.♔xf1 bxc5 35.h4 ♘c4 36.♔e2 ♘e5 37.♔e3 ♔f6 38.♔f4 ♘f7 39.♔e3 g5?

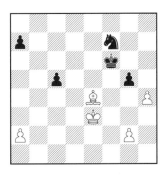

On the back foot throughout and now in time-trouble, Fischer cracks. Just one move before the time control, Black fatally allows White to create an advanced passed h-pawn. This is likely to tie down Black's king (or knight) to passive kingside defence, while White's king freely invades on the queenside.

Fischer perhaps shied away from the passive, 39...♘e5 40.♗c2, when White might still press. Svetozar Gligoric, however, spotted the rather more active 39...♘h6, heading for f5 and possibly drawn endgames, such as after 40.♗c2 (or 40.a4 ♘f5+) ♘f5+ 41.♗xf5 gxf5 42.g3 ♔g6 43.♔d3 ♔h5 44.♔c4 ♔g4 45.♔xc5 ♔xg3 46.h5 f4 47.h6 f3 48.h7 f2 49.h8♕ f1♕.

40.h5 ♘h6 41.♔d3 ♔e5 42.♗a8 ♔d6
Defence is now impossible. White also wins, after 42...♔f4

43.♔c4 ♔g4 44.♗f3+ ♔h4 45.♔xc5 g4 46.♗e4 ♔xh5 47.a4.
After the text-move, with Black's knight tied down on the kingside, White wins by forcing Black's king into passivity on c6, followed by the advance of his a-pawn to a5 and a final attack on Black's a-pawn.

43.♔c4 g4 44.a4 ♘g8 45.a5 ♘h6 46.♗e4 g3 47.♔b5 ♘g8 48.♗b1 ♘h6 49.♔a6 ♔c6 50.♗a2

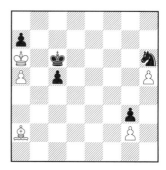

Black is helpless against the most exact preliminary, ♗c4, followed by ♔xa7.
1–0

In the twelve months or so following his Santa Monica triumph, Spassky's stock remained high. Through 1967, Spassky's most important aim, of course, was to ensure that, going into the make or break 1968 Candidates' matches, he reached peak form. His 1967 tournament results compared well with those of his most important rivals and he remained on track to battle for the big prize. Then a bomb dropped. In an inexplicable mega-huff, Bobby Fischer walked out of the 1967 Sousse Interzonal.

This bizarre step, midway through the event, when Fischer was already so far ahead that he could scarcely have failed to take 1st place, had he remained, boosted everyone else's Candidates' hopes, not least Spassky's. As a gesture, it was pointless. None of the eventual Candidates, of course, either sought or wished for such an outcome. Writing in *Chess Life & Review*, even Fischer's great friend, Svetozar Gligoric, could only lament that Fischer had brought it all on himself. It was tragic for Fischer and chess.

Fischer's absence immediately installed Spassky as clear favourite to win the 1968 Candidates' match series. The field itself remained superbly strong but it robbed chess history of one of its most tantalizing 'what if' moments. Spassky impressively stepped up to the mark, to repeat his 1965 Candidates' triumph, this time consecutively defeating Geller (+3=5), Larsen (+4=3-1) and Korchnoi (+4=5-1). Quoted in *Spassky's 100 Best Games*, Korchnoi acknowledged that he had been 'decisively' beaten, routinely outplayed 'in the middlegame'.

Korchnoi hotly tipped Spassky to defeat Petrosian. A much more experienced and tougher opponent than in 1966, the 32 year-old challenger had played better chess in those years than the champion. Spassky's (post-1961) co-analyst and coach, Bondarevsky, moreover, had been a calmly affable friend as well as an invaluable technical assistant. To Leonard Barden, Spassky credited Bondarevsky with doing much 'not only for my chess knowledge and understanding of positions, but also for my character'.

Spassky's openings were much better prepared for the 1969 match.

Unlike 1966, he rarely ran out of hard-hitting ideas in his chosen range of exclusively powerful main lines and eschewed any resort to irregular openings. He and his team also recruited Nikolai Krogius, a psychologist as well as a grandmaster, who added considerable steel to his mental approach. Spassky eventually ran out the deserved winner, by a comfortable two point margin (+6=13-4).

In a lengthy article, included in the second of two indispensible biographical works, *The Games of Tigran Petrosian*, edited by Eduard Shekhtman, Petrosian largely echoed Korchnoi's assessment of Spassky's middlegame strength. Petrosian considered that the main element in the challenger's match strategy 'comprised - active piece play'; and that Spassky consistently 'displayed rare skill in maintaining ... tension in the position, constantly finding ways to keep the opponent on edge'.

Petrosian appears to have felt such pressure most acutely in Games 4, 19 and 21, in which he lost to an opponent, who, he acknowledged, played 'like a world champion'. Games 19 and 21 effectively decided the match. Petrosian's energy had drained and he confessed to trying to over-force matters and making a 'stupid choice of opening' in both of those games. Punishment came unusually swiftly after a model Spassky attack in Game 19.

B.Spassky – T.Petrosian

Game 19, World Championship, Moscow 1969

Sicilian Defence

1.e4 c5 2.♘f3 d6 3.d4 cxd4 4.♘xd4 ♘f6 5.♘c3 a6 6.♗g5 ♘bd7 7.♗c4 ♕a5 8.♕d2 h6

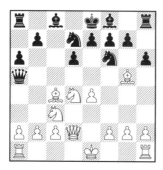

Petrosian's choice of a Najdorf Variation isn't really 'stupid', of course, except perhaps in the sense that Spassky enjoyed playing against it. B.Spassky-L.Polugaevsky, USSR Championship, Riga 1958, had previously gone 8...e6 9.0–0–0 b5 10.♗b3 (10.♗d5!? b4!, is fine for Black) 10... ♗b7 11.♖he1 ♗e7 12.f4 ♘c5 13.e5 dxe5 14.♗xf6 ♗xf6 15.fxe5 ♗h4 16.g3 ♗e7 17.♗xe6, and White won.

9.♗xf6 ♘xf6 10.0–0–0 e6 11.♖he1 ♗e7
With the bishop pair and a prickly, so-called 'small' pawn centre, Petrosian plans to castle kingside and absorb any attack by White. Spassky enjoys space, leads in development and has a clear plan: to play ♔b1, followed by f4, with an e5 break and / or a g4-g5 flank attack, in mind. Black might have played

...♗d7, followed by 0–0–0, with his king (perhaps) a little safer. Generally, however, Black still lacks concrete counterplay.

12.f4 0–0 13.♗b3 ♖e8 14.♔b1 ♗f8 15.g4

Spassky offers a frightening and genuinely speculative gambit. Black can

21. Boris Spassky, Amsterdam 1973

scarcely decline: or if 15...b5 16.g5 hxg5 17.fxg5 b4 18.♘d5, and if 18...exd5 (or 18...♘xd5 19.exd5 e5 20.g6) 19.gxf6 dxe4 20.fxg7 ♗xg7 21.♖g1, soon over-running Black. White might also have played 15.e5 dxe5 16.fxe5, and if 16...♘d7 17.♕f4 ♘c5 18.♘e4, with a comfortably risk-free pull but wants much more.

15...♘xg4 16.♕g2 ♘f6 17.♖g1 ♗d7 18.f5

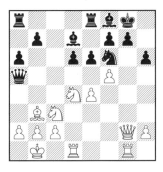

The key follow-up: White creates light square havoc around Black's king and opens the f-file. After 18...e5 19.♘f3, Black would now face multiple winning threats, including ♖xd6, ♕g6 and ♕d2 (winning either f- or h-pawn).

White also stands well, after 18...exf5, as in the computer line 19.♘xf5 ♗xf5 20.exf5, and if 20...♖ac8 (or 20...♕xf5 21.♖df1 ♕e5 22.♕xb7 ♕e7 23.♕g2, threatening ♘d5) 21.♘d5 ♕d8 22.♘xf6+ ♕xf6 23.♕g6 ♗e7 24.♖de1 d5 25.♗xd5 ♖ed8 26.♖xe7 ♕xg6 27.fxg6 ♖xd5 28.a3.

The computer also favours White after 18...♕e5 19.♘f3, and if 19...♕c5 (or 19...♕f4 20.♖d4 ♗c6 21.fxe6 fxe6 22.♘d5) 20.♕h3 ♔h8 21.♘g5 ♗e7 22.fxe6 fxe6 23.♗xe6 ♗xe6 24.♘xe6 ♕e5 25.♘g5.

As a result, Petrosian tucks his king gingerly into the corner and instead 'hopes'.

18...♔h8 19.♖df1 ♕d8

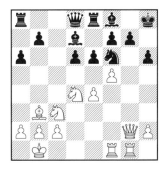

White now crowns his attack with five crushing tactical blows. But what else? White also remains in complete command, after either: 19...♕e5 20.fxe6, and if 20...♗xe6 (or if 20...fxe6 21.♘f3 ♕h5 22.♕g3) 21.♗xe6 fxe6 22.♘f3 ♕h5 23.♕g3, strongly threatening e5; 19...exf5 20.♘xf5, and if 20...♗xf5 21.♖xf5 ♖e5 22.♖xf6 (or 22.♖xe5 ♕xe5 23.♗xf7) 22...♖g5 23.♕xg5 hxg5 24.♖xf7; or 19...e5 20.♘de2.

20.fxe6 fxe6

White now sacrifices a second pawn to gain a staging post to the kingside (on e4) for his knight. Black is, however, also quite lost after 20...♗xe6 21.♗xe6 fxe6 22.♘ce2, and if 22...e5 (or if 22...g5 23 ♘f4) 23.♘f5 g5 24.♕h3, with overwhelming threats on the light squares and in the f-, g- and h-files.

21.e5 dxe5 22.♘e4 ♘h5

Clearly forced, or if 22...♘xe4

23.♖xf8+, and mates. Now, however, White's queen decisively lands on g6.

23.♕g6 exd4

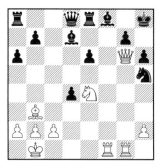

Petrosian permits an attractive, one move killer. The alternative was to allow the even more strikingly beautiful conclusion: 23...♘f4 (or if 23...♕h4 24.♘f3) 24.♖xf4 exf4 25.♘f3 (threatening ♘fg5), 25...♕b6 26.♖g5! (threatening ♘f6), 26...♕d8 27.♘e5, now threatening ♘f7+, and wins.

24.♘g5 1–0

Or if 24...hxg5 (or 24...♘f6 25.♖xf6) 25.♕xh5+ ♔g8 26.♕f7+ ♔h7 27.♖f3, and mates.

Professional Sport in a New Information Age

'Only one writer could have invented him: Franz Kafka ... Poor Bobby? Poor Boris. One wonders who is more to be pitied: a state-owned gladiator or a freelance Samurai'

Arthur Koestler, in his *Introduction* to Harry
Golombek's *Fischer versus Spassky* (1973)

The year 1972 marked a watershed in chess. That year's prize fund for the so-called 'Match of the Century', between Bobby Fischer and Boris Spassky, at Reykjavik, broke all records. At stake was a purse of some $250,000 (worth well over $1m today). From 1972 onwards, top-class chess began to gain widespread popular acceptance as a professional sport, in which its elite practitioners met in wholly committed combat, just as in, say golf, boxing or tennis.

It also clearly got better paid, too. And not just because of the additional Reykjavik frisson of an East-West showdown between an American and Soviet Russian, at the height of the Cold War, though that added spice. With the full glare of the world's media on the match, even non-chess players were gripped by a spectacle, in which they could clearly perceive that success in the top-class game demanded not just exceptional levels of skill but also extraordinary reserves of both physical and mental endurance.

Gone were the days when a part-time player might expect to ascend to the chess summit. Through the 1950s and 1960s, the number of strong players and events just continued to grow and the corresponding battle to stay on top of ever-increasing sources of complex international information only markedly intensified. Even such a peculiarly near-full-time and certainly generously supported 'part-timer' as Mikhail Botvinnik, would have struggled. Chess now required total commitment.

Bobby Fischer set the initial bar high, although he clearly owed a debt to the most recent Soviet full-timers: Smyslov, Tal, Petrosian, Spassky and others. Fischer's immediate world title successors, Anatoly Karpov and Garry Kasparov, drove his example and developed his professionalism even further, including through the increasing adoption of such innovations as the employment of business managers, agents and advisers (in addition to chess coaches and trainers) that has since become widespread.

Total Commitment

Bobby Fischer

22. Bobby Fischer: Amsterdam, early 1972

B obby Fischer (1943-2008) burst on to the international chess scene in his early teens in a manner that was then quite exceptional. It foreshadowed the way many of the world's top players have since begun to emerge, at a very young age, in the 21st century. US junior champion (1956 and 1957), US Open champion (1957) and US champion (1957-58), Fischer became a world championship Candidate and the world's youngest ever grandmaster, aged 15.

Already tipped as a future world champion, Fischer dropped out of High School to pursue a destiny, which he, too, believed in but knew would be far from easy. In the 1950s, and even the more prosperous 1960s, economic returns in the professional game were borderline parlous. While a few might earn a reasonable income, prize funds for professional players, even in the strongest competitions, tended towards the miniscule. In those decades only communist state professionalism really flourished.

In *Endgame*, Fischer's perceptive biographer, Frank Brady, quotes a UPI wire report, in which, just after he had become a Candidate, even Fischer himself seemed to recognise the impossibility of his dream. In response to one interviewer, he replied, 'One thing is certain – I am not going to become a professional chess player'. Driven more by raw emotion, however, the young Fischer could never rid himself of his boundless love for the game. Best leave it to those well-subsidised Soviets? No!

From his earliest years, Fischer studied the game voraciously, evincing an unusually total commitment. Brought up in a tight-knit, low income, one parent family, Fischer nevertheless enjoyed his mother's ongoing support. Partly through her, he obtained much pro bono help from two excellent New York coaches, Carmine Nigro (from 1951) and Jack Collins (from 1956). New York's two world-class Chess Clubs, the Manhattan and Marshall, home to some of the strongest players outside of the USSR, also stood by him.

In his mid- to late-teens, moreover, not just a player of world-class, Fischer was also extremely well-read in chess history and more up to date on the game's theory, including Russian sources, than even most of the best Soviets. Aware that he posed a real threat to the Soviet grip on the world championship, however, he nevertheless found it rather more difficult to get his hands on the crown. Fischer's first two attempts to qualify for a title challenge, at the 1959 and 1962 Candidates' tournaments, both ended in failure.

Aged only 16, in the 1959 Candidates' (played at various Yugoslavian venues), Fischer could still objectively put his share of 5th/6th places down to youthful inexperience. Tal, who won, simply outclassed him. Aged 19, at the 1962 Curaçao Candidates', however, Fischer's 4th place came as a huge disappointment. While he alleged that the Soviets played as a team against him (by agreeing a number of quick draws against each other and thereby conserving energy), in truth, he simply hadn't himself played well enough.

Back home, Fischer won consecutive US championships, in 1962-63 and 1963-64 (his fifth and sixth, to date), scoring a scarcely credible, 11/11, in the latter. While a US championship wasn't quite on a par with its USSR equivalent, this was nonetheless extraordinarily special. In most fans' eyes and even in those of many of the chess world's elite, Fischer, still just aged 20, was already the world's best player. He then took an unexpected eighteen month competitive break, however, which signalled the start of a worryingly stop-go relationship with chess that endured for the rest of his life.

Fischer's 1963-64 US Championship clean sweep was certainly no fluke. It was not just the score that impressed but the extraordinarily high quality of the games that he played. The merest slip against him saw him power up a gear. Playing White, Robert Byrne, set out with an apparent determination to create a risk-free symmetry, offer exchanges and agree to a stone-cold draw. Fischer, however, found a way to force complications, in which Byrne went wrong, on his 14th move, allowing Fischer to conjure up one of his most memorably dazzling combinations.

R.Byrne – R.Fischer

US Championship, New York 1963-64

Grünfeld Defence

1.d4 ♘f6 2.c4 g6 3.g3 c6 4.♗g2 d5 5.cxd5 cxd5 6.♘c3 ♗g7 7.e3 0-0 8.♘ge2 ♘c6 9.0-0 b6 10.b3 ♗a6 11.♗a3 ♖e8

According to Fischer, in *My 60 Memorable Games*, Black has various ways to establish 'dead-eye' equality, based on completing his development and playing the solid ...e6. He instead speculates on essaying the combative central pawn break ...e5.

12.♕d2 e5

While 'a bit worried about weakening my d-pawn', Fischer judged that 'the tremendous activity obtained by my minor pieces would permit White no time to exploit it'. Black obtains good prospects for his bishops, on the a6–f1 and long dark square diagonals, and for his knights, which exert pressure against White's potentially exploitable d3 and e4 light squares.

13.dxe5 ♘xe5 14.♖fd1?

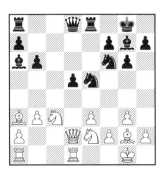

Byrne's fateful mistake: this is the wrong rook to play to the correct square. Without the benefit of hindsight, however, it was not yet easy to appreciate why White's pawn on f2 might require more protection. Correct was 14.♖ad1, when the game remains in rough balance. Fischer then intended 14...♘e4, and if 15.♘xe4 dxe4 16.♗xe4 ♕xd2 17.♖xd2 ♘c4 18.♗xa8 ♘xd2 19.♖d1 ♘c4 20.bxc4 ♖xa8, but Averbakh subsequently noted the crushing improvement, 20.♗c6, and if 20...♘xa3 21.♗xe8 ♗xe2 22.♖d7, and White wins.

So Black is left with either of two alternatives, 14...♕c8 and ...♕d7, over which countless person and subsequently engine hours have been invested, without establishing any clear consensus, other than that, while Fischer's judgement, in playing ...e5, was perfectly good, White has balancing chances. After the text-move, however, Fischer unerringly takes White apart.

14...♘d3 15.♕c2?!

Had White's other rook been on d1, Black's knight would have had to retreat. Fischer's reply, however, refutes White's concept entirely. White now simply had no better than to allow Black to consolidate his crushing grip on d3, after: 15.♘d4 ♘e4 (key), and if 16.♘xe4 dxe4 17.♗b2 ♖c8, 'with a bind'; 15.♘f4 ♘e4 16.♘xe4 dxe4 17.♖ab1 ♖c8, and if 18.♘xd3 ♗c3 19.♕e2 ♗xd3 20.♕g4 f5; or 15.f3 ♗h6 16.f4 ♗g7, again threatening ...♘e4 (Fischer).

15...♘xf2 16.♔xf2 ♘g4+ 17.♔g1 ♘xe3 18.♕d2 ♘xg2

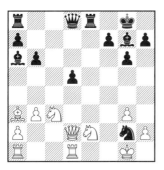

Byrne had only considered 18...♘xd1 19.♖xd1, simply missing Fischer's deadly intention. With this and his next move, Black impressively clears both the long light and dark square diagonals, leading to the White king's ensnarement in an inescapable web of across the board mating threats.

19.♔xg2 d4 20.♘xd4 ♗b7+ 21.♔f1

Black also wins at once, after either 21.♔g1 ♗xd4+ 22.♕xd4 ♖e1+, or the equally stunning 21.♔f2 ♕d7, and if 22.♖ac1 ♕h3 23.♘f3 ♗h6 24.♕d3 ♗e3+ 25.♕xe3 ♖xe3 26.♔xe3 ♖e8+ 27.♔f2 ♕f5 (Fischer).

21...♕d7 0–1
Sadly Byrne didn't permit his opponent to demonstrate the further remarkable variation: 22.♕f2 ♕h3+ 23.♔g1 ♖e1+ 24.♖xe1 ♗xd4, and wins. After 22.♘db5 ♕h3+ 23.♔g1 ♗h6, Black, of course, wins mundanely.

Despite his magnificent 1963-64 US Championship win, Fischer ruled himself out of competing at the 1964 Amsterdam Interzonal. Fischer would have been odds-on favourite to finish first, let alone take one of the six qualifying places for the 1965 Candidates' match series, but instead went on an exhibition tour of the USA. Perhaps still embittered by his Curaçao result, Fischer's seemingly odd choice (we don't really know his exact reasoning) meant that he could no longer challenge for the world title, until 1969, at the earliest.

Happily, Fischer came back to the board, at Havana 1965, playing from New York, by cable. In 1966, he then scored outstandingly well, at Santa Monica and the Havana Olympiad. As he also won his 7th and 8th US Championships, in 1965-66 and 1966-67, Fischer seemed once more on course to contend for that elusive world title. Following two further outstanding 1st places, at Monaco and Skopje, early in 1967, Fischer seemed certain to sail through that year's Sousse Interzonal.

Fischer began playing, at Sousse. Sadly, however, while comfortably ahead, on 8.5/10 (in a 22 round marathon), he suddenly took umbrage with several of his main rivals and the organisers over what was really no more than a relatively minor scheduling issue, and promptly departed from Sousse. Despite painstaking organisational (and diplomatic) efforts, it proved impossible to get Fischer back to the board. The earliest date that he might challenge for the world title receded by yet another three years.

Thankfully, Fischer resumed his international career, this time fairly quickly, scoring two excellent 1st places, at Netanya and Vinkovci, both in 1968. Slightly worryingly, he hardly played at all, in 1969. In 1970, however, miracles happened. Fischer first defeated Petrosian, 3-1, in the USSR v Rest of World Match, at Belgrade. Shortly afterwards, he won the unofficial Blitz World Championship, at Herceg Novi, and placed 1st in another two very strong tournaments, at Rovinj/Zagreb and Buenos Aires.

Fischer then played in the 1970 Siegen Olympiad, scoring an outstanding, 10/13, a total that was only just bettered by new world champion, Boris Spassky. While it was now abundantly clear that Fischer was Spassky's natural challenger, he hadn't, however, actually entered the 1969-72 qualifying cycle. To widespread relief, Pal Benko then generously transferred his own Interzonal qualifying place to his American colleague. Fischer finished fully 3.5 points ahead of the rest of the field, at Palma 1970, taking 1st place, on a blistering 18.5/23.

Hot favourite to win the subsequent Candidates' match series, Fischer first swept Mark Taimanov aside, at Vancouver (May 1971), by a 6-0 score that was quite as astonishing as it was unexpected. Two months later, in the Denver semi-final, Fischer then did it again, 6-0, against the unfortunate Bent Larsen. Taimanov and Larsen might, of course, have snatched at least the odd half-point or so. To their great credit, like Fischer, they only battled to win. Fischer's chess, however, seemed completely surreal, as if played in a parallel universe.

The high quality of Fischer's play was exceptional. While also rather better prepared in the opening, there really was no matching his middlegame drive. Fischer repeatedly outplayed, out-calculated and out-pummelled both Taimanov and Larsen. Highly creative, Fischer's game was also remarkably error-free, while always consistently hard-hitting. His win in Game 1 against Larsen was conducted wholly on the grand scale. Larsen unwittingly walked into complications that Fischer quite evidently mastered much better than he did.

R.Fischer – B.Larsen

Game 1, Candidates' Semi-final, Denver 1971

French Defence

1.e4 e6 2.d4 d5 3.♘c3 ♗b4 4.e5 ♘e7 5.a3 ♗xc3+ 6.bxc3 c5 7.a4 ♘bc6

R.Fischer-K.Darga, Berlin 1960, had earlier gone 7...♕c7 8.♘f3 b6 9.♗b5+ ♗d7 10.♗d3 ♘bc6 11.0-0 c4 12.♗e2 f6 13.♗a3

reaching the same position as in the Larsen game after 12 moves (but with Black's b-pawn still on b7). Fischer went on to win a tense battle, included in *My 60 Memorable Games*, after 13... fxe5 14.dxe5 ♘xe5 15.♖e1 ♘7c6 16.♘xe5 ♘xe5 17.f4 ♘c6 18.♗g4 0-0-0 19.♗xe6 ♗xe6 20.♖xe6.

Fischer's notes to the Darga game suggest that 13.♖e1 is a 'solid but less aggressive alternative'. My guess is that Fischer subsequently considered this to be good whether Black's b-pawn was on b6 or b7, with the same idea (as against Larsen) of continuing (after the Darga sequence) 13.♖e1, and if 13... fxe5 14.dxe5 ♘g6 15.♗a3 ♘gxe5 16.♘xe5 ♘xe5 17.♕d4.

8.♘f3 ♗d7 9.♗d3 ♕c7

R.Fischer-W.Uhlmann, Stockholm 1962, had instead gone 9...♕a5 10.♕d2 f6 11.0-0 fxe5 12.♘xe5 ♘xe5 13.dxe5 0-0 14.c4, inviting an exchange of queens and a battle, in which White hopes to make something of his bishop pair (the game was drawn).

10.0-0 c4 11.♗e2 f6 12.♖e1

Larsen, who rarely ever played the French Defence, must have prepared this line specially. R.Fischer-E.Mednis, US Championship 1962-63, had gone 12.♗a3, when Fischer suggests that Mednis may have safely accepted the gambit pawn (with 'Black's b-pawn ... still on b7'). Mednis instead 'got a cramped game' after 12...0-0 13.♖e1!, with the idea, 13...fxe5 14.♘xe5! (Fischer), though Mednis sensationally won.

12...♘g6 13.♗a3 fxe5 14.dxe5 ♘cxe5 15.♘xe5 ♘xe5 16.♕d4

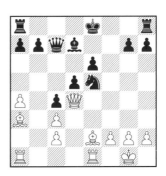

In his preparations, Larsen may have underestimated (or possibly over-looked) the strength of this fine move, the clever complement to White's earlier ♖e1 (and equally strong with Black's b-pawn either on b6 or b7). White's queen occupies a crushing central post, obtaining more than sufficient dark square compensation for a pawn and powerfully threatening ♗h5+.

White can no longer rely on 'copying' play in the Darga game, as after 16.f4 ♘c6 17.♗g4 0-0-0 18.♗xe6 ♗xe6 19.♖xe6, Black simply replies 19...♕xf4 (because Black's b-pawn is not on b6 but b7).

16...♘g6 17.♗h5 ♔f7

Cleverly caught out in the opening, Black resorts to desperate measures. With his king on f7, Black clearly risks a perilous White breakthrough in the f-file. White, however, also stands well after 17...0-0-0 18.a5!, and if 18...e5 (or if 18...♔b8 19.♗c5) 19.♕xa7 ♘f4 20.♖ab1 ♕b8 21.♕xb8+ ♔xb8 22.a6 ♘xh5 (or 22...♗c6 23.♖xe5) 23.♖xb7+ ♔c8 24.♗d6, with winning pressure.

18.f4 ♖he8 19.f5 exf5 20.♕xd5+ ♔f6 21.♗f3!?

Fischer errs on the side of safety rather than play the promising, if near incal-culable, 21.♗d6. He perhaps consid-ered that White retains a safe, if slight, advantage after the text-move anyway. In fact, however, he allows his oppo-nent to get back in the game most in-geniously.

After 21.♗d6, while the tactics are ex-tremely tricky (modern engine analy-sis helps), White almost certainly pre-vails, such as after (illustrative main ideas only):

21...♕d8 22.♗f3, and if 22...♗c6 23.♕d4+ ♔f7 24.♗d5+ ♗xd5 25.♕xd5+ ♔f6 26.♖f1 ♕d7 27.g4 ♘h4 28.♖ab1 b6 29.♗e5+ ♔e7 30.♗f6+ gxf6 31.♖be1+; or 21...♕b6+ 22.♗c5 ♕c6 (or if 22...♕c7 23.h4, and if 23...♖e6 24.♗d4+ ♔e7 25.♕xf5) 23.♕d4+ ♔g5 24.♗f3 ♕c7 25.♗e7+ ♖xe7 (or if 25...♔h6 26.♕d2+ f4 27.♕d5) 26.♖xe7 ♘xe7 27.♕xg7+ ♘g6 28.h4+ ♔f4 29.♕d4+ ♔g3 30.♕f2+ ♔f4 31.♖e1, and mates.

21...♘e5 22.♕d4 ♔g6 23.♖xe5

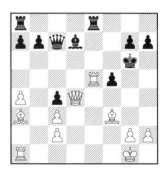

Black's king is distraught but safe enough. The players now speed down a line, in which White eventually obtains a rook and two bishops for his queen. White is unlikely to lose – here, as is so often the case, White's rook and bishops are a source of formidable defensive as well as attacking power. White is not, however, favourite to win either - due to the near equally formidable power of Black's queen.

23...♕xe5 24.♕xd7 ♖ad8 25.♕xb7 ♕e3+ 26.♔f1 ♖d2

Larsen chooses the most forcing continuation. After 26...h6, White might still worry Black, by playing 27.♕a6+ ♔h7 28.♕a5, and if 28...♖d2 29.♕xf5+ ♔h8 30.♗h5.

27.♕c6+ ♖e6 28.♗c5

Fischer no doubt foresaw this clever defence very many moves in advance. Otherwise he would simply be lost.

28...♖f2+ 29.♔g1 ♖xg2+ 30.♔xg2 ♕d2+ 31.♔h1 ♖xc6 32.♗xc6 ♕xc3 33.♖g1+ ♔f6 34.♗xa7 g5

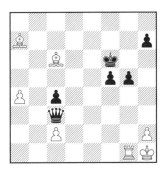

Fischer no doubt also (long ago) foresaw that he could reach positions like this and judged (correctly) that White runs no real risk of losing. White's a-pawn, a critical trump, is a potential game winner that need only advance a move or two to connect with White's powerful bishops and threaten to advance to the 8th rank.

With that in mind, Black should perhaps have preferred 34...♕xc2, to free his c-pawn, so that it might itself advance and act as an effective counterbalance, such as after the plausible conclusion: 35.a5 ♕d2 36.a6 c3 37.♗c5 c2 38.a7 c1♕ 39.♖xc1 ♕xc1+ 40.♔g2 ♕d2+ 41.♗f2 ♕g5+ 42.♔f3 ♕h5+ 43.♔e3 f4+ 44.♔d2 ♕a5+, and Black draws by perpetual check.

35.♗b6 ♕xc2 36.a5 ♕b2

Having allowed White's a-pawn to advance, Black now finds it more difficult both to stop that pawn and to activate his c-pawn. He might, however, still have survived, by playing 36...♕a2, and if 37.♗b7 ♕b2 38.♗d8+ ♔e5 39.a6 c3 40.♗xg5 c2.

37.♗d8+ ♔e6 38.a6 ♕a3

Here, 38...♕f2, and if 39.♗xg5 c3 40.♖a1 c2, might still also have saved Black. Now he is lost.

39.♗b7 ♕c5

Black's c-pawn is a crucial tempo short on the c-file. White's advancing a-pawn still wins, however, even after 39...♕b3 40.♖e1+, and if 40...♔d6 41.♗e7+ ♔c7 42.♗c5 ♕b5 (or if 42...c3 43.♗g2) 43.♖e5 ♔d7 44.♗g1 ♕xe5 45.a7.

40.♖b1 c3 41.♗b6 1-0

After the Taimanov and Larsen matches, no one expected even the ultra-solid, ex-world champion, Tigran Petrosian, to pose an insuperable obstacle to Fischer in the Candidates' final. He was, however, expected to put up a stubborn defence. And so it proved, at least initially. After one win each, followed by three consecutive draws, however, Petrosian's early good form and morale unexpectedly vanished. Fischer sealed a confident victory with four further consecutive wins.

Psychologically, this must have been a most difficult match for Petrosian. Fischer had won all twelve of his games against Taimanov and Larsen. Petrosian, who had consecutively despatched Robert Hübner and Viktor Korchnoi in his two previous Candidates' matches, may not have lost any games but he only won two. How then to adjust to such a formidable scoring machine, as Fischer? Despite starting quite well, Petrosian couldn't ultimately cope with Fischer's inimitable pressure.

As against Taimanov and Larsen, Fischer was once again a little better in the opening and too strong in the middlegame, against Petrosian, although he had to bide his time before the tough ex-world champion finally cracked. Petrosian, in fact, played at least as well as Fischer, in the first five games, not least in the opening. Fischer won Game 1, but Petrosian clearly won the openings theoretical debate. In Game 2, Petrosian gained a clear advantage from the opening and, this time, won brilliantly.

In the last four games, however, the quality of Petrosian's play in the opening (especially) markedly dipped, which enabled Fischer to subject his opponent to much more early pressure than in the first half of the match. As Fischer's middlegame play remained as superb throughout as it had been against Taimanov and Larsen, this helped him subject Petrosian to a form of sustained torture, with which Petrosian just couldn't cope. He went out, in the end, with a whimper.

Game 7, Fischer's most memorable in his final winning streak, speaks both for Petrosian's torrid problems and Fischer's exceptional brilliance. Petrosian unwisely opted for a line, with which he had successfully kept Spassky at bay, in their 1969 world championship match. Clearly prepared, Fischer hit hard with a powerful 12th move improvement. Soon on the back foot (the new concept was good), Petrosian wriggled but couldn't shake off Fischer's well-nigh unplayable combinational persistence.

In mid-1971, Soviet grandmasters Boleslavsky, Polugaevsky, Shamkovich and Vasiukov presented a joint report on Fischer's strengths and weaknesses, to Petrosian and Spassky. This highlighted Fischer's superbly clear planning, strategic and tactical gifts, his directly classical playing style and his outstanding precision in endgames. The problem for the Soviets, however, (with a nod to Karl Marx) was not just to understand Fischer's world, but rather to figure out how best to confront a giant who repeatedly produced such consistently wonderful chess games.

R.Fischer – T.Petrosian

Game 7, Candidates final, Buenos Aires 1971

Sicilian Defence

1.e4 c5 2.♘f3 e6 3.d4 cxd4 4.♘xd4 a6 5.♗d3 ♘c6 6.♘xc6 bxc6 7.0–0 d5 8.c4
White seeks to exchange pawns twice on d5, leaving Black with a potentially vulnerable IQP. The attempt to finesse this plan, by playing 8...d4, can be met by the energetic 9.e5. In their 1969 match, Petrosian twice successfully neutralised Spassky's more modest 8.♘d2.

8...♘f6 9.cxd5 cxd5 10.exd5 exd5
After 10...♘xd5, White plays 11.♗e4, with ♘c3 pending.

11.♘c3 ♗e7 12.♕a4+

In place of the older 12.♗e3, followed by ♗d4, Fischer's excellent new idea injects a little extra spice into White's

play. After the natural interposition, 12...♗d7, White plans either 13.♕d4 or 13.♕c2, followed by ♗e3–d4, when Black's bishop seems somewhat misplaced. After some thought, Petrosian instead opts for a brave, if unclear exchange sacrifice. Fischer declines, judging that the longer-term dynamic and structural elements in White's game already tell heavily in his favour.

12...♕d7 13.♖e1
Fischer instinctively rejects 13.♗b5 axb5 14.♕xa8 0–0, and if, say 15.♕a5 d4 16.♘xb5 ♗b7, believing that he needn't court complications. In such positions, Black's lively bishops and lead in development offer compensation of a murky, double-edged kind that Petrosian frequently favoured.

13...♕xa4 14.♘xa4 ♗e6 15.♗e3 0–0
Black's severely constrained IQP lacks vitality and his game is decidedly passive. White's queen's knight and bishop exert considerable pressure on the queenside dark squares. After the text-move, White exchanges Black's livelier bishop, ensuring an enduring

advantage. White also stands well, however, after 15...♘d7 16.♗d4, and if 16...0–0 17.f4 (or possibly 17.a3, and if 17...a5 18.f4).

16.♗c5 ♖fe8 17.♗xe7 ♖xe7 18.b4
White controls c5 and may ultimately create a dangerous passed b-pawn. Black's immobile a-pawn is also a target. The attempt to contest control in the open c-file, by playing 18...♖c7, only backfires, after 19.♖ac1, and if 19...♖xc1 20.♖xc1 ♖b8 21.a3.

18...♔f8 19.♘c5 ♗c8 20.f3 ♖ea7

Black struggles for activity. After 20...♘d7, seeking to exchange knights, White retains a clear advantage, by playing 21.♖ec1, and if 21...♘e5 22.♗f1. White is also much better after 20...♖xe1+ 21.♖xe1 ♘d7 22.♖c1 (Garry Kasparov), and if 22...♔e7 23.♘xd7, followed by ♖c5.

21.♖e5 ♗d7 22.♘xd7+
Fischer voluntarily exchanges his 'good' knight for Black's ostensibly 'bad' bishop to ensure that Black remains passive. A strikingly concrete

transformational idea, Fischer plans to strengthen his positional grip, by a rook incursion in the c-file, followed by the advance of his king, via f2, towards its potentially most commanding (d4) post. Fischer judges that Black can scarcely ever hope to solve his a-file problems, by playing ...a5, as this is only ever likely to permit White to achieve a (winning) passed pawn on b5.

22...♖xd7 23.♖c1 ♖d6
White's rook now reaches the powerful 7ᵗʰ rank. Black daren't, however, allow White's rook to reach c6, as this would force Black's rook to return to wholly abject defence on a7.

24.♖c7 ♘d7 25.♖e2 g6

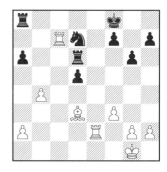

Deprived of any readily convincing queenside or central choices, Petrosian turns to the kingside, in the hope that he might eventually exert some countervailing pressure on that flank.

26.♔f2 h5 27.f4 h4 28.♔f3 f5 29.♔e3 d4+
Even if this move only further weakens

Black's d-pawn, and allows White to dream of a decisive doubling of rooks on the 7th rank, Black can hardly allow White's king to occupy d4 (followed by ♖ec2–c6).

30.♔d2 ♘b6

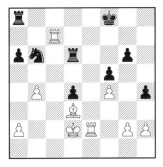

In a last desperate bid for activity, Black allows White to double his rooks on the 7th rank. White's immediate threat was to play ♗c4, followed by ♔d3, surrounding Black's d-pawn.

After 30...a5 31.b5, and if 31...♘f6 32.♗c4 ♘e4+ 33.♔d3 ♖b8 34.g4, White breaks through on the kingside (Kasparov).

31.♖ee7 ♘d5 32.♖f7+ ♔e8 33.♖b7 ♘xb4

Black allows mate, but must surely also lose anyway, after either 33... ♖b6 34.♖xb6 ♘xb6 35.♖g7, or 33...♖b8 34.♖a7, and if 34...♖a8 (otherwise ♖h7) 35.♖xa8+ ♔xf7 36.♗c4.

34.♗c4 1–0

Or if 34...a5 35.♖h7 ♖f6 36.♖h8+ ♖f8 37.♗f7+.

Fischer achieved a whopping 88% success rate (+17=3-1) in his three 1971 Candidates' matches. No wonder all of the Soviets quaked in their boots. As the 1972 Match of the Century loomed ever closer, the whole world sensed that a seismic power shift was imminent. Soviet grandmasters and world champions had dominated chess for almost three decades but how could anyone stop Bobby Fischer. At least Boris Spassky still had a slim plus score against him.

At the beginning of 1972, however, most chess fans simply wondered whether FIDE (and any sundry others) would actually succeed in getting the unpredictable challenger to turn up and play against Spassky. Early signs were promising. First, Iceland won an open tender process to hold the match, to which both parties agreed without much fuss. Fischer then began to train intensely, at a retreat in the Catskill Mountains, where his regime included challenging physical as well as chess training routines.

Fischer seemed relaxed, fit, well-prepared and up for battle. But, as the match neared, he began to show last minute signs of unease about the (already) signed and agreed match contract. Almost without warning, Fischer suddenly demanded that he receive a share of the gate receipts on top of the already agreed share of TV and film rights. The Icelanders, who had budgets to balance, understandably baulked. Fischer refused to fly to

Iceland for the scheduled match start. What next?

In rapid response, FIDE President, Max Euwe, announced a two day match postponement but Fischer still wouldn't budge. Step forward, wealthy London financier, Jim Slater, who then guaranteed $125,000 to double the prize fund, which Fischer warmly welcomed. Upping the patriotic ante, US Secretary of State, Henry Kissinger, also personally implored Fischer to play. To everyone's relief, Fischer was finally persuaded that he really ought to turn up.

With Fischer and Spassky both now in Reykjavik, the two protagonists, who had the utmost respect for each other, could finally communicate, more or less directly. Both dearly wanted this match to take place. After some further, nervous give and take, Game 1, in fact, actually commenced, if a week or so behind schedule. In that game, however, Fischer rashly over-pressed, converting a dead-level endgame into a quite unnecessary loss, and he flared up all over again.

Fischer now railed against the positioning and noise of the cameras filming the event, which the organisers genuinely sought to address. Without bothering to check what they'd done, however, the challenger decided it wasn't enough. In a continuing strop, Fischer forfeited Game 2. Long

suffering Chief Arbiter, Lothar Schmid, fortunately persuaded both players to play Game 3 in an ante-room. Fischer won Game 3, following which he returned to play out the rest of the match on the main stage (with no cameras).

Game 3, Fischer's first ever win against Spassky, broke a significant psychological barrier. Ignoring the Game 2 forfeit, the score between the players, before Game 3, favoured Spassky (+4=3). Following an audacious opening innovation, in Game 3, that set a recurring match pattern, Fischer brilliantly outplayed his opponent. By Game 6, an unnerved Spassky trailed by a point. By Game 13, Fischer had stretched his lead to three. Following a win in Game 21, Fischer finally took the world title by a well-merited, four point margin (+7-3=11).

The East-West political symbolism of the match was stark but should not be over-stressed. The protagonists were not two stereotypical Cold War combatants. Even to the non-chess player, something much more humanly gripping was afoot. This human interest derived predominantly from the challenger's obviously troubled psyche, as patently vulnerable as it was frequently difficult. Spassky's compelling sportsmanship and obvious fellow feeling for Fischer perhaps only ultimately kept this historic show on the road. We owe him much.

B.Spassky – R.Fischer

Game 3, World Championship, Reykjavik 1972

Modern Benoni

1.d4 ♘f6 2.c4 e6 3.♘f3 c5 4.d5 exd5 5.cxd5 d6 6.♘c3 g6 7.♘d2 ♘bd7 8.e4 ♗g7 9.♗e2 0–0 10.0–0 ♖e8 11.♕c2

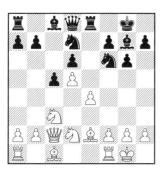

None of this would have surprised Spassky. S.Gligoric-R.Fischer, Palma de Mallorca 1970, had gone 11.a4 ♘e5 12.♕c2 g5 13.♘f3 ♘xf3+ 14.♗xf3 h6 15.♗d2 a6 16.♗e2 ♕e7 17.♖ae1 ♕e5 18.♔h1 ♕d4 19.f3 ♘h5 20.♘b5?! (a dubious choice) 20...axb5 21.♗xb5 ♕e5 22.♗c3 ♕e7 23.♗xe8 ♕xe8 24.♗xg7 ♔xg7 25.b4 cxb4 26.♕b2+ ♕e5 27.♕xb4 ♘f4, with a firm grip on the kingside dark squares (Black won). Fischer's startling reply to Spassky's slight move order twist, however, almost certainly came as a shock.

Black now offers his knight for capture on h5, judging that Black's bishop pair and easy kingside development will compensate for his broken kingside pawns. No doubt ready to confront a repeat of plans based on ...♘e5, followed by ...g5, Spassky

brooded for some 30 minutes (not a good sign) before taking up Black's challenge.

11...♘h5 12.♗xh5 gxh5 13.♘c4

Caught out, it seems, by Fischer's bold concept, Spassky reacts listlessly. White eventually only manages to exchange this knight, on g4 (via e3), rounding out Black's kingside pawns with, at best, equality. More promising is 13.a4, and if 13...♘e5 14.♘d1 ♕h4 15.♘e3 (or first 15.♖a3), when S.Gligoric-L.Kavalek, Skopje Olympiad 1972, continued 15...♘g4 16.♘xg4 hxg4 17.♘c4 ♕f6 18.♗d2 ♕g6 19.♗c3, with a slight edge for White (who won).

13...♘e5 14.♘e3

Black's game is also sufficiently active after 14.♘xe5 ♗xe5 15.♘e2 ♕h4, when the attempt to wrest an initiative, in A.Goryachkina-M.Vokac, Pardubice 2011, only rebounded in Black's favour, after 16.f4 ♗g7 17.♗d2 ♕e7 18.♗c3 ♕xe4 19.♕xe4 ♖xe4 20.♘g3 ♖e3 21.♗xg7 ♔xg7 22.♘xh5+ ♔g6 23.♘g3 ♗f5 24.♖ae1 ♖ae8 25.♖xe3 ♖xe3 26.♔f2 ♖d3 (though White held).

14...♕h4 15.♗d2 ♘g4 16.♘xg4 hxg4 17.♗f4 ♕f6 18.g3?

Why Spassky didn't play 18. ♗g3 (or 17.♖ae1), is a mystery. White's pawn on e4 now becomes a long-term target. Black can also advantageously gain space by advancing his queenside pawn majority. White's enduring problem is that he can no longer expect to play f3 (to bolster e4 and maintain a healthy central pawn chain), without allowing the structurally disruptive reply ...gxf3.

18...♗d7 19.a4 b6 20.♖fe1 a6 21.♖e2 b5 22.♖ae1 ♕g6 23.b3 ♖e7 24.♕d3 ♖b8 25.axb5 axb5 26.b4 c4

Black's powerful passed c-pawn will remain a constant thorn in White's side for the rest of the game, severely constraining White's defensive options. In all likelihood, White can no longer expect to hold his rickety e-pawn, as Black has a virtually free attacking hand on the kingside and in the centre.

27.♕d2 ♖be8 28.♖e3 h5 29.♖3e2 ♔h7 30.♖e3 ♔g8 31.♖3e2

What else could White do? White's sole remaining hope is that, after his e-pawn drops, he might retain drawing chances, due to the presence of op-

posite colour bishops in the resultant queen and bishop endgame.

31...♗xc3 32.♕xc3 ♖xe4 33.♖xe4 ♖xe4 34.♖xe4 ♕xe4 35.♗h6

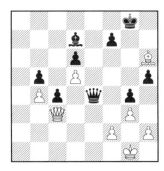

Black's queen and bishop, however, cannot be prevented from lining up with checkmating force on the h7–b1 diagonal. White can briefly slow down the process but his chronically weak light squares determine his end. White has no real counterplay. Black also wins quickly, after 35.♕f6 ♕b1+ 36.♔g2 ♗f5, and if 37.♕g5+ ♗g6 38.♗xd6 f6, followed by ...♗e4+.

35...♕g6 36.♗c1 ♕b1 37.♔f1 ♗f5 38.♔e2

White's king makes a last, vain dash towards the centre. Black, however, keeps queens on the board and simply hunts down White's monarch there, too.

38...♕e4+ 39.♕e3 ♕c2+ 40.♕d2 ♕b3 41.♕d4 ♗d3+ 0–1

Or if 42.♔e3 ♕d1, forcing mate or the win of White's bishop.

Resolute Bite

Anatoly Karpov

23. Anatoly Karpov, in 1977

Sadly, having become a globally recognised celebrity and established chess as a sport that could attract a popular following and substantial sponsorship, Bobby Fischer effectively 'retired' from the game after Reykjavik. We didn't know this at the time (neither did he) but it gradually crept up on everyone. No one could coax Fischer back to the board. He even walked away from an astronomical $5m purse, guaranteed by the Philippines, to host his scheduled 1975 world title defence in that country.

As the years went by, it became clear that US chess history was repeating itself in the most melancholy way. Just as Paul Morphy had turned his back on the game, in mid-19th century, an equally troubled, Bobby Fischer, did, too. Unlike Morphy, Fischer did, at least, pick up the pieces for one last reprise of his glorious mastery. In 1992, fully twenty years on from their Reykjavik battle, he and Spassky met in a somewhat incongruous, so-called 'Return World Championship Match'. Fischer again won (+10=15-5), after which his chess dried up completely.

Anatoly Karpov (b 1951) was the main and worthy beneficiary of Fischer's 1975 chess abdication. A new kind of wholly committed, chess sports-kid on the Soviet block, Karpov had grown up in and imbibed all the lessons of the Fischer era. Drop the 'state' before 'professional'. While he enjoyed all the early benefits of old-style Soviet chess coaching and training, Karpov began to leave much of the more outmoded baggage of that old 'school' behind, as he entered his late-teens and twenties.

The young Karpov was clear that Fischer had decisively changed the game's character. In his early biographical, *Chess is My Life*, co-authored with Aleksandr

Roshal, for example, Karpov asserted that 'Fischer returned the sharpness to chess, made it tougher ... raised universalism ... demonstrating amazing technique ... splendid combinational and positional play, a feel for the initiative, and an ability to attack ... most characteristic ... his competitive nature [and] exploitation ... of every chance to the last'.

Karpov felt driven to the firm conclusion that 'the competitive side in chess will continue to prevail ... over the creative ... an enormous role ... played by the availability of information [continually forcing players] to seek something new, and to change their favourite systems and variations'. Already with many tough matches to his name, he added that 'psychology in chess has become very important especially in matches ... to understand yourself ... your opponent ... to utilise this knowledge [well] at the board'.

Tough and hard working, Karpov developed at pace. Botvinnik briefly helped train him, when first brought to his notice, aged 12. By 1968, he was World Junior Champion. Among subsequent heights, he tied 1st/2nd equal, with Leonid Stein, at Moscow 1971, and by sharing 1st/2nd places, with Viktor Korchnoi, at the 1973 Leningrad Interzonal, he became a world title Candidate. Through 1974, Karpov consecutively defeated Lev Polugaevsky (+3=5), Boris Spassky (+4=6-1) and Viktor Korchnoi (+3=19-2), to become Fischer's challenger, a huge threat.

Despite his mere 23 years, Karpov had already demonstrably shown that only Fischer might match him in strength. In mid-1974, having just defeated Spassky in the Candidates' series, he already clearly merited his promotion to top board in the USSR team at that year's Nice Olympiad. In those years, he played with a remarkably sure strategic and tactical touch and with unusual rapidity. With a powerful team behind him, moreover, Karpov's depth of theoretical preparation, especially with White, matched anyone's.

Karpov successfully aspired to Fischer's universality and wholly committed battling mode. While his greatest strength arguably lay in logical planning and superior strategy, he neither drew back from tactics, when logic required such paths, nor was he incapable of executing the very finest of chess combinations. After going one down, in Game 2 of their 1974 match, Korchnoi severely criticised his provocative opening choice. In every aspect of that wonderful battle, however, Karpov was quite simply deadly.

A.Karpov – V.Korchnoi

Game 2, Candidates final, Moscow 1974

Sicilian Defence: Dragon

1.e4 c5 2.♘f3 d6 3.d4 cxd4 4.♘xd4 ♘f6 5.♘c3 g6 6.♗e3 ♗g7 7.f3 ♘c6 8.♕d2 0–0 9.♗c4 ♗d7

After the alternative, 9...♕a5 10.0–0–0 ♗d7 11.h4 ♘e5 12.♗b3 ♖fc8, Karpov had already impressively shown his strategic, theoretical and combinational, anti-Dragon mettle twice. A.Karpov-A.Whiteley, European Team Championships, Bath 1973, had continued calmly, 13.♔b1 ♘c4 14.♗xc4 ♖xc4 15.♘b3, ♕d8 16.♗h6 ♕f8 17.♗xg7 ♕xg7 18.g4 ♗e6 19.♘d4 ♘d7 20.h5, with a powerful attack (White won).

Prior to that, A.Karpov-E.Gik, Moscow University Championship 1969, had brilliantly gone 13.h5

13...♘xh5 14.♗h6 ♗xh6 15.♕xh6 ♖xc3 16.bxc3 ♕xc3 17.♘e2 ♕c5 18.g4 ♘f6 19.g5 ♘h5 20.♖xh5 gxh5 21.♖h1 ♕e3+ 22.♔b1 ♕xf3 23.♖xh5 e6 (or if 23...♘g6 24.♕xh7+ ♔f8 25.♖h1! - Karpov) 24.g6 ♘xg6 25.♕xh7+ ♔f8 26.♖f5 ♕xb3+ 27.axb3 exf5 28.♘f4, and White (again) won.

10.h4 ♖c8 11.♗b3 ♘e5 12.0–0–0 ♘c4

Korchnoi follows a then current main line, only to be mightily wrong-footed by White's 19th move. Blocking alternatives, based on ...h5 (at various points), are also possible.

A.Karpov-A.Sznapik, Dubai Olympiad 1986, however, later brilliantly continued 12...h5 13.♗g5 ♖c5 14.♔b1 b5 (14... ♖e8 may be best) 15.g4 hxg4 16.h5 ♘xh5 17.♘d5 ♖e8 18.♖xh5 gxh5 19.♕h2 ♖c4 (or if 19...♖xd5 20.♗xd5 ♕b6 21.♘f5 ♗xf5 22.exf5 ♘xf3 23.♕xh5, with 'unpleasant consequences' - Karpov) 20.♗xc4 bxc4 21.♕xh5 f6 22.f4 ♘f7 23.♗h4 ♕b8 24.♖h1 c3 25.b3 ♕b7 26.f5 ♘e5 27.♘e6 1–0.

13.♗xc4 ♖xc4 14.h5 ♘xh5 15.g4 ♘f6 16.♘de2

White has several other interesting alternatives (both here and at move 14). This retreat, however, has the advantage of minimising the risk of running into any structurally damaging exchange sacrifice on c3, while simultaneously retaining options to play this knight (via f4 or g3), towards the kingside.

16...♕a5 17.♗h6 ♗xh6 18.♕xh6 ♖fc8 19.♖d3 ♖4c5

Korchnoi sank into deep thought before playing this move. No doubt ready to meet either of White's then known alternatives (19.♖d5 and 19.g5), he was apparently caught out by Karpov's more critical choice. By further protecting c3, White's rook (on d3) minimises any risk of structurally damaging exchange sacrifices on c3, and supports the threat of g5. Black attempts a lateral 4th rank defence, but it fails. Botvinnik suggested 19...♕d8, but after 20.♘f4, and if 20...♕f8 21.♕h2, White's twin threats of ♘fd5 and g5, maintain lasting pressure.
Black also suffers after 19...♗e6 20.g5 ♘h5 21.♘f4, and if 21...♕e5 22.♘xh5 gxh5 23.♕xh5, with 'an appreciable advantage' (Karpov). A.Ioffe-A.Reshko, Leningrad 1980, then later went 23...♔f8 24.♕xh7 ♕xg5+ 25.♔b1 ♔e8 26.♕h2 ♕a5 27.♖xd6 exd6 28.♕xd6

1-0. Black also fails to trap White's king, after 21...♖xc3 22.bxc3 ♖xc3 23.♘xh5, and if, say 23...♕a3+ 24.♔d2 ♖xd3+ 25.cxd3 ♕b2+ 26.♔e3 gxh5 27.♕xh5, with a winning advantage.

20.g5 ♖xg5 21.♖d5
This fine move, coupled with White's even more dramatic 24th move, wholly refutes Black's defensive idea. Black's knight on f6 will inevitably fall, leading to a crush in the h-file.

21...♖xd5 22.♘xd5 ♖e8 23.♘ef4 ♗c6 24.e5 ♗xd5

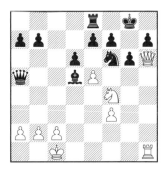

Or if 24...dxe5 25.♘xf6+ exf6 26.♘h5, and mates.

25.exf6 exf6 26.♕xh7+ ♔f8 27.♕h8+ 1-0
Or if 27...♔e7 28.♘xd5+ ♕xd5 29.♖e1+, winning Black's queen.

In refusing to defend his world title, Fischer claimed that he had only 'resigned' FIDE's 'version' and actually remained 'world champion'. His refusal to play in FIDE's scheduled 1975 title defence was, in his eyes, solely FIDE's fault. At an emergency meeting of its General Assembly, in early 1975, FIDE had voted down one of his two remaining, 'non-negotiable' match conditions. The first, that the winner should be the first to score 10 wins (draws not counting), was approved. The second, that the champion should retain the title, in the event of a (highly unlikely) 9-9 score, was considered unfair and rejected.

Karpov strongly objected to both proposals. He may, however, have accepted any FIDE decision to safeguard his challenge but wasn't even put to that test. Why Fischer couldn't bring himself to accept FIDE's compromise ultimately defies all rationality and resulted only in the most tragic own goal. Towards the late-1970s, Frank Brady judged that 'Fischer was depressed [and] in retrospect ... upset at having

passed on the chance to acquire a portion of that $5m purse in 1975 ... having to make ends meet was wearing'.

Despite being given plenty of opportunity to re-think his position, by the ever patient (and scrupulously fairminded) FIDE President, Max Euwe, Fischer wouldn't budge. Accordingly, Karpov became the first (and still only) world champion ever to have won the title, without having to play either in a match, or, as in 1948, a match-tournament. This inevitably raised an unfortunate question mark against Karpov's world title credibility, even if such doubts were entirely misplaced. He was soon to dispel them completely.

While Karpov waited for his first scheduled challenger to emerge from the 1975-78 world championship qualifying cycle, he embarked on a highly active period of participation in top international tournaments and team

24. Anatoly Karpov (r.), Max Euwe and wife, Caro Bergman: Max Euwe's 75th birthday reception, Amsterdam 1976

events. During this period, the new champion chalked up Bobby Fischer-like triumph upon triumph. He also remained open to private negotiations to contest some kind of match, against Fischer, but what little ensued in respect to these matters, sadly went nowhere.

From 1975 to early 1978, Karpov scored an outstanding eight 1st places and one share of

1ˢᵗ/2ⁿᵈ places in the strongest international tournaments. He also won
the 1976 USSR Championship, almost
as an afterthought. Such dominance
matched anything that had been
achieved by any other great player.
Karpov, moreover, played like a world
champion, combining the dedicated,
all-round, Botvinnik-inspired energy
and rigour of the old Soviet school,
with the freer, more intensely committed and competitive dash of the
emerging, post-Fischer era.

As Fischer dropped out, Viktor Korchnoi (1931-2016) found an extraordinary new lease of life, in his late
forties, to become Karpov's first challenger. Remarkably, in 1978, Korchnoi
posed an even greater threat to Karpov
than he had in their 1974 Candidates'
final. Feeling his career to be unduly
hindered by Soviet officialdom, Korchnoi had since defected to the West and
been roundly denounced as a 'traitor'.
Still fit, extraordinarily hard working,
on the right side of 50 and with deep
scores to settle, Korchnoi determined
to do all-out battle.

No love was lost, in the1977-78
Candidates' match series, between
Korchnoi and all of three Soviet opponents: he consecutively defeated Petrosian (+2-1=9), Polugaevsky (+5-1=7) and
Spassky (+7-4=7). Although the Petrosian match was a mutually nervous affair, Korchnoi's clear superiority over
all three matches sent shivers down
the spine of the Communist Party. Just

as they had, in the 1972 Match of the
Century, the USSR experienced a real,
if different sort of Cold War frisson, in
1978. Korchnoi, though no American
foe, was perhaps even worse, a reviled
'enemy' of the USSR and temporarily
'stateless'.

Fortunately for the Soviets, their
state-funded gladiator remained
clearly higher rated and the bookies'
favourite. Yet the 1978 match, which
took place in Baguio City in the Phil-
ippines, proved to be as close a contest
between the two players, as in their
1974 Candidates' match. Aged 47, Korchnoi, who really had hit an incom-
parably high career peak, recovered a
three point deficit to force a 5-5 tie (in
wins), only to lose the next and decisive 32ⁿᵈ match game, to go down, 6-5
(in wins), with 21 draws.

Note that FIDE kept faith with the
'unlimited' match principle, except
that they sensibly reduced Fischer's
'first to ten wins' requirement to a
more practical 'six'. Hearteningly, the
1m Swiss franc prize fund (worth double today) compared well with Reykjavik. Karpov (and team) won more of
the key openings theoretical, psychological, combinational and technical
battles, if only marginally. Korchnoi's
Open Defence, against the Spanish
Opening, which featured eight times,
proved to be a key Achilles Heel, in Korchnoi's armoury, twice breached early
on in the match.

A.Karpov – V.Korchnoi

Game 14, World Championship, Baguio City 1978

Spanish Opening

1.e4 e5 2.♘f3 ♘c6 3.♗b5 a6 4.♗a4 ♘f6 5.0–0 ♘xe4 6.d4 b5 7.♗b3 d5 8.dxe5 ♗e6 9.c3 ♗c5

The players resume a theoretical battle begun in Games 2 and 4 of the match (both drawn). Karpov turned to 9.♘bd2, in Games 8 and 10, and to 9.♕e2, in Game 12 (in which Karpov scored a win and two draws).

10.♘bd2 0–0 11.♗c2 ♗f5

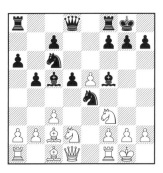

Bent Larsen had used this move in a famous win against Bobby Fischer, at the 2nd Piatigorsky Cup, Santa Monica 1966. Older alternatives include:

11...♘xd2 12.♕xd2, and if 12...f6 13.exf6 ♖xf6 14.♘d4 ♘xd4 15.cxd4 ♗b6 16.a4 ♖b8 17.axb5 axb5 18.♕c3 ♕d6 19.♗e3, as in Em.Lasker-A.Rubinstein, St Petersburg 1914, in which White's bind on the queenside dark squares and still mobile 3–2 kingside pawn majority offer White slightly the better chances (White won);

11...f5, and if 12.♘b3 ♗b6 13.♘bd4 ♘xd4 14.♘xd4 ♗xd4 15.cxd4 f4 16.f3 ♘g3 17.hxg3 fxg3 18.♕d3 ♗f5 19.♕xf5 ♖xf5 20.♗xf5 ♕h4 21.♗h3 ♕xd4+ 22.♔h1 ♕xe5 23.♗d2 ♕xb2 24.♗f4, as in the utterly confusing, V.Smyslov-S. Reshevsky, USSR v USA Radio Match 1945, which may well be better for White (who won); and

11...♘xf2 12.♖xf2 f6 13.exf6 ♕xf6, English amateur, Vernon Dilworth's romantic, if perhaps slightly risky offer of knight and bishop for rook plus a pawn and a certain kingside initiative.

12.♘b3 ♗g4

Korchnoi continues in Larsen's footsteps but no doubt due to White's fine follow-up play (and especially White's new, 17th move), later switched to 12...♗g6, in Game 6 between the same players, at Meran 1981. That game continued 13.♘fd4 ♗xd4 14.cxd4 a5 15.♗e3 a4 16.♘c1 a3 17.b3 f6, with unclear complications (Black won).

A.Karpov-A.Jussupow, Moscow 1983, however, later saw 16.♘d2 a3 17.♘xe4 axb2 18.♖b1 ♗xe4 19.♖xb2 ♕d7 20.♗d3 ♗xd3 21.♕xd3 ♖fb8 22.♖fb1 b4 23.h3 h6 24.♖c1 ♖b6 25.♕b1 ♖ab8 26.♖c5, with pressure on the queenside dark squares and in the c-file (White won).

13.h3 ♗h5 14.g4 ♗g6 15.♗xe4 dxe4

16.♘xc5 exf3 17.♗f4

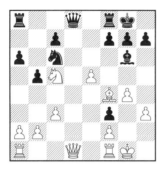

This is a significant discovery, apparently missed by Korchnoi in his analysis, in *The Encyclopaedia of Chess Openings*. To save Black's pawn on f3, Korchnoi must now exchange queens, leaving White with a clear lead in development, control in the d-file and prospects of eventually winning Black's pawn on f3. After 17...♕e7, White plays 18.♕d5 ♘a5 19.b4 ♘c4 20.♕xf3, and if 20...♘xe5 21.♗xe5 ♕xe5 22.♘d7, winning.

17...♕xd1 18.♖axd1 ♘d8 19.♖d7 ♘e6 20.♘xe6 fxe6 21.♗e3 ♖ac8

Black has no active prospects. After an imminent ♔h2–g3, White will tie Black down to long-term defence of his f-pawn and prepare the ground for the future advance of his h- and g-pawns. Exchanging one pair of rooks, by playing 21...♖f7, and if 22.♖fd1 ♖xd7 23.♖xd7 ♖c8 24.♗c5, only entrenches White's domination on the 7ᵗʰ rank.

22.♖fd1 ♗e4 23.♗c5 ♖fe8 24.♖7d4 ♗d5 25.b3 a5 26.♔h2 ♖a8 27.♔g3 ♖a6
Black embarks on a manoeuvre that effectively forces White to give up an exchange for two pawns, obtaining good winning prospects. After the passive alternative 27...a4, and if 28.c4 bxc4 29.bxc4 ♗c6, however, White can play 30.♗b4 (with a3 in mind), and if 30...a3 31.♖1d3 ♖a4 32.♗d2, with continuing good prospects on the kingside.

28.h4 ♖c6 29.♖xd5 exd5 30.♖xd5 ♖ce6 31.♗d4 c6 32.♖c5 ♖f8

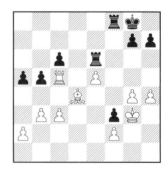

This move loses. Karpov can now win one of Black's queenside pawns, after which he will also eventually win Black's f-pawn. Black had to play 32...♖d8, and hope to hold the difficult endgame that arises after 33.♔xf3 ♖d5 34.♖xd5 (not 34.♔e4? ♖exe5+) 34...cxd5. Karpov then intended 35.a3, followed by b4 (creating 'a fortress on the queenside') and the subsequent advance of White's king-side pawns (to create two connected passed pawns in the e- and f-files).

33.a4 bxa4 34.bxa4 g6 35.♖xa5 ♖ee8 36.♖a7 ♖f7 37.♖a6 ♖c7 38.♗c5 ♖cc8 39.♗d6 ♖a8 40.♖xc6 ♖xa4 41.♔xf3 h5 Korchnoi sealed this move, but White now has three good pawns for the exchange and is clearly winning.

42.gxh5 gxh5 43.c4 ♖a2 44.♖b6 ♔f7 45.c5 ♖a4 46.c6 ♔e6 47.c7 ♔d7 48.♖b8 ♖c8 49.♔e3 ♖xh4 50.e6+ 1–0 Or if 50...♔xd6 (or 50...♔xe6 51.♗g3) 51.♖xc8 ♖c4 52.♖d8+ ♔xc7 53.e7, and wins.

Still defying his years, Viktor Korchnoi consecutively defeated Petrosian, Polugaevsky and Hübner, in the 1980-81 Candidates' matches to win through to a second title challenge. At Meran 1981, however, Karpov comfortably defeated his 50 year-old opponent (+6-2=10). The twenty year age difference may have weighed heavier than before. The vehemence of a deplorably cynical Soviet campaign to harass Korchnoi's wife and son, however, which must ultimately have emanated from the upper echelons of the Communist Party, perhaps loomed even larger.

Five years on from Korchnoi's defection to the West, in early 1976, there was certainly no excuse (if ever there was one) for the USSR to continue to deny Korchnoi's wife and son the right to emigrate and join him. Despite widespread international condemnation, including direct intervention by FIDE's president (Fridrik Olafsson), Soviet functionaries all too vindictively played on the family's vulnerability. The Party, moreover, also continued to ban Soviet players from competing against Korchnoi, in all but formally organised FIDE events.

These melancholy years coincided with an increasing sense of pending Soviet social, economic and political implosion not just within the Party but widely. The late-1970s and early 1980s, indeed, marked a particularly sclerotic period in which old school reactionaries still ruled most roosts before gradually giving way to the rise of the reformist spirit of Mikhail Gorbachev. After Meran, the Korchnoi family eventually obtained the requisite exit visas and the anti-Korchnoi playing ban ceased. Amelioration coincided, however, only with Korchnoi's gradually declining threat at a chessboard.

Through 1981-84, Karpov continued to win event after event in ever more brilliant displays of his wonderful chess. Entering his thirties, Karpov remained in peak playing condition and clear world number one. As Korchnoi's form faded, however, a new and impeccably home-grown Soviet star, Garry Kasparov (b 1963), emerged to replace him as challenger, marking the start of an entirely new rivalry that would persist for much more than a decade.

Karpov and Kasparov were both children of the new, much better re-munerated, post-Fischer age of total commitment and the first Soviet world champions no longer reliant on old-style state professional support. They benefited, too, from the way old-style Soviet politics was beginning to crum-ble. As long as elite sports stars con-tinued to perform well and didn't rock too many political boats, they gained increasing personal freedoms, not least to retain most of their increasing earnings.

The professional game had quite radically changed. In *Chess is My Life*, Karpov summed it up this way: 'Botvin-nik could permit himself long breaks ... and altogether didn't play a great deal. Nowadays a player can't permit himself this ... if you don't play for half a year, you begin to sense deterioration ... the feeling of something having been lost, and you lose confidence ... as if you have to begin studying something ... For this reason a player endeavours to compete in events more or less regularly'.

Karpov and Kasparov both played the game this way. According to Kar-pov, to Botvinnik, chess theory 'was still to a considerable extent virgin land', which allowed him to develop and introduce 'entire new systems'. In the much faster-moving, information-rich territory that typified late-20ᵗʰ century chess, however, the dynamic had changed. The modern top player had a good grasp of systems. He or she now had to work ceaselessly to unearth ever more concretely detailed varia-tional underpinnings.

Through the 1980s and beyond, Karpov and Kasparov remained exem-plars in keeping on top of this continu-ously runaway challenge. Making the best use of dedicated, ever costlier and expanding coaching and analytical teams, Karpov and Kasparov gener-ated by far the most creative and tell-ingly innovative ideas in those years. When they met in their first world title match, at Moscow 1984-85, Karpov was marginal favourite. Few, however, foresaw the highly unusual course of what turned out to be an interminably almighty battle.

As in 1978 and 1981, the race was to be first to score six wins, draws not counting. After only nine games, how-ever, Karpov had sprinted to a 4-0 lead and already the match seemed over. Somehow Kasparov dug in, although he first went 0-5 down, after Game 27. Surprisingly, Karpov couldn't then nail that last crucial win. After wins in Games 47 and 48 (and five months match duration), Kasparov closed to 3-5, at which point FIDE president, Florencio Campomanes, dramatically halted the match, declaring it 'ended without decision'.

What exactly happened still isn't wholly clear. Campomanes, who un-questionably had the authority to act as he did, seems to have been pressed by the Soviet organisers to find some face-saving way to stop what had cer-tainly become an over-lengthy contest of rapidly escalating cost and patently diminishing sporting validity. Both players initially complained but after private 'discussion' with Campomanes, hastily convened during a break in the middle of the Moscow Press Conference at which the decision had just been announced, they both abided by it.

Campomanes's decision at least drove matters not irrationally forward. Karpov retained his title. Kasparov gained a re-match, to begin later in 1985, in which the title would go to the winner of an old-style, maximum of 24 games contest. Should he lose that match, Karpov obtained a right, in turn, to his own re-match. Inimical to conventional budgeting and always at risk of descent into 'never ending' chaos, the 'unlimited' match concept was henceforth condemned to oblivion. Game 9 was one of the best played in this most strangely 'indecisive' first match.

A.Karpov – G.Kasparov

Game 9, World Championship, Moscow 1984

Queen's Gambit: Tarrasch

1.d4 d5 2.c4 e6 3.♘f3 c5 4.cxd5 exd5 5.g3 ♘f6 6.♗g2 ♗e7 7.0–0 0–0 8.♘c3 ♘c6 9.♗g5 cxd4 10.♘xd4 h6 11.♗e3 ♖e8 12.♕b3

Karpov called this move, 'the key to Black's position': by directly targeting Black's d- and b-pawns, White lures Black's queen's knight to the side of the board, thereby increasing White's grip on the key (d4) blockading square. Kasparov had successfully defended against all of 12.♕a4, 12.♕c2, and 12.a3, against Beliavsky, Korchnoi and Smyslov, in his 1983 Candidates' matches.

12...♘a5 13.♕c2 ♗g4 14.♘f5 ♖c8

So far, as in Game 7, which continued 15.♘xe7+ ♖xe7 16.♖ad1 ♕e8, and was eventually drawn: Karpov's reply is a significant improvement. Karpov's 14th move had only recently been introduced, in L.Portisch-M.Chandler, OHRA Amsterdam 1984, which indicated that White might retain the more active prospects, after 14...♗b4 15.♗d4, and if 15...♗xc3 16.♗xc3 ♖xe2 17.♕d3 (17.♕d1 may also be good).

15.♗d4 ♗c5 16.♗xc5 ♖xc5 17.♘e3 ♗e6
After his 17th move, Karpov considered that 'the opening dispute has concluded in White's favour'. In this position, Black's IQP is more a target than strength, forcing Black on to the defensive.
The dynamic, but doubtful 17...d4 18.♖ad1 ♘c6 19.♘xg4 ♘xg4 20.e3, and if 20...♘ge5 21.♕b3 d3 22.f4 ♘g4 23.♘e4, only favours White.

18.♖ad1 ♕c8 19.♕a4 ♖d8 20.♖d3 a6 21.♖fd1 ♘c4 22.♘xc4
Structurally, White clearly stands well. Black's game, however, remains

25. Kasparov v Karpov, Moscow 1984

remarkably resilient. Black defends comfortably, for example, after the imprecise pawn grab, 22.♘exd5 ♘xd5 23.♘xd5 ♗xd5 24.♗xd5 ♖dxd5 25.♖xd5 ♖xd5 26.♖xd5 ♘b6, and if 27.♕d4 ♘xd5 28.♕xd5 ♕c1+ 29.♔g2 ♕xb2.

22...♖xc4 23.♕a5 ♖c5 24.♕b6 ♖d7 25.♖d4

Karpov found it hard to settle on a clear plan around here. He considered that he might have caused Black more problems by earlier playing 19.♕b1, with the idea of ♖d3 and ♖fd1, or later 23.♕b3. Here, instead of meekly allowing queens to be exchanged, he recommended 'prophylactic measures such as 25.h3 or 25.a3'.

25...♕c7 26.♕xc7 ♖dxc7 27.h3
White retains his structural edge, but as long as Black can defend his IQP and prevent any significant advance by White on either flank,

he retains excellent drawing chances. Here, too, White achieves no more than dead equality after the premature pawn capture, 27.♘xd5 ♘xd5 28.♗xd5 ♗xd5 29.♖xd5 ♖xd5 30.♖xd5 ♖c2, and if 31.♖d8+ ♔h7 32.♖d7 ♖xb2 33.♖xf7 ♖xe2.

27...h5 28.a3 g6 29.e3 ♔g7 30.♔h2 ♖c4 31.♗f3 b5 32.♔g2 ♖7c5 33.♖xc4 ♖xc4 34.♖d4 ♔f8 35.♗e2 ♖xd4 36.exd4 ♔e7 37.♘a2 ♗c8 38.♘b4 ♔d6 39.f3 ♘g8 40.h4 ♘h6 41.♔f2 ♘f5 42.♘c2 f6

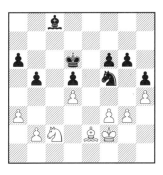

This move was sealed. Kasparov plans ...g5, seeking further simplification, by an exchange of pawns on g5 or h4. Karpov preferred 42...♗d7. While Kasparov has so far defended robustly, his inactive bishop, hemmed in by its own a-, b- and d-pawns, remains a little concerning. White may still also hope for an advantageous kingside break, such as after 42...♘g7 43.g4, and if 43...f6 44.♗d3 g5 45.♗g6 hxg4 46.h5, with a powerful, outside passed h-pawn (Karpov).

43.♗d3 g5 44.♗xf5 ♗xf5 45.♘e3 ♗b1 46.b4 gxh4?

Close to his drawing goal, Kasparov falls into the most extraordinary trap. After the correct retreat, 46...♗g6, White still has no clear winning path and Black's defence might, indeed, hold. In reply, Karpov now offers one of the most surprising pawn sacrifices ever played at high level. White wins quite brilliantly, by force.

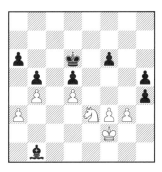

47.♘g2 hxg3+

Black must accept. After 47...♗g6, White recaptures on h4 with his knight and must eventually win Black's remaining h-pawn, by playing his king to h3, followed by ♘g2–f4, and ♔h4.

48.♔xg3 ♔e6

Black has no better move. However Black plays, he will ultimately be unable to prevent White's king and knight from penetrating deep into the heart of the kingside and either eventually overcoming Black's f-pawn or winning a variety of king and pawn endgames, such as after 48...♗g6 49.♘f4 ♗f7 50.♔h4, and if 50...♔e7 51.♘xh5 ♗xh5 (or 51...♔e6 52.♘g7+ ♔e7 53.♔g4 ♔d6) 52.♔xh5 ♔f7 53.♔h6 ♔e7 54.♔g7 ♔e6 55.♔g6.

49.♘f4+ ♔f5 50.♘xh5 ♔e6

The difference in relative strength of White's king and knight compared to Black's king and (now truly) 'bad' bishop is quite glaring. After 50...♗a2 51.♘g7+, followed by ♘e6–c5, White wins Black's a-pawn.

51.♘f4+ ♔d6 52.♔g4 ♗c2 53.♔h5 ♗d1

Black chooses to swap f-pawns but even this can't stem White's flow. After 53...♗b1, White plays 54.♔h6 ♗c2 55.♔g7 f5 56.♔f6, forcing 56...♗d1, anyway.

54.♔g6 ♔e7

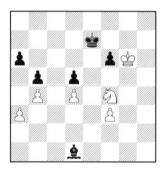

Nor can Black survive after 54...♗xf3 55.♔xf6, and if 55...♗e4 56.♘e6, followed by ♘c5.

55.♘xd5+ ♔e6 56.♘c7+ ♔d7 57.♘xa6 ♗xf3 58.♔xf6 ♔d6 59.♔f5 ♔d5 60.♔f4 ♗h1 61.♔e3

Black has achieved some activity, but only at the expense of going two pawns down and the rest is easy.

61...♔c4 62.♘c5 ♗c6

Or if 62...♔c3 63.♘e4+ ♔b3 (or 63...

♔c4 64.♘d6+) 64.d5 ♗g2 65.d6 ♗h3 66.♔d4 ♔xa3 67.♔c5, and wins.

63.♘d3 ♗g2 64.♘e5+ ♔c3 65.♘g6 ♔c4 66.♘e7 ♗b7 67.♔f5 ♗g2 68.♘d6+ ♔b3 69.♘xb5 ♔a4 70.♘d6 1-0

Kasparov's remarkable achievement in hauling back three wins from a perilous 0-5 score, in the 'undecided', 1984-85 world title match, made him marginal favourite in the title re-match that began, in September 1985 (again in Moscow). Having learned much, greatly tightened his match strategy and grown considerably in confidence, Kasparov fulfilled the favourite's role, winning by a deserved, two point margin (+5-3=16), in a thrilling contest. Over two title matches, however, the world's two best players only managed to 'equalise' (+8-8=56). This rivalry had a promising future.

Through 1986-90, Kasparov and Karpov contested three further world championship matches. At London-Leningrad 1986, Karpov's stipulated re-match, Kasparov again ran out victor, though only narrowly (+5-4=15). Karpov was then required to meet Andrei Sokolov in an unusually constituted super-final Candidates' play-off (necessitated by the congested nature of all these rapid fire title events), which he duly won comfortably (+4=7). The two K's shaped up a fourth time, at Seville 1987, tying (+4-4=16), with Kasparov retaining the title.

Karpov then had to contest a full Candidates' match series: he consecutively defeated Johann Hjartarson, Artur Yusupov and Jan Timman to set up his fifth and final title match against Kasparov, at Lyon-New York 1990. Kasparov again won narrowly (+4-3=17), thereby concluding one of the greatest world title rivalries in chess history. They both played magnificently. Kasparov 'won' by an overall margin of only two points (+21-19=104). The two might even have contested at least one further title match but for an unforeseen schism.

Karpov, still world number two, but entering his forties, was being chased down by a younger generation. He lost to Nigel Short (b 1965), in one of the two 1992 Candidates' semi-final matches. Short then defeated Timman in the Candidates' final, to earn the right to challenge Kasparov. Short and Kasparov, however, then shockingly abandoned FIDE, to play (at London 1993) for a 'new' world title, organised by a breakaway Professional Chess Association (PCA). In a hastily organised replacement (FIDE) title match (played in the Netherlands / Indonesia 1993), Karpov defeated Timman (+6-2=13).

This unfortunate disunity persisted well into the 2000s. Some top players played in only one or other of two rival world title series. Most played in both. Kasparov's PCA title retained a little extra 'sparkle', as Kasparov remained clear world number one. The

sad fact was, however, that both titles diminished in stature and organisational chaos ensued. Kasparov and Karpov, FIDE champion (until 1997), eyeballed each other closely but never found a way to play what might have been a most exciting sixth 'title' match.

At least the two Ks still faced off in many tournaments. Here, too, their rivalry was dominant. They both played in and won so many of the great tournaments played in the post-Fischer years, however, that it becomes hard to draw useful comparisons about who performed 'best'. In *Anatoly Karpov's Best Games*, Karpov contents himself with the statement that (up to 1994) he had played 'in around two hundred tournaments and matches (not counting team competitions, rapid-plays and blitz tournaments) and won well over a hundred of them'.

The year 1994 marked a special moment in Karpov's tournament career: he won, at Linares, scoring an undefeated, 11/13, well ahead of what many still consider to have been one of the strongest ever tournament fields. Kasparov and Alexei Shirov (8.5) finished in a share of 2nd/3rd places, fully 2.5 points adrift. Two future world champions, Vladimir Kramnik (7) and Vishy Anand (6.5), also took part. Karpov was proud of this achievement, in which just about everything worked well for him, as in this very fine win, against Kramnik.

A.Karpov – V.Kramnik

Linares 1994

Meran Defence

1.d4 d5 2.c4 c6 3.♘f3 ♘f6 4.♘c3 e6 5.e3 ♘bd7 6.♗d3 dxc4 7.♗xc4 b5 8.♗d3 a6 9.e4 c5 10.d5 c4 11.dxe6 fxe6 12.♗c2 ♗b7 13.0-0 ♕c7 14.♘g5 ♘c5 15.e5

The players sprint down a main line of Reynolds' Variation (10.d5). Karpov now essays an apparently 'new' temporary gambit idea. How deeply he had analysed this line at home, however, he doesn't make clear. Black must accept, as after 15...♕c6 16.f3, and if 16...♘fd7 17.♕e2, Black can't contemplate the natural 17...0-0-0, because of 18.♘f7.

15...♕xe5 16.♖e1 ♕d6 17.♕xd6 ♗xd6 18.♗e3

Simple development tells. Black's e-pawn will soon fall anyway. After 18...♘d3 19.♗xd3 cxd3 20.♖ad1, White will soon net both Black's e- and d-pawns, while the rash 18...♘g4, allows 19.♗xc5 ♗xc5 20.♖xe6+, and if 20...♔d7 21.♖d1+ ♔c7 22.♘ce4, with game-winning threats.

18...0-0 19.♖ad1 ♗e7

Black must sadly retreat this piece, or else suffer a material imbalance after 19...♖ad8 20.♖xd6 ♖xd6 21.♗xc5 ♖d2 22.♖c1, which is in White's favour.

20.♗xc5 ♗xc5 21.♘xe6 ♖fc8 22.h3

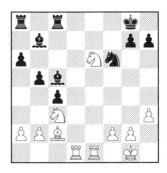

This is one of those wonderfully deep little moves, for which Karpov was famous. Black has an apparently healthy bishop pair and 3-2 queenside pawn majority but cannot readily put these ostensible 'advantages' to useful effect. White's well-placed rooks and powerful knight on e6 dominate too many key squares. Karpov's modest flank move envisages g4 and raises the prospect of dangerous space-gaining play on the kingside. White achieves nothing after 22.♘xc5 ♖xc5, and if 23.♖e7 ♖b8.

Kramnik now reacts too passively. With hindsight, Black's best is probably 22...♖ab8, and if 23.g4 ♗f3 24.♖d2, either 24...♗b4 or 24...h6, rather than 24...b4 25.♘a4 ♗a7 26.g5, as in V.Topalov-J.Lautier, Dos Hermanas 1994, which may still be in White's favour (though the game was drawn). Black can't safely play 22...b4, as after 23.♘a4 (a recurring resource), the retreat 23...♗a7, allows 24.♘xg7, with advantage to White.

22...♗f8 23.g4 h6

This move allows White to throw his f-pawn into the attacking mix, but Black also struggles after 23...♗f3 24.♖d4, and if 24...b4 25.♘a4, which again hurts.

24.f4 ♗f3 25.♖d2 ♗c6

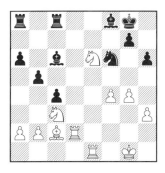

Now White can harry Back's knight but 25...b4 26.♘a4, was still unpalatable, such as after 26...♖ab8 27.♘xf8 ♖xf8 28.♘c5 a5 (28...♖fd8 29.♖xd8+ ♖xd8 30.♘xa6) 29.♗f5 ♖fd8 30.♗e6+ ♔h8 31.♖xd8+ ♖xd8 32.♗xc4 ♖d2 33.♖e5, threatening g5.

26.g5 hxg5 27.fxg5 ♘d7 28.♘xf8 ♘xf8

Another Black piece goes backwards. Black can't, however, allow 28...♖xf8

29.♖e6, when White forces material gain.

29.♖d6 b4 30.♘e4 ♗e8

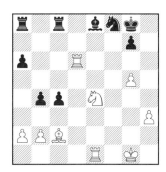

Kramnik has finally got in ...b4 securely. White's kingside menace and more active pieces, however, pose more serious problems than anything Black is likely to achieve on the queenside. After the text-move, White can manoeuvre his knight to a powerful outpost on f5. Karpov considered that 30...♗d7, and if 31.h4 ♖c6 or 31.♘g3 ♖e8, offered better defensive chances, although White might even then make promising ground on the kingside, such as after, say 31.♔g2, and if 31...♖e8 32.h4 ♗b5 33.♔g3 ♖e5 34.♔f4 ♖ae8 35.h5.

31.♘g3 ♖d8 32.♘f5 ♖xd6 33.♘xd6 ♗g6

Now also plagued by serious time shortage, Kramnik offers a pawn in a last, desperate bid for counterplay that Karpov simply refutes. After 33...♗d7, however, White retains a clear advantage, by playing 34.g6, threatening ♗e4, followed by ♗d5+.

34.♗xg6 ♘xg6 35.♘xc4 ♖d8

Karpov rejected the alternative, 35... ♖f8 36.♖e4, and if 36...♘f4 37.h4 ♔h7 38.♘e5, as no better than 'suicide'.

36.♖e4 b3 37.axb3 ♖d3 38.♔g2 ♖xb3 39.h4 ♘f8 40.♖e8 1-0 (Time forfeit)

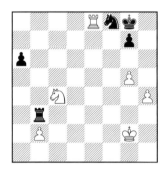

After 40...♔f7 (or if 40...♖b4 41.♖c8 ♔f7 42.h5), Karpov would have sealed 41.♘d6+. It is, however, perhaps unfortunate that he didn't have to demonstrate the win, which is almost certainly there (although much work remains necessary), after the move repetition, 41...♔g8 42.♘c4 ♔f7, and now 43.♖e3.

The Eyes Have it

Garry Kasparov

Following a one-sided, 1986 exhibition match defeat (0.5-5.5), against Kasparov, Tony Miles lamented that he had lost not just to 'a world champion [but to] a monster with 22 eyes who sees everything'. In *Tony Miles: 'It's Only Me'*, Geoff Lawton concludes that this match finally caused Miles to abandon all hope that he might challenge for the world title. A year later, Miles acknowledged that while 'on a good day' he might aspire 'to be about number three in the world [to] be better than that you'd have to be completely devoted to chess, which I'm not'.

Garry Kasparov (b 1963) not only embodied super-human chess 'devotion' but was also blessed with boundless natural talent. In his autobiographical *Child of Change*, Kasparov recounts that, in 1973, a precocious ten year-old from Baku, he was singled out for inclusion in Botvinnik's school for top young Soviet talents. Kasparov stood out, in Botvinnik's judgement, 'because of his ability to calculate variations very skilfully and for many moves ahead'. Botvinnik's mentoring was hugely beneficial.

26. *Garry Kasparov: 'retired' 2007*

Kasparov acknowledged: 'There is no price I can set on the value [Botvinnik] gave me'. Not even Karpov, the most notable talent to emerge from the first (eighteen month) incarnation of Botvinnik's school, ten years earlier, derived such good fortune. By the early 1970s, Botvinnik had retired from competitive chess and was able to invest much more of his time to such teaching. This was conducted largely by correspondence, with two or three face to face meetings annually, and continued, in Kasparov's case, for the next five years.

Kasparov recalls that Botvinnik, an inspiring, as well as formidably knowledgeable chess professor, 'never tried to impose his own style on his pupils [merely] to show the right direction [and] take the mystery out of chess ... always trying to reduce problems ... to a manageable scale'. Kasparov learned 'how to study chess, to find new ideas ... good ideas in all positions ... a scientific method, learning the old moves, then trying to improve ... finding new openings, new variations, new methods in the middlegame, a new plan of the whole game'.

Outside 'formal lessons', Botvinnik also taught Kasparov to appreciate the disciplined processes required for optimum tournament preparation. For Botvinnik, again to quote Kasparov, this was always 'a highly professional business, with periods set aside for study and analysis, careful preparation of opening moves and variations, as well as exercise to promote physical and mental fitness'. Botvinnik's 'regime' was apparently 'a bit like that of a boxer in training for a championship fight'.

Towards the close of the 1970s, Botvinnik and a growing number of other discerning judges already considered Kasparov to be Karpov's likeliest challenger in waiting. Botvinnik had early on noted and wisely indulged Kasparov in the young player's 'wish to emulate the dynamic style of ... Alekhine'. By around 1980, Kasparov certainly played much of his best chess in the richly complex and grand combinative manner of his great Russian forebear. His rise to the absolute top was exceptionally rapid.

Aged only 16, Kasparov made his first major international breakthrough, at Banja Luka 1979, where he headed a strong field, by a full two points. He then won the 1980 world junior championship and played second reserve for the winning USSR team, at the 1980 Malta Olympiad. At Moscow 1981, in his first 'super' tournament, he shared 2nd/3rd places, with Polugaevsky, behind only Karpov. Later that year, he shared 1st/2nd places, in the near equally competitive USSR Championship, with Lev Psakhis.

In 1982, Kasparov won effortlessly at Bugojno and in the Moscow Interzonal, which helped ensure 2nd board place, behind Karpov, in the victorious USSR team, at the subsequent Lucerne Olympiad. Through 1983 and into early 1984, while sailing through the Candidates' matches (by comfortable 3 or 4 point margins), Kasparov also dominated in yet another 'super' tournament, at Niksic 1983. Karpov and Kasparov, were by then world numbers one and two respectively in the world rankings.

As already noted, Kasparov survived the perils of the players' extraordinarily extended 1984-85 title match, but proved Karpov's superior in the 1985 Moscow re-match. While Kasparov harked back to Alekhine, Karpov echoed much of Capablanca's intuitively strategic artistry, Both, however, were even more distinctively all-round, late-20th century, model chess professionals, capable of playing exceptionally well in all styles and outstandingly well-prepared in the opening.

Game 16 symbolised the stylistic nature of the struggle, at Moscow 1985. Kasparov won with an audacious piece of opening preparation that, with hindsight, was objectively doubtful. In a similar match situation (Kasparov sensed a breakthrough moment), an Alekhine might also have employed such a tempting, highly double-edged gambit, far less so a more coldly sober, Capablanca or Karpov. Modern engines immediately spot the problem (on White's 12th move) but computers were still not yet especially strong, in those years.

A.Karpov – G.Kasparov

Game 16, World Championship, Moscow 1985

Sicilian Defence

1.e4 c5 2.♘f3 e6 3.d4 cxd4 4.♘xd4 ♘c6 5.♘b5 d6 6.c4 ♘f6 7.♘1c3 a6 8.♘a3 d5 9.cxd5 exd5 10.exd5 ♘b4 11.♗e2

Game 12 had gone 11.♗c4 ♗g4 (a Kasparov improvement on a previously played 11...b5) 12.♗e2 ♗xe2 13.♕xe2+ ♕e7 14.♗e3 ♘bxd5 15.♘c2, leading to a quick draw. After the text-move, Karpov probably expected 11...♘bxd5 12.♘xd5 ♘xd5 13.0–0, when, ahead in development, White might hope to develop a slight edge.

11...♗c5

Kasparov's shock gambit novelty, although it is, in fact, flawed: neither analytic team had apparently noticed the clever and sole advantageous reply, 12.♗e3, and if 12...♗xe3 13.♕a4+ ♘d7 14.♕xb4 ♗c5 15.♕e4+ ♔f8 16.0–0, as in A.Karpov-J.Van der Wiel, Brussels 1986, which is clearly better for White (Black held).

12.0–0 0–0 13.♗f3 ♗f5 14.♗g5

With straightforward development, White gets nowhere. Black exerts unpleasant pressure on the h7–b1 diagonal, particularly on the d3 and c2 squares and White's knight on a3 remains disconnected from the centre. White lacks good options. After, for example, 14.♗e3 ♗xe3 15.fxe3 ♗d3, and if 16.♖f2 ♖e8 17.♕d2 a5 18.♖e1 ♕b6 19.b3 ♖ac8, only Black sets a blistering pace.

14...♖e8 15.♕d2 b5 16.♖ad1

Karpov makes a brave decision to hang on to his d-pawn. But it comes with undoubted downsides. Black's knight lands powerfully on d3, from which it can scarcely be budged. Behind it, White's d-pawn remains hugely vulnerable, while Black's dark square bishop can also hope to exploit d6, as an additional attacking base.

Perhaps White should have tried to bail out, by abandoning his extra pawn and playing 16.d6. Then if, say 16...♖a7 17.♖ad1 ♖d7 (not 17...♘d3 18.♗e2, and if 18...♘xf2 19.♖xf2 ♗xf2+ 20.♔xf2 b4 21.♕f4, with advantage to White) 18.♕f4 ♗d3 19.♗xf6 ♕xf6 20.♕xf6 gxf6 21.♖xd3 ♘xd3 22.♗c6, and White fights.

16...♘d3 17.♘ab1

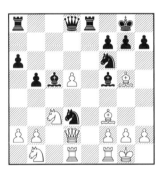

Sadly for White, 17.♗e2, hoping to dislodge Black's knight, fails to 17...♘xf2 18.♖xf2 b4, gaining critical control of e4, and Black wins.

17...h6 18.♗h4 b4 19.♘a4

White's knights reel from the power exerted by Black's inexorable takeover of ever more space in the centre and on the flanks. White's knight stands self-evidently poorly posted on a4. Black also stands well, however, after 19.♘e2 ♕b6, and if 20.♘c1 ♘e5.

19...♗d6 20.♗g3 ♖c8 21.b3 g5

This further fine move markedly limits

White's scope for kingside manoeuvre as well as (indirectly) on the queenside. White can't now play 22.♘b2, allowing 22...♘xb2 23.♕xb2 g4, and Black wins. Any attempt at a kingside break, such as after, say 22.h4 ♘e4 23.♗xe4 ♗xe4 24.hxg5 (or if 24.♗xd6 ♕xd6 25.hxg5 ♘f4) 24...♗xg3 25.fxg3 ♕xd5, and if 26.gxh6 ♖e6, moreover, also only rebounds in Black's favour.

22.♗xd6 ♕xd6 23.g3 ♘d7 24.♗g2

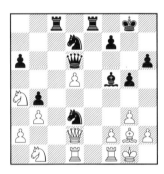

White's options remain severely limited. After 24.♘b2 ♘7e5 25.♗g2 a5 26.♘xd3 ♘xd3, Black retains a powerful knight on d3, and if 27.a3 bxa3 28.♕a2 ♘b2 29.♖c1 ♖xc1 30.♖xc1 ♕b4, followed by ...♖e1, White almost certainly loses.

24...♕f6 25.a3 a5 26.axb4 axb4 27.♕a2

Karpov prefers not to tempt fate, by playing 27.h3, which only invites 27...h5, and if 28.♔h2 h4 29.gxh4 gxh4 30.♖g1 ♔h8 31.♖df1 ♖g8. In such positions, Black clearly enjoys all sorts of attacking threats against a defence that is chronically hampered by the continuing plight of White's out-of-play knights on the queenside.

27...♗g6 28.d6 g4

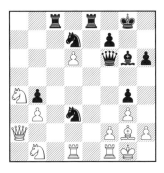

Kasparov mercilessly reinforces his bind, rather than immediately capture Black's d-pawn.

After 28...♕xd6, White might still struggle, by playing 29.♘d2. After the text-move, however, White cannot even play that move because of Black's crushing reply, 29...♖e2.

29.♕d2 ♔g7 30.f3

White has run out of good moves. Black's bind is total and everything loses. White would be quite as fatally wounded, after 30.h3 h5, followed shortly by ...♕xd6.

30...♕xd6 31.fxg4 ♕d4+ 32.♔h1 ♘f6 33.♖f4 ♘e4

While White's knights remain wholly impotent, off-side spectators, Black's superior forces simply crash through the White king's flimsy defences.

34.♕xd3 ♘f2+ 35.♖xf2

Or if 35.♔g1 ♘h3+ 36.♔h1 ♕xd3 37.♖xd3 ♖e1+, and wins.

35...♗xd3 36.♖fd2 ♕e3 37.♖xd3 ♖c1

38.♘b2 ♕f2 39.♘d2

Or 39.♖xc1 ♖e1+.

39...♖xd1+ 40.♘xd1 ♖e1+ 0–1

The two great K's scarcely had time to draw breath before they were once again back at the board to contest their third title match, at London/Leningrad 1986. In that short, inter-title match period, Kasparov managed to squeeze in (and comfortably win) two six game matches against two of the top western grandmasters, Jan Timman (4-2) and Tony Miles. These contests mirrored two played between his first and second title matches, in which he had soundly defeated the other two top western players, Ulf Anderssen (4-2) and Robert Hübner (4.5-1.5).

Kasparov and Karpov completely dominated chess in these years. Kasparov, however, was now clearly beginning to draw ahead of Karpov in the world rankings and was firm favourite to retain his newly won crown, at London/Leningrad. At first, Kasparov seemed set for a quick victory. Three points ahead after Game 16, however, he lost the next three games to a determined Karpov rally. Kasparov eventually steadied, to win Game 22, and see out victory by the narrowest margin (12.5-11.5).

The London/Leningrad title match was the first title match between two Soviets to be staged at least partly outside the USSR. Ever since the

Fischer-Spassky match, every world title match had attracted widespread global media coverage, as well as increasingly attractive prize funds. In *Child of Change*, Kasparov notes that even the rouble prize funds that applied in the first two Karpov-Kasparov matches were quite tidy sums. London/Leningrad attracted an overall £1m bid to host the match (£600,000 alone by London).

By 1986, Kasparov was already really quite wealthy, certainly in Soviet terms. Moreover, still aged only 23, his long-term earning power was potentially huge, as world champion. That year, Kasparov engaged a British manager, Andrew Page, who helped grow his international commercial interests, into the 1990s - a path smoothed by Mikhail Gorbachev's 1985 appointment as General Secretary of the Communist Party of the USSR and his *Glasnost* and *Perestroika* reform programmes.

One year on, at Seville 1987, Kasparov and Karpov again clashed, in the first ever title match between two Soviets to take place completely outside the USSR. At Seville 1987, Karpov almost recovered the title. Following some unexpectedly wayward Kasparov form, Karpov went into the final match game, if perhaps a little fortuitously, one point ahead. Kasparov, however, achieved a magnificent winning save, to win and tie the match (12-12), thereby retaining his title.

The players then enjoyed their first 'normal' three year respite from title match play. Due to the curious nature of their 'undecided' 1984-85 match and the clauses that triggered the 1985 and 1986 re-matches, the years 1984-1987 had witnessed four, rather than two title matches. Few complained, as we were privileged to experience the world's two best players (by far) knocking consistently wonderful lumps out of each other. Both were now free to play in a lot more tournaments, in which they were equally supreme.

Between Seville 1987 and his 1990 title defence, Kasparov either won outright or tied $1^{st}/2^{nd}$ in all nine 'super' tournaments he contested. Karpov's record was almost equally good. Both tied

27. Garry Kasparov (l.), Anatoly Karpov, Jan Timman: Amsterdam 1986

fittingly in the 1988

USSR Championship and at Skelleftea 1989. Karpov also comfortably won the 1988-89 Candidates' match series, to set up the players' fifth and final title match, at New York/Lyon 1990, which enjoyed a fabulous $3m prize fund, to be split 5/8 to the winner and 3/8 to the loser.

Kasparov was firmer favourite than before. The struggle, as expected, however, was hard. By winning Game 20, Kasparov went two points ahead, following which two draws got him to the minimum 12 points necessary to retain his title. Karpov won Game 23, reducing the final losing margin to only one point. Game 20 was a splendid contest, played out on the ultra-sharp battlefield of Zaitsev's Variation of the Spanish Opening, a line developed by Karpov's long-time second (Igor Zaitsev).

G.Kasparov – A.Karpov

Game 20, World Championship, Lyon 1990

Spanish Opening

1.e4 e5 2.♘f3 ♘c6 3.♗b5 a6 4.♗a4 ♘f6 5.0–0 ♗e7 6.♖e1 b5 7.♗b3 d6 8.c3 0–0 9.h3 ♗b7 10.d4 ♖e8 11.♘bd2

White can't exploit (Zaitsev's) 10th move, by playing 11.♘g5 ♖f8 12.f4, which leads after 12...exf4 13.♗xf4 ♘a5, and if 14.♗c2 ♘d5 15.♕h5 h6, to positions that are fine for Black.

11...♗f8 12.a4

Nor do Zaitsev players fear 12.♘g5 ♖e7, and now either 13.d5 or 13.f4, although the more restrained 12.a3, remains a popular choice.

12...h6 13.♗c2 exd4 14.cxd4 ♘b4 15.♗b1 c5

In this highly complex and mutually unbalanced line, White has two strong centre pawns and potentially menacing bishops trained on Black's kingside. Black, who enjoys Modern Benoni-like compensation, aims to control the e5 square, neutralise White's centre pawns and rapidly mobilise his majority of pawns on the queenside.

Game 2, played in the New York stage of the match, saw 15...bxa4

16.♖xa4 a5 17.♖a3 ♖a6 18.♘h2 g6 19.f3, an important (Kasparov) innovation that reinforces White's centre and reduces targets for possible counterattack. Play then continued 19...♕d7

20.♘c4 ♕b5 21.♖c3 ♗c8 22.♗e3 ♔h7 23.♕c1 c6 24.♘g4, leading to an eventual win for White, which completely shook Karpov's faith in that line.

16.d5 ♘d7 17.♖a3 f5

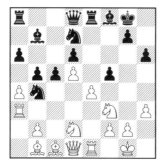

Black's sharpest course, seeking to undermine White's e- and d-pawns directly. The move had recently featured in, J.Timman-A.Karpov, Game 9, Candidates' final 1990. Kasparov now repeats Timman's 18th move. Earlier in the match, he had tried the equally critical 18.exf5, which led to two highly eventful draws, after 18...♘f6 19.♘e4 ♗xd5 (Game 4) and 18...♗xd5 (Game 22).

In their 1986 title match, Kasparov twice defeated Karpov, after 17...c4, a major alternative that targets d3 for a Black knight (though often at the cost of losing Black's b-pawn). The second of these games (Game 16) continued, 18.♘d4 ♕f6 19.♘2f3 ♘c5 20.axb5 axb5 21.♘xb5 ♖xa3 22.♘xa3 ♗a6 23.♖e3 ♖b8, with unclear complications, if few fond memories for Black.

18.♖ae3 ♘f6

Karpov improves on 18...f4 (played against Timman), after which Kasparov intended 19.♖a3, keeping the rook active along the 3rd rank and not impeding the White queen's access to the d1–h5 light squares. Timman had instead replied weakly: after 19.♖3e2 ♘e5, Black (who won) simply stood well.

White obtains excellent play for a pawn after 18...fxe4 19.♘xe4 ♘xd5 20.♖3e2.

19.♘h2 ♔h8

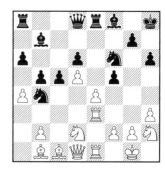

Both players still clearly considered 19...fxe4 20.♘xe4, and if 20...♘fxd5 21.♖g3, threatening ♗xh6, too risky for Black. Kasparov's reply to the text-move apparently surprised Karpov. G.Kasparov-A.Karpov, Euwe memorial, Amsterdam 1991, later saw the more urgent and probably critical, 19...♕d7, which continued 20.exf5 ♖xe3 21.fxe3 ♗xd5 22.♘g4 ♗e7, and was eventually drawn.

20.b3 bxa4 21.bxa4 c4

Positions like this defy exact analysis. Kasparov insists on continually keeping his underlying gambit idea in play. Karpov continues to reject its acceptance. This may, however, have been the point for Black to risk the complications arising, after 21...fxe4 22.♘xe4 ♗xd5, and if 23.♘xf6 ♖xe3 24.♖xe3 ♕xf6 25.♗d2 ♕f7 26.♗c3, which, according to Kasparov (after very considerable home reflection) remains 'very unclear and double-edged'.

22.♗b2 fxe4 23.♘xe4 ♘fxd5 24.♖g3 ♖e6 25.♘g4

Due allowance must be given to both players for the extreme complexity each faces. White has dangerous play for his pawn and may even be close to a win, although perhaps only after 25.♘f3

and if: 25...♘f4 26.♘d4, and if 26...♖e5 27.♕g4 ♘bd3 28.♗xd3 ♘xd3 29.♘e6 ♕e7 (or 29...♕f6 30.♗xe5 ♕xe5 31.f4 ♕b2 32.♕f5) 30.♗xe5 dxe5 31.♕g6 ♘f4 32.♘xf8 ♖xf8 33.♕d6; or 25...♘d3 26.♘eg5, and if 26...♖xe1+ 27.♘xe1 ♔g8 28.♕c2 (Kasparov).

In turn, Black might still hold, at this point, by playing 25...♘d3, such as after the amusing (but logical) drawing line, 26.♗xd3 cxd3 27.♕d2, and if 27...♕e7 28.♘xh6 ♖xe4 29.♖xe4 ♕xe4 30.♘f7+ ♔g8 31.♘h6+ ♔h7 32.♘f7 (again Kasparov). Karpov now certainly under-estimates the strength of Kasparov's crushing 26th-28th moves, which crash through Black's remaining defences.

25...♕e8 26.♘xh6 c3

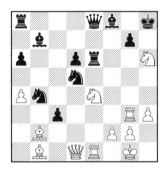

Black hopes to negate White's pressure on the long dark diagonal but it is already too late to repair the damage done to his kingside defences as a result of Black's imprecise 25th move. No better was 26...♖xh6 27.♘xd6, and if 27...♕h5 (or if 27...♕d7 28.♕g4 ♕xg4 29.♘f7+) 28.♖g5 ♕xd1 29.♘f7+, winning material.

27.♘f5 cxb2 28.♕g4 ♗c8

Although a bishop to the good, Black's three queenside pieces (rook, bishop and knight) contribute little to Black's cause. By contrast, all of White's forces are optimally placed for a breakthrough that can no longer be prevented. White also wins, after 28...g6 29.♔h2, threatening ♕h4+, followed by ♘g5, and if 29...♔g8 30.♘exd6 ♗xd6 31.♖xe6 ♗xg3+ 32.fxg3 ♕xe6 33.♘h6+; or if 28...♘c3 29.♘f6 ♖xe1+ 30.♔h2, and soon mates.

29.♕h4+ ♖h6

Or if 29...♔g8 30.♔h2, again threatening ♘g5, and wins.

30.♘xh6 gxh6 31.♔h2

White's knight now threatens to move to f6, g5 or d6, leaving Black completely defenceless.

31...♕e5 32.♘g5 ♕f6 33.♖e8 ♗f5 34.♕xh6+

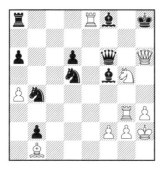

Kasparov concludes with a crushing queen sacrifice.

34...♕xh6 35.♘f7+ ♔h7 36.♗xf5+ ♕g6 37.♗xg6+

Time trouble! White's most aesthetic and immediately decisive continuation was rather 37.♖xg6, and if 37...♖xe8 38.♖g3 mate.

37...♔g7 38.♖xa8 ♗e7 39.♖b8 a5 40.♗e4+ ♔xf7 41.♗xd5+ 1–0

Kasparov next defended his title against Nigel Short, who had defeated Jon Speelman, Boris Gelfand, Karpov and Timman, in an unusually extended series of Candidates' matches, to become challenger. Sponsored by *The Times*, in London 1993, their title match, however, was to be controversially organised by Short and Kasparov's recently constituted *Professional Chess Association*. Established earlier that year, the PCA had arbitrarily declared that it would henceforth take the world title completely out of FIDE's hands and run an entirely new PCA qualification cycle.

FIDE, however, flatly refused either to recognise any 'PCA' champion or to abandon its world title 'ownership'. Flexing its own muscle, FIDE staged an alternative 'official' title match, to run concurrently with the London match: contested by Timman, losing 1993 Candidates' finalist, and Karpov, higher rated of the two losing Candidates' semi-finalists. In 1993, Kasparov and Karpov decisively won these respective 'PCA' and 'FIDE' crowns. They also defeated parallel PCA and FIDE challengers, in 1995 and 1996. The PCA then lost its major sponsor (*Intel*) and its cycle dramatically ceased.

In 1993, both Kasparov and Short firmly believed that the future beneficial development of top-class chess required a complete break from FIDE. Their ambition, however, was breathtakingly huge. It may have been one thing to establish a body to represent the interests of top players, acting in tandem with FIDE – along the lines of a prior, *Grandmasters Association* (GMA), launched in 1987. It was, however, an extraordinary stretch for two players, acting initially almost entirely alone, to expect to completely bypass FIDE. Many top-class players were openly critical. Most felt uneasy.

Why a revised GMA template didn't attract Kasparov or Short, in 1993, isn't entirely clear. On the whole, the GMA had worked quite constructively with FIDE and successfully brokered a lucrative *World Cup* tournament series, in the late-1980s, before it ran out of steam. While throughout its own brief existence, the PCA gave us some excellent chess – two PCA title matches, one PCA Candidates' match series and a wonderful string of *Intel*-sponsored Rapid tournaments – it also led to an extremely messy FIDE / PCA world title split that took many long years to unravel.

The disputatious organisational background to the 1993 match probably helped raise the profile of Short's challenge. The challenger, however, was already well-known to the UK public and excitement ran high. Kasparov was favourite but Short had a game that might easily lead to a surprise. Played for an amply rewarding £1.7m prize fund, the match was a huge TV and print media success. Short was the first British player to challenge for the world title since the naturalised, Anglo-Hungarian, Isidor Gunsberg, lost to Steinitz, at New York 1891-92, which added historical spice.

Aged 30, higher-rated and already with five successful world championship matches behind him, Kasparov comfortably triumphed (+6-1=13). The champion's greater all-round resourcefulness, enterprise and merciless execution whenever he got a chance showed up particularly strongly in the middlegame. While the 28 year-old challenger played much better than the one-sided score might suggest, Short seemed sadly fated to let slip many more (occasionally gilt-edged) opportunities than Kasparov and paid a high price.

Kasparov's openings were all also exceptionally well-chosen. With White, Short continually hammered away against Kasparov's favourite Najdorf Variation of the Sicilian Defence but without making much headway. Playing White, Kasparov fared much better, employing a more varied mix of 1.e4 and 1.d4 main lines. In Game 15, Kasparov adopted what he called his 'favourite opening', one largely originated by Botvinnik, whose ideas he had absorbed in his youth. Hard enough to play Kasparov, but Botvinnik, too – Short stumbled!

G.Kasparov – N.Short

Game 15, PCA World Championship, London 1993

Queen's Gambit

1.d4 d5 2.c4 e6 3.♘c3 ♘f6 4.cxd5 exd5 5.♗g5 ♗e7 6.e3 0–0 7.♗d3 ♘bd7 8.♘ge2 ♖e8 9.0–0 ♘f8 10.b4

This gambit idea is only possible because Short has delayed ...c6, a move that is virtually standard in this line (and often played at move 5). White would now stand well after 10...♗xb4 11.♗xf6 gxf6 12.♘xd5 ♕xd5 13.♕a4, and if 13...♗h3 14.♘f4 ♕a5 15.♕xa5 ♗xa5 16.♘xh3. J.Timman-N.Short, Amsterdam 1992, had instead recently gone 10.♕c2 c6 11.f3 (reaching a frequent theoretical battleground) 11...♘h5 12.♗xe7 ♖xe7 13.♕d2, with an eventual draw.

10...a6 11.a3 c6 12.♕c2 g6 13.f3

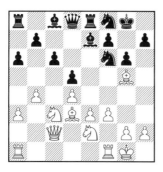

White embarks on the dynamic plan whose early development owes most to Botvinnik. With his king's knight on e2 (rather than on f3), White aims to establish a space-gaining, e4/d4 central pawn duo, while simultaneously

containing Black's 4-3 queenside pawn majority. With a White knight on f3, White tends to rely on the more purely technical / positional plan of conducting a minority queenside attack (based on playing a4, followed by b4-b5) rather than create immediate threats in the centre.

13...♘e6 14.♗h4 ♘h5

Short relies on an exchanging but somewhat passive strategy. Black's plan seems solid enough but lacks any real punch on either of the flanks or in the centre. Bolder and perhaps more critical was 14...a5, as White's apparently natural reply, 15.b5, can then be successfully met by the energetic 15...c5, and if 16.dxc5 ♗xc5.

15.♗xe7 ♖xe7 16.♕d2 b6

According to Kasparov, this was a serious error. Black aims to develop his bishop to b7, connect his major pieces and eventually get in a freeing ...c5. The last part of this plan, however, proves exceptionally hard to achieve, entailing a high risk that (with Black pawns on a6 and c6) Black will be left with 'a permanent weakness on the b6 square'.

It is, however, hard to see how Black might otherwise complete his queenside development satisfactorily, without allowing White to get in e4 eventually (rather as in the game). After 16...a5 17.b5, and if 17...♕d6 18.bxc6 bxc6 19.♖fb1, for example, White is clearly much better. Perhaps 16...♘hg7 is a better try, although after 17.♗c2, White maintains a clear edge.

17.♖ad1 ♗b7 18.♗b1 ♘hg7 19.e4 ♖c8 20.♗a2 ♖d7 21.♘f4

Kasparov was rightly pleased with this move. White has a clear advantage but it is far from easy to convert. It might initially seem counter-intuitive to exchange a pair of knights (while sitting on a significant space advantage). By doing so, however, Kasparov greatly activates his queen, which (from f4 and subsequently e5), soon dominates the kingside dark squares.

The move's tactical justification, lies in the line 21...dxe4 22.♘xe6 ♘xe6 23.fxe4, and if 23...♖xd4 (or 23...♘xd4 24.♕f2 c5 25.♗xf7+ ♔g7 26.♗d5 ♗xd5 27.♘xd5) 24.♕f2 ♖d7 25.♗xe6 fxe6 26.♖xd7 ♕xd7 27.♘a4 ♖d8 28.♕xb6, with considerable advantage for White (Kasparov).

21...♘xf4 22.♕xf4 ♘e6 23.♕e5 ♖e7 24.♕g3 ♕c7

Although gasping for manoeuvring space, Black still fights. He can't safely break in the centre, by playing 24...dxe4, as after 25.fxe4, and if 25...♘xd4 26.♕f2, White has too many game-winning threats.

25.♕h4 ♘g7

Nor can Black break out on the queenside, by playing 25...c5, which allows 26.dxc5, and if 26...dxe4 27.♗d5, threatening ♗xb7, followed by ♘d5, and wins.

26.♖c1 ♕d8 27.♖fd1 ♖cc7 28.♘a4 dxe4

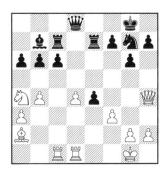

Apparently in Kasparov's time trouble, though still under much pressure, Short seems to have snatched at this move in the misguided belief that he had set a clever trap. Black had nothing better than to attempt to defend the severely cramped positions arising after 28...♖cd7 29.e5. Black is now almost certainly lost.

29.fxe4 ♕e8

Black had hoped for 30.♖e1 c5, but

this is easily side-stepped. After 29…
♖cd7, Kasparov would have maintained White's pressure, by playing
30.♔h1, and if 30…♘e6 31.♗xe6 ♖xe6
32.♕xd8+ ♖xd8 33.e5, with a likely
winning endgame (not least because
of the baleful plight of Black's pawn
on b6).

30.♘c3 ♖cd7 31.♕f2 ♘e6 32.e5 c5

White's knight threatened to take a decisive jump, via e4, either to f6 or d6.
There was no other way (though it fails)
to prevent this.

**33.bxc5 bxc5 34.d5 ♘d4 35.♘e4 ♕d8
36.♘f6+ ♔g7 37.♘xd7 ♖xd7 38.♖xc5
♘e6 39.♖cc1 1–0**
Or if 39…♗xd5 40.♕f6+, and wins.

Kasparov's next PCA title challeng-
er was the young Indian star, Vishy
Anand (b.1969), who defeated Oleg
Romanishin, Michael Adams and
Gata Kamsky, to win the 1994-95 PCA
Candidates' match series. In his mid-
twenties, Anand led the charge of a new
generation of young players, including

notably Kamsky, Boris Gelfand, Vassily
Ivanchuk and Vladimir Kramnik, from
whom it seemed likely to expect a successor to Kasparov. For the moment,
the world number one still held them
at bay, but several of these youngsters
were beginning to best him occasionally in tournaments.

The players met, in 1995, in a dramatic location: on the 107ᵗʰ floor of the
New York World Trade Center. At stake
was a $1.5m prize fund, put up by *In-
tel*, who had also sponsored all of the
PCA Candidates' matches (and a prior
Interzonal). No doubt primarily due
to Kasparov's international celebrity,
the match made an impressive media impact. The hugely media friendly
and talented Anand, however, was also
a hit. India's strongest ever player,
Anand enjoyed incisive analytical skills
and blitz speed reactions. Kasparov
had a match on his hands.

A child of the Kasparov era, Anand
excelled almost as much as Kasparov
himself in his ability to conjure up rich
middlegame complexity from a deep-
ly-researched range of soundly-based
modern openings. Not unlike Karpov,
Anand played in a compellingly natural, directly classical style that was
founded ultimately on an enviably intuitive grasp of what simply worked
in a game. Robustly self-confident but
also able to reflect wisely on his own
play, Anand was certainly not an opponent that even a fired-up Kasparov
might expect to blast from a chessboard with ease.

Quite the contrary: after eight straight draws, in which Kasparov's game had seemed less fresh than his opponent's, Anand deservedly won Game 9, to take a one point lead, at New York. At this point, Kasparov arguably had the good fortune to enjoy a 48 hour break in the contest: the defending champion and his team perhaps put this period to the best use ever made of such time in any world championship match. On his return to the board, Kasparov dramatically triumphed.

In Game 10 (see below), Anand ran into a most brilliant piece of opening preparation that completely demolished one of his main match defences. In Game 11, Kasparov then switched from defence (against Anand's 1.e4), with his 'known' favourite Sicilian: Najdorf to a quite unexpected Dragon Variation, in which he deployed another ambitious new plan and again won. Anand's spirit slumped. Following a draw in Game 12, Anand then wearily lost Games 13 and 14. Kasparov ran out winner, with four further draws (+4-1=13).

Aged 32, Kasparov showed that he still possessed greater energy, better nerves and deeper reserves of fighting spirit than others, which, allied to his equally pre-eminent openings preparation and playing skills, ensured that he remained clear top-ranked player and the world champion in its truest (not just PCA) sense. Karpov's FIDE title paled in stature, even after he, too, fended off a challenge by a dangerous youngster, in 1996, against Kamsky. Then disaster ensued: following a post-PCA world title match review, *Intel* ended its PCA sponsorship.

Without a PCA sponsor (no replacement was found), Kasparov's dreams of launching a second (non-FIDE) world title cycle were effectively over. *Intel*'s association with chess hadn't been deemed a failure. For whatever reason, Intel simply wished to move on. Whether *Intel*'s decision had been significantly influenced by the fact that FIDE had stubbornly refused to desist from running its 'official' title events wasn't ever made clear. Notably, however, widespread cherry picking went on: Anand and Kamsky played in both PCA and FIDE cycles.

Moreover, adding to Kasparov and the PCA's woes, the youthful President of the (Russian) Republic of Kalmykia, Kirsan Ilyumzhinov, who had succeeded Campomanes as FIDE President, in 1995, demonstrated that he was perhaps even more determined than his predecessor, to reinstate FIDE's absolute world title leadership rights. Kasparov struggled to find a legitimate challenger for his (post-PCA) crown. Let Game 10, from the 1995 title match, however, stand as a glorious, if bittersweet memory of the PCA's legacy just before its demise.

G.Kasparov – V.Anand

Game 10, PCA World Championship, New York 1995

Spanish Opening

1.e4 e5 2.♘f3 ♘c6 3.♗b5 a6 4.♗a4 ♘f6 5.0–0 ♘xe4 6.d4 b5 7.♗b3 d5 8.dxe5 ♗e6 9.♘bd2 ♘c5 10.c3 d4 11.♘g5

A Mikhail Tal inspiration, this sensational sacrifice was first offered in Game 10 of the 1978 Karpov-Korchnoi world title match, causing a surprised Korchnoi to spend almost three quarters of an hour, before declining. Exceptionally well-primed, against Anand, Kasparov reached move 18 in no more than about 5 minutes and had almost certainly judged the position after the players' 21st moves, as effectively winning.

What if Black accepts the sacrifice? Kasparov-Shirov, Linares 2001, perhaps points to Kasparov's likely intention: play continued 11...♕xg5 12.♕f3 0–0–0 (or if 12...♔d7 13.♗d5) 13.♗xe6+ fxe6 14.♕xc6 ♕xe5 15.b4 ♕d5 16.♕xd5 exd5 17.bxc5 dxc3 18.♘b3 d4 19.♗a3 g6 20.♗b4 ♗g7 21.a4 ♔d7 22.axb5 axb5 23.♖fd1 ♔e6 24.♖ac1, and

White eventually won in a still complex endgame.

11...dxc3 12.♘xe6 fxe6 13.bxc3 ♕d3 14.♗c2

Another Tal suggestion, which involves an audacious rook sacrifice that Kasparov and his team had analysed remarkably deeply.

After 14.♘f3, Game 10, in the Karpov-Korchnoi match, had gone 14...♕xd1 15.♗xd1 ♗e7 16.♗e3, with a slight pull. Game 6, in the Kasparov-Anand contest, saw the more active 14...0–0–0 15.♕e1 ♘xb3 16.axb3 ♔b7 17.♗e3 ♗e7 18.♗g5 h6 19.♗xe7 ♘xe7 20.♘d4 ♖xd4 21.cxd4 ♕xb3 22.♕e3 ♕xe3 23.fxe3, and was soon cagily drawn.

14...♕xc3 15.♘b3 ♘xb3

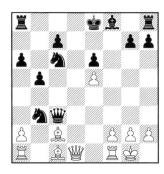

Anand agonised for some 45 minutes before this move. It seems certain that he and his team had either underestimated White's chances or simply missed something. Black has no completely safe way to decline White's rook offer. After, for example, 15...♖d8 16.♗d2 ♕xe5 17.♖e1 ♕f6 (or 17...♕d5 18.♕g4) 18.♘xc5, forcing 18...♖xd2, White stands well.

16.♗xb3 ♘d4

Black loses after the immediate 16...♕xa1, to the spectacular

17.♕h5+, and if 17...g6 18.♕f3 ♘d8 (or if 18...♕xe5 19.♕xc6+ ♔f7 20.♕f3+ ♔g7 21.♗f4) 19.♕f6 ♖g8 20.♗xe6 ♖g7 (or 20...♗g7 21.♗f7+) 21.♗a3 ♕xf1+ 22.♔xf1 ♗xa3 23.♗d5; White also wins, in this line, after 17...♔d7 18.♗xe6+ ♔xe6 19.♕g4+, and if 19...♔f7 20.♕f3+ ♔e6 21.♕xc6+ ♗d6 22.exd6 ♕e5 23.♗d2. Black's king is fatally stranded, after 16...♘xe5 17.♗f4 ♗d6 18.♗xe6.

17.♕g4 ♕xa1 18.♗xe6 ♖d8

Anand prevents ♗d7+, but cannot simultaneously defend against White's equally threatening reply. No better was 18...♗c5 19.♗d7+, and if 19...♔f7 20.e6+ ♔g8 21.♕h5 g6 22.♕xc5 ♘e2+ 23.♔h1 ♘xc1 24.♖xc1, or if 19...♔f8 20.♗h6 ♕xf1+ 21.♔xf1 gxh6 22.♕h4 ♔g7 23.♕f6+ ♔g8 24.♕xh6, in both cases winning for White.

19.♗h6 ♕c3

Black's queen rather desperately journeys to g6 and eventual exchange into a dubious endgame. After 19...♕xf1+ 20.♔xf1, however, and if 20...gxh6 21.♕h5+, he is mated.

20.♗xg7 ♕d3 21.♗xh8 ♕g6

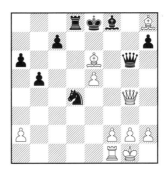

Up to here, Kasparov had scarcely paused for breath and was over an hour ahead on the clock. Only now did he begin to slow down to prevent any possibility of error. A pawn ahead and poised to rush forward his kingside pawns much more rapidly than Black might advance his own queenside pawns, White should win with due care.

22.♗f6 ♗e7 23.♗xe7 ♕xg4 24.♗xg4 ♔xe7 25.♖c1

Before advancing his pawns, White exploits a golden opportunity to obstruct the possible advance of Black's c-pawn.

25...c6 26.f4 a5 27.♔f2 a4 28.♔e3 b4 29.♗d1

White now denies Black any real hope

of creating mischief with his a- and b-pawns. Now, for example, after 29...b3 30.axb3, and if 30...♘xb3 (or 30...axb3 31.♖b1) 31.♗xb3 axb3 32.♖b1 ♖b8 33.♔d3 ♔e6 34.♔c3, White wins Black's b-pawn.

29...a3 30.g4 ♖d5 31.♖c4 c5 32.♔e4 ♖d8 33.♖xc5 ♘e6 34.♖d5 ♖c8

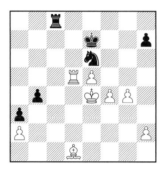

White simply has too many kingside pawns. White also wins quickly, after 34...♖xd5 35.♔xd5 ♘xf4+ 36.♔c4, and if 36...♔e6 37.♔xb4 ♔xe5 38.♔xa3.

35.f5 ♖c4+ 36.♔e3 ♘c5 37.g5 ♖c1 38.♖d6 1–0

Or if 38...b3 39.f6+ ♔f8 40.♗h5, and Black will be mated.

Mastery in the Modern Computer Age

'*Chess should be something personal ... a game ... life, a human creation ... I had these discussions with seconds, yes, I know I am worse according to the computer [and] I know I am risking too much, but I like my position and I don't care*'

Vladimir Kramnik, interviewed by Dirk Jan Ten Geuzendam
in *New In Chess* (2/2019)

The computer rapidly developed into an indispensible tool for the serious player through the 1990s and into the 2000s. Database game collections and analytic engines became ever more up-to-date and accessible, incorporating increasingly sophisticated information capture and software tools and links to the internet. Allied to equally astonishing leaps in PC and laptop performance, including marked cost reductions, such changes revolutionised traditional methods of training, coaching and game preparation.

Computers, of course, only act as an aid to decision-making. They don't 'think'. They merely 'compute'. Our challenge is to make best use of their extraordinary powers in a constant quest to extend our own understanding of what makes 'good' moves actually tick. This is no trivial task. It often leads to such exasperated cries from the heart, as Kramnik's. Going into the 21st century, three players have negotiated these treacherous waters better than most: Vladimir Kramnik, Vishy Anand and Magnus Carlsen.

In addition to the considerable contributions made by these three giants, this chapter also considers Judit Polgar's thoroughly heartening impact in spearheading a welcome gender-neutral trend, both at the top and more widely. Like Kramnik, Anand and Carlsen, Polgar grew up with computers. She also notably joined the elite in her early teens. Top-class chess is becoming an ever younger men and women's game, in which more and more leading players consider 'retirement' before their thirties are out.

These days, given the marked competitive intensity and full-time dedication required of a modern professional player, little room remains at the top even for the most heroic 'amateur'. Wilhelm Steinitz would surely have been in his element. Less so Tarrasch, Euwe, or perhaps even the great Botvinnik, who all pursued separate professional lives outside chess. This chapter concludes with a nod to AlphaZero, the first chess playing machine to be fired by an artificial intelligence algorithm and to the future.

Deeply Combative Artist

Vladimir Kramnik

W ith the demise of the PCA and no replacement sponsor for *Intel* prepared to finance a full-blown (non-FIDE) Candidates' match series, Garry Kasparov's breakaway from the world body was fast miring in sand. Talks took place for a while about the prospect of a reunification title match between the two 'rival' champions, Kasparov (PCA) and Karpov (FIDE), but these fizzled out. FIDE then ditched its own Candidates' and world title match cycle, opting instead for a radical KO mini-match tournament replacement.

28. Vladimir Kramnik: Corus tournament 2005

FIDE's new event was not itself unwelcome. Few, however, much liked the KO principle underpinning it as a means of deciding a 'true' world champion. Knock-out outcomes, based mostly on mere two game eliminators, played at Classical time rates, followed by Rapid and Blitz tie-breaks, introduced far too much randomness. FIDE's first (1997-98) version established Vishy Anand (its winner) as challenger for Karpov's FIDE crown. In a brief eight game title match played not long after that main KO event, Karpov won 5-3.

Kasparov meanwhile continued to seek sponsors for a more conventionally lengthier Candidate's cycle for 'his' (ex-PCA) version of the crown. But he could only eventually secure funds for a (single) 1998 'qualifying' match, between Vladimir Kramnik, and Alexei Shirov. Although odds-on favourite to win, Kramnik lost (3.5-5.5), for which he pocketed $200,000, as loser. Shirov's sole winner's prize was the promise of a large share of the $1.9m prize fund for a (pre-agreed) title match that then failed to take place.

These were chaotic years at the elite level. That Kasparov should have to resort to organising his 'challenger' by means of a makeshift 'eliminator', limited to only two players, itself caused frowns. After Kramnik's unexpected loss, however, the sponsor quite shockingly compounded the embarrassment by declining to support Shirov's challenge. Whether funds would have materialised for the generally expected (and, most probably, the actually desired) Kramnik challenge, remains unclear.

By the mid-1990s, Vladimir Kramnik (b 1975), like Vishy Anand, a player whose early promise had 'potential Kasparov successor' written all over it, seemed destined for greatness. For a brief period, in 1996, he even tied with Kasparov for top spot in the world rankings. Kramnik's match play, however, wasn't then as consistently excellent as in tournaments. Kramnik had previously also lost key matches (both in 1994) to Gata Kamsky, in the quarter finals of the PCA Candidates' series, and to Boris Gelfand, in the FIDE Candidates' semi-finals.

Most ascribed such wobbles to a certain Bohemian streak in Kramnik's youthful lifestyle. Kramnik's loss to Shirov, however, appears to have jolted him into serious change. At London 2000, when he played Kasparov for the world title, Kramnik was physically and mentally as well as technically ready for battle. He was, however, quite lucky to get this chance. In 1999, following the Shirov match debacle, Kasparov obtained sponsorship for a second Anand challenge. Declaring loyalty to FIDE, however, Anand wouldn't accept.

Kasparov invited Kramnik to replace Anand. The original sponsor of the 'Anand' match, however, then dropped out. The (London based) *Braingames Network* saved the worst of Kasparov's sponsorship blushes: towards the end of 2000, the players eventually met to contest Kasparov's first title match in five years, with a $2m prize fund at stake. Aged 37, and much stressed by his failure to negotiate reunification match terms with FIDE (his main goal, at that time), Kasparov was ripe for a crash, against an opponent, whom he had long singled out as his likeliest eventual successor.

Kasparov may not have been quite at his best, at London. Kramnik's sustained superiority, however, was evident throughout. Kramnik won comfortably (+2-0=13), with no need to play the scheduled final 16th game. The challenger struck a huge, early psychological blow, in Game 1, by blunting Kasparov's main match weapon: the Spanish Opening. Kramnik's deeply prepared adoption of the so-called Berlin Wall Endgame, which seems not to have been anticipated by the champion, brought Kasparov nothing but heartbreak.

All four games featuring the Berlin Wall Endgame were drawn. Worse, Kasparov didn't seem to have an alternative to the Spanish Opening that he felt happy with. As Kasparov, moreover, also routinely seemed insecure, playing Black, he was handicapped in the opening as never before in a match. In his two decisive games, Kramnik impressively deployed 1.d4, gaining enduring initiatives: in Game 10, Kasparov's Nimzo-Indian caved in; in Game 2, Kramnik gradually ground down Kasparov's Grünfeld Defence.

V.Kramnik – G.Kasparov

Game 2, World Championship, London 2000

Grünfeld Defence

1.d4 ♘f6 2.c4 g6 3.♘c3 d5 4.cxd5 ♘xd5 5.e4 ♘xc3 6.bxc3 ♗g7 7.♘f3 c5 8.♗e3 ♕a5 9.♕d2 ♗g4

Kasparov relies on a line that brought him success, in A.Yermolinsky-G. Kasparov, Wijk aan Zee 1999, which now went 10.♖c1 ♗xf3 11.gxf3 e6 12.d5 exd5 13.exd5 ♘d7 14.c4 ♕b6 15.♗h3 f5 16.0-0 ♕d6 17.♗f4 ♗e5 18.♖fe1 0-0-0, with good play for Black (who won). With his next two moves, however, Kramnik shows that he was ready for this. Subsequently 9...0-0 and 9...♘c6, became more common.

10.♖b1 a6 11.♖xb7

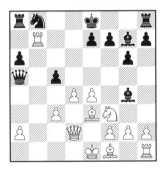

This is a critical capture, which (perhaps surprisingly) hadn't been tried before. White hopes to coax an early queen exchange and build on the strengths of his bishop pair and slightly more active pieces to develop an endgame initiative. The stem game in this line, J.Timman-V.Ivanchuk, Linares

1992, had previously gone 11.♖b3 b5 12.d5 ♘d7 13.c4 b4 14.♕c2 ♕c7, leading to double-edged play (and an eventual draw).

11...♗xf3 12.gxf3 ♘c6 13.♗c4 0-0 14.0-0 cxd4 15.cxd4 ♗xd4 16.♗d5 ♗c3

Either here, or on the previous move, Black might, and perhaps should have fallen in with White's plans, as it is far from certain that the positions that arise after 16...♕xd2 17.♗xd2, and say 17...♖fc8 (or 17...♘e5 18.♗b4) 18.♔g2, offer White more than the very slightest of pulls. Kasparov instead opts for an unclear gambit course, based on reaching a queen, and (opposite colour) bishop middlegame; he hopes for ample compensation on the kingside dark squares.

17.♕c1 ♘d4

With this and his 19th move, Kasparov achieves the desired opposite colour bishops and forces an exchange of White's active rook on the 7ᵗʰ rank. Black might still have brought about an exchange of queens, by playing 17... ♖ac8, although after 18.♗b6 ♕b4 19.a3 ♕b2 20.♕xb2 ♗xb2 21.a4, White's game seems livelier.

18.♗xd4 ♗xd4 19.♖xe7 ♖a7 20.♖xa7 ♗xa7 21.f4

White battles for control of the dark squares. If he can maintain the integrity of his e- and f-pawn duo, keep at least one major piece on the board and continue to train his light square bishop on Black's vulnerable f7–pawn, his extra pawn might eventually count in such positions, notwithstanding the existence of opposite colour bishops.

21...♕d8 22.♕c3 ♗b8 23.♕f3 ♕h4 24.e5 g5 25.♖e1

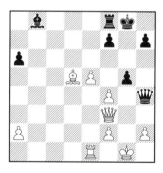

Kasparov, who had long foreseen this position, trusted that Black's ... g5 thrust, allied to his very concrete queen and bishop manoeuvres (to h4 and b8), should successfully undermine White's f4 and e5 points. White, however, now unexpectedly returns

his extra pawn, enabling him to reach a highly promising rook + opposite colour bishop endgame. Black cannot safely reply 25...gxf4, as this only lames his bishop and invites 26.e6, and if 26...fxe6 27.♖xe6, with even more serious middlegame problems.

25...♕xf4 26.♕xf4 gxf4 27.e6 fxe6 28.♖xe6 ♔g7

White's e6 pawn break also pays an immediate endgame dividend. Due to the threat of a powerful White discovered check, Black can't hang on to his a-pawn.

29.♖xa6 ♖f5 30.♗e4 ♖e5 31.f3 ♖e7 32.a4

Black may already be lost. White's dangerously advancing passed a-pawn operates on the most distant file from the kingside and will therefore constantly stretch Black's defences. Black's split kingside pawns are also both potentially at risk to attack by White's king, via either the centre or kingside.

32...♖a7 33.♖b6 ♗e5 34.♖b4 ♖d7

White's king now decisively penetrates on the kingside. Kasparov, in acute time shortage, had apparently intended 34...♗d6 35.♖c4 ♖c7, to force a rook exchange, but missed the deadly reply 36.♗c6, tying up his pieces completely.

35.♔g2 ♖d2+ 36.♔h3 h5 37.♖b5 ♔f6 38.a5 ♖a2 39.♖b6+ ♔e7

Black blunders a piece away but must be lost anyway. One plausible conclusion: 39...♔g7 40.a6, and if 40...♗d4 41.♖g6+ ♔f8 42.♗b7 ♖a5 (White threatened ♖g5) 43.♖d6 ♗e3, when White can even win the pure opposite colour bishop endgame after 44.♖d5 ♖xd5 45.♗xd5 ♔g7 46.♔g2 (heading for the centre) 46...♔f6 47.h4, nicely dooming either Black's bishop or h-pawn.

40.♗d5 1-0

Or if 40...♖e2 (or 40...♖xa5 41.♖e6+) 41.a6 ♗d4 42.a7 ♗g1 43.♖e6+ ♖xe6 44.a8♕, and wins.

By around 2000, computers could already defeat virtually all humans. They were, however, still not yet clearly invincible against the world's absolute best. In 1997, Kasparov had lost a famous match (2.5-3.5) against the mightily powered *IBM* monster, *Deep Blue*. That result, however, was the closest of calls and far from a definitive test. The company then summarily retired and dismantled its machine. *Deep Blue* had hugely out-performed against its commercial and research expectations but it ducked any rematch.

In 2002, Kramnik took up the next man v machine challenge. Leading chess software company, *Chessbase*, organised a *Brains in Bahrain* battle, in which Kramnik faced a formidable piece of newly developed software: *Deep Fritz*, running on a *Compaq* laptop. Given the enormous technological advances made since 1997, Kramnik's chances seemed slim, but he nonetheless managed to tie (4-4) and pocket $800,000. His 'opponent' was soon released in a commercial version and after one or two upgrades routinely able to trounce anyone.

Back in the purely flesh and blood chess world, Kramnik inherited two ongoing problems: how best to maintain the integrity of 'his' crown (now christened 'Classical'); and how best to 'reunify' it with FIDE's. Fortunately few baulked at the thought that Kramnik, preceded by Kasparov, Karpov and all the other recognised world champions right back to Steinitz, embodied the 'truest' world title bloodline. Without a credible path to 'true' reunification, however, many feared that this short-term consensus might quickly unravel.

Fortuitously, all of the various actors somehow managed to focus on seeking ways forward. In 2000, the *Braingames* group had presciently provided for a *Braingames* Candidates' match-tournament, with the losing player in the 2000 world championship signed up to play in it. In 2002, this event took place (though without Kasparov), under a successor group, *Einstein*, in turn underpinned by a generous French sponsor. Early in 2004, Kramnik duly met its winner, Peter Leko, in a 14 game match for his 'Classical' world title, at Brissago, in Switzerland.

Behind all this lay the (May 2002) *Prague Agreement*, to which Kramnik, FIDE and Kasparov all signed up. FIDE continued to hold its biennial series of KO World Cup 'FIDE title' tournaments. All agreed that FIDE's 2002 'world champion', Ruslan Ponomariov, should meet Kasparov in a match to decide who should play against the eventual winner of the Kramnik-Leko match, in a reunification title decider. Kasparov abandoned a bid to be rematched directly with Kramnik.

Much of this happened: first up, Kramnik-Leko took place. In an enthrallingly close contest, Kramnik dramatically won the final game to tie (+2-2=10) and retain his title (there was no tie break clause). A formidably correct technician and openings expert, Leko was one of the most difficult of opponents to win games against. Self-confessedly risk averse, however, he could have done with some of Kramnik's exceptional combinative spark and gritty determination, which only just saved the champion's title.

Aged 14 years, 4 months and 22 days, Leko (b 1979) had been the youngest ever grandmaster, in his day. Unusually, he and Kramnik were rather good friends. They even shared the same manager, Carsten Hensel, at Brissago. Sponsored by the Swiss tobacco company, *Danneman*, the match strongly echoed the up and down nature of the Kasparov-Karpov match, at Seville 1987, in which Kasparov also had to win the final match game. Kramnik's 'equaliser' was both powerfully controlled and strikingly brilliant.

V.Kramnik – P.Leko

Game 14, World Championship, Brissago 2004

Caro Kann Defence

1.e4 c6 2.d4 d5 3.e5 ♗f5 4.h4 h6 5.g4 ♗d7 6.♘d2 c5 7.dxc5 e6

White's 6th move was apparently new. White plays for a slight space advantage but Black's solid structure is extremely hard to break down. Here, Black can also play the later discovery 7...♕c7 (or 7...♘c6), seeking first to induce 8.f4, before replying ...e6, in an attempt to loosen a further White kingside pawn.

8.♘b3 ♗xc5 9.♘xc5 ♕a5+ 10.c3 ♕xc5 11.♘f3 ♘e7 12.♗d3 ♘bc6 13.♗e3 ♕a5 14.♕d2 ♘g6

As played, Kramnik can now successfully consolidate an edge by occupying d4.

Leko drew back from the double-edged alternative, 14...d4, and if 15.cxd4 (or if 15.♗xd4 ♘xd4 16.cxd4 ♕d5) 15...♘b4, and if 16.0–0 ♗b5 17.♗xb5+ ♕xb5 18.♖fc1 ♘bd5, sacrificing a pawn for dynamic compensation based on Black's grip on d5. He later felt he should have played this way but a pawn is a pawn, of course.

15.♗d4 ♘xd4 16.cxd4 ♕xd2+
Black again opts for simplification. After the murkier 16...♕b6, and if 17.a4 (to prevent ...♗b5) 17...a5 18.0–0, (or perhaps first 18.h5), White probably still has a pull but Black might complicate.

17.♔xd2 ♘f4 18.♖ac1 h5
Black now prefers activity to exchanges, such as after 18...♘xd3 19.♔xd3 ♔e7, and if 20.♖c7 b6 21.♖hc1 ♖hc8 22.♔e3 ♔d8 23.♖7c3 ♖xc3+ 24.♖xc3 ♖c8, which only seem likely to lead to a dangerously passive bishop v active knight endgame: White might continue to press for a kingside breakthrough, for example, with such ideas as h5, ♘h4, f4–f5, and ♔f4.

19.♖hg1 ♗c6

Black struggles, however, to achieve anything concrete. White also stands well after either 19...♘h3 20.♖g3, and if 20...hxg4 21.♖xg4 ♘xf2 22.♖xg7 ♘xd3 23.♔xd3 ♖c8 24.♖xc8+ ♗xc8 25.♔e3, or 19...g6 20.gxh5, and if 20...♘xd3 21.♔xd3 ♖xh5 22.♖c7 ♖b8 23.♖gc1.

20.gxh5 ♘xh5 21.b4
Black momentarily holds on the kingside but now comes under queenside pressure by White's aggrandising a- and b-pawns.

21...a6 22.a4 ♔d8?

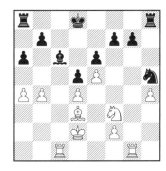

Leko has defended tenaciously but now he badly miscalculates. Black should play 22...♔e7, when White's best may be 23.a5, and if 23...♖hc8 24.♔e3 ♗e8 25.♖c5, with a commanding spatial advantage, but no clear breakthrough. Post mortem analysis confirmed both players' judgement that 22...♗xa4 almost certainly loses, to 23.♖c7, and if 23...♗b5 24.♗b1 b6 25.♘g5 0–0 26.♗h7+ ♔h8 27.♗c2 ♔g8 (or 27...♗e8 28.♖a1, threatening ♖b7) 28.♗d1 ♘f4 29.♔e3 ♘g6 30.h5 ♘h4 31.♗g4 ♖ac8 32.♘xe6.

Black's chances are no better in this line, after either 24...0–0 25.♖g5, and if 25...♘f4 26.♔e3 ♘e2 27.♗d3 ♗xd3 28.♔xd3 ♘f4+ 29.♔e3 ♘g6 30.h5 ♘h8 31.h6 g6 32.♖g1, or earlier 23...♗c6 24.♘g5, and if 24...0–0 25.♗h7+ ♔h8 26.♗c2 (threatening both ♘xf7+ and ♗d1) 26...♗e8 27.♖xb7.

23.♘g5 ♗e8 24.b5 ♘f4

Leko apparently intended 24...axb5, but missed the crushing reply, 25.♗xb5, which exploits the momentary weakness of Black's pawn on f7, to win a pawn after: either 25...b6 26.♖b1 ♔e7 27.♗xe8 ♖hxe8 28.♖xb6 ♖eb8 29.a5; or 25...♘f4 26.♔e3 ♘g6 27.♗xe8 ♔xe8 28.♘xe6 fxe6 29.♖xg6. After the text-move, White builds up game-winning pressure in the c-file.

25.b6 ♘xd3 26.♔xd3 ♖c8

Black must either contest the c-file or perish on the 7ᵗʰ rank, after 26...♖xh4 27.♖c7 ♖c8 28.♘xf7+ ♗xf7 29.♖xf7 ♖h3+ 30.f3, and wins.

27.♖xc8+ ♔xc8 28.♖c1+ ♗c6

Or if 28...♔b8 29.♖c7 ♖xh4 (or 29...♗xa4 30.♘xf7 ♖xh4 31.♘d6) 30.♘xf7 ♗xf7 31.♖xf7 ♖h3+ 32.♔c2, and White's back rank mating threats decide.

29.♘xf7 ♖xh4 30.♘d6+ ♔d8 31.♖g1

Black has managed to close the c-file and retain material equality but his kingside collapses. Purely passive defence, such as after 31...♖h2 32.♔e2 ♖h4 33.♔e3 ♖h3+ 34.f3 ♖h7 35.a5, and

if 35...♔d7 (or 35...♔e7 36.♖g4) 36.♖g6 ♔e7 37.♖g4 ♔d7 38.♖f4, threatening ♖f7+, and wins, is clearly hopeless. Leko instead resolves on a last, desperate dash with his rook to the queen-side, in the hope of achieving counter-vailing play along White's 4ᵗʰ rank.

31...♖h3+ 32.♔e2 ♖a3 33.♖xg7 ♖xa4 34.f4

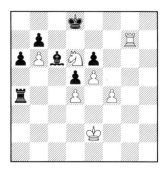

Kramnik, however, threatens to create a crushing passed e-pawn. White would now win quite brilliantly after 34...♖xd4 35.f5 (the key breakthrough), and if 35...exf5 36.e6 ♖e4+ (or else e7–e8=♕+, and wins) 37.♘xe4 fxe4 38.♖c7, threatening ♖xc6, followed by b7. Denied this possibility, Black's rook must now unfortunately nudge White's king fatally towards f6 and the eventual entanglement of Black's king in an inescapable mating net.

34...♖a2+ 35.♔f3 ♖a3+ 36.♔g4 ♖d3 37.f5

White now either forces mate or extracts a decisive material gain, such as after 37...exf5+ 38.♔xf5 ♖h3 39.e6 ♖f3+ 40.♔e5 ♖e3+ 41.♔f6 ♖f3+ 42.♘f5, threatening ♖c7, followed by e7+.

37...♖xd4+ 38.♔g5 exf5 39.♔f6 ♖g4 40.♖c7 ♖h4 41.♘f7+ 1–0

Or if 41...♔e8 42.♖c8+ ♔d7 43.♖d8 mate.

The Brissago match successfully delivered a 'Classical' world champion to compete against the winner of the (promised) FIDE-organised contest between Kasparov and Ponomariov. FIDE, alas, then began to go rogue. The world body first dropped Ponomariov but paid no more than lip service to his possible replacement by Ponomariov's 2004 FIDE World Cup champion successor, Rustam Kasimdzhanov. This left Kasparov, still clear world number one, without any formal route back to a possible title challenge, and also Kramnik in limbo.

These were not FIDE's best years. Acting on a suddenly declared impulse to organise future world championships on a double round-tournament basis, FIDE announced that its first such 'championship' would be decided, at San Luis (Argentina) 2005. FIDE even 'invited' Kramnik to participate. As playing at San Luis, however, would have required Kramnik to put his Classical title at stake, in breach of FIDE's duty to provide him with a reunification match opponent (in accord with the *Prague Agreement*), Kramnik protested. FIDE backed down.

Kramnik held too many trumps. Early in 2005, Kasparov had announced his retirement from chess, following

which Kramnik stood out as the chess world's unchallenged top draw. Moreover, as mooted by Carsten Hensel, Deputy Prime Minister of Russia and President of the Russian Chess Federation, Alexander Zhukov, no doubt helped persuade FIDE President, Ilyumzhinov, to sort out this unseemly mess fast. FIDE at last accepted that it must host a reunification match: to be contested by Kramnik and FIDE's San Luis 'champion', Veselin Topalov, at Elista (Kalmykia) 2006.

A dangerous opponent, Topalov scored a fine, 10/18, at San Luis, 1.5 points ahead of 2nd/3rd placed Anand and Svidler. Topalov and Kramnik both shared the same birth year and had vied at the top since the late-1990s. Topalov's exceptional fighting spirit, tactical ingenuity and theoretical preparedness were second to none. Throughout 2005, moreover, Kramnik's form slumped, due to a serious illness that eventually forced him to take a few months' complete break, early in 2006.

Kramnik, it seems, suffered from a rare rheumatic disorder, which had apparently always been latent. Fortunately Kramnik's break enabled him to discover sufficiently effective means to manage the condition and return to full strength at the board. Despite a series of outstanding results on his return, however, Kramnik still clearly trailed Topalov in the world rankings as they sat down to play, at Elista: Topalov ranked world number one; Kramnik lagged fourth.

Kramnik nevertheless won - and deservedly – though only after winning a Rapidplay tiebreak (2.5-1.5), which probably shouldn't have been necessary. The players tied (+3-3=6) over the initial twelve Classical games. Topalov, however, scored one of his wins (Game 5) by an undue 'forfeit'. Topalov's team had accused Kramnik of 'possibly' consulting electronic devices during (allegedly) over-frequent visits during play to his (fully vetted) personal rest room. Though lacking in merit, these egregious claims were astonishingly upheld by the Appeals Committee.

Kramnik refused to play Game 5, in protest. Disastrous for the game's international image, the bizarre episode was instantly christened 'Toiletgate'. FIDE President, Ilyumzhinov, was (this time) sent packing from a meeting, in Sochi, with Vladimir Putin. Shamefacedly (but creditably) Ilyumzhinov replaced the two main culprits on the Appeals Committee, both FIDE Vice-Presidents. As Kramnik had omitted to confirm his protest 'in writing' (in strict accordance with the match rules), however, his forfeit regrettably continued to stand. Outraged, Kramnik only continued to do battle (one forfeit point down), on the advice of his team's lawyer, formally 'under protest'. Had he then lost the match, he would have retained strong legal grounds for a successful appeal against the outcome to the International Court of Arbitration for Sport. Fortunately that proved unnecessary. The 'right' man won a contest, which almost instantly became a battle for right moral conduct as much as checkmate, with just about every neutral now rooting firmly for Kramnik.

The legality of the judgement by the (old) Appeals Committee aside, the conduct of Topalov's team, led by his manager, Silvio Danailov, remains hard to grasp. Their actions were, at best, tasteless, at worst, self-defeatingly bad. They certainly underestimated the resulting huge swing in world-wide support for Kramnik. At first struggling to regain his composure, Kramnik lost Games 8 and 9, to go 4–5 down. He incisively won Game 10, to 'level', however, and then never looked back.

V.Kramnik – V.Topalov

Game 10, World Championship, Elista 2006

Catalan Opening

1.d4 ♘f6 2.c4 e6 3.♘f3 d5 4.g3 ♗b4+ 5.♗d2 ♗e7 6.♗g2 0–0 7.0–0 c6 8.♗f4 ♘bd7 9.♕c2 a5

This is one of Black's most reliable responses to the main line Catalan, allowing both sides much scope to vary their plans. Black's 9th move, slightly more ambitious than the more popular and solid choice, 9...b6, bids for a greater share of queenside space and is sometimes followed up by a later ...b6, followed up by ...♗a6.

10.♖d1 ♘h5 11.♗c1 b5

Black continues on the theme of gaining queenside space. After 11...f5, another good move, Black plays a kind of Dutch Defence. Players intent on concealing their ultimate strategic choices even further into the early middle-game often play 10...h6.

12.cxd5 cxd5 13.e4

Play now becomes concrete. Reasoning that Black's advancing a- and b-pawns offer White potential play on the momentarily weakened light squares behind them, Kramnik breaks in the centre in an attempt at exploitation. Similar intent lies behind another idea, 12.♘e5, though this time directed primarily against Black's vulnerable pawn on c6.

13...dxe4 14.♕xe4 ♖b8 15.♕e2 ♘hf6

This knight recentralisation is an essential preliminary to contesting White's light square pressure. After the incautious 15...♗b7 16.♘e5, and if 16...♘hf6 (or if 16...♗xg2 17.♔xg2, winning an exchange) 17.♗xb7 ♖xb7 18.♘c6 ♕e8 19.♘xa5, Black loses a pawn.

16.♗f4 ♖b6 17.♘e5 ♘d5

Black must again avoid 17...♗b7 18.♗xb7 ♖xb7 19.♘c6, with obvious advantage. As played, Black hopes to solve most of his light square problems by blocking the power of the light square Catalan bishop. By exchanging this bishop, however, White now successfully changes the nature of the position into one in which White can play to win Black's b-pawn.

18.♗xd5 exd5 19.♘c3 ♘f6

T.Radjabov-V.Topalov, Wijk aan Zee 2007, later saw the radical 19...♘xe5 20.dxe5 d4, leading to the clever draw by repetition (subsequently repeated by others), 21.♗e3 dxe3 22.♕xe3 ♗g5 23.♕c5 ♗e7 24.♕e3 ♗g5 25.♕c5 ♗e7 26.♕e3. Topalov had no doubt subjected the critical alternative, 22.♖xd8

exf2+, and if 23.♔xf2 ♖xd8 24.♖d1, to powerful computer analysis and concluded that Black's rook + two bishops offer sufficient dynamic compensation for White's queen. Maybe!

20.♘xb5 ♗a6 21.a4 ♘e4

White's knight on b5 is awkwardly pinned and Black can hope to regain his pawn by subjecting it to further attack. In doing so, however, he must still tread carefully, as his a-pawn is vulnerable, such as after 21...♕e8 22.♗d2, and if 22...♗xb5 23.axb5 ♕xb5 24.♕xb5 ♖xb5 25.♖db1 (or possibly 25.♖a2) 25...♗d8 26.♘c6 ♘e4 27.♗xa5.

As played, Black covers d2 to prevent this but allows White's king's rook to exert pressure along the 7ᵗʰ rank.

22.♖dc1 ♕e8 23.♖c7 ♗d8 24.♖a7 f6?

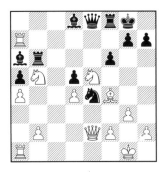

Topalov either tires badly or sees ghosts. He may have distrusted the slightly worse endgames likely to arise after 24...♗xb5 25.axb5 ♕xb5 26.♕xb5 ♖xb5 27.♖a2. Post mortem analysis, however, confirmed that Black then

obtains good drawing chances, by continuing 27...g5 28.♗e3 f5, and if 29.♖a8 ♗c7 30.♖xf8+ ♔xf8 31.f3 ♗xe5 (possibly also 31...♘c5) 32.dxe5 ♘c5 33.♗xg5 ♘d3. At any rate, Black had to play this way. White now gains a pawn and wins in a powerful middlegame.

25.♘d7 ♖f7 26.♘xb6 ♖xa7 27.♘xd5 ♖d7 28.♘dc3 ♖xd4 29.♖e1
Black no longer has any real counterplay. White's pieces are all actively placed and White threatens f3, blasting open the e-file.

29...f5 30.♕c2 ♖b4 31.♘d5 ♖xb5
A last, desperate throw, but inadequate: no better was 31...♗xb5 32.axb5 ♖xb5 33.♕c4, and if 33...♔h8 34.f3 ♖xb2 35.fxe4 ♕h5 36.h4 ♕f3 37.♕f1, and wins.

32.axb5 ♕xb5 33.♘c7 ♕c4 34.♕d1 ♗xc7 35.♕d7
Regaining Black's bishop on c7, due to the threat of ♕e8 mate.

35...h6 36.♕xc7 ♕b4
Allowing queens to be exchanged is tantamount to resignation. By playing 36...♕d4 and retaining queens on the board, however, Black could hope for no more than simply to prolong his agony.

37.♕b8+ ♕xb8 38.♗xb8 ♘d2 39.♖a1 g5 40.f4 ♘b3 41.♖a3 ♗c4 42.♗c7 g4 43.♗xa5 1-0

Exceptional Predatory Stealth
Vishy Anand

S hortly after the Topalov match, Kramnik lost a second contest against *Deep Fritz*. Duly upgraded and now virtually unbeatable against all humankind, the computer ran out clear winner (4-2). The match took place, in Bonn's splendid Art and Exhibition Hall, to a blaze of intense international media excitement. Humanity, it seemed, had finally bowed to the machine's exponentially increasing playing skill. Kramnik's reward for going down in this last ditch cause: 500,000 euros.

Rather more weightily, Kramnik also soon lost his world title. Kramnik agreed to play in FIDE's second 'world championship' tournament, at Mexico City 2007, but only as part of an agreed two stage process that would re-establish future battles for the world's greatest individual accolade, on a settled 'Classical match' basis. The Mexico City winner was to be recognised as the 'undisputed' champion. If that 'champion' were not Kramnik, the two were to meet in a fully recognised Classical title match decider.

Carsten Hensel considers it one of Kramnik's greatest achievements that FIDE agreed to his insistence that the Classical world title must continue to be decided only on its traditional match play basis. As it happened, Anand (9/14) won at Mexico City, a point ahead of 2nd /3rd tied, Kramnik and Gelfand. At Bonn 2008, Anand then defeated Kramnik (the 14th champion) by a splendid two point margin (+3-1=7), to become the 15th champion, in the distinguished Classical line that stretched (via Kasparov, Karpov et al) all the way back to Steinitz.

Aged 38, Anand unusually conceded five years to Kramnik but he did have a marginally higher world ranking. More significantly, Anand had been here before, having previously played against Kasparov, in their 1995 PCA title match. During the unfortunately lengthy fracture between FIDE and Kasparov (and then Kramnik), Anand forged a broadly neutral but brilliant course: he became FIDE world champion, by defeating Shirov (+3=1), in the final of the FIDE KO World Championship 2000.

Both played in a thoroughly modern, enterprisingly universal, classically direct style, employing subtly strategic, tactical and combinational elements, backed up by a wealth of deeply prepared opening ideas. Kramnik perhaps laced his enterprise with a tendency towards intuitively creative and aesthetic paths. Anand more often evinced a calmer, Petrosian-like tendency towards correctly controlled ambition and menacing stealth. Both could explode with in-spired combinative energy if positions required this.

Both Kramnik and Anand were also backed up by the large and talent-ed support teams now a longstanding fixture in such con-tests. These teams worked hard with

29. Vishy Anand v Vladimir Kramnik: World Championship match 2008

their principals to get them into optimum mental, physical and technical (es-pecially in-depth opening preparatory) shape, in anticipation of an unremitting contest. Margins were tight. Anand triumphed largely due to an exceptionally well-chosen choice of openings that told against the handicapping consequences of two particularly debilitating (openings preparatory) Kramnik blind spots.

Kramnik's first major problem arose through an apparent failure to antici-pate Anand's adoption of a relatively new and highly complex line of the Meran Defence, against which he twice (stubbornly) confronted a maelstrom of incred-ible complexity, lost clock-time, missed odd improvements and crashed disas-trously. Anand (and team) had invested masses of highly productive computer time in analyses of a deeply nuanced kind that (once the match had begun) Kram-nik's team couldn't hope to replicate. Anand won both games superbly.

Ahead by two points, Anand all but ended Kramnik's resistance with a third crushing win, in Game 6, which pointed to Kramnik's second openings weak-ness. Kramnik (and team) had apparently over-concentrated on preparing a Black repertoire to meet Anand's expected favourite (1.e4). Primed with many wickedly challenging new ideas, Anand, however, came to the match with 1.d4 his main weapon. White's wonderfully understated 9ᵗʰ move, in Game 6, packed plentiful venom.

V.Anand – V.Kramnik

Game 6, World Championship, Bonn 2008

Nimzo-Indian Defence

**1.d4 ♘f6 2.c4 e6 3.♘c3 ♗b4 4.♕c2 d5
5.cxd5 ♕xd5 6.♘f3 ♕f5 7.♕b3 ♘c6
8.♗d2 0–0 9.h3 b6**

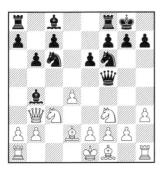

White's novel 9th move, in place of the known 9.e3, prepares g4 (followed by a kingside fianchetto) and poses the question whether Black's queen will be well-posted on g6.

Kramnik sidesteps that challenge. But it later became clear that Black might safely play 9...a5 10.g4 ♕g6, and if 11.a3 a4 12.♕c4 ♗xc3 13.♗xc3, then either 13...♕e4 (Michael Adams), or 13...♘d5 (Sergey Karjakin), with chances for both sides.

**10.g4 ♕a5 11.♖c1 ♗b7 12.a3 ♗xc3
13.♗xc3 ♕d5 14.♕xd5 ♘xd5 15.♗d2**

Against Kramnik's more cautious approach, White has obtained the bishop pair, slightly more flexible pawns and sufficient extra space in which to press a little. White's pressure in the c-file is especially valuable, as it makes it dif-

ficult for Black to achieve a potentially freeing ...c5 break.

15...♘f6 16.♖g1 ♖ac8 17.♗g2 ♘e7

Kramnik provokes White's (excellent) reply, which bolsters White's pressure on c5; but he aims to gambit a pawn on that square, in an enterprising bid to obtain sufficiently compensating piece activity.

18.♗b4 c5

Kramnik fully backs his ambitious judgement, though it doesn't work out as well as he probably hoped. Perhaps he should have contented himself with either of the more cautiously defensive alternatives, 18...♖fe8, and if, say 19.g5 ♘fd5 20.♘e5 ♘f5 (or 20...♘g6), or 18...♘fd5, and if 19.♘e5 ♖fe8.

**19.dxc5 ♖fd8 20.♘e5 ♗xg2 21.♖xg2
bxc5 22.♖xc5 ♘e4 23.♖xc8 ♖xc8 24.♘d3
♘d5 25.♗d2 ♖c2 26.♗c1**

After a lengthy flurry, Black's rook and knights have obtained fine posts in the centre and c-file. White's game, however, lacks any real weakness. Anand will soon eject Black's rook from c2, after which he can expect to make further gradual progress by carefully edging forward his e- and f-pawns, with a view to eventually re-engaging his temporarily poorly-placed rook more usefully along the 2ⁿᵈ rank.

26...f5 27.♔d1 ♖c8 28.f3 ♘d6 29.♔e1 a5 30.e3 e5

Kramnik dynamically gambits a second pawn, hoping to re-energise his knights on the central light squares weakened by this radical course. Black can probably safely bank on eventually regaining at least one of his two sacrificed pawns, as White will struggle to restore harmony in his position without jettisoning at least some of his extra material. It may, however, have been better to play the more solid queenside clamping move, 30...a4, while still possible.

31.gxf5 e4 32.fxe4 ♘xe4 33.♗d2 a4

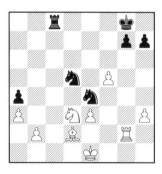

As White can now unravel his still somewhat awkwardly placed pieces to establish an incontrovertibly winning advantage, Kramnik considered this move (which arrives too late) a fatal error. Black gets nowhere, after 33...♖c2, because of 34.♖e2, followed by ♔d1. Kramnik later suggested 33...♖e8, and if 34.♗c1 ♘d6 35.f6 g6, when (although a pawn down) he might still hope to battle.

34.♘f2 ♘d6 35.♖g4 ♘c4 36.e4 ♘f6 37.♖g3 ♘xb2

Black's activity is effectively spent and White now decisively mobilises his e- and f-pawns. Black also loses after 37...♘xe4 38.♘xe4 ♖e8 39.♗c3 ♖xe4+ 40.♔f2, and if 40...♘e5 41.f6 g6 42.♖g5 ♘d7 43.♔f3 ♖e6 44.♖a5.

38.e5 ♘d5

Or if 38...♖e8 39.♗c3, and if 39...♘c4 40.e6 ♘d6 41.♘g4, and wins.

39.f6 ♔f7

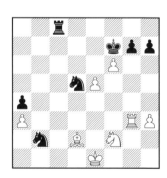

White's e- and f-pawns are unstoppable. White also wins quickly after 39...g6 40.♘e4, threatening e6.

40.♘e4 ♘c4 41.fxg7 ♔g8
Or if 41...♖g8 42.♘d6+ ♘xd6 43.exd6, and if 43...♔e6 44.♗h6 ♔xd6 45.♖f3.

42.♖d3 ♘db6 43.♗h6 ♘xe5 44.♘f6+ ♔f7 45.♖c3 ♖xc3 46.g8♕+ ♔xf6 47.♗g7+ 1–0

Anand next defended his title against Veselin Topalov, who had earned his right to a challenge by defeating the 2007 FIDE World Cup winner, Gata Kamsky, at Sofia 2009 (by 4.5-2.5). Such a 'one-off' decider was a pragmatic choice. FIDE had accepted the principle of deciding the world title by match play, but it hadn't yet decided on a settled qualification format for the challenger. FIDE eventually reinstated Candidates' matches for the post-2010 world championship cycle (after which they were replaced by Candidates' tournaments).

The Topalov-Kamsky match may have been rough-hewn; no one, however, truly decried Topalov his second bite at the 'Classical' crown. Defeated in the 2006 reunification title match, Topalov had to 'sit out' FIDE's world title tournament, at Mexico City 2007, apparently due to a rather bizarre rule that disbarred the reunification match loser from playing there. Since Kasparov's 2005 retirement, Kramnik, Anand and Topalov had been the world's stand-out players. Through most of 2007-2009, Topalov was world number one.

The two parties duly crossed swords, at Sofia 2010. Home advantage, however, failed to fire Topalov, although his one point losing margin was closer than Kramnik's against Anand. On the whole, Anand deservedly defended his title (+3-2=7). Anand's superiority in the opening proved pivotal. Just as he had pin-pointed (and superbly exploited) one or two omissions in Kramnik's repertoire, Anand did much the same against Topalov, although margins, as ever, were tight.

Both players performed at the cutting edge of person/computer interactive mastery. Topalov's Achilles' heel, however, lay primarily in his dogged attachment to a relatively restricted range of favourite opening systems. While Topalov (and team) had prepared these generally well-principled choices to a remarkable degree of depth and precision, they were nonetheless rather more predictable than Anand's more varied systems, which allowed him more often to pounce.

As against Kramnik, Anand's less predictable switch from his lifelong favourite (1.e4), to a wide range of deeply researched 1.d4 openings, brought dividends. Anticipating certain Topalov responses against the Catalan Opening, in Games 2 and 4, Anand confronted his opponent with disagreeably powerful innovations. Topalov misguidedly opted for enterprising counter-attacking ideas that had served him well in the past (and thought that he he understood well), only to be outplayed superbly.

Anand particularly considered that his play, in Game 4, went like a 'dream'. Topalov unwittingly followed a line that Anand had anticipated well beyond Topalov's preparation horizon. After White's excellent 17th move, Anand was already aware that Black's queenside pawns were at risk and that bids to retrieve them lacked substance. Anand's pre-game notes even included the thought that a White knight might eventually land on g4, with fatal consequences on the kingside, as happened.

V.Anand – V.Topalov

Game 4, World Championship, Sofia 2010

Catalan Opening

1.d4 ♞f6 2.c4 e6 3.♞f3 d5 4.g3 dxc4 5.♗g2 ♗b4+ 6.♗d2 a5 7.♕c2 ♗xd2+
Topalov opts for Black's most double-edged line. Smyslov's old favourite, 7...♞c6, and if 8.♕xc4 ♕d5 9.♕xd5 (9.♕d3 is perhaps critical) 9...exd5 10.♞c3 ♗e6, is a more conventionally reliable positional alternative.

8.♕xd2 c6 9.a4 b5 10.♞a3
V.Kramnik-V.Topalov Game 1, World championship, Elista 2006, had previously gone 10.axb5 cxb5 11.♕g5 (regaining the gambit pawn immediately) 11...0-0 12.♕xb5 ♗a6 13.♕a4 ♕b6 14.0-0 ♕xb2 15.♞bd2 ♗b5 16.♞xc4 ♗xa4 17.♞xb2 ♗b5 18.♞e5 ♖a7, with roughly equal chances (White won). Anand's perhaps unexpected alternative allows Black to hold on to the pawn in exchange for an active queenside and central initiative.

10...♗d7 11.♞e5 ♞d5 12.e4 ♞b4 13.0-0 0-0 14.♖fd1 ♗e8

Black's queen's knight and bishop are far from optimally developed and he strains to maintain the integrity of his far advanced and potentially quite rickety queenside pawns. Moreover, after the text-move, White's strong d4/e4 central pawn duo supports an immediate d5 break that threatens to undermine Black's grip on many of his most critical light squares.

Black should probably prefer, 14...♕b6, as in the (later) game, Wang Yue-V.Kramnik, Khanty-Mansiysk 2010, which continued 15.d5 ♖a7 16.dxc6 ♞4xc6 17.♕d6 bxa4 18.♞exc4

♛b4 19.♖ac1 ♗e8 20.♛xb4 axb4 21.♘b5 ♖d7, with Black still battling (and was eventually drawn).

15.d5 ♛d6

Topalov hopes to defend by plugging the d6 and c5 dark squares that have been freed by White's pawn break. If Black instead exchanges pawns on d5, he suffers serious pawn structural deterioration, after either 15... exd5 16.exd5 f6 (or if 16...cxd5 17.axb5) 17.dxc6 ♛xd2 18.♖xd2, and if 18... ♘8xc6 (not 18...fxe5 19.c7) 19.♘xc6 ♗xc6 20.♗xc6 ♘xc6 21.axb5, or 15... cxd5 16.exd5 exd5 17.axb5.

16.♘g4 ♛c5 17.♘e3

After this powerful (home-prepared) knight move, Anand clearly swings matters his way. White threatens to exchange pawns on c6, leading to renewed pressure on Black's queenside light squares (especially b5 and c4). White now develops a definite edge, not just in the centre but on both flanks.

17...♘8a6 18.dxc6 bxa4

Black also suffers after 18...♗xc6 19.axb5 ♗xb5 20.♘axc4, and if 20... ♗xc4 21.♖ac1, regaining White's bishop with a definite advantage.

19.♘axc4 ♗xc6 20.♖ac1 h6

After this move, White establishes a powerful knight on d6 and cuts off Black's queen from its most natural defensive square (e7). Topalov later advocated 20...♛e7, although White can still then manoeuvre a knight to d6, by playing 21.♘xa5, and if 21...♗b5 22.♘ac4 ♖fd8 23.♘d6, with continuing pressure.

21.♘d6 ♛a7

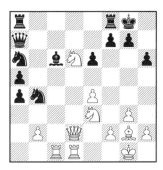

This temporarily decentralising retreat fatally encourages White to embark on a combinative conclusion. Black's chances of defence, however, are also slim, even after 21...♛g5, covering h6, after which White can choose from a range of testing continuations, including 22.h4, and if 22...♛e7 23.♘ec4, threatening both ♘xa5 and ♘e5.

22.♘g4 ♖ad8

Topalov resignedly invites White's crushing finale; or he perhaps just missed some fine point. Black had to play 22...f6. Even then, however, after the clever 23.♖c4, followed by ♛c1, White exerts extreme pressure on Black's awkwardly placed bishop on c6.

23.♘xh6+ gxh6 24.♛xh6 f6 25.e5 ♗xg2 26.exf6

So far, all forced: due to the threat of ♕g6+, followed by f7, and wins, Black can't now retrieve his bishop before giving up an exchange on d6.

26...♖xd6 27.♖xd6 ♗e4

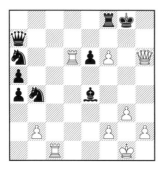

But consider the alternative 27...♗d5. This try loses to the fiendish, 28.♕g6+ ♔h8 29.♖c4!, and if 29...♗xc4 30.♖d4!, mating quickly, a quite brilliant conclusion that might easily have been missed at around move 20.

28.♖xe6 ♘d3

Black may have three minor pieces for a rook (and three important pawns) but one of these pieces languishes completely out of play (on a6) and together they all lack coordination. The text-move only postpones the inevitable for one more move. After the immediate 28...♕h7, White wins by playing 29.♕g5+, and if 29...♗g6 30.f7+ ♔g7 31.♕f6+ ♔h6 32.♖c4, and mates.

29.♖c2 ♕h7 30.f7+

As White's rook (on c2) defends White's f-pawn, this is now quite as decisive as the equally powerful 30.♕g5+.

30...♕xf7 31.♖xe4 ♕f5

Or if 31...♘xf2 32.♖f4

32.♖e7 1-0

Or if 32...♖f7 33.♖c8+ ♕xc8 34.♕g6+ ♔h8 35.♕h5+ ♔g7 36.♖xf7+, and mates.

In 2012, Anand (42) met Boris Gelfand (43) in his next title match. Some eyebrows were raised at the players' ages: weren't they both just a little on the old side? In an age when players in their teens, twenties and thirties increasingly dominated, Magnus Carlsen (20), recent world number one, would probably have been the people's challenger. Citing objections about the selection criteria and event format, however, Carlsen had declined to play in the 2011 Candidates' matches and ruled himself out.

These two 'forty plus' veterans, however, remained at a technical and physical peak and their match-up was merited. Gelfand had, indeed, come through an especially punishing qualifying route. To win the 2011 Candidates', he had defeated Shakhriyar Mamedyarov, Gata Kamsky and Alexander Grischuk. Prior to that, he had obtained his right to play in the Candidates' by winning the 2009 FIDE KO World Cup, leaving Judit Polgar, Maxime Vachier-Lagrave, Dmitry Jakovenko, Sergei Karjakin and Ruslan Ponomariov all in his wake.

The 2012 title match was Gelfand's biggest chess moment. Like Anand, an ever-present in the world elite for two decades, Gelfand first became a Candidate, in 1991. Up for his first ever title challenge, he had nothing to lose and was bound to prove a handful. The contest was staged in Moscow's prestigious State Tretjakow Gallery. A jewel among Moscow's museums, the Tretjakow Gallery houses the world's foremost collection of Russian fine art. At stake was an equally exquisite prize fund of some $2.55million.

The match was exceptionally tight. The players tied (+1-1=10), in the twelve main games played at Classical time rates. In the dramatic, four game Rapid match tie-break, Anand, who was close to a loss in one of the drawn games, just edged victory (+1=3). Anand's relative superiority in rapid-play perhaps eventually told. Going

30. Vishy Anand: Tata Steel tournament 2013

into the match, results between the two, at Classical time rates, had been largely level (overwhelmingly draws). Anand led 8-1, at rapidplay.

Throughout the match, however, Anand also seemed to show just a little more creative resourcefulness, ambition and energy, especially with White. Both players' deeply prepared Black defences held in all but the two decisive, 7th and 8th match games. Anand, however, missed a golden opportunity earlier on. Having outplayed his opponent and on the verge of a win, in Game 3, Anand went seriously wrong, allowing Gelfand to escape with a study-like draw in the midst of a mutually challenging time scramble.

Recognising his opponent's great strengths, Anand explained to the press that Gelfand had been exceptionally 'good in controlling play ... kept on playing unexpected ... very intelligent choices [that defused] the greater part of my preparation [and] was very effective in neutralising me.' Gelfand, in turn, accepted defeat with admirably dignified grace. *New in Chess* quotes him as saying, 'I came to play a big match [and] am proud of my achievement ... the title is not the main thing ... the effort is much more important'.

Having been outplayed in Game 7, Anand was aware that he had to hit back quickly; he did this with aplomb, in Game 8. Perhaps tempting fate, Gelfand allowed Anand to reprise the fuzzily complex line that had almost brought White the full point, in Game 3 (1.d4 ♘f6 2.c4 g6 3.f3 d5 4.cxd5 ♘xd5 5.e4 ♘b6 6.♘c3). In Game 8, rather than repeat 3...d5, Gelfand instead opted for transposition into lines of the King's Indian Defence, but this choice rapidly ran into problems.

Due to the peculiarities of the move-order (3...c5 4.d5), Anand was able to opt for another fuzzy, but perfectly playable manoeuvre (♘g1-e2-c3), delaying the development of White's knight (on b1). This suited Anand, who was simply keen to depart from known theory with a complex game. Gelfand, however, then seemed gripped by an undue impulse to punish his opponent by means of an overly ambitious kingside counter that proved quite disastrously flawed.

V.Anand – B.Gelfand

Game 8, World Championship, Moscow 2012

King's Indian Defence

1.d4 ♘f6 2.c4 g6 3.f3 c5 4.d5 d6 5.e4 ♗g7 6.♘e2
After the more popular and readily understandable, 6.♘c3, and if 6...0-0 7.♗g5 (or 7.♗e3) 7...h6 8.♗e3, followed by ♕d2, play transposes into standard King's Indian lines.

6...0-0 7.♘ec3 ♘h5

Gelfand invites the double-edged reply, 8.g4 ♘f6 9.h4, leading to obscure complications that might either favour the attacker or just prove self-weakening. Ignoring all such temptation, Anand instead aims for a solid plan to increase pressure on the kingside dark squares. Gelfand perhaps later regretted not opting for 7...e6, and if 8.♗e2 exd5 9.cxd5, when both sides can continue along more conventional lines.

8.♗g5 ♗f6
This move, too, surprised Anand, who now felt encouraged. Black rarely exchanges his powerful dark square bishop voluntarily in such positions. He has an ambitious idea. But why should it work? After 8...h6 9.♗e3 f5, Anand intended 10.exf5 gxf5 11.♕d2, which he felt favoured White. Peter Leko advocated 8...f5, with the idea of ...f4, followed by ...♘d7-e5, to prevent which Anand would no doubt also have exchanged pawns on f5.

9.♗xf6 exf6 10.♕d2

Anand again prefers solidly purpose-ful development. He rejected the more directly confrontational 10.g4 ♘f4 11.♕d2 g5 12.h4 ♘d7 13.♕h2, because of the unclear gambit resource, 13...h5, and if 14.hxg5 fxg5 15.gxh5 ♘e5, when he could see no clear way to break down Black's central dark square and kingside blockade.

10...f5 11.exf5 ♗xf5

The attempt to bully White on the king-side, by playing 11...♕h4+ 12.♔d1 ♘g3, clearly fails to 13.♕f2 ♘xf5 14.♕xh4 ♘xh4 15.♘b5, threatening both ♘c7 and ♘xd6.

12.g4 ♖e8+

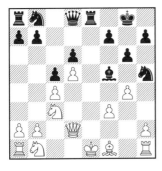

Black drives White's king to d1. But as Black's bishop can't remain on f5, Gelfand only succeeds in nudging White's monarch towards complete safety in the centre (on c2), after which White can expect to rapidly centralise rooks and dominate play on the king-side. Anand thought that Black had to play 12...♗xb1 13.♖xb1 ♘g7, although after 14.h4, and if 14...h5 15.♔d1 ♘d7 16.♔c2 ♘e5 17.♗e2, he considered that White clearly stood better.

13.♔d1 ♗xb1 14.♖xb1 ♕f6?

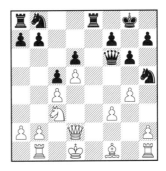

Having apparently missed White's clever 17th move refutation, Gelfand unwittingly blunders. After the game, he confessed that he didn't really be-lieve in either of Black's two dispirit-ingly passive alternatives (...♘f6 or ...♘g7), but he no longer had anything better.

15.gxh5 ♕xf3+ 16.♔c2 ♕xh1 17.♕f2 1–0

Black's queen is quietly but effectively trapped. White threatens ♗d3, forcing a decisive gain in material, after ei-ther 17...♘a6 18.♗d3, and if 18...♘b4+ 19.♔d2 ♘xd3 20.♔xd3 ♕xb1+ 21.♘xb1, or 17...♘c6 18.dxc6 ♕xc6 19.♗d3.

All Round Momentum

Magnus Carlsen

Having defeated Gelfand, Anand enjoyed little more than a year's break before having to meet Magnus Carlsen (b 1990), in his fourth, and final title defence. The young Norwegian superstar, top in the world rankings, since January 2010, belonged to a new generation brought up completely in the computer age. Aged 22, Carlsen (2870) was odds-on to win, at Chennai 2013. Aged 43, Anand (2775) was not just out-rated but also double his age. Carlsen won comfortably (+3=7), with no need to play either of the final two scheduled match games.

Carlsen emphatically showed that he had the tighter and more powerful all round game. Anand lamented afterwards that he simply couldn't get to grips with a determinedly slippery opponent, who was full of surprises and made few mistakes. A chameleon-like master of all styles and modes of play, Carlsen successfully sought primarily original paths, with a view to giving full reign to his universally versatile, hard-hitting mastery.

Carlsen's principal match plan seemed to be to steer for positions in which both sides had to think for themselves. While he and his coaching team studied theory as well as any rival, Carlsen tended to see this aspect of the game mainly as an essential stepping-stone to real contests that took place beyond learned horizons. Carlsen had developed such wide-ranging, deeply creative instincts from his earliest primary school years. In 50:50 situations, he wins more often than most.

Interviewed in *New in Chess* (2006), Simen Agdestein, Carlsen's earliest biographer and coach, observed that 'in a time of information overflow ... the new champion could be the one that handles this best'. Predicting a bright future for his precociously gifted young charge, already two years a grandmaster, he noted how Carlsen had long wished 'to know everything'. Carlsen used computers well. His abiding aim, however, was to have fun, while making interesting things happen in games.

In his book, *Wonder Boy - How Magnus Carlsen became the youngest grandmaster in the world*, Agdestein explains how the very young Carlsen thrived in a highly supportive familial, coaching and learning framework that accented unabashed 'joyfulness'. While Carlsen was allowed ample space in which to discover and develop his own special chess talent, his close-knit family ensured that he remained well-rooted in his local community.

Carlsen was neither home-schooled nor hot-housed. From around 2000, however, as his early talent, wide-ranging chess curiosity and voracious work ethic became ever clearer, he began to play in a series of increasingly strong open international tournaments, usually accompanied by his father, Henrik, but also often by other family members, trying to inject as relaxed an off-board

31. Magnus Carlsen: Tata Steel tournament 2013

social atmosphere as possible into the more serious chess proceedings.

This certainly worked. In 2004, aged 13 years and three months, Carlsen became one of only a select few players to have gained the grandmaster title at such an exceptionally young age. From that point, he only rapidly got even stronger. With his father as manager, Carlsen began to attract invitations to ever more elite tournaments. In 2007, he qualified for a place in the Candidates' matches, in which, after tying at Classical time rates (3-3) and then at Rapidplay (2-2), he only went out, in the Blitz tie-break, against Levon Aronian.

By April 2008, Carlsen placed fifth in the world rankings. By November 2009, rated 2801, he ranked world number two, only nine points behind VeselinTopalov. By that date, only five players (Kasparov, Topalov, Kramnik, Anand and Carlsen) had ever broken the formidable 2800 ratings barrier. From January 2010, the world's top-ranked player, Carlsen subsequently retained that spot through the 2010s and into the 2020s. Early in 2013, he won a splendidly competitive Candidates' tournament, at London.

Although run close, at London, by Vladimir Kramnik, who only lost on the narrowest of tie-breaks (5-4 to Carlsen on overall wins), Carlsen remained clear favourite to defeat Anand, at Chennai 2013. Most experts and fans tipped him heavily. Carlsen seemed to have just a little bit extra in every skill in the game: calmly confident, self-possessed, boundlessly creative, thoroughly prepared, razor-sharp in calculation and utterly accurate in judgement, he also simply fizzed with energy.

Game 9, at Chennai, adds an additional twist of calculated risk, controlled aggression and psychology into that mix. Two points behind, Anand chose a sharp favourite, in a final bid to get back into the match. Ready for this, however,

Carlsen startled his opponent, on his 7th and 8th moves, which took play into decidedly unclear territory. 'Theory' often gives a very slight nod to White structures in such middlegames but this was new ground. Both players absolutely gave their all; Carlsen, as so often, snatched the full point.

V.Anand – M.Carlsen

Game 9, World Championship, Chennai 2013

Nimzo-Indian Defence

1.d4 ♘f6 2.c4 e6 3.♘c3 ♗b4 4.f3 d5 5.a3 ♗xc3+ 6.bxc3 c5 7.cxd5 exd5

After the more usual 7...♘xd5 8.dxc5, and now either 8...♕a5 or 8...f5, play is dynamically balanced. Carlsen's pawn recapture stakes a strong claim on d5, and allows easy piece development, but comes with a potentially static, pawn structural downside. White can now aim to achieve an attacking central (e4-e5) pawn advance, often backed up by the further menacing advance of White's f- and g-pawns to the fourth and even fifth ranks.

8.e3 c4 9.♘e2 ♘c6 10.g4 0-0

No doubt buoyed by considerable human/computer preparation, Carlsen castles directly into White's attack. He hopes to hold in the centre and on the kingside, while generating queenside counterplay. Black plans ...♘a5-b3, followed by the advance of his a- and b-pawns. White plans ♗g2, 0-0 and ♘g3, followed eventually by advancing his e-pawn.

V.Korchnoi-A.O'Kelly de Galway, Bucharest 1954, one of the few relevant stem games in this line (no doubt known to both sides), had earlier gone 10...♘a5 11.♘g3 (or if 11.♗g2 ♘b3 12.♖a2 h5) 11...♘b3 12.♖a2 h5 (hoping to break White's attack before it gains alarming strength) 13.g5 ♘xc1 14.♕xc1 ♘g8 15.h4 ♘e7 16.e4 ♕c7 17.♔f2 ♗e6, and was eventually drawn.

11.♗g2 ♘a5 12.0-0 ♘b3 13.♖a2 b5

Carlsen, however, clearly had other plans. Steinitz-like, he leaves his kingside pawns untouched unless absolutely forced to move them. Such moves as ...h5 (and perhaps also ...h6) may have strategic point but might also prove weakening. Carlsen rather aims to stand completely fast on the kingside, while aiming for a rapid queenside pawn break (on b4), but will that be sufficient?

14.♘g3 a5 15.g5 ♘e8 16.e4 ♘xc1

There was much post-mortem debate about whether Black should have retained this knight and instead played 16...♘c7, with the possible continuation 17.♗e3 ♖a6 18.e5 b4, perhaps followed by 19.axb4 axb4 20.♖xa6 ♘xa6, and if 21.f4 bxc3 22.f5, reaching a position in which both sides may (or may not) have roughly balanced attacking and defensive chances. Black is, however, still going to get in the ...b4 pawn break, come what may.

17.♕xc1 ♖a6 18.e5

Anand stakes all on advancing his e- and f-pawns as rapidly as possible, which is both readily understandable and can hardly be bad. Kasparov suggested the more cautious preliminary 18.♖b2, and if 18...♘c7 19.e5 ♕e7 20.♖b1, but after 20...♖b6, Black is again poised to play ...b4, and retains activity.

18...♘c7 19.f4 b4 20.axb4

Anand decides to eliminate a pair of rooks. After the immediate 20.f5, retaining both pairs of rooks on the board, Black's best might be 20...g6, seeking to induce the response 21.f6 b3, followed by ...♕d7 (and ...♖b6), when Black's powerful b-pawn is a threatening beast.

20...axb4 21.♖xa6 ♘xa6 22.f5

Sadly, for Anand, who badly needed to win, the more careful attempt to maintain White's attack, by playing 22.cxb4 ♘xb4 23.f5, only appears to peter out to rough, but fairly clear equality, after 23...♕b6, and if 24.♕c3 ♘c6 25.♗xd5 ♘xd4 26.♔g2 g6 27.fxg6 hxg6 28.♘e4 ♗e6.

After Anand's dangerous, if more speculative and quite unfathomably complex choice, Black's most accurate continuation might have been 22...g6, and if 23.f6 b3. Either way, however, Black's b-pawn seems destined to prove a mighty thorn in White's side for the rest of the game.

22...b3 23.♕f4 ♘c7 24.f6

After another Kasparov suggestion 24.♕h4

Black may have had to find the remarkable computer resource (quickly noticed, at the time) 24...g6 25.♕h6 ♗xf5 26.♖xf5 ♕e7!, when Black's powerful b-pawn appears to be fully worth a minor piece: such as, for example, after 27.♖f1 (or if 27.♗e4 ♖a8 28.♗b1 ♕f8 29.♕xf8+ ♔xf8 30.♖f1 ♔g8, threatening ...♖a1, ...b2 and ...♘b5) 27...♖a8, and if 28.♖b1 ♖a2 29.♗h3 ♘e6 30.♗xe6 ♕xe6 31.♕h4 ♕c8, threatening ...♖c2 and ...b2 (note how, in this line, White's queen is fatally tied to the h-file, to prevent the mating idea ...♕h3).

24...g6 25.♕h4 ♘e8 26.♕h6

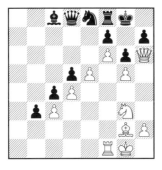

Anand's determination to play until his very last winning chance disappears commands the utmost admiration. With his 26ᵗʰ move, White steels himself to allow Black to gain an extra queen (scarily with check). Anand realised, of course, that this was his only remaining winning try and that after his only sensible alternative, 26.♘e2 ♗e6 27.♘f4 ♕a5, Black holds, even after 28.♘xe6 fxe6 29.♗h3 ♘c7 30.f7+ ♖xf7 31.♖xf7 ♔xf7 32.♕xh7+ ♔f8, when White must take the draw by perpetual check.

26...b2 27.♖f4 b1♕+ 28.♘f1??

Chess can be cruel. Anand had hoped (against hope) that by instead retreating his bishop he might still mate. There isn't any mate, however, and unable to find one, Anand simply used up virtually all of his remaining clock-time and energy. And cracked.

After 28.♗f1, it transpires that both sides must agree to the spectacularly forced (and, indeed, honourable!) draw: 28...♕d1 29.♖h4 ♕h5 (only move) 30.♘xh5 gxh5 31.♖xh5 ♗f5 32.g6 (even more accurate than 32...♗h3 ♗g6, and if 33.e6 ♘xf6 34.gxf6 ♕xf6, which should also suffice) 32...♗xg6 33.♖g5 ♕a5 (or if 33...♘xf6 34.exf6 ♕xf6 35.♖xd5 ♕f3 36.♖c5 ♕xc3 37.♖xc4, with equality) 34.♖g3 ♕a3 35.♗g2 ♕a1+ 36.♔f2 ♕b2+, forcing perpetual check (but not 36...♕a5 37.h4, threatening h5, and White presses).

28...♕e1 0–1

Anand had noticed the quite brilliant conclusion 28...♕d1 29.♖h4 ♕h5 (forced) 30.♖xh5 gxh5 31.♘e3 ♗e6 32.♗xd5, and if 32...♗xd5 33.♘f5, followed by ♘e7+, and wins.

Now, however, after 29.♖h4 ♕xh4, White simply loses a rook.

Not yet to be out-done, Anand almost immediately bounced back by comfortably winning the 2014 Candidates' tournament, at Khanty-Mansiysk. At Sochi 2014, however, Carlsen again won their second title contest, with relative ease (+3-1=7). While Anand narrowed the deficit, won one game and played one extra round, this second defeat effectively ended his many distinguished years of either holding or battling for the world title. Carlsen's fast rising contemporary, Sergei Karjakin, runner-up to Anand, at Kanty-Mansyisk, reversed these standings, at the Moscow 2016 Candidates' tournament.

By far the oldest player, at Moscow, Anand (46), finally bowed to the travails of age. Scoring 8.5/14, Karjakin (25) this time firmly relegated Anand (7.5) into a share of 2nd/3rd places with another exciting young prospect, Fabiano Caruano (23). The forthcoming Karjakin-Carlsen title match signalled a definite generational shift at the summit in chess. Karjakin became the world's youngest ever grandmaster at the extraordinarily young age of 12 years and 7 months (still a record, as I write). The over-40s vanguard, comprising Anand, Kramnik and Topalov, was at last in world title decline.

Both born in 1990, Karjakin and Carlsen had long been measured only against each other's prodigious achievements. Carlsen's rather more naturally talented and securely intuitive gifts matured more quickly. Karjakin's clear-sighted analytical powers, exceptional work ethic and icy competitive steel, however, strongly suggested that he might eventually catch up. When the two players clashed, at New York 2016, the outcome over the twelve Classical games was a far from surprisingly hard-fought tie (+1-1=10). Carlsen, however, prevailed (+2=2) in the Rapidplay tie break.

Sadly for Karjakin, Carlsen was not just the higher-rated player at Classical chess but also at Rapidplay. In 2014, Carlsen held all three world titles (Classical, Rapid and Blitz), a feat that he later repeated in 2019. The 2016 result echoed the 2006 and 2013 world championships, in which the clear Rapidplay favourites, Kramnik (against Topalov) and Anand (against Gelfand) also won Rapidplay tie-breaks. 21st century world title aspirants require absolute mastery at Rapidplay (and Blitz) to deal with such modern tie break demands, or risk failure at the very last hurdle.

Tie breaks nonetheless inevitably entail heightened risk and strain on anyone's nerves. More relieved than elated by his tie break success against Karjakin, Carlsen openly acknowledged that his overall margin of victory had been tight. In Game 8, Carlsen had even engineered a largely self-inflicted crisis, by overplaying his hand and losing, to fall one point behind in the main Classical games, with only four games remaining. Carlsen only just managed to restore parity by winning an epic Game 10.

Game 10 is an excellent example of Carlsen's unrelenting desire to judiciously vary his openings and niggle opponents. In Game 10, Carlsen's choice of opening didn't seem to promise very much. It hadn't, however, been especially tested, which forced both players to play almost from scratch. Up to around Black's 21st move, Karjakin's game was objectively

fine but he over-thought matters, fell behind on the clock and struggled to calculate clearly, eventually stumbling into a difficult endgame, in which Carlsen's technique was superb.

M.Carlsen – S.Karjakin

Game 10, World Championship, New York 2016

Spanish Opening

1.e4 e5 2.♘f3 ♘c6 3.♗b5 ♘f6 4.d3 ♗c5 5.c3 0-0 6.♗g5 h6 7.♗h4 ♗e7 8.0-0 d6 9.♘bd2 ♘h5 10.♗xe7 ♕xe7 11.♘c4 ♘f4 Black's 7...♗e7, a known (and sound) manoeuvre, sets up this relieving dark square bishop exchange. The energetic 11...f5, and if 12.♗xc6!? (or if 12.♘e3 fxe4 13.dxe4 ♘f4) 12...bxc6 13.♘fxe5 ♘f4 14.♘xc6 ♕e8, with good play for a sacrificed pawn, may also be perfectly good.

12.♘e3 ♕f6 13.g3 ♘h3+ 14.♔h1 ♘e7 15.♗c4 c6 16.♗b3 ♘g6 17.♕e2 a5 18.a4 ♗e6 19.♗xe6!?

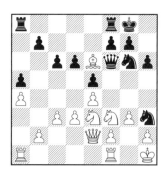

Following mutually cagey manoeuvring, White takes a committal plunge (19.♘d2 might, however, have been

best). After Black's more or less forced reply (otherwise White's gains f5 for his knight), White doubles Black's e-pawns, which may (or may not) prove to be a long-term structural weakness. Objectively, Karjakin retains sufficient solidity and activity in the half-open f-file. He had, however, already fallen markedly behind on the clock.

19...fxe6 20.♘d2 d5?!
Karjakin misses 20...♘xf2+, and if 21.♔g2 ♘h4+ 22.♔g1 (not 22.gxh4? ♕g6+, and Black wins) 22...♘h3+ 23.♔h1 ♘f2+, drawing immediately. White should avoid 21.♔g1 ♘h3+ 22.♔g2 ♘hf4+ 23.gxf4 ♘xf4+ 24.♖xf4, which, after either recapture on f4, only benefits Black. White should, however, now play 21.f3, with the slightly better, long-term prospects.

21.♕h5?! ♘g5?
Still nervily on edge, Karjakin now misses 21...♘xf2+ 22.♔g2 (or if 22.♔g1 ♕g5 23.♕xg5 ♘h3+ 24.♔g2 ♘xg5, with an edge for Black) 22...♕f7! (threat-

ening ...♘f4+!) 23.♔g1 (or if 23.♕e2 ♘h4+!) 23...♕f6!, threatening ...♕g5!, which forces the surprise draw by repetition, 24.♔g2 ♕f7, etc.

22.h4 ♘f3 23.♘xf3 ♕xf3+ 24.♕xf3 ♖xf3 25.♔g2

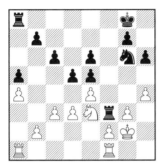

Famed for his superb defensive skills, Karjakin no doubt hoped that he should hold this relatively simplified endgame. But he no longer retains any meaningful kingside activity and must sit back wholly passively and 'wait'. In these circumstances, Black's doubled e-pawns are, indeed, weak. With rooks on the board, moreover, White also has a variety of probing (and eventually breakthrough) prospects, in the centre and on both flanks.

25...♖f7 26.♖fe1 h5 27.♘f1 ♔f8 28.♘d2 ♔e7 29.♖e2 ♔d6 30.♘f3 ♖af8 31.♘g5 ♖e7 32.♖ae1 ♖fe8 33.♘f3

By initially concentrating power in the e-file, White has cleverly forced Black's rooks into purely defensive positions and induced ... h5 (weakening g5). If Black hadn't played ...h5, however, White would eventually have played h5

himself, gaining significant kingside space. With the text-move, White envisages making further dynamic gains by playing d4.

33...♘h8 34.d4 exd4 35.♘xd4 g6 36.♖e3 ♘f7

Black would prefer to prevent White's space-gaining reply but daren't risk 36...e5, which only chronically loosens his central pawns, such as after 37.♘b3, and if 37...b6 38.♖d1 ♔e6 39.exd5+ cxd5 40.♖ed3 ♖d8 41.c4 d4 42.f4, when Black's d-pawn must fall, or if 42...♖ed7 43.c5, and White wins.

37.e5+ ♔d7 38.♖f3 ♘h6

Or if 38...g5 39.hxg5 ♘xg5 40.♖f6 ♘e4 41.♖h6, with a continuing grip on the game.

39.♖f6 ♖g7 40.b4

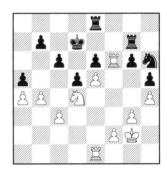

Black has rid himself of his doubled e-pawns but White's extra acres of space and punishing piece pressure are decisive. White might now try 40.c4, threatening to exchange pawns on d5, followed by an attack in the c-file, or in the d-file, after 40...dxc4. On the last move of the first time control, however, Carlsen instead opts for the eminently secure and strategically powerful alternative to dominate further key squares (c5 and b6).

40...axb4 41.cxb4 ♘g8 42.♖f3 ♘h6 43.a5 ♘f5 44.♘b3 ♔c7 45.♘c5 ♔b8 46.♖b1 ♔a7 47.♖d3 ♖c7 48.♖a3 ♘d4 49.♖d1 ♘f5 50.♔h3 ♘h6 51.f3 ♖f7 52.♖d4 ♘f5 53.♖d2 ♖h7 54.♖b3 ♖ee7 55.♖dd3 ♖h8 56.♖b1 ♖hh7?!

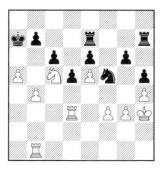

Carlsen's plan has played out much as expected. White now probes for the most favourable moment to pull the trigger on a potentially winning b5 break (possibly preceded by a timely g4 advance). Having rushed his king to the a-file, Black has so far defended well but now miscalculates. White's b5 break now leads by force to the win of Black's e-pawn.

57.b5 cxb5 58.♖xb5 d4

Black abandons his e-pawn, which was, in any case, indefensible after 58...♖h8 59.♖b6, and if 59...♖he8 60.g4 ♘h6 61.♖db3, and wins.

59.♖b6 ♖c7 60.♘xe6 ♖c3 61.♘f4 ♖hc7 62.♘d5

This is good enough, but 62.♖xg6, and if 62...♖xd3 63.♘xd3 ♖c3 64.♖f6, was even more directly effective.

62...♖xd3 63.♘xc7 ♔b8 64.♘b5 ♔c8 65.♖xg6 ♖xf3 66.♔g2 ♖b3 67.♘d6+ ♘xd6 68.♖xd6 ♖e3

A dejected Karjakin rejected the more robust 68...♔c7, because of 69.♖xd4 ♖b5 70.e6 ♖xa5 71.e7 ♖e5 72.♖d5!, but missed 72...♖xe7 73.♖xh5 ♔c6, when White still faces some practical problems. White might also opt, however, for 70.♖a4, and if 70...♖xe5 71.♔f3 ♔d7 72.a6 bxa6 73.♖xa6, when, since Black's h-pawn must eventually fall, White's win should be relatively easy.

69.e6 ♔c7 70.♖xd4 ♖xe6 71.♖d5 ♖h6 72.♔f3 ♔b8 73.♔f4 ♔a7 74.♔g5 ♖h8 75.♔f6 1–0

By the mid-2010s, the reunified world title cycle had settled into a two year series of eight-player, double-round Candidates' tournaments, followed by a twelve game title match (with Rapid, Blitz and Armageddon play-offs, as required). This arrangement used the FIDE World Cup, Grand Prix Series and Rating System as feeders (top two from each) into the Candidates' tournament, which also included the defeated player from the previous title match and one FIDE wild card.

Faster moving than the three year cycle of the mid- to late-20th century, this shorter cycle keeps world champions on their toes and fits well with the wider demands of other professionally organised chess. Since Karpov first made the point, in the late-1970s, top-class players must continually train and play frequently or risk rapid decline in a modern (post-Fischer) professional environment. One of the virtues of the new cycle is that it allows space for participants to compete in a diverse range of other non-title events.

Some critics nonetheless specifically decry the truncation of the Classical section of the newly designed title match to only twelve games. While the history of world championships contains wild swings from various 'unlimited' to 'limited' match formats, this arguably streamlines too much. Carlsen's next title defence, against Fabiano Caruana (b 1992), at London 2018, only fuelled this debate. The players reeled off twelve straight draws, in the first ever title match to feature no wins at all, at Classical time rates.

Formally, of course, tie-breaks kicked in. Carlsen, the significantly higher-rated Rapid player, then drubbed his opponent (3-0), at Rapidplay. To become Classical world champion, however, without winning even one Classical game, still somehow grates. Some contend that the world's best Rapid and Blitz players might even enjoy a perverse incentive to play solely for draws, in such short title matches, so that they might unduly profit by their superiority at Rapid and Blitz.

It should, at once, be stressed that the twelve Classical draws, at London 2018, were all generally very hard-fought. Far from boringly bloodless, this was a difficult contest in which both players probed hard and missed occasionally excellent chances in often highly tense games. Caruana, moreover, didn't complain but drew the rather more appropriate professional conclusion that he must work even harder on his all-round Classical and Rapidplay strength.

Debates about match formats will, of course, never cease. Irrespective of its initial twelve draws, the actual course of the Carlsen-Caruana match was compelling throughout. When they met, Caruana, clear world number two, trailed Carlsen only by three insignificant points in the Classical rankings. Two giants clashed but landed no game-winning blow against the other in the Classical contests. Caruana began with a loss in the Rapid tie-break but, playing White in the second game, he could certainly hope to strike back.

After an excellent start, however, Caruana began to over-force a definite edge on the queenside. Going, it seems, nervously (and unnecessarily) for a doubtful conversion into a winning attack, he fatally ignored king safety and began to collapse. Having soaked up White's early pressure,

Carlsen hit back with all of the defensive and counterattacking resources he could muster, demonstrating deadpan panâche against an opponent whose Rapidplay skills just weren't up to his outstanding mark.

F.Caruana – M.Carlsen

Rapid tie-break Game 2, World Championship, London 2018

Sicilian Defence: Sveshnikov

1.e4 c5 2.♘f3 ♘c6 3.d4 cxd4 4.♘xd4 ♘f6 5.♘c3 e5 6.♘db5 d6 7.♘d5 ♘xd5 8.exd5 ♘e7

The players had already tested the lines arising after 8...♘b8 9.a4 ♗e7 10.♗e2 0-0 11.0-0 ♘d7, and now 12.♗d2 (Classical Game 8) and 12.b4 (Classical Game 10). Both games led to hard fought draws, in which White perhaps obtained a slight opening pull before the onset of unclear complications.

9.c4 ♘g6 10.♕a4 ♗d7 11.♕b4 ♕b8

Some five months later, F.Caruana-M. Carlsen, Grenke 2019, went 11...♗f5 12.h4 h5 13.♗g5 ♕b8 14.♕a4, leading eventually to a draw, although White perhaps enjoyed another slight opening pull. S.Karjakin-M.Carlsen,

Gashimov Memorial 2019, played two weeks before that game, saw 14.♗e2 a6 15.♘c3 ♕c7 16.g3 ♗e7 17.♗e3 e4 18.0-0 0-0 19.♗xh5 ♘e5 20.♗e2 ♕d7 21.♕a4 ♕c8 22.c5 dxc5 23.♘xe4 c4, with good play for a pawn (Black won).

12.h4 h5 13.♗e3 a6

Two years later, the internet encounter, Carlsen,M-Gelfand,B, Legends of Chess 2020, went 13...b6 14.♗e2 ♗e7 15.g3 a6 16.♘c3 b5 17.cxb5 axb5 18.0-0 0-0 19.♗xh5, when Black failed to achieve sufficient compensation for the sacrificed pawn and eventually lost.

14.♘c3 a5

Within two months or so of the Caruana-Carlsen title match, the young Dutch player, Jorden van Foreest, bravely tempted fate by repeating White's first 14 moves in this line against Carlsen, only to meet the full-blooded novelty, 14....f5. J.Van Foreest-M.Carlsen, Tata Steel 2019, then continued, 15.0-0-0 ♗e7 16.g3 0-0 17.♗e2 e4 18.♘d4 (18.♗xh5 looks critical) 18...♗f6 19.♗xf6 ♖xf6 20.♕b6

32. F.Caruana v M.Carlsen: Grenke tournament, Karlsruhe 2018

♘e5 21.♔b1 ♗e8, with at least full equality (Black won).

15.♕b3 a4 16.♕d1 ♗e7 17.g3 ♕c8 18.♗e2 ♗g4 19.♖c1

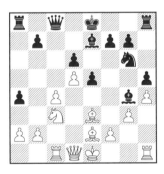

White angles for an ambitious c5 break. This idea, however, would have been more in place in response to 18...0–0, to deter ...♗g4, which (with Black castled) would allow an exchange of bishops on g4, followed by h5.

White should instead have preferred the more straightforward 19.♗xg4, and

if 19...♕xg4 20.♕xg4 hxg4 21.♔e2, with a comfortable, queenside structural edge; or if 19...hxg4 20.♕e2, keeping open the option of 0–0–0 (as well as c5).

19...♗xe2 20.♕xe2 ♕f5 21.c5!?

With the Rapidplay clock ticking down, Caruana's judgement starts to go around here. Opening up the position like this, with White's king still in the centre (and White's king's rook undeveloped) carries no little risk. White might still have played more soundly to his long-term structural advantages, by castling kingside.

21...0–0 22.c6!?

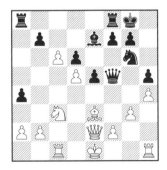

White should now have probably preferred 22.cxd6 ♗xd6 23.0–0, even if it leads to no more than equality after 23...e4, releasing e5 for occupation by a Black minor piece.

22...bxc6 23.dxc6 ♖fc8 24.♕c4 ♗d8 25.♘d5

It was now too late for 25.0–0, which allows 25...♘e7, and if 26.♘d5 ♘xc6.

25...e4 26.c7?

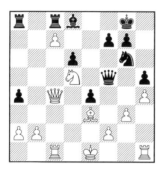

Nerves shot completely, White now simply blunders away his passed c-pawn and loses. Even here, he might still have resisted, by playing 26.♗d4, and if 26...♖a5 (or 26...♕f3 27.0–0 ♘xh4 28.gxh4, with no more than a draw) 27.♘e3 ♕f3 28.0–0, when it remains unclear whether Black can achieve much, by sacrificing either bishop or knight on h4.

26...♗xc7 27.♘xc7 ♘e5 28.♘d5

Or if 28.♕d5 ♖ab8, and wins.

28...♔h7 0–1

White cannot prevent the crushing ...♘d3+.

After retaining his title, at London 2018, Carlsen once again began to pull clearly ahead of allcomers in the world rankings. From Biel 2018 to Stavanger 2020, he recorded an unprecedented unbeaten run of 125 consecutive Classical games, scoring impressively (+42=83). Not just unbeatable at Classical time rates, Carlsen also took the 2019 world titles, at Rapid and Blitz. Through 2020, as virtually all over the board chess shut down, due to international lockdowns in response to the world-wide spread of the Covid-19 pandemic, Carlsen was equally dominant in online formats.

In the enforced absence of almost all professional over the board chess, *The Play Magnus Group* (together with *Chess24*) launched its first online *Magnus Carlsen Chess Tour*, to help fill in a huge gap for the eight elite players who played in it. A Rapid event, with a novel, tennis-like, mini-set format, it consisted of four knock-out legs and one grand final for the top four qualifiers. Magnus won this series, as well as an equally novel *Clutch Chess International* KO Rapid, organised by the Saint Louis Chess Club not long after.

These, and other online events, broadcast with expert commentary live on the internet, attracted large audiences. So much so, that later in 2020, the *Play Magnus Group* was able to launch successfully on the Oslo Stock Market, with a mission to grow the game in the internet era as a global portal offering extensive online news, playing, coaching, teaching and publishing services. The company's 'brand ambassador', Carlsen is a key board member, alongside his father, Henrik, and Espen Agdestein, his manager (since 2009).

This team had a long-proven record of successful chess promotion and development of the Magnus 'brand'. It made an early international breakthrough, by negotiating a major modelling contract with the global clothing group, *G-Star Raw*, which was as good for Magnus's image as it was a commercial master-stroke. Like Anand, in India, one of Norway's most celebrated sportsmen, Magnus's considerable accomplishments have sparked an explosion in numbers of Norwegian chess players, sponsorship and media interest in chess.

How commercially successful such partnership, sponsorship and service provision activities offered by *The Play Magnus Group* and any other similar online rivals might be in the future, not least when the pandemic relents and over the board chess returns, remains to be seen. Elite professional online Rapid and Blitz competition, however, backed up by astute, media-savvy live commentary, certainly seems poised to thrive. As I conclude this book, almost half-way through 2021, new waves of the Covid virus still threaten havoc and lockdowns remain. I have no crystal ball.

FIDE nonetheless remains hopeful that its Covid-induced postponement of Carlsen's scheduled 2020 world title defence will take place towards the end of 2021, in Dubai. To that end, FIDE 'successfully' managed to complete the

'2020' Candidates' tournament (but only) one full year after it commenced. Due to a rapid rise in Covid-19 in Russia, FIDE were forced to suspend the Ekaterinburg event half-way through. Deemed safe to conclude, only in April 2021, Ian Nepotmnachtchi (b 1990), ran out convincing winner, scoring 8.5/14.

While we await events on the Carlsen-Nepotmnachtchi match, let's look back to the 8th Altibox tournament, at Stavanger 2020, one of very few over the board tournaments that actually took place that year during an extremely brief and localised lull in the pandemic's virulence. In a bid to encourage fighting chess, in this six player, double round event, each round featured a Classical game, followed, only if drawn, by an Armageddon decider. All Classical wins scored 3 points. Armageddon wins scored 1.5 (with 1 point to the loser).

At Stavanger 2020, Carlsen once more triumphed, scoring 19.5 points, ahead of second-placed, 17 year-old, Alizera Firouzja (18.5), currently the hottest tip among the chess world's youngest aspirants for an eventual tilt at the world title. All eyes, however, were inevitably drawn to Carlsen's second Classical game against, Jan-Krzysztof Duda (22), another young rival, who had magnificently ended Carlsen's run of 125 undefeated Classical games, in their first encounter. In one of Carlsen's best Stavanger games, revenge came sweetly.

M.Carlsen – J-K.Duda

8th Altibox, Stavanger 2020

Queen's Gambit: Meran Variation

1.d4 d5 2.c4 c6 3.e3 ♘f6 4.♘c3 e6 5.b3 b6 6.♗b2 ♗b7 7.♗d3 ♘bd7 8.♘ge2

In this line, this knight more commonly develops to f3, to exert pressure on e5. Here, however, Black has fianchettoed his queenside bishop early, rather than play the more direct ...♘bd7, ...♗d6, ...0–0 (which raises the possibility of an early ...e5). This slower development allows White to speculate on the manoeuvre, ♘ge2–g3, which, by eyeing the f5 square, indirectly inhibits ...e5.

8...♗d6 9.0–0 0–0 10.♘g3 c5 11.cxd5 cxd4

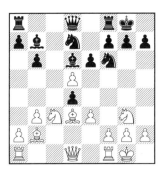

Black has gone for an early ...c5 break. How familiar either player was with this little-played line, however, isn't certain. White must find a useful middlegame future for his knight on g3, such as after, say 11...♘xd5, and if 12.♘xd5 ♗xd5 13.e4 ♗b7 14.e5 ♗c7 15.♖e1, with e4 and h5 beckoning.

Black hopes to deny White's knight any such prospect, while rapidly completing his development.

12.♘ce4 ♗xg3 13.♘xg3 dxe3 14.dxe6

With his 11th and 12th moves, Carlsen opts for an interesting gambit. For a pawn, White gains a lively bishop pair, the more active development and potential play against Black's slightly weakened kingside and isolated e-pawn.

14...exf2+ 15.♖xf2 fxe6 16.♕e2 ♘c5

A.Pashikian-M.Matlakov, Gjakova 2016, had gone 16...♖f7 17.♕xe6 ♗d5 18.♕f5 ♕e7 19.♕g5 h6 20.♕h4 ♘e8 21.♕xe7 ♖xe7 22.♘f5, with a marked White advantage, which (I suspect) may certainly have been known (at least) to Carlsen. That game suggests that Black can't equalise, by immediately returning the gambit pawn.

17.♗c2 ♗a6 18.♕e1 ♕e8?

Duda opts to hold on to the pawn but White's initiative only grows after this somewhat awkwardly passive rejoinder. The livelier 18...♘d5, and if 19.♖xf8+ (but not 19.b4?! ♖xf2 20.♔xf2 ♕e7, which is certainly no worse for Black) 19...♕xf8 20.♘h5 ♕f7 21.♘xg7 ♘f4, was probably critical.

19.♖d1 ♖c8

Without an alleviating exchange of rooks on the f-file, Black is hard pressed to hold back the disruptive advance of White's b-pawn. White is also clearly better after 19...♖d8 20.♖xd8 ♕xd8 21.b4, and if 21...♘d3 22.♕xe6+ ♔h8 23.♖d2, or if 19...♗b7 20.b4 ♘cd7 21.♗a4 ♖d8 22.♖e2, with a winning advantage in both cases.

20.b4 ♘b7

Black still has his pawn but this is a patently ugly retreat. Unfortunately 20...♘cd7 21.♗a4, and if 21...♘d5 (or if 21...b5 22.♗b3 ♘d5 23.♖e2) 22.♖xf8+ ♔xf8 23.♘e4, hardly improves matters for Black.

21.♘e4 ♘d5

Perhaps 21...♘h5 offered slightly better practical chances. Even then, however, after 22.♖dd2, and if 22...♕e7 23.♕d1 ♕xb4 24.♘g5 ♖xf2 25.♗xh7+ ♔h8 26.♖xf2, Black's misery clearly continues.

22.♖xf8+ ♕xf8

Black also suffers after 22...♔xf8 23.♖d2 ♕e7 24.♕g3, and if 24...♗c4 25.a3 (simplest), when Black is unlikely to be able to transfer sufficient of his offside queenside forces to defend against White's overwhelming power on the kingside. After the text-move, White might now have won even more quickly, by playing 23.♗b3, which threatens ♘g5 (even after 23...h6).

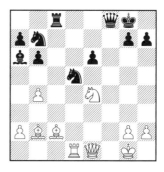

23.♗b1 ♕xb4

This loses at once. Black had to try 23...h6, even if White's attack must still surely prevail, after 24.♘g3, and if, for example, 24...♕f7 25.♖xd5 exd5 26.♘f5 ♖e8 27.♕g3 ♖e6 28.♗xg7, threatening ♘xh6+.

24.♘f6+ ♔h8

Or if 24...gxf6 25.♕xe6+ ♔f8 26.♕xc8+, and wins.

25.♕xe6 ♖a8 26.♕xd5 1–0

After 26...♕xb2, White wins either by playing 27.♕e4, and if 27...g6 28.♕e7, or 27.♕h5, and if 27...h6 28.♕g6.

Gender Attack

Judit Polgar

I t's time to spotlight women in chess, which throughout its long history has largely been dominated by men. Nowadays women's chess enjoys its own top rank individual and team events, including world titles, and a growing reputation, in which the very best women increasingly compete with the very best men. There are no gender-based reasons to suggest that a woman can't become world number one other than perhaps outmoded societal constructs. Only glass ceilings exist.

33. *Judit Polgar: Chess Classic, Mainz 2008*

While no woman may yet have shattered the ultimate chess glass ceiling, Judit Polgar (b 1976) has nonetheless broken many a mighty pane of the toughest plate glass. Breaking Bobby Fischer's then existing record, Polgar became the youngest ever chess grandmaster, in 1991. She soon also joined the world's chess elite, in which she remained throughout the 2000s. Ranked 8th in the world (July 2005), she qualified for a place in the 2005 FIDE World Championship Tournament.

Apart from playing in two Women's Chess Olympiads, in 1988 and 1990 (helping Hungary twice to win gold), Polgar abjured competition in women-only events. She was simply much too high-rated even to briefly pause her elite career to play in the women's world championships. Given that she was virtually always the only (not just the first) woman ever to compete regularly at the elite level, her ground-breaking achievements have inspired a legion of young women and, indeed, men.

Women's playing strength and interest only really began to grow apace, as women fought for and gained more of the societal rights, freedoms and equalities necessary to establish greater parity with 20th century men. At London 1927, FIDE organised its first individual women's world championship, alongside the first Chess Olympiad. Its winner, Vera Menchik (1907-1944), who held the title until her untimely death in a German V1 rocket attack, was the first woman able to take on and (occasionally) defeat several of the world's very best men.

The USSR then dominated women's chess for a very long stretch, with its powerhouse increasingly in its Georgian Republic. Nona Gaprindashvili (b 1941) held the women's world title, from 1962-1978, followed by fellow Georgian, Maia Chiburdanidze (b 1961), champion, from 1978-1991. These two great players, both strong grandmasters, formed the core of a long, all-conquering USSR women's Olympiad team.

Following the brief Hungarian interlude, in 1988 and 1990, the next women's powerhouse was based firmly in China, which had invested hugely in chess in the post-Mao years. Had Polgar stayed in the women's game, she would have been hot favourite to succeed Chiburdanidze for the women's world title. Instead the highly gifted Xie Yun (b 1970), also a strong grandmaster, became the first Chinese player to win the women's world title, ending Chiburdanidze's long reign.

Without Polgar, Hungary's women's team diminished in strength. Polgar, however, was a unique talent. In January 1989, she became the world's top-rated woman player, a distinction she retained until her 2014 retirement. In 1991, aged only 15, she sensationally won the Hungarian championship, one of the chess world's strongest tournaments. At Budapest 1993, Polgar even more sensationally defeated Boris Spassky in a match, scoring (+3-2=5). Polgar's star thereafter shone brightly for two decades.

Polgar's primary stylistic instincts were for the initiative and attack. She calculated variations exceptionally well, played quickly and soundly, with plenty of fight. Theoretically well-versed, she tended to favour a wide range of combative, frequently very sharp openings, as in one of her most famous wins against Vishy Anand. Both sides were almost certainly well booked-up for this contest. Polgar's subtly 'quiet', 17th move, however, may have caught Anand out.

J.Polgar – V.Anand

Dos Hermanas 1999

Sicilian Defence: Perenyi Attack

1.e4 c5 2.♘f3 d6 3.d4 cxd4 4.♘xd4 ♘f6 5.♘c3 a6 6.♗e3 e6 7.g4 e5 8.♘f5 g6
With 7.g4, Polgar opts for an all-out attacking line introduced by her late-Hungarian colleague, Bela Perenyi. If

Black wishes to avoid the main lines, he can also hazard the lively alternative, 8...h5, and if 9.g5 (or 9.♗g5 hxg4) 9...♘xe4 10.♘xg7+ ♗xg7 11.♘xe4 d5 12.♘g3 d4.

9.g5 gxf5 10.exf5 d5 11.♕f3

Perenyi's original idea and the critical test: a fortnight earlier, A.Shirov-V. Anand, Monte Carlo 1999, had gone 11.gxf6 d4 12.♗c4 ♕c7 13.♕d3 dxe3 14.fxe3 b5 15.♗b3 ♗b7 16.♘d5 ♕a5+ 17.c3 ♘d7 18.0-0-0 ♘c5 19.♕c2 0-0-0, and Black won. Sporadic attempts have since been made to revive White's chances in this line, usually commencing 14.0-0-0 exf2 15.♗xf7+ ♔xf7 16.♕d5+ ♔xf6 17.♘e4+ ♔e7, and now either 18.f6+ or 18.♘d6, but without much success.

11...d4 12.0-0-0 ♘bd7 13.♗d2

Polgar later won the high stakes (FIDE World Championship) battle, J.Polgar-R.Kasimdzhanov, San Luis 2005, after 13.♗xd4 exd4 14.♖xd4 ♗g7 15.♖g1 ♔f8 16.♕e3!?, although 16.♗c4, and if Black's N/f6 moves, 17.♕h5, may have been best. Black should, however, perhaps prefer 14...♗c5, as in N.Matinian-D.Navara, Legnica 2013, which then continued 15.♖d2 ♕c7 16.gxf6 ♘xf6 17.♗c4 ♗e7 18.♗b3 0-0 19.♖e2 ♔h8 20.♖g1 ♗d6 21.♕g2 ♗f4+ 22.♔b1 ♗h6, and Black won.

The later Rapid game, P.Leko-V.Anand, Nice 2008, saw 13.♗c4 ♕c7 14.♗xd4 exd4 15.♖he1+ ♔d8 16.♖xd4 ♗c5 17.♖dd1 ♖e8 18.gxf6 ♖xe1 19.♖xe1 ♘xf6 20.♖d1+ ♔d7 21.♗xf7 ♕xh2 22.♘d5, and White won, but Black can certainly improve, by playing either 21...♖c8 or 20...♔e8.

13...dxc3 14.♗xc3 ♗g7

Two pieces ahead, Black hopes to return one of them for development's sake. Even if a computer might try to hang on to both pieces, by playing the ugly (non-human) retreat, 14...♘g8, the reply 15.f6, would then clamp down on an enormous swathe of Black's game and looks (at least) humanly scary!

15.♖g1 0-0

Black's king heads for a (reasonably) secure bolt-hole on h8, which seems both consistent and strategically sound. Polgar considered it risky! Black might also consider 15...♕c7, and if 16.gxf6 ♗xf6 17.♕e2 ♘b6, although if Black wished to develop like this way, it might have been better introduced by playing ...♕c7, at move 13.

16.gxf6 ♕xf6 17.♕e3!

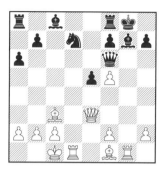

It is not clear how far either player may have home-prepared this line. This highly subtle manoeuvre, however, might easily have slipped Anand's detection. White hopes to demolish Black's hold on e5, for which it is essential to have White's queen on e3. The same plan fails after either 17.♔b1 ♔h8 18.♕e3 (as f4 hasn't been played), or 17.♕g3 ♔h8 18.f4, allowing 18... ♗h6 (which, with White's queen on e3, would lose to ♖xd7).

17...♔h8 18.f4 ♕b6?!

Anand now definitely slips. Though well nigh impossible to assess, far less calculate accurately, Black obtains better defensive chances after 18...♖e8. White's best try may then be 19.♗c4, and if 19...♗h6 20.♔b1 ♗xf4 21.♕f3 (or possibly 21.♕e4), with continuing unclear complications.

19.♕g3 ♕h6

Black deliberately invites White's reply (White's rook is inviolable on d6), in the hope of bolstering his centre (by playing ...f6). Black's resulting central light

square weaknesses, however, eventually prove fatal. Perhaps better was 19...♖g8, and if 20.♗c4 ♘f6, although White still presses, after 21.♕d3 (possibly also 21.♗xe5, and if 21...♗xf5 22.♗xf7), and if 21...exf4 22.♗d4 ♕c6 23.♗xf7.

20.♖d6 f6 21.♗d2 e4

Black relieves the pressure on e5, but allows White's light square bishop to infiltrate on the weakened central light squares. No better, however, was 21... ♘c5, and if 22.fxe5 ♘e4 23.exf6 ♘xg3 24.fxg7+ ♕xg7 25.♖xg3 ♗xf5 26.♖xg7 ♔xg7 27.♗h6+ ♔h8 28.♗xf8 ♖xf8 29.♗g2, winning a pawn.

22.♗c4 b5

Black's poorly coordinated forces are in a terrible tangle. Black certainly has no time for 22...♘b8, hoping to find a better post for his knight on c6, because of 23.♗c3, and if 23...♗d7 24.♖xf6 ♖xf6 25.♕xg7+ ♕xg7 26.♗xf6, and mates.

23.♗e6 ♖a7

Black also struggles to disentangle after 23...♘c5 24.♗e3, and if 24...♘xe6

25.fxe6 ♕g6 26.♕h3 ♕e8 (26...♕h6
27.♕xh6 ♗xh6 28.e7 ♖e8 29.♖xf6 ♗g7
30.♖f8+ ♖xf8 31.exf8♕+ ♗xf8 32.♗d4+)
27.f5 ♖g8 28.♖d2 ♗b7 29.♖dg2 ♕f8
30.♖g4, followed by ♖h4, and wins; or
if 24...♘b7 25.♖b6 ♘d8 26.♔b1 ♘xe6
27.fxe6 ♕g6 28.♕h3 ♕e8 29.f5, with
a crushing bind (both widely quoted
lines at the time).

24.♖c6 a5

White controls the centre. Black's self-
blocking f-pawn gets in the way of any
sensible kingside or central development. Unwilling to submit to the kind
of suffocating lines (with White pawns
on e6 and f5), as in the previous note,
Anand attempts to create a queenside
diversion, which, however, fails to
shake White's iron grip on the game.

25.♗e3 ♖b7 26.♗d5 ♖b8 27.♖c7 b4 28.b3

White neatly prevents any further
advance by Black's queenside pawns,
threatens Black's e-pawn and leaves
Black without any good move. Rather
than resign, Anand continues, at the
cost of a piece, with a final quixotic tilt
at White's furthest advanced f-pawn.

**28...♖b5 29.♗c6 ♖xf5 30.♖xc8 ♖xc8
31.♗xd7**

Black is undone by an elegant skewer.
White finally equalises the piece count
and her advantage is now overwhelming.

**31...♖cc5 32.♗xf5 ♖xf5 33.♖d1 ♔g8
34.♕g2 1–0**

After Black's e-pawn falls, Black's king
follows.

The Polgar family - Judit's parents,
Laszlo and Klara, and her two sisters,
Zsusza (b 1969) and Zsofi (b 1974) -
hugely influenced the development of
chess education. All three sisters were
home-schooled, majoring in chess,
while also studying in accordance
with the formal school curriculum.
The sisters studied chess with Laszlo,
himself a master, each other and many
strong players and coaches. They rarely touched base with schools except
to take formal exams in the academic
subjects required by the state educa-
tional system.

This brave, but ultimately successful experiment has since been copied
widely. Since Judit raised the bar for
precocious chess advancement, virtually all of the world's subsequent elite
players have followed a not dissimi-
lar trajectory. Unless you are already
a grandmaster, able to juggle school
with regular play on the professional
circuit, by the age of around 14 or so,
you can probably nowadays abandon

any realistic hope of reaching the very top-class.

Back in 1970s Communist Hungary, in which such departures from strict Party policy were very largely discouraged, many considered the path chosen by the Polgars a huge gamble. Laszlo Polgar, however, had a strong teaching background. Strong-willed and, as it turned out, also a good manager, he and his equally well-qualified and highly supportive wife, made it all work. One of the more 'western-leaning' of the Warsaw Pact states, Hungary quietly allowed space for the Polgar project.

Serendipity also chipped in. At Buenos Aires 1978, the Hungarian Olympiad team had become overnight national heroes by wresting gold from the mighty USSR, which had won all of the biennial Olympiads since first playing, in 1952. Chess in Hungary was accordingly popular, well-funded and exceptionally competitive, as the Polgars grew up. Through the 1980s, all three sisters attracted many international invitations, not just individually but also as a celebrity 'threesome'.

Together the Polgar sisters most famously formed the three board core of the winning Hungarian team, at the 1988 and 1990 Women's Chess Olympiads. As Judit gradually migrated into the ranks of the absolute top-flight, however, Zsusza turned rather more to women's chess, eventually winning the women's world title, by defeating Xie Jun (8.5-4.5), at Jaén 1996. Following

34. *Zsusza Polgar, in 2011*

her marriage in 1999, Zsofi opted largely to withdraw from competitive chess to pursue other interests.

For Judit and Zsusza, of course, motherhood led to unavoidable chess adjustments and time-outs. Following the birth of a son (2001) and daughter (2006), however, Judit nonetheless twice returned to the board, hardly even missing one chess beat. Zsusza was rather less fortunate. In 1999, FIDE controversially turned down her request to postpone her scheduled Women's world title defence, due to the birth of a son (and certain other match wrangles). When she declined to play, FIDE withdrew her world title.

Not yet 40, when she retired in 2014, Judit perhaps reflected that her very best years had probably passed. She may have recalled her individual loss, at Gibraltar 2012, against the extraordinarily gifted young Chinese player, Hou Yifan (b 1994). At Gibraltar, already a grandmaster (2008) and Women's world champion (2010-12), Hou tied 1ˢᵗ/2ⁿᵈ with Nigel Short, scoring 8/10 (though she lost on a tie break). The future of women's chess seemed secure in others' hands.

Such early retirements, however, may more mundanely reflect the unusual intensity of 21ˢᵗ century elite chess, in times when ever more players begin their effective professional careers in their very earliest teens. Polgar had already survived at the top for two decades. The first woman ever to qualify for a short leet World Championship Tournament (2005)

and then a Candidates' match series (2007), where she lost to Evgeny Bareev, Polgar's reputation had long been sky high and secure among the great names in chess history.

In 2011, Polgar advanced to the quarter-finals of FIDE's (KO) World Cup, where she lost to the eventual tournament winner, Peter Svidler. On that journey, she eliminated the number one seed, Sergei Karjakin, against whom she succeeded in landing yet another great blow for gender equality. In their sole decisive game (of two), Karjakin went for a solid 'Berlin Wall' endgame, which wrecking-ball, Polgar, quite demolished.

J.Polgar – S.Karjakin

FIDE World Cup, Khanty-Mansiysk 2011

Spanish Opening

1.e4 e5 2.♘f3 ♘c6 3.♗b5 ♘f6 4.0-0 ♘xe4 5.d4 ♘d6 6.♗xc6 dxc6 7.dxe5 ♘f5 8.♕xd8+ ♔xd8 9.♘c3 ♔e8

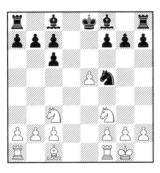

Both sides have a wide variety of ways to approach this far from trivial

'endgame'. Kramnik twice shattered Kasparov's dreams, at London 2001, by playing 9...♗d7, followed by an eventual shift of Black's king, via c8 (and the move ...b6) to safety on b7. Black's king also often finds safety on e8, as in the main text.

In the earliest games played in this line, the little-known German, Fritz Riemann's first thought was to conserve the bishop pair, by playing 9...h6, followed by ...♗e6. The famed battle, S.Tarrasch-Em.Lasker, Hastings 1895, dramatically began in this vein: 9... h6 10.♗d2 ♗e6 11.♘e2 c5 12.♗c3 g5

13.♘d2 ♔d7 14.f4 ♔c6, followed by a queenside pawn-rush.

10.h3 h5 11.♖d1

Karjakin kept faith with this line. After 11.♗f4 ♗e7 12.♖ad1 ♗e6 13.♘g5, Anand,V-Karjakin,S, Khanty-Mansiysk 2014, continued with the uncompromising, 13...♖h6 14.♖fe1 ♗b4 15.g4 hxg4 16.hxg4 ♘e7 17.♘xe6 ♖xe6 18.♔g2 ♗xc3 19.bxc3 ♖d8 20.♖xd8+ ♔xd8 21.♖h1 ♘d5 22.♗g3 g5, and was eventually drawn.

11...♗e7 12.♘e4

Karjakin also built an impenetrable kingside blockade, in F.Caruana-S. Karjakin, Shamkir 2014, after the equally striking 12.♘e2 ♘h4 13.♘xh4 ♗xh4 14.♗e3 ♗e7 15.♖d2 h4 16.♖ad1 ♖h5 17.♗f4 a6 18.♘d4 c5 19.♘e2 ♗e6 20.♘c3 ♖d8 21.♘d5 ♖d7 22.♘xe7 ♖xd2 23.♖xd2 ♔xe7, and the draw was agreed very shortly.

12...♗d7 13.b3 h4 14.♗g5 ♖d8 15.c4 b6 16.♖d2 ♗c8 17.♖xd8+ ♔xd8 18.♖d1+ ♔e8 19.♗f4 c5?!

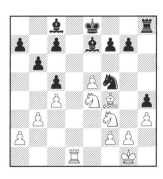

This move, however, doubtfully plac-

es all of Black's queenside pawns on potentially vulnerable dark squares. Polgar now has a good choice between playing 20.♘c3, in an attempt to coax ...c6 (to cover d5 and b5, but weakening d6) or, as played, to speculate on a more ambitious e6 pawn break (to free White's bishop for an attack against Black's vulnerable queenside pawns). Karjakin subsequently discovered the dynamic improvement 19...♖h5, which led to a continuing rough balance, in D.Navara-S.Karjakin, Wijk aan Zee 2012, after 20.♔f1 ♗d8 21.♘fg5 ♗e7 22.♘f3 ♗d8 23.♘fg5 ♗e7 24.♖d3 c5 25.♘f3 ♗b7 26.♘c3 ♗xf3 27.♖xf3 ♘d4, (Black even won).

20.e6 ♗xe6?

With his a-, b- and c-pawns all worryingly static, dark square targets, Black should probably have tried to mix things up, by playing 20...fxe6, and if 21.♗xc7 ♗b7 22.♘fg5 ♘d4 23.♗b8 ♗xe4 24.♘xe4 ♘c6.

21.♗xc7 f6 22.♗b8 a6 23.♗a7 ♗d8 24.♘c3 ♔f7

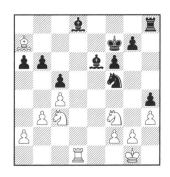

Black must now lose a pawn. After

24...♘e7 25.♘a4 ♘c8, Karjakin's probably intended defence, Polgar could play 26.♗xb6 ♘xb6 27.♘xb6 ♗xb6 28.♖d6, regaining her piece (due to a surprise skewer), with a clear advantage.

25.♘a4 b5 26.♘xc5 ♗c8 27.cxb5 axb5 28.a4

Black retains the bishop pair but White's pieces are all much more active than Black's. White's outside passed a-pawn, moreover, is a potential game-winner, not least while Black's rook remains far from the centre and queenside.

28...bxa4 29.bxa4 ♖e8 30.♖b1 g5 31.♗b6 ♗e7 32.a5 ♗xc5 33.♗xc5 ♖e6 34.♖b6 ♘g7 35.♗e3 ♘f5 36.♖b8 ♖e8 37.♖a8 ♗b7

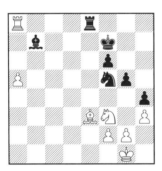

White now wins by force. But even after 37...♘xe3 38.fxe3, and if 38...♗b7

39.♖a7 ♖e7 40.a6 ♗e4 41.♖xe7+ ♔xe7, Black chances are bleak; White's outside passed a-pawn is then almost certainly bound to draw Black's king towards it, leaving the kingside free for a decisive White break.

38.♖a7 ♖e7 39.♗c5 ♖d7 40.a6 ♗c6 41.♖xd7+ ♗xd7 42.♘d2 ♔e6 43.♘c4 ♗c6

Or if 43...♔d5 44.♘a5 ♗c6 45.♘xc6 ♔xc6 46.a7, after which White will again rapidly activate his king and win on the kingside, while Black's king tends to White's a-pawn.

44.♘b6 ♘d6 45.♗xd6 ♔xd6 46.a7 ♔c7 47.a8♕ ♗xa8 48.♘xa8+ ♔b7 49.f4 1–0

After Black captures White's knight, White gobbles up Black's g- and h-pawns, and wins.

Artificial Intelligence

AlphaZero

As computers now so clearly outperform even world champions, it's timely to revisit a very old debate about the game's longer-term health. A century or so ago, Capablanca and Lasker, among a few others, occasionally fretted that top-class players had so mastered technique that the game faced an imminent drawing death. They were quite wrong then and remain so today. Throughout its long history, chess has actually enjoyed remarkably continuous regenerative powers. Despite huge leaps in knowledge, vast challenges remain both for humans and their silicon friends.

In reality, not even the strongest computers do more than still chip away at the game's daunting vastness. Brute force powers of calculation, hugely expanded in the last few decades, may have given modern engines their most recent cutting edge over humans. But this still doesn't remotely enable them to calculate 'everything'. Conventional engines rather respond to so-called 'handcrafted', decision-making algorithms, which, integrated with digitised 'look-up tables' of all sorts, enable the creation of intelligent short cuts to swift and high quality move generation.

Of course, humans still 'think', which computers can't do. This enables us to manage their outputs quite cleverly. Rather than play against computers, we increasingly consult them. For some time now, all top players have hired engine-intelligent coaches, invested heavily in computer skills and set to work in teams to delve ever more deeply into the labyrinthine complexities of openings, middle-games and even endgames. A very select few even enjoy occasional links to some of the world's leading supercomputer research facilities. Managed well, all such intelligence undoubtedly helps at the practical board face.

Thankfully such vast computer work probably still, very broadly, at least, cancels out at the absolute top, leaving scope for the expression of stylistic difference and true battles of skill as undiminished as ever before. Computers have definite limits. Players must still make many difficult judgements about what they consider to be any machine's 'conclusions', when its computations 'cease', as they must do. Due to the game's non-trivial depth, this is usually still at some quite 'unclear' point, leaving even world champions to face multiple, often unanticipated problems, 'on their own', in their over the board games.

Computers best help improve our chess understanding. They provide no unduly clear-cut solutions. Steinitz, perhaps the first great player to grasp the sheer vastness of the game's inexorably puzzling character, used that fundamental insight to fire up his extraordinary capacity for research, calculated risk-taking, objective review and constant innovation. Modern computers inhabit that same place, helping us push forward the knowledge bequeathed to us by all previous chess generations in a faster-moving 21st century.

Whether and how far computers may further influence future chess trends remains uncertain. At one extreme, they might, indeed, eventually develop in ways that lead to a levelling of skills sufficient to bring about the game's death by a thousand draws, albeit more than a century after this prospect was initially mooted. On the other hand, they might simply continue to better inform and inspire us, leading to a sharpening in play. Probably most of us still lean towards the latter, more confident prognosis. The game presently seems perfectly healthy.

This debate, however, has recently sharpened, following the exploits of a radically new chess engine, AlphaZero. Early in 2018, AlphaZero sensationally debuted by drubbing one of the world's strongest conventionally programmed engines, Stockfish 8. Behind the bare match statistics (+155-6=839), impressive as they are, lies an even more significant breakthrough in computer programming. Having been fed only the rules of the game, AlphaZero is the first chess-playing machine to 'learn' how to play chess by playing countless games against itself (or others) and drawing 'lessons'.

AlphaZero has a core *neural network*, which instructs it solely to make moves and assess outcomes in terms of the *percentage probabilities* of success in winning games. As it computes the data that flows from its incessant games, the machine refines these numbers into ever improving signifiers of move success. Evolved by *Deep Mind*, a company that specialises in the development of Artificial Intelligence (AI) techniques, AlphaZero remains a non-commercially available research engine. The company aims to achieve successful AI software transfer from such 'simplified' game-playing to 'the real world'.

In its AlphaFold off-shoot, for example, *Deep Mind* recently achieved what Venki Ramakrishnan, Nobel prize winner and President of the Royal Society called 'a stunning advance' in the prediction of protein unfolding, a critical process that underpins life. AlphaZero itself evolved from AlphaGo, the first machine to demonstrate clear superiority over the best Go players. By demolishing Stockfish 8, AlphaZero made an equally impressive impact in the chess world, as much because of its magnificent playing style as its points score.

Some of AlphaZero's best games against Stockfish 8 point to a truly virtuosic blend of profound strategic vision and attacking dynamism. AlphaZero and the leading conventionally programmed engines, including the Stockfish family, of course, all perform at a significantly higher level than the best humans.

AlphaZero, however, occasionally plays with a flair that can only best be described, as it has been by many elite players, as uniquely inspirational. The most lauded game played in the Stockfish 8 match is an undoubted masterpiece.

While it might not be entirely beyond an elite human player to play like this, it would be far from easy to match AlphaZero's consistently high levels of insight, accuracy and precision through an entire game of such challenging complexity. From its novel, gambit-based start, AlphaZero develops an exceptionally fine initiative that unfolds on the back of the most subtly judged spatial, containment and line-break strategies and the most delicately maintained optimum coordination of every single one of White's forces throughout.

After plain admiration, the best way to react to such brilliance is to commit to greater effort to ramp up one's own, never-ending quest to aspire to create and incorporate ever more virtuosity in one's own game. The present world champion and his team are on record as enthusiastically responding to AlphaZero's impact in exactly that way, much as, I am sure, all the great players in this book would have reacted (or might still do). Work hard! Experiment! Review! Innovate! Steinitz's exhortations ring through the ages. There remains much creative chess work to be done. Enjoy it!

AlphaZero – Stockfish 8

1000 game match 2018

English Opening

1.♘f3 ♘f6 2.c4 e6 3.♘c3 ♗b4 4.♕c2 0–0 5.a3 ♗xc3 6.♕xc3 a5 7.b4 d6 8.e3 ♘e4 9.♕c2 ♘g5 10.b5 ♘xf3+ 11.gxf3 ♕f6

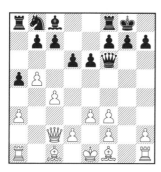

To a human, both sides have played

the opening slightly oddly, which may have had something to do with the fact that neither computer was permitted access to a digitised 'openings book'. With White's tacit encouragement, Black has gone pawn hunting: mutually playable, if unclear.

A more humanly played game might have seen Black opt for more conventionally rapid development and the erection of solid central blockading pawns (such as on b6, d6, c5/e5, with ...♗b7 and ...♘bd7). With White, most humans would probably have played the natural ♗b2 earlier (incidentally covering f6).

12.d4 ♕xf3 13.♖g1 ♘d7 14.♗e2 ♕f6 15.♗b2 ♕h4 16.♖g4 ♕xh2 17.♖g3 f5 18.0-0-0 ♖f7

Having grabbed two pawns, Stockfish 8 stops short at taking a third. Apparently it considered that the text-move, followed by the retrieval of its queen from its far-flung kingside adventures gives Black an edge. Neither machine believed Black achieves anything at all (and possibly far less), by succumbing to the further, ultra-materialistic pawn grab, 18...♕xf2 19.♖dg1, and if, say 19...g6 20.♖1g2 ♕e1+ 21.♗d1, with very definite compensation for White.

19.♗f3 ♕h4 20.♖h1 ♕f6 21.♔b1 g6 22.♖gg1 a4?!

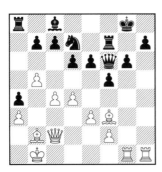

According to correspondence chess grandmaster, Arno Nickel, who deeply analysed this game, in an online *Chessbase: Schachnachrichten* article, using Stockfish 8 and the subsequently improved Stockfish 10, to probe the various machines' decisions to depths

of around 20 moves or so, it is only here that Stockfish 8 plays a clearly second-rate move. Stockfish 10 urged the immediate 22...♖g7, which Stockfish 8 rejected. Then if 23.a4 (to prevent ...a4), Black has time to stiffen his defences, by playing ...♕f7, followed by ...♘f6 and ...♗d7.

23.♔a1 ♖g7 24.e4

Strong human players would, I am sure, now certainly sense that White has excellent play for two pawns. Severely lacking in queenside space, Black encounters significant obstacles to his further development on that flank; simultaneously Black can scarcely move any of his (extra) kingside pawns without offering clear targets for White. With the text-move and his next several moves White gains even more space on the queenside and creates serious problems for Black in the centre.

24...f4 25.c5 ♕e7 26.♖c1 ♘f6 27.e5 dxe5 28.♖he1 e4?

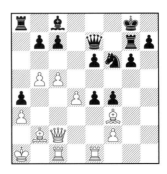

Stockfish 8 can't avoid opening the e-file, to the advantage of White's rooks. Analysing more deeply, Stockfish 10

preferred 28...♘d5, and if 29.c6 ♖b8 30.♗xd5 exd5 31.♖xe5 ♕f8 32.cxb7 ♗xb7 33.♕xa4, which it considered, in one of its most critical lines, to be only slightly better for White (to a depth of just over 22 moves). AlphaZero now launches further line-opening strikes that bring Black to the brink in the centre.

29.♗xe4 ♕f8 30.d5 exd5 31.♗d3 ♗g4 32.f3 ♗d7

White's 30th and 32nd moves are both very fine. The former freed White's dark square bishop for highly threatening action on the long dark diagonal. The latter, a poisoned offer, leads to a mighty, no doubt game-winning assault on f6, in the event of 32...♗xf3 33.♖f1 ♗e4 34.♖xf4 ♖f7 35.♖cf1, though the preliminary 35.c6, and if 35...bxc6 36.♖cf1, may even be stronger.

33.♕c3 ♘h5 34.♖e5 c6 35.♖ce1 ♘f6 36.♕d4 cxb5 37.♗b1

Despite his (now) three extra pawns, Black is in obvious danger of complete dark square collapse and can scarcely do anything constructive either with his pawns or hopelessly hamstrung

pieces. Having doubled rooks in the e-file and settled his queen powerfully on d4, White now threatens to switch his light square bishop to a2 to target Black's highly vulnerable d-pawn.

37...♗c6 38.♖e6 ♖f7 39.♖g1 ♕g7 40.♕xf4

AlphaZero begins to cash in on his almighty bind. Black's classically 'bad' bishop, completely obstructed by its own light square pawns, is an obvious dud and White's pin on f6 is horrific.

40...♖e8 41.♖d6 ♘d7 42.♕c1 ♖f6

Black resolves on a doubtful piece sacrifice but had no better choice. After the purely passive 42...♘f6 43.♕g5 ♖ef8, White simply piles on the kingside pressure, by playing 44.♕h4, and if, say 44...♗d7 45.f4 b4 46.f5, winning quickly.

43.f4 ♕e7 44.♖xf6 ♘xf6 45.f5

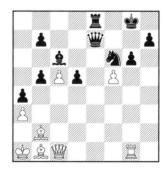

White needed this pawn to effect the final and decisive breakthrough. Black must now exchange queens (and lose a piece) or worse will clearly befall his king before very much longer.

45...♕e3 46.fxg6 ♕xc1 47.gxh7+ ♔f7 48.♖xc1 ♘xh7

Or if 48...d4 49.♖f1, threatening both ♗xd4 and ♖xf6(+), and wins. According to Nickel, Stockfish 10 saw all of this from move 37. Computers!

49.♗xh7 ♖e3 50.♖d1 ♔e8 51.♔a2 ♗d7 52.♗d4 ♖h3 53.♗c2 ♗e6 54.♖e1 ♔d7 55.♔b2 ♖f3 56.♖e5 ♖g3 57.♖e3 ♖g2 58.♔c3 ♖g4 59.♖f3 ♔e8 60.♖f2 ♖g3+ 61.♔b4 ♖g4 62.♖d2 ♗d7 63.♔a5 ♖f4

64.♗e5 ♖f3 65.♖d3 ♖f2 66.♗d1 ♗c6 67.♔b6 1–0

Be aware, in passing, that AlphaZero's novel AI 'motor' hasn't condemned conventionally handcrafted engines to technological oblivion. Many lively debates about how best to assess and benefit from the availability of such quite differently programmed engine types remain ongoing.

Acknowledgements

While able to access much of the material required for this book from the resources of my own library and online, I am also indebted to much additional source material provided by: David Archibald and the Library of the Edinburgh Chess Club; the collections at the National Library of Scotland (Edinburgh) and the Mitchell Library (Glasgow); and Chess Scotland historian, Alan McGowan. I am also grateful for the support and encouragement of Daniël Van Heirzeele and the wider 'Thinkers Publishing' team throughout.

Of course, I also owe a huge debt to the creative achievements of every chess player who has ever played a part, big or small, in the development of chess thought. Many other great names, and lesser lights, too, might have been added to the primary trailblazers that I highlight in this book, but lines had to be drawn somewhere. Thanks to all players who have ever attempted to push the game's boundaries. Ideas matter not merely points.

Special thanks are also due to my wife, Elaine, daughters, Katie and Sally, and Aaron. The views expressed in the book are my own, as are any errors. I dedicate this book to the memory of one of my earliest chess collaborators, Danny Kopec (1954-2016), who once even conspired (in 1978) to introduce me to the great Mikhail Botvinnik.

Bibliography

I have confined the bibliography only to those sources that I directly consulted in writing this book, divided into 'Main', 'General' and 'Periodicals & Online Resources'. 'Main' sources primarily include major works either written about the players or by the players themselves. Sources in the other two categories primarily informed wider and / or deeper context, opinion or fact: some significantly marked *.

Certain 'Main' sources - *Lasker's Chess Manual* is a good example – inevitably inform major thoughts that apply to more than one chapter. Where that applies in chapters, other than the chapter to which the source has been principally 'assigned' below, I have generally made it plain by source references and / or quotations that appear in the main text of the book. Years contained within [...] denote first publication dates, where deemed essential.

I suggest that any reader who might wish to undertake further research into any aspect of the book's near 200 year span of chess history consider the list only as a starting point. Chess has an extraordinarily vast written record and I have certainly indulged in much other reading that touches on many aspects of the book's subject matter. Follow your own instincts: but always critically!

Main Sources

Chapter 1

Anderssen, Adolf: *Aufgaben für Schachspieler (Verlag J.Urban Kern 1842)*
Bachmann, Ludwig: *Schachmeister Steinitz, Vols I-IV, 2ⁿᵈ Edition (Edition Olms 1980)* [1920-28]
Bird, Henry: *Chess History and Reminiscences (London 1893)*
Bogoljubow, Efim: *Mikhail Chigorin, Selected Games (Batsford 1987)* [1926]
Edge, Frederick: *Paul Morphy, The Chess Champion (London 1859)*
Gotschall, Hermann von: *Adolf Anderssen, der Altmeister deutscher Schachspielkunst (Elibron Classics 2006)* [1912]

Lawson, David: *Paul Morphy, The Pride and Sorrow of Chess (University of Louisiana at Lafayette Press 2010)*

Landsberger, Kurt: *William Steinitz, Chess Champion (McFarland 1993)*

Landsberger, Kurt: *The Steinitz Papers (McFarland 2002)*

Löwenthal, Johann: *Morphy's Games of Chess (London 1860)*

Pritchett, Craig: *Steinitz Move by Move (Everyman Chess 2015)*

Staunton, Howard: *The Chess Tournament – London 1851 (Batsford 1986) [1852]*

Steinitz, Wilhelm: columns in *The Field (1873-1882)*

Steinitz, Wilhelm: *International Chess Magazine, Vols. I-VII, 1885-91 (Moravian Chess Reprint)*

Steinitz, Wilhelm: *The Modern Chess Instructor, Part 1 (New York 1889)*

Walker, George: *Chess and Chess Players (London 1850)*

Chapter 2

Brinkmann, Alfred: *Siegbert Tarrasch Lehrmeister der Schachwelt (Walter de Gruyter 1963)*

Forster, R, Negele, M, Tischbierek, R (eds): *Emanuel Lasker, Vol 1 (Exzelsior Verlag 2018)*

Hannak, Dr J: *Emanuel Lasker Biographie eines Schachweltmeisters (Schach Archiv 1952)*

Kamm, Wolfgang: *Siegbert Tarrasch, Leben und Werk (Verlag Fruth 2004)*

Lasker, Emanuel: *Common Sense in Chess (London 1896)*

Lasker, Emanuel: *Mein Wettkampf mit Capablanca (1921)*

Lasker, Emanuel: *Lasker's Manual of Chess (Dover 1960) [1932]*

Reinfeld, Fred & Fine, Reuben: *Lasker's Greatest Chess Games 1889-1914 (Dover 1965) [1935]*

Soltis, Andrew: *Why Lasker Matters (Batsford 2005)*

Tarrasch, Siegbert: *Dreihundert Schachpartien (Edition Olms 1984) [1894]*

Tarrasch, Siegbert: *Die Moderne Schachpartie (Edition Olms 2003) [1912]*

Tarrasch, Siegbert: *The Game of Chess (Dover 1987) [1931]*

Tartakower, Savielly: *Die hypermoderne Partie (Edition Olms 1981) [1925]*

Chapter 3

Alekhine, Alexander: *Das New Yorker Schach Turnier 1927 (Walter de Gruyter 1963)*

Alekhine, Alexander: *The Book of the New York International Chess Tournament 1924 (Dover 1961)*

Alekhine, Alexander: *On the Road to the World Championship 1923-27 (Pergamon 1984)*

Alekhine, Alexander: *My Best Games of Chess 1908-23 & 1924-1937 (G. Bell & Sons 1927 & 1939)*

Alekhine, Alexander: *World Chess Championship 1937 (Batsford 1993)*

Capablanca, José Raúl: *World Championship Matches 1921&1927 (Dover 1977)*

Capablanca, José Raúl: *Chess Fundamentals (1921)*

Euwe, Max & Prins, Lodewijk: *Capablanca Das Schachphänomen (Schach Archiv 1979) [1949]*

Golombek, Harry: *Capablanca's 100 Best Games of Chess (G. Bell & Sons 1947)*

Golombek, Harry: *Richard Réti's Best Games (Batsford 1997) [1954]*

Keene, Raymond: *Aron Nimzowitsch, A Reappraisal (Batsford 1999) [1974]*

Kotov, Alexander: *Alexander Alekhine (Batsford 1975)*

Nimzowitsch, Aron: *My System (Batsford 1987) [1925]*

Nimzowitsch, Aron: *Chess Praxis (Dover 1962) [1929]*

Reinfeld, Fred: *Hypermodern Chess (Dover 1958 [1948]*

Réti, Richard: *Modern Ideas in Chess (Dover 1960) [1923]*

Réti, Richard: *Masters of the Chess Board (Batsford 1993) [1933]*

Skinner, L, Verhoeven, R & Jefferson, N: *Alexander Alekhine's chess games 1902-42 (McFarland 1998)*

Winter, Edward: *Capablanca (McFarland 1989)*

Chapter 4

Botvinnik, Mikhail: *One Hundred Selected Games (Dover 1960)*

Botvinnik, Mikhail: *Best Games 1947-70, 4th Edition (Batsford 1992)*

Botvinnik, Mikhail: *Achieving the Aim (Pergamon 1980)*

Botvinnik, Mikhail: *Half a Century of Chess (Pergamon 1984)*

Bronstein, David: *The Chess Struggle in Practice (Batsford 1980) [1956]*

Cafferty, Bernard: *Spassky's 100 Best Games (Batsford 1972)*

Clarke, Peter: *Mikhail Tal (G. Bell & Sons 1961)*

Clarke, Peter: *Tigran Petrosian (G. Bell & Sons 1964)*

Euwe, Max: *From My Games 1920-37 (Dover 1975) [1939]*

Golombek, Harry: *The World Chess Championship 1948 (BCM Reprint 1982)*

Keene, Raymond & Levy, David: *Siegen Chess Olympiad (Chess 1970)*

Münninghof, Alexander: *Max Euwe, The Biography (New In Chess 2001)*

Shekhtman, E: *The Games of Tigran Petrosian Vols. 1&2 (Pergamon 1991)*

Smyslov, Vassily: *My Best Games of Chess 1935-1957 (Routledge & Keegan Paul 1958)*

Smyslov, Vassily: *125 Selected Games (Pergamon 1983)*

Sosonko, Genna: *Russian Silhouettes (New In Chess 2009)*
Sosonko, Genna: *Smyslov on the Couch (Elk and Ruby 2018)*
Sosonko, Genna: *The Rise and Fall of David Bronstein (Elk and Ruby 2017)*

Chapter 5

Brady, Frank: *Endgame, Bobby Fischer's remarkable Rise and Fall (Broadway 2011)*
Edmonds & Eidinow: *Bobby Fischer Goes to War (Faber 2004)*
Fischer, Bobby: *My 60 Memorable Games (Faber 1969)*
Golombek, Harry: *Fischer Versus Spassky (Barrie & Jenkins 1973)*
Karpov, Anatoly & Roshal, Aleksandr: *Anatoly Karpov Chess is My Life (Pergamon 1980)*
Karpov, Anatoly: *Anatoly Karpov's Best Games (Batsford 1996)*
Kasparov, Garry with Trelford, Donald: *Child of Change (Hutchinson 1987)*
Kasparov, Garry: *On Modern Chess, Parts 2-4 (Everyman Chess 2007-10)*
Kasparov, Garry: *On Garry Kasparov, Parts 1-3 (Everyman Chess 2011-14)*
Keene, Raymond: *Kasparov Short 1993 (Batsford 1993)*
King, Daniel: *World Chess Championship 1995 (Cadogan 1995)*
Lawson, Dominic: *The Inner Game (Pan 1993)*
Lawton, Geoff (compiler): *Tony Miles, 'It's Only Me' (Batsford 2003)*
Plisetsky, Dmitry & Voronkov, Sergei: *Russians versus Fischer (Pergamon 2005)*
Soltis, Andrew: *Bobby Fischer Rediscovered (Batsford 2003)*
Sosonko, Genna: *Evil-Doer, Half a Century with Viktor Korchnoi (Elk and Ruby 2018)*

Chapter 6

Agdestein, Simen: *Wonderboy (New In Chess 2004)*
Anand, Vishy: *My Best Games of Chess (Gambit 1998)*
Anand, Vishy: *My Career, Vols 1&2 (ChessBase DVDs 2008)*
Hensel, Carsten: *Vladimir Kramnik The Inside Story of a Chess Genius (Quality Chess 2018)*
Karolyi, Tibor: *Judit Polgar The Princess of Chess (Batsford 2004)*
Keene, Raymond & Morris, Don: *The Brain Games World Chess Championship (Everyman 2000)*
Kramnik, Vladimir & Damsky, Iakov: *Kramnik My Life and Games (Everyman 2000)*
Polgar, Susan with Paul Truong: *Breaking Through, How the Polgar Sisters Changed the Game of Chess (Everyman 2005)*

Sadler, Matthew & Regan, Natasha: *Game Changer (New In Chess 2019)*

Shahade, Jennifer: *Chess Bitch, Women in the Ultimate Intellectual Sport (Siles Press 2005)*

General

Dvoretsky, Mark: *School of Chess Excellence, Vols 1-4 (Edition Olms 2003)*

Eales, Richard: *Chess The History of a Game (Batsford 1985)*

Euwe, Max: *The Development of Chess Style (G. Bell & Sons 1968)**

Gobet, Fernand: *The Psychology of Chess (Routledge 2019)**

Hartston, William: *The Kings of Chess (London Pavilion 1985)*

Hooper, David & Whyld, Ken: *The Oxford Companion to Chess (OUP 1984)*

Kasparov, Garry: *On My Great Predecessors, Parts 1-V (Everyman Chess 2003-06)*

König, Imre: *Chess from Morphy to Botwinnik (G. Bell & Sons 1952)**

Pandolfini, Bruce (ed): *The Best of Chess Life & Review, Vols, 1&2 (Simon & Schuster 1988)*

Pritchett, Craig: *Heroes of Classical Chess (Everyman Chess 2009)**

Pritchett, Craig: *Giants of Innovation (Everyman Chess 2011)**

Pritchett, Craig: *Great Chess Romantics (Everyman Chess 2013)**

Vidmar, Milan: *Goldene Schachzeiten (Walter de Gruyter 1981) [1960]**

Winter, Edward: *Chess Explorations (Cadogan 1996)*

Winter, Edward: *Kings, Commoners and Knaves (Russell Enterprises 1999)*

Winter, Edward: *A Chess Omnibus (Russell Enterprises 2003)*

Winter, William: *Kings of Chess (Carrol & Nicholson 1954)*

Periodicals & Online Resources

Periodicals: *Chess (from 1960s)*, New In Chess Magazine (from 1980s)* & SchachMagazin 64 (from 1980s)**

Websites: *ChessBase Schach Nachrichten / Chess News, Edward Winter's Chess Notes & The Week in Chess*

Software tools: *Chessbase*

Note on photographic sources and attribution

The 34 photographs of the main players who feature in the book were sourced principally from Wikipedia Commons and are all either clearly in the public domain (by age) or made freely available for use under a variety of (broadly similar) attribution and licensing arrangements. Photographs 15-17, 19-24 and 27 are held in the Dutch National Archives. Photograph 18 is held in the German Federal Archive.

Photographs 25 and 26 are © 2007 SMSI Inc –Owen Williams, The Kasparov Agency; numbers 29 and 33 are attributed to Ygrek; 28 to Steenslag; 30 to Stefan64; 31 to Frans Peeters; and 32 to GF Hund – under licences CC BY-SA 3.0, CC BY 3.0, Attribution-Share Alike 2.0 Generica, CC BY-SA 3.0, Attribution-Share Alike 2.0 Generica and CC BY-SA 4.0, respectively.

The original authors of most of the older photographs remain 'unknown', though number 3, is an engraving by D.J. Pound, and number 7, held in the Hermitage Museum (digital collection) is attributed to Dmitry Spiridonovic. Other known authors include: J.D. Noske (15), Ulrich Kohls (18), Harry Pot (16-19), Bert Verhoeff (21 and 22), Koen Suyk (23) and Bart Molendijk (27).

The photograph of the book's author is by Sally Pritchett.

About the Author

C raig Pritchett (b 1949) is a former national champion and international master (1976), who represented Scotland in nine Chess Olympiads (1966-1990), including four times on top board (1974-1980). Gold medal winner on top board for Scotland at the European Seniors (60+) Team Championship in 2011, he continues to compete regularly at Senior and Open events.

Chess Correspondent for the Scottish newspaper *The Herald* (1972-2006) and *East Lothian Life* (since 2005), he has taught and written widely on chess, specialising latterly on the historical development of chess thought and the fascinatingly wide differences in players' chess styles.

A University of Glasgow graduate in Modern History and Politics and a Chartered Public Finance Accountant, he also worked for many years in UK central government audit. President of his local Dunbar Chess Club, he has also long been associated with three major chess clubs: Edinburgh West, Barbican 4NCL and SK Berlin-Zehlendorf.

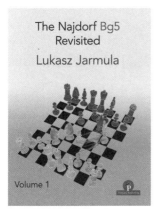

THE NEW STANDARD IN
CHESS PUBLISHING

**Your Jungle Guide To
Unbalancing Your Opponents**

Tips & Tricks of Young Chess Guns

Dorsa & Borna Derakhshani

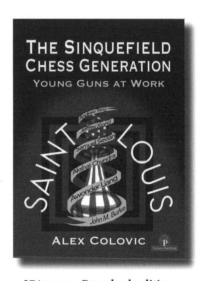

**THE SINQUEFIELD
CHESS GENERATION**

YOUNG GUNS AT WORK

ALEX COLOVIC

420 pages - Paperback edition

This book in front of you assists all players in their efforts to improve, and along their way, our young chess guns provided fresh insights how to trap and trick your opponent in the opening and early middlegame. With the many computer-assisted learning tools available, the player's capacity to improve is limitless. Their final product offers the reader an insider's candid view of how to unbalance the game in the modern age of chess.

274 pages - Paperback edition

The idea was to write about the best players in the USA born at the turn of the century. These players grew and blossomed thanks to the continuous and generous support by the world's biggest chess patron Rex Sinquefield and the Saint Louis Chess Club. Their success changed the scenery of American chess, set new standards and propelled the country as the promised land for new talents. Grandmaster Alex Colovic will be your guide along this fascinating journey.

P
Thinkers Publishing

Always One Move Ahead!